Durkheim and Violence

S. Romi Mukherjee

Library of Congress Cataloging-in-Publication Data

ISBN 978-1-4443-3275-9

A catalogue record for this book is available from the British Library.

Set in 10 on 12 points, Times by Macmillan India
Printed in Singapore by C.O.S. Printers Pte Ltd

International Social Science Journal

Durkheim and Violence

S. Romi Mukherjee

Abstracts

Introduction: on violence as the negativity of the Durkheimian: between anomie, sacrifice and effervescence

S. Romi Mukherjee

In this introductory article I contextualise, historically and theoretically, the rapport between Durkheimianism and violence. Telescoping Durkheimian theories of anomie, sacrifice and effervescence, I demonstrate how both Durkheim and Mauss, arguably the most prominent members of the French School of Sociology, found themselves constantly reflecting on violence in all its forms while never outlining an explicit theory of violence. Violence was thus the dark spot of their enterprises, at once omnipresent but disavowed. I weave together the various fragments of their oeuvres that illuminate the ground of the Durkheimian theory of violence and also examine the precise reasons for its lack of clear theorisation. I conclude with some remarks on Durkheim and fascism. Therefore, this article serves to supplement and set the stage for the articles that appear in this volume, pieces that in their own ways grapple with similar problematics while also moving beyond them and charting new directions in Durkheimian studies.

Durkheim's theory of violence

Mike Gane

Emile Durkheim (1858–1917) developed a wide-ranging foundational sociology that has often been read as lacking a theory of politics, power and violence. This article argues that this view can be contested and outlines a reading of Durkheim's work that reveals that it places power and violence at the centre of its concerns through the concept of social energy. The discussion examines aspects of Durkheim's work on education, the family, gender, suicide, politics and war. It argues that Durkheim's theory centres on the way that social energies are produced and distributed. The heart of the theory suggests that in social development social energy can be centralised and concentrated in an absolute form, and as societies become more complex and institutionally balanced energies are dispersed towards the individual and this shift is the underlying cause for the move towards the cult of the individual and human rights. But this is not an inevitable progression as societies can experience tensions that shift social energies into tyrannical forms.

Durkheimism: a model for external constraint without a theory of violence

Jacques Plouin

Durkheimism is often regarded as being unconcerned with the question of violence because it considers manifestations of violence to be a residue of irrationality. However, the Durkheimian model places great importance on the notion of coercion, which condenses the action of the social on the individual. The consistency of Durkheimism can be seen more clearly if we make a slight distinction between the Durkheimian model and Durkheim's work. In the model, instead of a social holism seen as an organic totality, we find relativism grounded in a sociological externalism, in which the only basis for sociology is the externality of social facts to individuals. The social is then no longer identified with an organic totality but with an ecosystem of plural, heterogeneous norms in which violence is not a residue of subjectivity but the effect of an always possible conflict between norms. The Durkheimian model can thus identify all forms of violence because it can proceed without a general theory of violence. We then obtain a new investigative tool: "look for forms or expressions of social coercion and violence and you will find social facts and underlying regularities to study".

Durkheim, the question of violence and the Paris Commune of 1871

Susan Stedman Jones

Through an examination of certain features of his thought and neglected aspects of his theoretical apparatus and of his historical era, Durkheim is defended against the accusation that he takes no account of violence. Indeed, rather than neglecting it, he has a wide conception of violence that focuses on the social. This was radical for his day for it moves the question of violence away from conservative ideas that violence was a permanent feature of human nature. An examination of some of his main concepts and ideas shows that, through his study of the main features of society, he is concerned with the establishment of positive social relations. The traumatic historical beginnings of the period in which he lived were a tragic inspiration and in turn lead him to criticise those theories that in different ways justify violence.

Durkheimian sociology, biology and the theory of social conflict

Jean-Christophe Marcel and Dominique Guillo

Durkheim's appropriations from the biology of his time are not simple concessions to the biologically influenced mood of his day, sitting uneasily with his sociological theory. Though tightly bound to the rest of his work, this biology nevertheless has a very particular content, quite different from what is today referred to by the term Darwinism or the theory of evolution. It consists of a conception of life centred on the idea of an ascending linear series of living forms, graduated according to their complexity of organisation. In this fundamentally morphological understanding, competition, conflict and dialectics are not driving principles in the functioning and development of organised bodies. A re-examination of this notion of biology enables us to understand the way that social conflict is theorised by Durkheim and, following him, by Halbwachs and Simiand, whose work shows a reference to such morphological thinking. This sheds light on the Durkheimians' conception of class relations and their rejection of Marxism and revolutionary socialism.

"Change only for the benefit of society as a whole": pragmatism, knowledge and regimes of violence

Ivan Strenski

By temperament and pragmatic intellectual conviction, Durkheim seems to have been averse to violence. His notion that suicide threatened the social whole or that the violence of social revolution was counterproductive, indicate as much. Yet in other areas of social life, such as in Durkheim's views of physical punishment and discipline in schools of his pedagogical work, or in his insensitivity to the fate of victims of religious and ritual sacrifice, an acceptance of violence, even death, appears to infuse his writings. Furthermore, there are also arguments to be made of the support that Durkheimian theory may have offered to regimes of French colonial domination during the Third Republic. Similarly, did Durkheim's societal thinking aid the rise of fascist organicism by offering it intellectual legitimacy? Such cases thus raise doubts about the consistency of Durkheimian thought with political violence or regimes of domination, like those explored by Michel Foucault. Among these matters I discuss whether there is a sense in which Durkheim may have been perceived as a supporter of schemes in which knowledge conspires to condition regimes of power, such those referred to as institutional violence.

Festival, vacation, war: Roger Caillois and the politics of paroxysm

S. Romi Mukherjee

I trace the evolution of Roger Caillois' theories of paroxysm and festival and his early sense of the political somatic structure of the social organism. I attempt to systematise his category of the paroxysmic, a mutation of Durkheimian effervescence, and examine it in relationship to his theory of the sacred as a vertiginous space of order/disorder. I then carefully explore Caillois' phenomenological anthropology that narrates the decline of the social and the sacred from the primitive to the modern and also critically explore his dialectic of festival, vacation and war. I demonstrate that Caillois' propositions, while grounded in the history of religions, reveal a political ontological hermeneutic that remains a vital critique of the modern nation-state.

Durkheim's concept of *dérèglement* retranslated, Parsons's reading of Durkheim re-parsed: an examination of post-emotional displacement, scapegoating and responsibility at Abu Ghraib

Stjepan G. Mestrovic and Ryan Ashley Caldwell

In a continued attempt to comprehend Durkheim's original understanding of anomie as a form of dérèglement or derangement, we begin with a discussion of how the experiences of abuse at Abu Ghraib fit his model of a deranged, anomic social system. To bolster our interpretation we show how this, more accurate, understanding of anomie as derangement is useful for understanding war crimes in general, an area where Durkheim's concept of anomie has been infrequently applied as a descriptor for research and analysis. Additionally, the concept of post-emotionalism is used to capture a number of related themes in this discussion pertaining to the sociology of knowledge: how and why original meanings of both the abuse at Abu Ghraib and Durkheim's concept of derangement have been taken out of context and result in displaced emotions, scapegoating and misplaced responsibility in intellectual discourse as well as the military justice system.

"A new kind of fear": Jean Baudrillard's neo-Durkheimian theory of mass-mediated suicide

Alexander Riley

The classical Durkheimian understanding of violence has been significantly augmented in recent decades by a neo-Durkheimian analysis of the dual nature of the sacred and mass-mediated ritual. A good deal of the post-1970s thought of Jean Baudrillard, including his controversial writings on the September 11, 2001 terrorist attacks, was centrally concerned with the ways in which the media shape the social experience of violence. In this chapter I argue that his theoretical reconceptualisation of the meaning of suicide, which can reasonably be described as Durkheimian in its essentials, offers a useful tool for making sense of the fascination exerted on viewers by some mediated acts of self-destructive violence.

From political emergencies and states of exception to exceptional states and emergent politics: a neo-Durkheimian alternative to Agamben

Ronjon Paul Datta

Agamben's *Homo Sacer* (1998) here serves as a stimulus for developing a neo-Durkheimian approach to the political. Durkheim's sociology of the sacred and government is read symptomatically to highlight the extent to which sacralisations refer to a real but underdetermined ontology of the social that threatens to break loose into violence against the mechanisms of rule that regulate institutions, actions and the broader normative terrain in which collective fates are thought about and problematised. This neo-Durkheimian approach is deconstructive of Agamben and reconstructive of an alternative to his state-focused conception of sovereignty, the political and sacralisation. The political field is reconceptualised as structured by the sacred difference between politics and rule, instantiated by a limen – a

door – through which the violence of politics may break, opening social life to the field of the contingency of history. This alternative thus shifts the focus from a political emergency to which states of exception, decided by state sovereignty, are a violent response, to exceptional states of an emergent politics grounded in the sacred power of popular sovereignty that may result in violence against rule.

On violence as the negativity of the Durkheimian: between anomie, sacrifice and effervescence

S. Romi Mukherjee

Introduction

A lacuna?

Coming shortly after the hundred and fiftieth anniversary of Durkheim's birth, this volume attempts yet again to rethink Durkheim. Rethinking Durkheim already presents itself as a problematic enterprise and opens up a field torn between historians who insist on treating Durkheim solely within the context of the Third Republic and his epoch and other theorists who find in Durkheim's corpus a set of potent tools with which to analyse and interpret contemporary phenomena that neither Durkheim nor his colleagues could have ever imagined or dared to. The present volume attempts to situate itself in the midst of this methodological debate and, hence, attempts in a polyvalent manner to engage the Durkheimian from a multiplicity of perspectives that seize the tradition in both its original context and its post-Durkheimian mutations.

However, this volume adds a new term to the rethinking of the Durkheimian: violence. Arguing that violence is the blind spot of the Durkheimian oeuvre, at once subtextually present, but never directly engaged by the sociologist, it asks how to account for Durkheim's relative inattention to violence and the attempt of subsequent theorists to fill this lacuna. If Durkheimian logics are pushed to their limits, is the result an inevitable confrontation with this blind spot? Although Durkheim

S. Romi Mukherjee teaches political theory and the history of religions at the *Institut d'Études Politiques de Paris* and the University of Chicago Center in Paris. He is also General Secretary of the *French Society of Durkheimian Studies*. Email: srmukher@uchicago.edu

may have not systematically confronted the production of violence, he was nonetheless interested in the spectrum of feelings attached to violence (melancholy, loss, grief, guilt, rage and so on) and their transformation or resolution. While such feelings functioned as the deep substrate of Durkheim's thought, they were never explicitly theorised, but rather were embedded in a series of Durkheimian concepts, among them being solidarity, sacrifice, anomie and effervescence. Ultimately, we must therefore ask (a) whether there exists a Durkheimian theory of violence and (b) whether such a theory can inform our understanding of contemporary forms of irrationalism?

While this blind spot may produce an ambivalent reading of Durkheim's relationship to violence, it is cannot be said to indicate Durkheim's own ambivalence to these questions.

Traces

Émile Durkheim came of age in an epoch of rupture and accelerating change. The son of a long line of rabbis, Durkheim was born on 15 April 1858 during Napoleon the Third's Second Empire. The Second Empire was typified by the grandiose and false ostentation of a burgeoning urban bourgeois and the simultaneous birth of a new under-class of impoverished *misérables* who found themselves uprooted and excluded from the nascence of modern Paris. With the

beginning of the urban transformations associated with the name of Baron Haussman, Paris
would be enveloped by a rising market economy
and swept up in the preliminary moments of
what we now call late capitalism. The Franco-
Prussian war may have been engineered by
Bismark but Napoleon too, in a classical
political ploy, used it to avert attention from
the economic and social inequities in France.
The Franco-Prussian war was an embarrassment and a blow to French pride, exacerbating
the already marked distinctions between the
bourgeoisie and the poor. Among the most
powerful repercussions of this failed war were
the 1871 uprisings of the Paris Commune. This
attempt to reclaim space, time and the city
would finish with a massacre and the deaths
of more than 40,000 communards. Hence, by
the age of 13, Durkheim had already endured
some of the most violent tremors of modern
French history.

From the ashes of the commune emerged
the Third Republic for which Durkheim would
later become an intellectual spokesman. It was
an entity that was just as fragile, fraught with
the ceaseless chaos of political factions prone
to infighting and rivalry. Total parliamentary
chaos was, nonetheless, kept at bay through
the impassioned desire to resurrect the glory of
France through republican virtues and the
promises of scientism, secularism and pedagogy.
It is against this backdrop that Durkheim
decided not to pursue the rabbinical life but
rather devote himself to his studies. He would
enter the École Normale in 1879 and slowly
begin to formulate the ground for what would
become arguably the most important of modern
disciplines, sociology.

In its Durkheimian guise, sociology was not
a merely descriptive enterprise; it was rather a
highly political domain intent on both diagno-
sing and correcting the ills of the society, the ills
of cohesion and the multitude of forces that
continually threatened to disintegrate the very
possibility of the social. As Durkheim matured
he would be terrified by the sacrificial political
rites that constituted the Dreyfus Affair and
moreover, he would be forced to deploy his very
particular brand of liberal-socialism against an
array of anarchists, intransigent Catholics,
reactionaries and royalists. Not unaffected by
anti-Semitism himself, Durkheim dreamed of

the social as a salve to the traumas of modernity
and a place of solace in which individuals could
feel themselves protected and morally unified.
The Durkheimian social (and its derivative
concepts, the sacred, the symbolic and solidarity) was an elaborately constructed theoretical
edifice that sought to surpass the identitarian,
religious and political divisiveness that had hitherto plagued modern France. It was an attempt to
surpass and suppress the seeds of violence.

By the early twentieth century Durkheim's
sociological revolution was well under way and
the seeds of its own eventual success firmly
planted. Among his greatest talents was team-
building and around his journal *L'Année Sociologique*, he amassed some of the brightest and
most penetrating minds of twentieth-century
thought; among them, Marcel Mauss, Henri
Hubert, Célestin Bouglé, Paul Fauconnet and a
host of other Durkheimians. The Durkheimian
project itself, albeit institutionally victorious,
was delicate in its own right, fragile by virtue of
its optimism in the human project and the moral
constitution of citizens. In his final days,
however, Durkheim was forced to ask if his
vision could ever really be implemented. Durkheim's son André would die in the Great War
in 1917. He himself died that year as well. As
Charles Lemert claims:

> Durkheim, shattered by the death of his son André on the
> Eastern Front, died (one supposes) of a broken heart. Or, it
> is possible that the Great War itself shocked Durkheim into
> the stroke from which he never recovered. Either way,
> whether it was the personal or the social tragedy in the years
> after 1914, Durkheim was in a fashion a doomed giant of
> French sociology. Had his son survived the war, the father
> may still not have survived the crushing evidence it
> represented: the war and its aftermath of absurdities
> brought on by the Versailles Peace Treaty in 1919, which
> ignored the basic rules of social accords – that peace is
> permanently made only when the settlement obeys the rule
> of proportionality between victors and vanquished. Had he
> lived to see Europe in the 1920s even, much less the 1930s,
> the experience would have almost certainly swept away all
> confidence that industrial societies could recapture the
> moral cohesion lost to the decline of the traditional order.
> (Lemert 2006, p.112)

In these last moments Durkheim surely lost the
resolve that had characterised his person
and work, a resolve ascetically distilled from
an equally ambivalent relationship to the
onslaughts of violence that he and his generation

lived through. Considering the epoch and the ferociousness of the sociological project and its agenda, it is surprising to apprehend, as Ivan Strenski suggests in his article in this volume, that almost everything we read about Durkheim indicates that he and his team were averse to violence and that these aversions grew out of a deeply entrenched view of the world and human nature. In other words, following Strenski, Durkheim and the Durkheimians produced a theoretical corpus that was the result of a deep disavowal, the product of an unwavering project for society that refused to integrate into itself the very violence that it registered. However, as this volume demonstrates, the violence that the Durkheimians may have been averse too was nonetheless present in the sediments of their texts and world-view. It was theorised by caveat, by silence and by a certain philosophical straining where, to varying degrees, it was implied as presence by its absence, or uncomfortably interpolated through other analytical tools that sought to absorb it. How do we begin to account for such antagonisms, tensions and paradoxes? In order to begin to respond to this question, the Durkheimian project must placed in its larger context.

Positivism and the Third Republic

Positivism, understood generally as the identity of thought and sensation with the real, created a dark spot and an excess that it simply could not integrate, tame, or master. As Gary Gutting argues, although by and large "French philosophers firmly rejected positivism, they still recognised the centrality of science for philosophical reflection" (Gutting, 2001, p. 26). Hence, one cannot speak of a pure French positivism, but rather of a republican scientism that opposed itself to the equally powerful strains of spiritualism (Bergson) and Idealism (Brunschwig). It should be recalled that, in both its Comtean and Durkheimian variants, in France, social "scientism" was not simply a philosophical or sociological enterprise, but one that was firmly embedded in the ideals, aspirations and practice of the Third Republic.

However, this particular strain of normative positivism, indebted to a sterilised strain of neo-Kantianism which, in jettisoning noumena, was believed to have settled the metaphysical question and, by translating experience into a series of empirical facts, was typified by its resistance to asking certain questions that would problematise its very foundations. Violence remained the most troubling of these questions. Such a scientism could, furthermore, never be adventurous, bodily or transgressive in so far as its doyens were advocates of the Third Republic's *status quo*. For instance, as Theodor Zeldin remarks, in the middle stages of the Third Republic, "philosophers were with time left increasingly free ... it was under the Third Republic that the philosophy teachers' pretensions to social superiority reached their highest level" (Zeldin 1980, p.211). While Durkheim may have been attempting to engineer a moral and political revolution, most of the philosophers of the Third Republic became somewhat too comfortable and thus became victims of liberal reason's complacency, content to believe that the illusion of progress would right all wrongs.

The intellectual ethos of the Third Republic may not have been rigidly positivist, but it also was positive in so far as it was the given; the reified, the ossified, the totalised, that which, like the liberal state, the ego, moralism and social facts, has too much presence. It became a self-satisfied geography of the smooth that denied the rough or ragged that it unsuccessfully tried to cover. If such roughness were to revenge itself on the smooth or the positive, a restless epistemological rupture would appear, one that would reveal the ultimate untenability of liberalism's philosophical assumptions. Violence is both rough and ragged and as the Third Republic entered into a period of decline, Durkheim's bastard epigones (such as Caillois, Bataille and Monnerot,) would overdetermine the ragged against the civilised malaise of the Republic as well its founding concepts: the moral, the person, the rational and the constrained.

Progress, civilisation and violence

The decline of the Durkheimian school of French sociology moved in tandem with the decline of the Third Republic and the advent of the crisis of civilisation of the 1930s. It was in the ashes of this crisis that Durkheimian sociology's blind spot was discovered and exploited and, more generally, that the cult of progress and optimism that characterised the republican spirit and its intellectual centre, the Durkheimian, was violently interpolated. In other words, it was the speed of progress that brought on civilisation's implosion, a speed that offered the veneer of plenitude. And as Paul Virilio remarks:

The invention of the boat was the invention of shipwrecks. The invention of the steam engine and the locomotive was the invention of derailments. The invention of highways was the invention of three hundred cars colliding in five minutes. The invention of the airplane was the invention of the plane crash ... I believe that the accident is to the social sciences what sin is to human nature. It's a certain relation to death that is the revelation of the identity of the object. (Virilio 1997, pp. 38–39)

Crises of civilisation are invisible. Like globalism, one only apprehends the condition of despair after the fact, after the total metastatisation of what appeared to be a subterranean or subcutaneous anomaly. By the mid-1930s the crisis was total, infecting every institutional and moral structure of the French nation and its spirit. The crisis was thus understood in not purely economic or political terms, but as a crisis of humanity, conscience, mastery and will. Hence, in the 1930s an array of dramatic narratives abounded concerning the crisis; narratives that sought to re-reconcile, to transcend and return civilisation to its rightful place. Under all these eschatological narratives of the end is the assumption that the human is itself a liminal passage to something else (ascent or fall). The human, like civilisation, is understood as trans, a stage that precedes something to come. But, in the 1930s the pervasive sentiment was that civilisation, like history, had entered a point of pure inertia, an immobility that preceded its death. Civilisation at its supposed apex was a state of deprivation; the deprivation of dreams, the deprivation of desires, the deprivation of destiny. What thus opened up was the "elsewhere" of the Durkheimian social/sacred dichotomy: reality was elsewhere. And both the apocalypse and redemption pointed to the possibility of an elsewhere that was the negativity of the human, of the Durkheimian – an elsewhere that functions as a primordial illusion that addresses the impossibility of giving the world a real final meaning, an elsewhere that binds us in a state of impossibility. The Durkheimian sociological revolution had reached a point of stagnation.

Hence, Durkheimian logics had to be perverted and reforged against the Durkheimian project itself; the sacred would become convulsive, constraint would come to flirt with fascism, the gift would be succeeded by a mad potlatch, exchange would be rendered impossible, morality would exist only to be transgressed and effervescence would run off the tracks in violent paroxysm. During the 1930s, the left Durkheimian tradition was born, a tradition that would not only create a precarious bridge between the Durkheimian and the post-modern, but also reignite a debate in Durkheimian scholarship between an orthodoxy that sought to resuscitate the Durkheimian project and rescue it from those who betrayed it by mystifying all that it registered and repudiated. This volume offers a tableau of this debate in both its early and late stages and from Durkheim to Halbwachs to Caillois to Baudrillard to Agamben, it re-poses the question of the use-value of violence within the Durkheimian frame, together with its limitations and insights. But today, far from the Third Republic and 1930s, concerns about civilisation's tenability and its dark underbelly continue to occupy scholarship, foregrounding the way in which society remains a delicate and fragile construct. And it goes without saying that violence is not just a figure of intellectual fashion, but a real question that social theory must grapple with in light of the current crisis of civilisation. Moreover, when confronting the various impasses of thinking through contemporary issues of society and violence, social theory finds itself immersed in the Durkheimian *dispositif* whether it cares to admit it or not. This volume therefore functions as one initial attempt to explicitly examine Durkheimian social theory's attempts to navigate such an impasse.

Social facts, sociology

Durkheim's scientism led him to believe that nothing exceeded the sealed universe of social facts and, as Sue Stedman Jones emphasises in this volume, eruptions of historical violence were *maladies*, but maladies that did not escape the interpretive methodology of the social fact. To ascribe to violence the status of the Durkheimian fact is to undercut and refuse theories of violence that pose conflict, rage and bloodshed as the ontological origin of being. In other words, in positing the transcendent *sui generis* nature of the social and the *homo duplex* that emerges within it, Durkheim was already refusing the existence of primordial violence and displacing its malefic effects to the abstract violence that society performs on its members. Violence could thus never be chthonian, subterranean or spiritual, but, as the articles in this volume all demonstrate, was always bound to a total nexus of the social, the psychic, the political, the juridical and the economic. Violence, for Durkheim, was not redemptive: it did not cleanse, purge, or channel, but infected total social life like a plague and functioned as a type of betrayal to the hidden contractual forces that guarded the social. Hence, in the beginning there was not violence but the circulating energies and emerging consciousness of the clan whose stalwart altruism and will to self-sacrifice would efficiently delimit the presence of violence through a disciplined and limited personhood that had internalised the social's deep moral core as something that was necessarily far greater than itself.

But Durkheimian sociology was not simple or utopian. It was, rather, cognisant of the heroic and impossible vision that it nurtured, one nonetheless worth striving for. On the one hand, *fin de siècle* France found itself absorbed with the moral question: the slackening of social ties, the weakening that emerged from the decline of religious institutions, the accelerating tides of consumer capitalism and the constantly fracturing Third Republic all contributed to the sensation of decline that masked itself as progress. The Third Republic, the Republic of professors, laboured to establish a new science of morality that would prescribe solidarism and civic fraternity. A moral science was needed to legitimise solidarism and sanctify socio-political cohesion against the imagined threat of violent upheaval.

Sociology is the symptom of a rupture, of a society that has lost its secret of cohesion and feels itself surrounded by forces that threaten its stability, coherence and illusory order. It is the product of a society that no longer treats the social as a given and finds little reassurance in the representations, institutions, customs and collective systems of belief (myth/ideology/ *doxa*) that contend to constitute the foundations of society. Sociology is born when these phenomena are no longer apprehended as natural, but instead as arbitrary and contingent.

Sociology in its Durkheimian incarnation was to be a corrective to disintegration and disorder, a neo-positivist war machine that aspired to confront and tame those forces of heterogeneity and deviation that threatened the core of the social. It aspired to be a corrective to violence. Moreover Durkheim, the sociologist of the Third Republic, the sociologist of the state, conducted this moral battle in the name of a series of centrist-liberal ideals: individual autonomy placed in the service of higher social causes, a reason that could liberate one from the threat of mania, excess and the passions, scienticism and progress and a moral education that would effectively socialise and ward off violent threats to democracy while fostering and preserving the social bond. Durkheim was already reflecting on the death of the social.

Moreover, although he was a socialist, Durkheim was a bourgeois thinker, one who believed in the virtues of constraint and the ascetic ideal and whose sociology was constituted in large part by appeals to moral, bodily and emotional regulation. In other words, he was always thinking about violence in its symbolic, epistemological and real forms. But while thinking about violence, his utopianism clashed with the definitive impossibility of exorcising it, the darkest of social facts, from the universe. Thus, the Durkheimian theory of violence is charged with ambivalence and resonating within it lies the inexorable tension between the psychic and disciplinary violence inflicted on the person to preserve *nomos* and the transgressions of anomie that not only indicate solitary states of internal violence and socio-economic states of upheaval but also the potential for real physical harm inflicted on the self and others.

Although the articles collected in *Durkheim and violence* do not claim to offer a complete genealogy of the Durkheimian embrace of and turning away from violence, they do move chronologically and gesture towards the possibility of a Durkheimian theory of violence. Introducing and setting the theoretical stage for a Durkheimian theory of violence proves to be no simple task. However, for hermeneutic purposes one can posit that the most rigorous Durkheimian confrontation with violence is oriented around three principal conceptual axes that merit re-discussion: the anomic, the sacrificial and the effervescent.

Fragments from a conflicted itinerary

The anomic, the abnormal: violence and evil

Whether transformed into a slogan, applied as a general term for malaise or rendered transparent to the entire course of modernity, "anomie" is much more than the simple absence of fixed law. It denotes a vast edifice of pathology, personality and political philosophy (that is, the question of how to organise the polis). It describes the horror of insatiability found in both the tectonics of individual desire and the precariousness of modern economies (where the only law is that of accumulation). It refers to delinquency, deviance and transgression. It is a spatial category that maps the hostile rapport between the centre and the margins, between the *doxa* and all that it casts out. It is, moreover, a moral category characterised by impiety, sacrilege, irreligion and immorality. In short, it can be posed as one of the most powerful frames for violence, be it in the form of suicide or crime. Nonetheless, the density of anomie was not lost to the generations that inherited Durkheim's legacy.

Roger Caillois and Georges Bataille, along with numerous other *non-conformistes des années 30*, would render it analogous to the larger *désordre établi* of the 1930s and synthesise it into the panoply of polemics against the crisis of civilisation, the dissolution of social ties that accompanied the loss of myth and the sacred and the critique of democracy and decadence. For these sociologists of the sacred, self-proclaimed anarcho-mystics and sorcerer's apprentices, anomie could only be remedied through the resurrection of a virile and vital sacred and the acted out conjunction of ritual and myth. The question that the College of Sociology (1938–1939), that group of post-Durkheimian sociologists of the sacred who sought themselves to incarnate the sacred, posed – "what is the modern counterpart to the sacred?" – emerges directly from the apprehension of anomie and the perceived rupture.

Sociologists such as Parsons, Dohrenwend and Allart would remain faithful to Durkheim's sociological realism but go further and empty anomie of its metaphysical aura and the *délire du sacré* that functioned as a response to it. It would be transformed into an analytic tool, a typology of norms and deviance that could be applied to any social (dis)organisation. However, the ultimate metamorphosis of the concept would arrive with Robert Merton's *Social theory and social structure* (1957), where anomie would cease to function as the crisis unleashed by modern democracy and late capitalism that turned on its creator, but would be composed of the lack of agreement on appropriate means to achieve culturally approved goals, group discord regarding how to unhinge obstacles. For Merton, anomie was an internal disequilibrium in social structure with an overdetermined set of goals and an equally underdetermined and de-institutionalised set of means. Unlike Durkheim, Merton was more interested in the social causes of anomie than in its consequences and consequentially delimited it, robbed it of its opacity and brought it into a conspiracy with late capitalism itself. Anomie scales and ratios (Sroles) would soon be used by many American sociologists and psychologists in their impossible quest to quantify deviation and normlessness. Criminologists would soon invoke the term to explain sociopathic states while social workers and sex therapists would explain everything from unemployment to marital infidelity with elaborate notions of welfare anomie and conjugal anomie. Popular derivations of anomie would continue to flourish until the mid-1960s when the concept, along with Durkheimianism itself, was eclipsed by the new theoretical paradigms of a generation of thinkers who conducted yet another war against the Enlightenment while feeling little nostalgia for the mythical Third Republic. Yet in the final analysis, anomie was always a cursed concept and, as Philippe Besnard remarks, it "was from the beginning a victim ... when an intellectual product owes its success more to the value of marketing than to its cognitive utility, its decline is inevitable" (Besnard, 1987, p. 387).

In Durkheim's own lifetime the stakes of deviance were very different and Durkheim's theory of anomie was nothing short of a theoretical attempt to ward off the violence of the mind, the violence of desire, the violence of modernity and the threat of violence *tout court*. Desperate to the abolish the threats of Nietzschean active nihilism, Jean-Marie Guyau's emancipatory anomie and the infinity that they so brazenly promised, Durkheim's corpus constructed itself as a recasting of social, psychic and bodily limits. A theorist of the inside or the social limit, the *idée force* that both implicitly and explicitly traverses the Durkheimian corpus is that of anomie and its multifarious consequences. But contrary to popular interpretation, anomie should not be reduced to mere social pathology or lawlessness. Rather, as Jean Duvignaud surmises, this operational concept is associated with the crisis of progress itself, a progress that acts on the interior of society, provoking momentary crises that correspond to efforts of readjustment and of re-adaptation, or simply testify to a general disequilibrium: "Anomie thus corresponds to a catastrophic phase of societies, engendered by a becoming that they themselves have incited by the determinism of progress and industrial production" (Duvignaud 1965, pp. 16–17).

Anomie is a dynamism caught within the fluxes of anarchy and *liberté triste*; it is the gradient that spans radical revolutionary individualism, bourgeois atomised individualism and the mortifying melancholia and ennui of massification where, as Denis Hollier quips, "Being is being bored".

The problem of establishing a precise definition of anomie has forever plagued the social sciences, theology and the history of religions. Anomie is a derivative of the Greek *anomia* that itself derives from the adjective *anomos*, literally meaning without *nomos* (law or culture). However, this simple definition scours the signifier of any real content. Immediately one asks what constitutes the law that is lacking; is *nomos* a civic or polity-based law? Is it divine law? Is it a wilful or voluntary suspension of law? Is it sin or is it crime? Or is it simply the oscillation between stability and instability, the cohesion and dispersion that characterises human life? Is it a synonym for mutation?

For Durkheim things were seemingly less complicated but by no means simple. All that was not useful and threatened republican euphoria and solidarity with explosive or paralysing dystopia participated not only in the machinations of the left-sacred but also emerged from the dark desert of anomie where all becomes dispersed. Dispersion is a laceration to the social body, a violent and literal tearing apart of tissue, organs and skin. Although existing on a gradient from metaphorical atomisation to real social violence, anomie was a general state in which all forms of disaggregation could be grouped. Moreover, it was a metaphysical site: anomie, as the movement towards non-form, nothingness and dissolution, forms the ground or rather groundlessness of being upon which society must be imposed. Anomie should, in principle, be thwarted by entrance into the symbolic, language and representation. But in Guyau and Nietzsche, the great enemies of representational regimes, Durkheim, one of the great arbiters of the symbolic, must have sensed the presence of real menace to the sociological revolution, one that carried within it the locus of violence.

Durkheim was an enemy of radical interiority and he would go on to completely distinguish himself from the Guyau–Nietzsche scourge and refine his critique of anomic immanence in *De la division du travail social* (1893). For Durkheim, only *conscience collective* was rightly *sui generis* and where Guyau asked that we become individual metaphysical workers, "*les ouvriers de nos croyances*", Durkheim, on the other hand, proclaimed:

The division of labour does not present individuals to one another, but social functions. And society is interested in the play of the later; in so far as they regularly concur, or do not concur, it will be healthy or ill. Its existence thus depends upon them and the more they are divided the greater its dependence. That is why it cannot leave them in a state of indetermination. (Durkheim 1947, p.407)

The *Division of labour* was Durkheim's first contribution to the rising field of the science of morality and an early formulation of the devastating effects of anomie. Here, anomie is an abnormal form and although the term is not theologically coloured, as a threat to morality and its correlate solidarity, Durkheim alludes to its original etymology, to evil and sin:

[Society] is the arbiter naturally designed to settle interests in conflict and to assign to each its suitable limits. Then it has the chief interest in order and peace; if anomy if evil, it is above all because society suffers from it, being unable to live without cohesion and regularity. A moral or juridical regulation essentially expresses then social needs that society alone can feel; it rests in a state of opinion and all opinion is a collective thing, produced by collective elaboration. For anomy to end, there must exist, or be formed, a group which can constitute the system of rules actually needed . . . this is what is called the corporation or occupational group. (Durkheim 1947, p.5)

Moreover, in the original 1893 introduction to the study (struck from later editions), Durkheim clearly responds to Guyau and hence, by extension, to Nietzsche:

The sentiment of obligation, that is the existence of duty, is in danger of being weakened in admitting there is a morality and perhaps a higher one, which rests on the independent creation of the individual, which no rule determines, which is essentially *anomic*. We believe, on the contrary, that *anomie* is the contradiction of all morality. (Durkheim 1947, p.431, n. 21)

According to Durkheim, it is impossible and dangerous to move beyond good and evil, and obligation, duty and sanction are the capstones of individual and social life. When shirked, the evil plague of anomie contaminates the previously healthy fabric of society. Obligation, duty and sanction are not simply imperatives. They are moral facts tied to the "rule of conduct to which a repressive diffuse sanction is attached" and "whether it stands alone or not", it "is moral" (Durkheim 1947, p.427). Morality corresponds to social density and anomic evil is its diffusion, dispersion and malfunctioning. Law, morality and virtue are hence synonymous with the social aggregate and all that forces one to take account of others is intrinsically moral. Anomie is, therefore, any disengagement from the environment and any resistance to integration in the social organism; any refusal of coherence (or conversely, too much integration in the organism; a coherence that destroys the individual's dialectical relationship to the social). The Durkheimians were not violent revolutionaries but patient reformers who believed that one is moral precisely because one is bound in this dialectic and "the state of nature of the philosophers of the nineteenth century, if not immoral, is, at least, *amoral*" (Durkheim 1947, p.39). Individualism or the duty of one towards oneself (the imperative of liberal regimes) can only be rendered moral if it converges with duty and obligation towards the social body. The slightest deviation from such a concurrence opens the floodgates to anomie and the negation of the social – violence in its many forms.

One must therefore remain aware of the fusion of one's occupational role and larger social interdependence, the wellspring of organic solidarity. Greater interdependence and hence, solidarism in the division of labour establish the conditions for moral, economic and social regulation. Following from this, anomie can only be exorcised from the social field through heightened solidarity:

If the division of labour does not produce solidarity in all these cases, it is because the relations of the organs are not regulated, because they are in a state of anomie. But whence comes the state? Since a body of rules is the definite form which spontaneously established relations between social functions take in the course of time, we can say, a priori, that a state of anomy is impossible wherever solidarity organs are sufficiently in contact or sufficiently prolonged (Durkheim 1947, p.368)

Anomie is an aberration in the well-oiled normative plan of *nomos* engendered by a rupture in social interaction. It emerges from the incapacity of the state apparatus to successfully ward off the solitude of specialisation, the atomisation of modern capital and labour, through the consecration of an ever-strengthening internal solidarity. The ultimate aim of fostering such solidarity is to ensure the orchestration of social functions and prevent individuals from ever experiencing themselves as self-sufficient. Dependence is a virtue and the labour and creative endeavour of one individual are transparent to the labour of another. One's work and creations are never one's own and, although Durkheim allows for moral and functional diversity, the products of one's labour must serve the social that reciprocally serves the state that is responsible for generating internal cohesion. The division of labour slowly reveals the *sui generis* nature of solidarity that, when joined by the juridical power of the state, can collectively retaliate against anomie; the criminal, Durkheim's supreme anomic, *offends* the sentiments of the social. Consequently he disrupts the division of labour and its moral and psychic force and incites everyone to oppose the attack,

for while opposite sentiments oppose each other, similar sentiments attract each other and as strongly do they attract as they themselves are intense . . . since it is common conscience which is attacked, it must be that which resists and accordingly the resistance must be collective. (Durkheim 1947, pp.102–103)

The criminal incurs public scorn for having failed in "obligations voluntarily contracted". In short, the social organ must dispose of its excreta and punish that which opposes collective consciousness. Social cohesion is thus also dependent upon the force of repressive law, prohibition and punishment. Crime is not simply an offence to collective sentiment, but an offence "against an authority in some way *transcendent*" (Durkheim 1947, p.85, my emphasis). Punishment, for Durkheim, is furthermore, not simply irrational vengeance but an essential principle for social cohesion and for the articulation and catharsis of violent emotions. Alienation from the objects of one's labour, instrumentalisation, unemployment, poverty and inequity are among the many causes of crime, delinquency and deviation. Durkheim's labourer is, however, immune to the forces of degradation and is without want or desire to see and become more:

For he feels he is serving something. For that, he need not embrace vast portions of the social horizon. It is sufficient that he perceive enough of it to understand that his actions have an aim beyond themselves. From that time, as special and uniform as his activity may be, it is that of an intelligent being, for it has direction and he knows it. (Durkheim 1947, pp.372–373)

Therefore, the problem was the attempt to embrace the social horizon or, rather, the drive to become more than human, to transcend finitude and a healthy respect for scarcity and believe that one can indeed become the cosmos.

Disciplining infinity

The years 1895–1896 signalled, as Philippe Besnard remarks, the "most anomic period in Durkheim's life" (cited in Fournier 2007, p.281). As Marcel Fournier explains, he was besieged by the plague on all fronts:

[D]omestic anomie resulting from the death of his father; progressive anomie from long-awaited professional, troubled by a "slightly severe" critique and the difficulty in creating a new journal; finally and above all, the indetermination of the object to which he was going to devote his life's work and a feeling of vertigo in the face of a new discovery in his scientific horizon. (Fournier 2007, p.281)

The plunge into the new discovery, that of religion was, however, temporarily forestalled by his own sociological attempt to come to grips with what he was feeling. In *Suicide: a study in sociology* (1897), Durkheim attempted to explain the terror of such indeterminations, expectations and vertigos. *Suicide* further explored anomic deviations through a series of provocative but empirically unsound analyses of the relations between social vitality and integration, modern industrial society, egoism, anomie and suicide. While most commentators telescope the correlation between economic crises and suicide or Durkheim's theory of types (egoistic, fatalistic, anomic), the key to unlocking the enigmatic and often contradictory theses on anomie that litter the pages of *Suicide* is what Durkheim describes at some length as *le mal de l'infini*. One must therefore move past the standard exposition of suicide as a symptom of weak social integration, a society that no longer holds individuals under its control and examine the infinity complex.

The infinity complex is a state of passion without limit, a hypertrophy of desire beyond measure and the desire for unrestrained expansion; it is the infinite of the dream, the infinite of desire wrapped simultaneously in egoism and the will to surpass and dissolve the ego itself through a becoming-totality. Durkheim perceived it as a disequilibrium that accompanies rapid economic expansion (progressive anomie) and crises (regressive anomie). He was, perhaps unknowingly, positing a libidinal materialism that associated the fluxes of desire with socio-economic transmutation. Both poverty and prosperity lead to anomic suicide but the proclivity to suicide does not always emerge from a crisis of scarcity or the ennui of overabundance. Rather, it is imbricated into a larger equilibrium of desire:

If therefore industrial or financial crises increase suicides, this is not because they cause poverty, since crises of prosperity have the same result; it is because they are crises, that is, disturbances of the collective order. Every disturbance of equilibrium, even though it achieves greater comfort and a heightening of general vitality, is an impulse to voluntary death. Whenever serious readjustments take place in the social order, whether or not due to a sudden growth of an unexpected catastrophe, men are more inclined to self-destruction. (Durkheim 1951, p.246)

Equilibrium denotes the state of rest and balance between need, desire, means and resources. In other words it describes a state where appetites and violent instincts are firmly repressed and controlled by a reality principle that curtails the desire for more and introduces an asceticism whereby the organism craves only what it needs to subsist and function in the social arrangement: "when the void created by existence in its own resources is filled, the animal, satisfied, asks nothing further" (Durkheim 1951, p.246). Society must establish firm regulations and a stringent set of checks and balances on desire itself in order to avert individuals reckoning with "insatiability and bottomless abyss". Unregulated and unlimited desires are anomic, producing states of morbidity and inflicting the most painful and renewed torture on their progenitors. That is, for Durkheim, one must not desire infinity or desire infinitely; individuals must not only accept finitude, but also resign themselves to finitude or be condemned to a state of perpetual unhappiness (Durkheim 1951, p.248). Morality is the cohesion of the social aggregate, a cohesion that may exist only when individuals divest themselves of the undulations of restless desire; the passions must be limited and harmonised with the other faculties by virtue of a moral regulative force. Accept your lot or succumb to the internal violence of anomie, an internal violence that threatens to externalise itself.

Unlike Rousseau, Durkheim assumed that in the "natural state", people would never consent to a limit on desire and expansion. Transgressive by nature, the natural state of desire is revolutionary. Furthermore, people cannot "assign themselves this law of justice. So they must receive it from an authority which they respect, to which they yield spontaneously"; namely, society (Durkheim 1951, p.249). Zygmunt Bauman describes this as the Durkheimian managerial posture, a sociology that liberates through mechanisms of social control. But there is, indeed, a theological substrate to such bureaucratisation as well as an overarching distrust of the individual; while society is composed of those individuals, in order to become a symbolic force to be obeyed, it must assume the function of the radical Other, the absolute Other that is God. Durkheim's clever idea to deify society would, nevertheless,

repeatedly encounter an obstacle: society as a collection of singularities could never be fully transcended by the absolute Other that was at the same time constituted by these singularities. The dilemma was always how to make society radically Other, so society could transform itself into something present and felt but remain transcendent. While the aggregate, the immanent-transcendent social would aspire to subjugate and control these singularities themselves, it could never channel the coefficients of desire circulating under its so-called transcendent guise. To limit ambitions and create an individual who respects regulations and is docile to collective authority through the internalisation of moral discipline would therefore be the only means of controlling the anomic ruptures and the desire for infinity that would actually translate into a desire to surpass the state formation itself. The race for an unattainable goal would necessarily call into question the segmentation and discipline of the social order and thus, open the way to violence and deviance. Transcending the body and the body's yoke would imply the possibility of transcending the yoke of the social body. To this, Durkheim would insist on the body's existence as subject to that of society (Durkheim 1951, p.252). The dilemma of the human animal is precisely its insatiability and will to expansion (material, psychic, libidinal, spiritual), its limitlessness, a sociological version of Hegelian "bad infinity," where beyond experienced pleasures one senses and desires others … "one thirsts for the non-existent … the result of it all is a state of disturbance, agitation and discontent, which inevitably increases the possibilities of suicide" (Durkheim 1951, p.271).

Hard school

Durkheim, however, had an answer. The central institution, the nucleus of moral order and regulation was the school system. Here the young would be socialised through a pedagogy that would obtain consensus and, through the spirit of discipline, attachment to social groups, autonomy and self-determination students would find themselves equipped to participate in the social organ's prolonged struggle against anomic forces. While "individuals are made aware of society and their dependence upon it through the state", "since this is far from them, it can exert only a distant, discontinuous influence over them" (Durkheim 1951, p.389). To remedy the evils of egoism and anarchy, a point of relay for state morality was of the highest necessity. The sociological revolution, its civilising process and the establishment of an unbreakable moral *habitus*, would require a pedagogical revolution as well. The classroom would be transformed into a foyer for moral energy and form the heart of the social organism. *L'éducation morale*, a collection of Durkheim's lectures on pedagogy, proposes an educational solution to the crisis of anomie: "Science should proceed prudently . . . pedagogy does not have the right to remain patient to the same degree; because it responds to vital necessities which cannot wait" (Durkheim 1938, p.1). The societal crisis is ever imminent and schools should be reconceived as buffering mechanisms, walls of radical resistance and barricades against anomic barbarism. Educators are the incarnation of *nomos* and the societal morality that they brandish attacks individualism with the law and the morals that fix our conduct. As authorities, educators exercise "on us all moral force which we recognise as superior to ourselves", and through regular discipline, they gain our consented obedience (Durkheim 1938, p.33). Morality is the synthesis of commandment and habit and, felt to be *sui generis* with the social itself, the spirit of discipline (scholarly, bodily, socially and so on) that education provides constructs the good and fundamental disposition of the moral temperament. Children will here be taught not simply how to read, write and reason, but also how to control their desires and manage their appetites. They will not feel this as an intrusion because they are filled with the religious and moral feeling of the school and its teachers; just as a priest interprets God, teachers interpret the moral ideas of their time and country (*patrie*). The child, having internalised these disciplinary mechanisms, will then become a contributing member to the social organism and go on to instil these virtues in future generations.

Therefore, the sensation of infinity appears only when the moral core of the institution begins to break down, where moral discipline has been robbed of its authority (Durkheim 1938, p.349). Durkheim rationally justifies the use of severe discipline (inspiring *douleur*) by the potential happiness that individuals will eventually feel as a result. Discipline, moreover, an instrument of victory, is the only means for one to realise one's nature and it must historically vary itself if humanity's vision of their nature shifts, but one must always avoid the lack of discipline that, once again, is morally incomplete (Durkheim 1938, p.59–60). For undisciplined individuals comprehend neither *devoir* nor prohibition nor the good, which is the moral ideal that flows through the secular *mana* of the school. Teachers must thus infect every student with this *mana*, bringing the young to become aware of themselves as moral agents dependent upon society, school, the state and the family. They themselves must ascend to the status of the sociological cleric who proffers morality and quashes anomic individualism under the mandate of the state. Without such directors of consciousness, society becomes an anomic flux, a space of explosive violence.

L'Essai sur la nature et fonction du sacrifice

At the turn of the century Durkheim was worried about his nephew Marcel Mauss. The young man lacked the celebrated discipline of his uncle. He was struggling to complete various essays and displayed few signs of being a young scholar with a promising academic career before him. According to Durkheim, Mauss was "ill suited for the intellectual life" and Durkheim was severe with his pleasure-seeking nephew who hankered after the "sweetness of life" (Fournier 2006, p.70). As the famous story goes, when Mauss was having drinks with his friends, he would duck under the café table at the slightest hint that his uncle was approaching. But Durkheim would not relent and enlisted Henri Hubert to "help him in the rescue operation" (Fournier 2006, p.70).

Hubert would become one of Mauss' dearest friends and collaborators. Their first major collective enterprise *L'Essai sur la nature et function du sacrifice* (1899), would not only be a spirited attack on Catholic annihilationism, the Aryan-Semitic thesis and Robertson Smith, but also come to figure as *the* text that not only solidified the sacred–profane binary as a key Durkheimian contribution, but more importantly introduced sacrificial discourse to contemporary scholarly debate. As Derrida, Girard, Burkert, Evans-Pritchard and a host of others have shown, one cannot think about sacrifice without engaging with Hubert and Mauss's landmark study. The two 26-year olds were fully aware of what they were doing and certainly anticipated the deep influence (and repercussions) that the study, a "Durkheimian theory of sacrifice", (Strenski 2002, p.163) would have. In an 1898 letter to Mauss, Hubert shed light on the stakes of the enterprise:

We shouldn't miss a chance to make trouble for these good, but badly informed, souls. Let's stress the direction of our work, let's be clear about our aims so that they are pointed, sharp like razors and so that they are treacherous. . . . Now, my friend, we are condemned to engage in a religious polemic. . . . Onward, I like combat. Let it spur us on. (Strenski 2002, p.165; Fournier 2006, p.71)

They were in fact condemned to the Republic, Dreyfussardism, civic virtues and anti-racism and the polemic operated on a series of socio-logical, religious and political fronts. Conduct-ing a fierce battle against such Catholic annihilationist *obscura*, Hubert and Mauss argued that there were limits to abnegation. Republicans, but also "prudent" and bourgeois thinkers they concluded, in a thesis that would be perfected in Mauss's theory of the gift, that the "ambiguity of sacrifice" was found in the commingling of disinterest and self-interest:

[T]his abnegation is not without submission and not without its selfish aspect. The *sacrificer* gives up something of himself but he does not give himself. Prudently, he sets himself aside. This is because if he gives, it is partly to receive. . . . Disinterestedness is mingled with self-interest . . . the two parties present exchange their services and each gets his due. For the gods too have the need of the profane. (Hubert and Mauss 1964, p.100)

The Catholic annihilationist imperative to self-immolation was antithetical to the Consti-tution of the Republic that depended rather on civic sacrifice and giving of oneself, not a total giving up of oneself. In a secular republic, expiation was no longer a primordial need nor a necessary mechanism to the proper function-ing of the social body. While the Christian ideal may "one of the most instructive to be met with in history" (Hubert and Mauss 1964, p.93), its instruction took the form of overdetermined

representations and dogma that alienated people as opposed to embracing them: what it asked of them was impossible and drastically out of place in the Third Republic. It could not be adapted to "proper bourgeois individuals who do not 'give up themselves'" (Strenski 2002, pp.166–167).

Moreover, following the lead of Sylvain Lévi, to whom their own text was greatly indebted, Hubert and Mauss defiantly rejected the Aryan-Semite distinction by not only affirm-ing the universal social nature of sacrificial rites but also by placing at the centre of the text Semitic, Vedic and Hindu rituals of all pedigrees. While Aryanists continued to believe that India served as the final destination and first home of the Indo-Europeans and thus, also the first home of myth, Hubert and Mauss argued that "the study of the Hindu sacrifice presents the whole gamut of the [sacrificial] practices – a rare instance – both those attributions to the gods and those concerning communication to the sacrifiers" (Hubert and Mauss 1964, p.41).

Moreover, in an ultimate inversion, they claimed that the Catholic Mass was identical to Hindu sacrifices and thus argued for the historical continuity of Aryan ritual life, or rather its deep embeddedness in the Semitic ritual system itself (Hubert and Mauss 1964, p.93–94). In blurring all of the boundaries, the Catholic Hubert and the Jewish Mauss transcended the Aryan-Semite divide through an exercise in socialist scholarship, one which hoped once and for all to expunge scholarship of its perverse myths of origins and roving racialist subtexts. And this was by no means a casual agenda. As Bruce Lincoln adds, Hubert, who reviewed all books on race for *L'Année sociologique* and insisted that the Germans were not actually Indo-Europeans, but were instead influenced by the Celts, "systematically combated all attempts to provide racism and anti-Semitism with scholarly apparatus, language and legiti-macy" (Lincoln 1999, p.127). Mauss and Hubert thus insisted on the "generic unity of sacrifices" (Hubert and Mauss 1964, p.13).

The curve: theory to the rescue of theology?

However, in the midst of these various polemics, Hubert and Mauss also proposed a novel methodological and theoretical paradigm for engaging the question of sacrifice. On one hand, in what now appears as run-of-the mill materialism, Hubert and Mauss dispensed with the hitherto dominant theologies of sacrifice by offering a purely sociological theory of sacrifice that understood ritual in only its social and economic dimensions. In classical Durkheimian fashion, this was yet another radical recasting of religious and spiritual life in civic life and, in fact, as Strenski advances, nothing short of "an attempt to justify social policy with global implications", a text that understood sacrifice as a matter of the state (Strenski 2003a, p.21). And while chided by both Catholic traditionalists and Sylvain Lévi for being "dogmatic" and falling prey to "abstraction" (Strenski 2003a, p.21 and Fournier 2006, p.74), the study was the first of its kind to evade both descriptive rhapsody and theological flight, proving that the choice of both discipline and method was also ideologically coded, informed by one's values and vision of social life. Stated simply, for Hubert and Mauss, "sacrifice is a social function because sacrifice is concerned with social matters" (Hubert and Mauss 1964, p.102).

The theory itself also broke new ground, although it was indebted to Robertson Smith's theory of sacrificial communion that reduced all sacrifice to the dual vectors of communion with the gods and social kinship in the collective imbibing of the sacrificial animal, libation, or meal (Robertson Smith 2002, pp.213–440). Nonetheless, Hubert and Mauss argued against Smith's desire to locate every possible kind of sacrifice in primitive simple form, (Hubert and Mauss, 1964, p.95) and, more specifically, criticised his errant misreading of the Latin *sacrificium – sacer facere –* which signifies not simply communion, but a dynamic and liminal process of making sacred, of transforming, of moving, displacing and acting upon. Therefore, for Hubert and Mauss, "Sacrifice is a religious act which, through the consecration of a victim, modifies the condition of the moral person who accomplishes it or that of certain objects with which he is concerned" (Hubert and Mauss 1964, p.13).

Moreover, the act, the elaborate transformative rite, moves the participants involved from one world into another through the destruction of the victim. Hence, in a secondary definition Mauss and Hubert add, "This proce-

dure consists in establishing a means of communicating between the sacred and the profane worlds through the mediation of a victim, that is, of a thing that in the course of the ceremony is destroyed" (Hubert and Mauss 1964, p.97).

The rite is thus animated in the form of an ontological curve that transports profane life into the sacred and then returns it to the profane. It is in the trajectory of the arc that the consecration occurs, where the "devotee who provides the victim" acquires a religious character which he did not have before" and rids himself of an unfavourable character; the devotee, *the sacrifier*, is changed internally, but also transformed in a spiritual economy that brings him into communication with the gods. He receives benefits and profits from the energies released through the destroyed victim (Hubert and Mauss 1964, pp.9–10). This is the ultimate end of the sacrifice. The sacrificial curve, furthermore, proceeds by way of a series of highly elaborate and ritualised steps that we can summarise as follows:

The beginning of the curve: the creation of a religious atmosphere in which only religious agents may function

1. Pre-sacrificial ceremonies in which the sacrifier is purified, sacralised and purged of his temporal and profane being (the shaving of the head, cutting of nails, ritual garments, anointing, and so on);
2. The introduction of the sacrificer (who is nearer the sacred and performs the rite), who functions as a guide into the fiery forces of the sacred and ensures that the sacrifier does not commit fatal errors. He is always already sanctified;
3. The sacralisation of the holy site and the ritual instruments by the sacrificer;
4. The choice of the victim, supplied by the sacrifier, instilled with a sacred character by the sacrificer and transformed from a profane mortal into the property of the gods while remaining in contact with mankind;
5. The creation of a chain of intermediaries and homologies:
   sacrifier → sacrificer → instrument → victim → gods;

The pinnacle of the curve

6. The sacrifice of the victim and the release of sacred energies from his body;
7. The ritual distribution and/or eating of the sacred portions (sacred shares) of the corpse, with the divine share going to the priest and the patron who ingest the sacred strength of the victim. This may also be accompanied by the sale of the corpse's skin. The destruction of unused shares;
8. The exit: the ritualised de-sacralisation of the holy site and the washing of instruments and utensils used;

The completion of the curve

9. The return to the profane where the sacrifier continues to profit from his benefits (Hubert and Mauss 1964, pp.19–49).

Unlike theories that concentrate on the choice of the scapegoat or the processes of sacralising the *homo sacer* previous to the rite itself, Mauss and Hubert, presaging the insights of Girard, insisted that the victim and his sacrificial aura were purely arbitrary, "made" and "indifferent to the current that passes through it"; like an empty vessel to which sacred powers are imparted to make it suitable, they are simply markers of passage, bloody screens of what could be a potentially equally arbitrary setting for communication (Hubert and Mauss 1964, p.97). The motor of the sacrificial rite was therefore not the victim but rather the priest who imparts the sacred and the beneficiary who profits from the energies released during the sacrifice. Hence, the theory of sacrifice was meticulously organised in a commodity-based model of a patron who pays a priest to make a sacred victim from which the patron will profit. Gone, thus, are the eternal return, the return to primordial chaos or the symbolic scapegoating of the barbarians who are always at the gates. Mauss and Hubert's sacrifice is a bourgeois rite and, indeed, the property of priests and patrons. Theory may have saved theology, but in lieu of Catholic total annihilation, Mauss and Hubert ask one to *give of*, only to gain indefinitely. And for their entire animus towards *homo economicus* they chose an unstable middle path between the socialist and the liberal, a middle path that, moreover, did not entirely resolve but merely deferred the question of violence.

Although staunchly arguing for the individual's sacrifice to the greater transcendent holism of the social and the Republic, what they too could not overcome was the central aspect of the sacrificial rite itself: violence. Hence, with *L'essai* they appear hopelessly torn between a desire to flee from the horror of the sacrifice by downplaying the identity and nature of the victim, while being unable to concede that there could be a sacrifice without a victim or loser and thereby to give credence to the Girardian rejection of the anthropology of sacrifice. In their attempts to liberalise and socialise violence, the result, as Strenski remarks in this volume, is a sanitisation of sacrifice and an uneasy admission that sacrifice is bloody, but that it is nonetheless useful.

Such sanitisation does reveal the dark spot of the Durkheimian sociological project itself, a dark spot that Mauss and Hubert were at pains to fully exorcise from their vision of civic sacrifice. And although Mauss would attempt a correction with the theory of the gift, the truth may have simply been that the perpetuation of social cohesion through those non-religious social practices linked to sacrifice (Hubert and Mauss, 1964, p.103) may not depend on how much one gives, but rather on how such giving is itself dependent upon the fact that *something* has to give. This dark spot or negativity of Durkheimian theory, fully present in both the sociological and religious texts, would be exploited and exploded by Durkheim's prodigal sons, among them Bataille and Caillois, and create the foundations of a Durkheimianism against itself; a Durkheimianism that set the stage for a historical *malentendu*.

Durkheim and sacrifice: impatience, fear, dread: penal forms

By 1899 Durkheim's sociological theory was already replete with visions of civic and secular sacrifice; the violence that society commits on individual consciousness calls individuals to sacrifice of themselves to uphold society and its moral core. Discipline, abnegation, rigour and restraint formed the *dispositif* of Durkheim's Republic, which was entirely dependent upon the spirit of individual sacrifice. As anomie loomed on the horizon Durkheim implored citizens to curb their egoism and longings, solidify family life and transform themselves into the strong and noble "institutional" men who were master "expiators" – teachers, intellectuals, secular clerics, citizens, the republican *paterfamilias*, reformers and so on (Stoekl, 1992, p.26) – that Durkheim envisioned as the guardians of the republican spirit. In other words, individuals were by nature sacrificed in so far as they were subjected and/or subjugated by social moral consciousness and, furthermore, subjected to the republican church, the school and the republican supra-consciousness, the state. Personhood, a sacred entity entirely divorced from the individual or the ego was the necessary product of self-sacrifice.

Interminably worried about his own nephew's descent into the wasteland of anomic moral chaos Durkheim, who had already reflected deeply on the question of sacrifice, oversaw the rescue mission and carefully watched over the progress of their first joint venture with a mix of impatience, fear, dread and expectation (Fournier 2006, p.73, 2007, pp.393–394). His attempts to discipline his nephew's labour were supplemented, however, by a series of very real intellectual concerns that indeed criticised the blind-spot in Hubert and Mauss' essay. In a celebrated letter of July 1898, Durkheim insists on the primacy of penal sacrifice, making *la vendetta* the origin of sacrificial rite (Durkheim 1998, p.154). *Pace* Van Gennep and others who rebuked him for his supposedly inert vision of a society without competition, Durkheim was thinking very seriously about the relationship between sacrifice, pain, destruction, conflict and social expiation. Even Frazer had overlooked the central function of sacrifice; for Durkheim, "the idea of destruction is essential to the sacrifice" (Durkheim 1998, p.154). Hence, Durkheim exhorted his young colleagues to confront the lacuna of Frazer's work and firmly establish a penal theory of sacrifice, without which the study would be incomplete. In response, Mauss would attempt to integrate his uncle's concerns into the plan of the text that he and Hubert had already decided upon (Durkheim 1998, pp.157–160), but his attempts to propitiate Durkheim would elicit another clarification by his uncle. Insisting again on the primacy of penal sacrifice, he would again posit that the nucleus of the institution of sacrifice lies in the elements of

"repression, obligatory destruction, imposition with the only end of destruction . . . the penal idea is the heart of sacrifice" (Durkheim 1998, p.162). Moreover, the taxonomy of sacrifice did not oppose Durkheim's conclusions in so far as

The penitence of a Christian is a penalty (*peine*), like the expiatory offering. All penalty is an expiation and all expiation is a penalty . . . to immolate a man in order to avenge moral outrage and to immolate a man in order to avenge a god, to appease a god, appears to me to be of the same nature. (Durkheim 1998, pp.162–163)

With the Dreyfus Affair weighing heavily on his spirit, Durkheim was not willing to allow his nephew to gloss over the vengeful and destructive dimensions of sacrifice in favour of a sketch of its socio-genesis. Durkheim countered that sacrifice was a penal phenomenon tied to archaic and modern institutions of expiation and various attempts to channel social violence. As for Mauss and Hubert's finished product, they mention the penal in the introduction and conclusion but, while feigning agreement with Durkheim's casual equation of penalty and sacrifice, they do not dwell on the *négativité du sacrifice* (Tarot 2008, p.299).

The circle

Durkheim surpassed the myth/ritual divide or, rather, fused the opposing terms through the introduction of the category of belief. But, as Strenski remarks, even though Durkheim actually wanted it both ways, ritual inevitably prevailed for the sociologist intent on bringing the gods down to earth (Strenski 2006a, p.151). Pickering, however, suggests that Durkheim maintained the primacy of belief over both myth and ritual, but gave ritual equal importance, finally lodging his thought in the interstices of the belief/ritual nexus and exploring how one category undergirds the other (Pickering 1984, p.65). But within these ambivalences, transformations and transcendences, ritual was a central concern to Durkheim and forms the contents of one of the lengthiest section of the *Elementary forms* (almost the entirety of Book II). Amongst his greatest and decidedly anti-Aryanist interventions was to demonstrate the rational basis of ritual, its universality, eternity and importance as a type of social cement. But, as Pickering further notes, Durkheim himself "played down his findings on ritual rather than having emphasized them ... ritual thus constitutes a forgotten chapter in Durkheim's work" (Pickering 1984, pp.322–323). Among the possible reasons for this was the dialectical nature of Durkheim's impossible vision of social progress; one where individuals would eventually liberate themselves from collective representations and incarnate social morality in a kind of self-sufficient solidarity that no longer depended on the representation for its renewal. But the path to such a vision was certainly obfuscated by the human institutions of exchange and transaction, and the need to render tangible and concrete the vectors of belief.

However, surprisingly, in the sections on sacrifice in the *Elementary forms*, he neither asserts the primacy of the penal and the penalty nor proceeds to correct the shortcomings of Hubert and Mauss. According to Strenski, Durkheim may have been at a loss and knowing that the theory of his disciples had displaced his own, the *Elementary forms* at best presented a "confused and derivative concept of sacrifice" (Strenski 2003a, p.23). But Durkheim's contribution on sacrifice in the *Elementary forms* should not be rejected as inferior to that of Mauss and Hubert. In the Durkheimian tradition, Mauss and Hubert's text may be the theory but Durkheim's writings on sacrifice in the *Elementary forms* are certainly an important supplement. In fact, as Alun Jones has revealed, Durkheim's Australian data conflicted with the conclusions of Hubert and Mauss; the victim was already sacred and not consecrated (Alun Jones 1981, p.198). On the one hand, Durkheim, unlike Mauss, was struggling to theorise a vision of purely disinterested republican sacrifice while simultaneously attempting to secularise sacrifice and guard it as a religious act. On the other, the theory of Smith had to be reappraised in light of Spencer and Gillian's data. For Durkheim, the most salient problematic concerned the paradox of the gods themselves:

The contradiction that Robertson Smith saw as inadmissible, a piece of blatant il-logic must still be explained. If sacred beings always manifested their powers in a perfectly equal manner, it would appear inconceivable that man should have dreamed of offering them favours. It is hard to see what they could have needed from him. (Durkheim 1995, p.348)

Durkheim's response is at once naturalistic and materialist. He embeds people in nature, aligning them with its rhythms and its cyclical "splendour and fading", only to conclude that, as ontologically contiguous with nature, "man can never take part in these spectacles as an indifferent watcher" and if he is to live, the gods, with which he also ontologically identified, "must not die ... in a word, he will make offerings" (Durkheim 1995, p.349). Hence, the sacrifice of the Arunta's "fecundating blood" is a cosmic act and, moreover, total in so far as physical and mental crises participate in the same rhythms of exuberance and entropy. However, Durkheim does not lapse into metaphysical speculation but immediately contends that

the sacred beings are sacred only because they are imagined as sacred ... in actuality it is in group life that these representations are formed and group life is by nature intermittent. They achieve their greatest intensity when individuals are assembled and in direct relations with each one another, at the moment that everyone communes in the same idea or emotion. Once the assembly is dissolved and each person has returned to his own existence those representations lose more and more of their original energy ... now they cannot weaken without sacred beings' losing their reality ... [it is] because the gods are in this state of dependence on the thought of man that man can believe his help to be efficacious. (Durkheim 1995, p.349)

In Durkheim's sacrificial schema, it is the gods who need the clan. In the logic of quid pro quo the Durkheimian tautology is remobilised once more. Sacrifice is a rite of social renewal and resurrection in which offerings are made to representations of the social (the gods) that are homologous to the clan itself in order to resolidify social foundations that wither in the rhythms of natural, cosmic and social life in which they are further imbricated and wholly identified. Reawakening the consciousness of the gods through the sacrificial offering is tantamount to revitalising social consciousness in each member of the group and hence, the entire ritual, albeit real and bloody, takes place in the consciousness of the clan member in a labyrinthine site of representation, reflection, mimicry and identification. Hence, sacrifice is at once "an act of communion" and "an act of offering" that "awakens in people the idea of a moral subject" (Durkheim 1995, pp.346–347). Hence, one can speak of the macro-circle of the sacrificial rite that cyclically rejuvenates the social and consciousness of the social and the micro-circle in which civic

Tug of war (2006) Photo of Tim Shaw's installation, "Rites of Dionysus" at the Eden Project, Gardens and Biomes in Cornwall, UK, by Drumaboy.flickr/Drumaboy

and interpersonal sacrifice are enmeshed in profane life, forming what Stoekl calls "smaller structures of reciprocity-reflection" (Stoekl 1992, p.34). Robertson Smith's contradiction is thus solved through the coextension of the gods and the clan and the self-reflexive nature of social representations to which offerings are made. In other words, all sacrificial rites give back to the social, creating a circular whirlwind of offerings in which nothing is lost and society writ large gains, triumphing over individual self-interest which is necessarily absorbed into the interests of society. The totemic principle dictates that *mana* be periodically recharged and with it the soul and belief of the clan.

But the problem of violence was still not solved and although the Arunta spill the vitalising blood of the Man-Kangaroo on sacred stones (Durkheim 1995, pp.334–335), pierce scrotum skin and engage in bloody ritual battle (Durkheim 1995, p.336), sacrifice, for Durkheim, is a positive rite through which, as Pickering remarks, "contrary to what might be thought, a sacrifice was not esteemed to be a sad affair. Usually only one person or creature suffers for the sake of others, who rejoice in anticipating the consequences of the rite" (Pickering 1984, p.334).

Yet does this make the enterprise in some way palpable? One could go even further and claim that, in the spirit of civic sacrifice, Durkheim had no recourse but to globalise sacrifice, transform it into a rational and conscious activity of the mind and replace the bloodthirsty god with a reasonable moral agent, society. The rite itself is arbitrary, masking a larger project. The participants in archaic sacrificial rituals had no idea what they were actually involved in:

Where could they have gotten the idea that with a few grains of sand thrown to the wind or a few drops of blood poured on a rock or on the stone of an altar, the life of an animal species or god could be maintained? When, from beneath these outward and seemingly irrational doings, we have uncovered a mental mechanism that gives them sense and moral import ... but nothing assures us that the mechanism itself is anything but a play of hallucinatory images ... it must be possible to establish that the effect of the cult is periodically to recreate a moral being on which we depend as it depends on us. Now, this being exists: it is society. (Durkheim 1995, pp.351–352)

Durkheim's own epistemological and sociological compromise, the attempt to delicately balance the forces of reason and ecstasy, prevents the sacrifice from going to the end, or rather brings Durkheim to downplay the possibility of mad ritual and, like his predecessors, sanitise the altar and the rocks of their blood by reconfiguring sacrifice as an essentially mental mechanism that should, from this moment onwards, be purely directed at the recreation of moral beings through moral means. In other words, the sacrifice cannot reach the paroxysmic moment of identification between the participant and the victim and reason or the profane are never fully surpassed (Stoekl 1992, p.50). If the world of the profane is the world of self-consciousness the sacrifice, while unleashing ecstatic energies, also plunges the cult into a moment of hyper–self-consciousness; the ultimate spinning of mental mechanisms. Moreover, as in all effervescent rites, the representation serves to ensure that violence does not spill over.

Therefore, Stoekl correctly surmises, "Durkheim's sacrifice is less a sacrifice than a recuperation" where the participant "knows himself in sacrificial exchange" and thus does not know himself sacrificially, if knowing oneself means pushing reason as far as it will go. By sacrifice the participant undergoes a force, a power, a death that cannot be translated into rational terms. In Durkheim's scheme the impossiblity of sacrifice does not overcome the participants, but is rather arrested in a pseudo-delirium interpreted and betrayed: "a recuperation of force, its retroactive depiction. It will once again save sacrifice by knowing that it is something else; the violence of the act will be mastered in the larger economy of the social or human representation" (Stoekl 1992, p.50). That is, Durkheimian rites are always metony-

mic – where the real and the concrete dimensions of physical abandon function as markers for the very moral processes that they seek to temporarily overcome in the throes of the ecstatic. The participant is thus trapped, unable to fully lose his head in frenzy and violence while simultaneously simulating such explosion in the effervescent ritual. The participant, in other words, is pushing up against the collective representation that is a vestige of himself and his essence.

Le don: humiliation and happiness

More than 25 years passed between Hubert and Mauss's *Essai sur le sacrifice* and the 1925 publication of Mauss's *Essai sur le don*. Although, we cannot speak of two Mausses, the foci of his interests, his intellectual concerns and the targets of his critique had substantially shifted during this period. Of particular importance was, as Tarot remarks, the fact that he had done away with the cumbersome weight of the sacred, which resisted the secularisation of modern societies, while also rejoining himself to Tylor's hypotheses which, abandoned too early, underscored how sacrifice must be understood as a gift to spirits (see Tarot 2008, pp.799–800). But although Mauss was at pains to affirm the primacy of the sacred/social, he did not necessarily abandon the sacred, but absorbed it into the total social fact and, just as Durkheim's *homo duplex* gave way to Mauss' *l'homme total*, the sacred was seamlessly merged into the holistic gestalt and dynamic substrate of archaic societies and the unconscious of modern ones. In *Le don* Mauss would find the ultimate expression of the total social fact, where

all kinds of institutions are given expression at one and the same time – religious, juridical and moral, which relates to both politics and the family; likewise economic ones, which suppose special forms of production and consumption, or rather, performing total services and distribution. This is not to take into account the aesthetic phenomena that these institutions manifest ... social "things" are in a state of flux. (Mauss, 2000, p.3)

While Durkheimian society may appear static and immobilised by the monolith of the social, Mauss' universe consisted of circulation, distribution, movement and flux.

The gift was also a response to a series of total and violent political cataclysms. As Jane Ellen Harrison observes, Durkheim was always at war with the English Utilitarians and an entire tradition of liberalism that spanned Rousseau to Spencer and all that emptied out the person and the moral role of participation through the imposition of a "negative concept of liberty" (Mauss, 2000, p.x). "Citizen Mauss" not only shared his uncle's convictions but radicalised and amplified them through his other vocation as socialist militant and journalist.

Following Durkheim's death another anti-liberal revolution was staged, but it certainly did not gain the approval of Mauss; he was appalled by the events of October 1917 and openly objected to the revolutionaries' use of force. He envisaged real socialism as a process of slow progress, gradual change, discipline and patience, and thus as the antithesis of the apocalyptic scenarios and catastrophes that characterised the Bolshevik revolution.

Mauss insisted that violence only be considered in its legal incarnation, without which it was simply sterile. Socialism required a legal and juridical framework to properly triumph and "violence is only legitimate by the law, through the legal order that reigns over it; it is not itself an order and less a law" (Fournier 1997, p.549). He maintained that force should only be called upon to apply sanctions in a political regime that, nevertheless, understands itself as constrained by law. He thus characterised fascism and its "older brother Bolschevism" (Fournier 1997, pp.510–511) as movements of brutality and not political thought and Lenin and Mussolini were simply victims of a "mythomania of a future society" (Fournier 1997, p.729). Furthermore, as David Graeber adds,

While exhilarated by prospects of a genuine socialist experiment, he was outraged by the Bolsheviks' systematic use of terror ... and most of all by their cynical doctrine that the end justifies the means, which, Mauss concluded, was really just the amoral, rational calculus of the marketplace, slightly transposed ... If the market could not simply be legislated away, even in Russia, probably the least monetarized European society, then clearly, revolutionaries were going to have to start thinking a lot more seriously about what this "market" actually was, where it came from and what a viable alternative to it might actually be like. It was time to bring the results of historical and ethnographic research to bear. (Graeber 2004)

And, refusing to allow the social-democratic spirit to be trammelled by the unholy trinity of liberalism, communism and fascism, Mauss began throughout the course of the early 1920s to examine the history of the social contract, from Xenophon to the Kwakiutl of the American Northwest (Karsenti 1994, pp. 10–12). These forays into primitive exchange would reveal to Mauss the existence of a pre-capitalist market contract, driven not by the laws of accumulation, profit and conspicuous consumption but rather by the laws of charity, loss and humiliation. And driven by the seemingly simple question, what rule of legality and self-interest ... compels the gift that has been received to be obligatorily reciprocated, *The gift* would brazenly challenge the very being of *homo economicus* while not dismantling liberality *tout court*; it would rescue *homo economicus* from an egoistic subjectivity that was enthralled by a certain market violence that levelled others in the name of profit. However, the gift was not without its own darkness and untenability as well.

Agonistic forms

Potlatch refers to a constellation of socio-biological processes; "to feed, to consume, system of exchange of gifts, place of being satiated ... a dominant idea of rivalry and competition between the tribe or tribes" (Mauss 2000, p.vi). For Mauss, it meant quite simply the collective ritual exchange of a system of total services, or rather, the agonistic exchange of wealth by collectivities that imposes the obligation of exchange on the other, forcing him into a contract in which he must reciprocate or risk losing face and lose his position in the social hierarchy:

what is noteworthy about these tribes is the principle of rivalry and hostility that characterises these rites and they go so far as to fight and kill chiefs and nobles ... they even go so far as to the purely sumptuary destruction of wealth that has been accumulated in order to outdo the rival chief ... There is total service in the sense that it indeed the whole clan that contracts on behalf of all ... but this "act" of service on the part of the chief takes on an extremely marked agonistic character. (Mauss 2000, p.6)

With the "gift of rivalry", nobles vie for power and prestige and secure their positions in a contested social hierarchy so that they and their clans may continue to prosper – potlatch, as Mauss begins, is a total service of the agonistic type, one which proves that the *acte gratuit* is impossible (Mauss 2000, p.7). There is no free gift and to receive is to lose through the rival chief's supra-loss, his greater expenditure. The chief or noble's ultimate dream, his perfect moment, would be then the giving of a Gift that could never be returned, a gift that would bless him with the favour of the spirits and good fortune and give to the other a shameful and unpayable debt; "in a certain number of cases, it is not even a question of giving and returning gifts, but of destroying, so as not to give the slightest hint of desiring your gift be reciprocated (Mauss 2000, p.37).

The order of the gift is thus a bustling field of tensions and social energies that seek to topple, outbid and trump one another. Gifts are not presents and although they are infused with *politesse* and ritual decorum, the rites of potlatch pit tribes against one another in a total symbolic war; not a war for resources, but a war of resources, earthly, spiritual, territorial and legal. Hence, the Kwakiutl would set fire to their family heirlooms, sink their riches into the sea and symbolically expend the structure of their societies. That is, as the noble or chief is transparent to the clan he is also transparent to its sub and super-structures that are all brought into play during the exchange. For Mauss, potlatch is not simply a juridical mechanism or an archaic ritual of sovereignty and power. Rather, it is mythological and shamanistic, since the

chiefs who are involved incarnate their ancestors and gods . . . [it is] an economic phenomenon . . . the effect of these transactions [is] enormous even today, when they are calculated in European values . . . a phenomenon of the *social* structure: the gathering together of tribes, clans and families, even of peoples, brings about a state of nerviness and excitement . . . *aesthetic* phenomena, which are extremely numerous . . . as well as the *juridical* status of the contracting parties . . . we must add this: the *material* purposes of the contracts, the things exchanged in them, also possess a special intrinsic power, which causes them to be given and above all to be reciprocated (Mauss 2000, p.38, my emphases)

The gamble during the potlatch is thus on the totality of the clan, its essence, its bedrock and its rapport with the cosmos. The contract is not simply collective, but ontological, risking the clan's origins, its mythic past, its ancestors and its sustenance – everything stands to be given up. But why dare lose the deep structure of the tribe? Why gamble with a total social fact?

The motor of the potlatch is not necessarily extravagant expenditure (this is merely its practice), but rather the play of honour and humiliation. Gift economies therefore derive their force from the elementary human sensations of shame, disgrace and embarrassment and herein rests their perceived superiority to both liberal and Marxian forms of exchange that remain trapped in a rationalism that denies the superior power of the symbolic or the "religious orientation of economic value ... something other than utility that circulates in societies of all kinds . . . a perpetual state of economic ferment " (Mauss 2000, p.72). In the triadic imperative of the potlatch, *donner, reçevoir, rendre*, the *mana* that circulates in the object (that special intrinsic power) is actually an index of honour and "men had learned how to pledge their honour and their name before they knew how to sign the latter" (Mauss 2000, p.38). The potlatch, a game of gifts, is thus a total test in which through the obligation to give, a chief must prove he

is haunted and favoured both by the spirits and good fortune, that he is possessed and also possesses it. And he can only prove this good fortune by spending it, sharing it out, humiliating others by placing them in the "shadow of his name" . . . all this under the pain of violating etiquette – at least for nobles – and of losing rank. (Mauss 2000, p.39)

The failure to give lavishly of one's fortune and favour may, moreover, have fatal consequences (Mauss 2000, p.40). Everything is placed on the line. However, it is not just the giver who is contractually obligated and committed; the receiver is also obliged to his humiliation, obliged to accept or risk being flattened:

One has no right to refuse a gift, or to refuse to attend the potlatch. To act in this way is to show that one is afraid of having to reciprocate. In reality, this is to already be "flattened" ... by accepting it one knows that one is committing oneself. A gift received "with a burden attached". (Mauss 2000, p.41)

And like the logic of Durkheimian effervescence, it is within the interstices of contracting, of taking on a social debt, that members of the clan become conscious of the transcendent social forces that mysteriously bind them. Through the ontological homologising of chief, society, totem and the clan's being, what is, in fact, being expended in potlatch are social forces – society gives itself up in order to re-establish itself. The power that forces gifts to be given, returned and endlessly distributed is the life-force of the social incarnated as well as its deep religious life. Hence, the material object given, the thing in itself is mingled: "souls are mixed with things; things with souls. Lives are mingled together" (Mauss 2000, p.20) and "mixed up with spirits", through which good luck is passed on, through which one obtains rank, wealth and a spirit (Mauss 2000, pp.44–45). To refuse the offering or to refuse to reciprocate would be tantamount to refusing the entire edifice of the social and its division of labour upon which one's capacity to exist as in individual is protected; to break the contract would be then to break being and Being. One must commit to the gift in order to remain a person and, jettisoning at once Catholic annihilationism and cold liberalism, Mauss concludes that in this archaic form of exchange by giving [*a gift*] "one is giving *oneself and* if one gives oneself, it is because one 'owes' oneself, one's person and one's goods – to others ... we have identified the circulation of things in these societies with the circulation of rights and persons" (Mauss 2000, p.46).

My liberty therefore is an affair of a perpetual debt that I owe to the Other and my claim to personhood and the very rights that allow for its expression and protection are contractually bound in my granting, my owing to the Other, the conditions for his personhood and rights. I guard my-self by owing it to the Other, by expending it and immolating it for the Other. The calculus of honour and humiliation, giving, receiving and reciprocating, safeguard social cohesion and institutional life. Each of us is the other's creditor.

But while drawing a series of social-democratic moral lessons from the example of potlatch, Mauss was also troubled by its dark spot. The potlatch can indeed go mad and the war of gifts, where one aspires to flatten out one's rival, can escalate into not only the glorious destruction of wealth, but the destruction of the Other as well. The principle of antagonism that founds the highly ritualised limits of the potlatch can consume and feed on the ritual life itself. And Mauss himself remained ambivalent as well, insisting that the full expression of the potential violence embedded

in the system of potlatch was an anomaly and constantly reiterating how the essence of the system was "noble, replete with etiquette and generosity" (Mauss 2000, p.37).

The paradox of the gift lies in its dual articulation of individual liberty and liberality and normative obligatory constraints; how it promotes what Caillé and the *Revue de M.A.U.S.S.* have dubbed the third paradigm (beyond individualism and holism): a perfect mechanism of giving to receive more that fuses the liberty of the individual in a social and socialist holism or game of association (Caillé 2007, p.19). In the *dispositif* of honour and shame one gains by losing and in being involuntarily obligated one enters into the paradox of an obligated liberty, or a free obligation. The gift is freedom circumscribed in an act of conditional autonomy; ostensibly, the gesture is free and disinterested, but such liberty only has meaning as an obligation or duty, indicating precisely the limits of such disinterested freedom. Constraint is intrinsic to the liberty of the gift (Karsenti 1994, p.28). Hierarchically organised prestige is accrued by forcing the equitable distribution of resources.

Moreover, interest is also imbricated in the social metaphysics of the gift or the force of things. Amongst Mauss' most controversial proposals in the *Essai* is that the objects that function as gifts contain within them *hau*, the spirit of things, a spiritual power embedded in the object given which is also the *hau* of the owner's soul that obligates reciprocation. The *taonga* or *hau* is singular and when I give a gift, I indeed give *of* my individual being, my nature and substance (Mauss 2000, pp.11–12). Here *mana* is not simply a means of speaking of wealth, honour or power, but rather the essence of a soul that comes into contact with the essences of other souls in the exchange of the gift. I give of myself while guarding myself and it is my self that circulates throughout the social in the form of the object that is ontologically identical to my self. But while giving of myself I also profit spiritually. The economy is animated by what people are willing to part with, but it is also understood that the gift may return to its original owner, its place of origin or "or produce ... an equivalent to replace it" (Mauss 2000, pp.13). Yet, while the gift autonomously circulates and seeks to come back to its point of origin, the owner of the gift still holds on to the gift and thus has a hold on the recipient of the gift as well. Moreover and more importantly, while *hau* may be that force that obligates me to reciprocate, it is also, as Marshall Sahlins argues, the profit yielded on the gift itself. As the object circulates it accrues metaphysical interest and its *hau* grows more empowered (Sahlins, 2004, pp.157–162). It should be noted that *hau* is also a verb meaning to "exceed, be in excess" (Sahlins, 2004, pp.162). The gift is thus a disinterested manifestation of the greatest self-interest.

Proof of *mana* – a programme?

With naive boldness, Mauss envisioned new societies of affluence where citizens, governments and political leaders would be constantly forced to offer proof of *mana* and, aware of the impossibility of liquidating egoism, he would ask that they give to one another without sacrificing themselves to one another (Mauss 2000, p.83). The rivalry of generosity would turn capitalist competition on itself and transform agôn into mass luxury. In replacing the liberal social contract with a social-symbolic contract with which, like law before the historical period, Mauss would seek to re-totalise life and re-attach morality to exchange and eliminate usury, exploitation and the intoxication of unbounded profit. In the end, what concerned Mauss was social well-being and happiness. Gift societies "were less sad, less serious, less miserly and less personal than we are" and Mauss saw no reason why we could not return to such a model of good health, friendship and hospitality (Mauss 2000, p.81). Happiness, like the individual, the social and the person, was an art to be cultivated or, as Mauss suggests, "*Politics*, in the Socratic sense of the word" (Mauss 2000, p.83).

Bataille's (mis)reading of Mauss would soon, however, destroy Socratic politics once and for all. While the Durkheimians privileged restraint, Bataille basked in excess. While the Durkheimians sought to sanitise sacrificial violence, Bataille overdetermined it as a founding ontological principle. While the Durkheimians wished to do away once and for all with Catholic annihilitionism, Bataille (a lapsed Catholic) searched for the annihilationist in the post-religious, replacing the hypocrisy of Catholic sacrifice, an economy of salvation, with an economy of pure loss, a sacrifice for its own

sake. While the Durkheimians sought to preserve republican social morality, Bataille called for the ultimate transgression. While the Durkheimians saw agonistic potlatch as an anomaly, for Bataille it was the only sacrificial rite. While the Durkheimians were bourgeois moralists, Bataille dreamt of sacrificing the bourgeois. While the Durkheimians bound their communities in the violence-limiting capacities of the totem and the representation, Bataille's anguished communities would be formed around the explosion of the representation and the totem as pure night and emptiness. While the Durkheimians sought redemption in the nonviolent giving of the self, for Bataille, violence was pure redemption and the "self" and "person" were contingent normative frames. In other words, Bataille would go the end.

Nonetheless, both Mauss and Bataille recognised the contradiction laden in the gift: it substituted material accumulation with the accumulation of power and while there may only be "dissipation for the giver", the loss "brings a profit to the one who sustains it"(Mauss 2000, p.70), but the unresolved problem remains. This is the merchant or sacrifiant's monopoly on power itself, which can be abused as readily as wealth and also, on the other hand, the fact that what is of more importance to gift economies is not what is given but rather what is kept and never squandered at all.

The gift eschews material profit for a different type of market all together, one where, as Maurice Godelier claims, "Power did not go to Big Men, who amassed women and wealth, but to Great Men, who held and inherited powers present in the sacred objects and secrets knowledge given to their ancestors by nonhuman divinities – the Sun, the forest spirits and others" (Godelier 1999, p.8).

In other words, in the Baruya societies that Godelier examined, like Bataille's infamous Aztecs, political power was desired more than material profit and those who wielded and guarded it garnered unprecedented influence over those below them. The gift is thus not necessarily a radical way out of capitalism but a displacement of the greed for money to the greed for *mana*.

The effervescent

In 1894 Alfred Dreyfus, a Jewish French artillery officer, was falsely accused of treason. A political maelstrom besieged France and divided its populace in two. The resulting Dreyfus Affair and the virulence of the anti-Dreyfusard movement created the conditions for the rebirth of the Catholic annihilationist reaction and, true to its origins, the advocates of this particular strain of sacrificial political theology grafted upon the figure of Dreyfus a series of sacrifices and, as Strenski further suggests, he then became the reservoir for a panoply of sacrificial mystiques, among them:

- "Judas-Dreyfus", the cosmic, theological and national traitor
- "True Jesus Dreyfus/false Jesus Dreyfus", a series of confused sentiments that rendered Dreyfus' agony heroic in Christ-like terms while guarding him as the living embodiment of Judas Iscariot
- "Scapegoat Dreyfus", the sacrificial immolation that would guarantee the preservation of the nation (Strenski 2002, pp. 95–118).

But regardless of the sacrificial discourse that enshrouded him, Dreyfus was not offered the luxuries of ancient *homini sacri*; he was abjectified, a filth that could be either Judas or Jesus. Dreyfus was not simply a name, a man, or a Jewish officer accused of treason, but also a sign, an icon and an index. Depending on one's political or religious orientation, Dreyfus was a marker of the Republic's shame and its simultaneous will to justice; he was both the sacrificer and the sacrificed; he was coded as the ultimate emblem of moral degeneration and also as the harbinger of the Republic's own moral disintegration; he was a form of abjection that needed to be cast out and purged, but also proof of a nation's capacity to render a man abject, transform him into a thing, even to himself. Dreyfus as abjectified. Sylvère Lotringer writes

people don't just become abject when they're treated like a thing, but because they become things to themselves. It is only then, when they're being invaded and exposed to the vertiginous experience of existing apart from the human race, that abjection comes about. ... Abjection doesn't result from a dialectical operation-feeling when "abjectified" in someone else's eyes, or reclaiming abjection as an identifying feature – but precisely when the dialectic breaks down. When it ceases to be experienced as an act of exclusion to become an autonomous condition, it is then and only then, that abjection sets in. (Lotringer 1999, p.10)

In the figure of Dreyfus crystallised not only a series of sacrificial logics, but also the base and collective impulse to cast out, exclude and set apart. The negative sacralisation of Dreyfus eclipsed his own personhood and, emptied of will and agency, exclusion was his autonomous condition. The concrete dimensions of the sign are of less significance than the effects that they elicit; few were actually concerned with the issue of Dreyfus' guilt. On the contrary, his name was the symbol of nation's capacity to collectively inflict moral, personal and physical injury. Theodor Herzl, who lived in Paris through the entire affair, was traumatised by the degradation of Dreyfus and the anti-Semitism of the anti-Dreyfusard mob. He soon concluded that no rapprochement between Jews and Christians would be henceforth possible and immediately published *L'état des juifs* [1896] (2008).

Although Durkheim was no stranger to anti-Semitism he refused to read these events as yet another struggle between Christians and Jews and "even if there was evidence that anti-Semitic nationalism was central to the right, he interpreted the attack on the Jewish community as the result of a lack of moral unity" (Fournier 2005, p.53). But, Durkheim also noticed the flowering of Dreyfusard solidarity, a new political religiosity that Péguy in *Notre jeunesse* (1957) called the *mystique Dreyfus*. According to Péguy, "our Christian mysticism culminates ... perfectly with our patriotic mysticism in our Dreyfus mysticism" (Péguy 1957, p.150) and the political was simply the domain of these various mysticisms translated into agitation. Moreover, it was precisely the degradation of such a politico-mystical core, particularly the degradation of the Dreyfus mystique, that unleashed the rise of tyrannical powers (Péguy 1957, p.154). The new religion, one animated by demonstrations, petitions, articles, polemics, heated debate and incessant intellectual exchange, testified to the unyielding presence of republican religiosity, one again born of effervescence and assembly. Moral stagnation and its symptoms (such as anti-Semitism, anti-Dreyfusardism, the will to exclude and the logic of the mob) could only be countered with a new effervescent religiosity that was characterised by the unrelenting moral agitation of intellectuals. In *L'individualisme et les intellectuels*, Durkheim's response to the Dreyfus Affair and, above all, his riposte against the reactionary right who paradoxically accused him of both anarchic individualism and totalitarianism, he pleaded for the mobilisation of social energies, the unceasing instrumentalisation of burgeoning effervescent forces:

The moral agitation that these events have incited is not extinguished and I am among those who think that it should not wane; because it is necessary. It is our past complacency which was abnormal and which constituted a danger. Whether we regret it or not, the critical period that opened with the fall of the old regime has not necessarily come to an end. It is much more important to be responsible than to abandon ourselves to a false security. The hour of rest has not come for us. There is too much to be done to render indispensable the perpetual mobilisation of our social energies. This is why I believe the politics of the last four years is preferable to what preceded them. They have succeeded in maintaining lasting collective activity of a considerable intensity ... the essential thing was to not let ourselves succumb to a state of moral stagnation (Durkheim 1997, p.44)

Religion is a response to not only slackening social bonds but also to the slackening moral constitution of a nation. Against moral stagnation, or the conditions that allow for the possibility of the Dreyfus Affair, Durkheim extolled the virtues of intense effervescent agitation that must, moreover, never slacken, even in times of peace; a production of the sacred that is wholly involved in the agitation of a slumbering politico-moral body, in quest of a religious absolute that is nothing more than a vision of collective political destiny. The sacred is not only the concentration and circulation of transcendent social energies but also the nucleus of the political; the social question and the political question are interwoven.

The Dreyfus Affair recast the political as an irreducibly violent, agonistic and hazardous process which, through the rising agitation of Dreyfusard cults and the symbolic constellation of the Dreyfus mystique, participated in the vituperations of the sacred. However, it is equally important to emphasise the radically pragmatic dimension of Durkheim's desire to bring effervescent energies to the service of the nation. The ontological transformation or liminal passage that effervescence initiates can be incited by moral outrage and subsequently function as the imperative to collective agitation. The sacred thus need not be overdetermined as a site of inexorable negativity, void, or non-being. Rather, it may simply be a question of riots, demonstrations, strikes, petitions

and various refusals and subversions that negate, moments of social becoming that are not indicative of any regression to the archaic or protest against the civilising process, but are instead permanent features of social and political life that inform social practices (Richman 2002, p.205).

Reminding participants of the vastness and density of the social, joining them to each other and wresting them from the throes of finitude, effervescence infects with the sensation of possibility. In effervescent assembly individuals explode the limits of their singular psyches and bodies; in traversing the limits of the sayable, the thinkable and the doable, effervescence, when successfully translated into moral agitation, opens the way to the infinite power of protest and the possibility of political change; transformations that accordingly traverse the limits of the sayable, thinkable and doable that circumscribe the social body or the nation.

Effervescence: against primordial chaos

The very act of congregating is an exceptionally powerful stimulant. Once the individuals are gathered together a sort of electricity is generated from their closeness and quickly launches them to an extraordinary height of exaltation. ... And since passions so heated and so free from all control cannot help but spill over, from every side there are nothing but wild movements, shouts, downright howls and deafening noises of all kinds that further intensify the states they are expressing. Probably because a collective emotion cannot be expressed collectively without some order that permits harmony and unison of movement, these gestures and cries tend to fall into rhythm and regularity and from there into songs and dances. But in taking on a more regular form, they lose none of their fury ... the effervescence often becomes so intense that it leads to outlandish behaviour; the passions unleashed are so torrential that nothing can hold them. (Durkheim 1995, pp.217–218)

Durkheim, who died in 1917, did not live to see the throngs of the wounded that littered Parisian streets but he had already presented a sociological and moral model of the Republic that found its origins in the body. Effervescence is a chemical reaction that engenders torrents of collective emotion, freeing the passions and collapsing the distinction between subject and object, but it is also a chemical reaction that threatens total slippage into horrifying formlessness. It is the apogee of social integration inaugurated by the flood of collective passions but, as Durkheimian argues, effervescence demonstrates that collective passions are not nomadic fluxes of life-forces that flourish and reproduce into infinity. On the contrary, passions require an object.

The forces of effervescence are real and impact on the physical, moral and psychic core of each clan member. They are real in so far as they are derived from the social field and the energies that circulate among group members, reminding them of their dependency upon others. However, *mana* cannot remain an abstract and free-floating substance. For order to come into unison where the conditions for social and individual flourishing are created, *mana* must take the form of an emblem, a totem, or representation, which serves as a rallying point. The explosion of collective emotion must attach itself to a symbolic form or risk the incommensurability that can potentially annihilate subjectivity. The symbolic form acts by inscribing itself and the emanating sacred onto the bodies of the participants. The powers ascribed to the totem serve inversely to determine one's conduct and it is only through symbolism that human life can objectify its moral exigencies by superimposing them upon nature (Durkheim 1995, pp.229–230). Without symbols, moral and emotional life remains inarticulate and non-signifying; pre-symbolic non-form poses a threat to the constitution of the clan whose very being and survival are bound in totemic life. But the totem remains an impersonal and empty vessel devoid of any inherent force – a territory to simply be used.

Unlike his detractors, for Durkheim effervescence posed no threat to republican *nomos*. It was at once its precondition and an experiential domain born of its organisation. Intensity is individuals in concentration and the contagion that such assemblies promote can effectively be de-pathologised when the sentiments of the crowd, forever threatening to break loose, are adequately channelled in the very collective representations that such assemblies aspire to re-embolden. Effervescence brings men into contact with the world that exceeds them or remains lost to spleen-time, those empty hours of lone anxiety; it enlivens, enhances, supplements and brings to a rousing crescendo the psychic and physical energies that lie asleep in the routine undulations of the profane. Intensities do not overflow the crowd and mobilise themselves against the social, but overflow into the individual from the outside, expressing the world and causing the individual to mutate from one who speaks of the social to one through whom the social speaks. The ontological transformation that stirs the individual in the effervescent mass is equally dependant upon the heightening of symbolic life, the cathexis of social energies into totemic imagos that are also ontologically identified with society:

The pious life of the Australian moves between two successive phases – one of utter colourlessness, one of hyper-excitement – and social life oscillates to same rhythm . . . by compressing itself almost entirely into circumscribed periods, collective life could attain its maximum intensity, therefore giving man a more vivid sense of the twofold existence he leads and the twofold nature in which he participates. But this explanation is incomplete. I have shown how the clan awakens in its members the idea of external forces that dominate and exalt it by the way in which it acts upon members. But I still must ask how it happens that those forces were conceived in the form of the totem. . . . The transfer of feelings takes place because the idea of the thing and the idea of its symbol are closely related. As a result, the feelings evoked by one spread contagiously to the other. The contagion, which occurs in all cases to some extent, is much more complete and more pronounced whenever the symbol is something simple, well defined and easily imagined. But the thing itself is difficult for the mind to comprehend – given its dimension, the number of its parts and the complexity of their organization (Durkheim 1995, p.221)

The thing itself is the totality of the social field and the energies that circulate through it. When represented, the thing itself enters into chiasma with the crowd simultaneously acting upon its members and absorbing them. The effervescent crowd avoids deteriorating into the hunting pack, or the crowd against itself, through the psychic girding of the symbolic. In the haze of the effervescent, sublime in so far as society defies calculation, the onslaught of depersonalisation and the dissolution of subjectivity can only be rendered creative and purposive through the mediation of collective representations. According to Durkheim a crowd without a realisable symbol lacks a nodal repository for unbridled energies and undoubtedly risks degenerating into the anomic criminal mass that Le Bon and Seghele so feared.

In other words, social energies must be transferred and submitted to the symbol to allow for the moral core of the social to be revealed. However, the collective representation opens individuals and free them from the torpor of delimited profane subjectivity, a passage that can only be comprehended and become nourishing and creative when mediated by symbolic life; the symbol reciprocates the energies transferred into it. Effervescent depersonalisation is a quasi-form of sacrifice, wherein closed existence temporarily suspends adhesion to the limit in order to be transformed by moral forces. Thrust outside, the effervescent participant is reduced to a pre-political, pre-national and pre-subjective point of energy in order to be, via the collective representation, raised to the heights of political and national responsibility, subjective and civic responsibility and an embodiment of social totality. Effervescence is the becoming-totem, becoming-social of the individual; a socialisation that transpires through the discharge and transference of libidinal forces that defy the homogenising practices of socialisation and bound libidinal economies that make up profane social life.

Effervescent effusion, as a collective cathexis and transference, provides a fleeting moment of social and moral crystallisation between individuals, symbolic life and moral spirit, one which inscribes itself in collective memory as therefore eases the trauma of the profane; the individual guards the memory of last assembly, a trace he shares with others, and pines for the next. Durkheim read the grammar of the crowd not in terms of degeneration, but as a "moral toning up" where moral power, immanent in ourselves, is metamorphosed into a transcendent field of social and symbolic relations.

It is the neurotic ego that wards off the possibility of cathexis through disallowing the libidinal investment of energies into an object; the psychic apparatus, constitutive of the living being as organism, purports to remain at low levels of excitation or constancy. The process of achieving such constancy is dependant upon operations of discharge and de-sublimation. The psyche is only able to tolerate a certain amount of stimuli and excitation before a breach is inflicted on the stimuli barrier, one that produces trauma. In an effort to reduce the build-up of such tension (the quest for constancy), the psyche or, more properly, the ego may choose to repress, sublimate, disavow, scotomise the stimuli and their source. The stimuli may also be internalised, accumulated and then discharged through a form of abreaction or one of its derivations. Social constancy, the preservation of *nomos*, depends equally on the firm placement of an object or symbolic regime to which *cathexis* can be directed.

Effervescence therefore corresponds to the social discharge of desires which is absorbed, distilled and redistributed within the collective representation. Following Durkheim, it is the presence of the symbolic order in the effervescent assembly that ensures that the force of the death drive, the quest for constancy and the zero-state do not deviate into the dangerous cathexes of sadism or aggression. Effervescent assemblies and festivals are, therefore, collective dramatisations of the interval between Eros and Thanatos; between the force that constructs greater and more coherent unities and seeks to preserve them and that which attempts to undo such unities and to destroy any coherence that may have been hitherto established. Durkheim's theory of effervescence can therefore be summarised as an attempt to recuperate the negative, to domesticate the violent and unbridled forces of the unconscious and the embodied through symbolism, while simultaneously acknowledging the social and material origins of these forces. Moments of effervescence effect less a return to primordial chaos or the time before time, than socially ground the non-signifying vituperations of a now de-radicalised negativity and violence. Nonetheless, although directed by totemic guardrails, effervescence is a form of unleashed violence and as, Friedland remarks "simply registering the totemic image is not enough" and moral force depends in its origins on "delirium, ecstasy" and "violence to the individual's mind and body" (Friedland 2005, p.245). Effervescence thus hinges on a dialectical release and capture: the totem incites violence only to reabsorb it and render it useful in the socio-moral functioning of the representation.

Effervescence, violence and social economies

The zero-state between Eros and Thanatos, the interval between the search for a reason to live and being for death, is not necessarily a politically subversive moment of revolutionary desire. Although effervescence unleashes torrential and uncontrollable passions, there is nothing orgiastic about the economies of effervescence. The inversion of sexual and social taboos, the hyper-excitement of physical and emotional concentration, the fury and the howling, do not challenge existing political and social regimes. These states of exaltation, where one discovers the art of losing one's self, dramatise and remobilise the energies from which the religious idea emerges, but it is a religious idea that resembles less the anti-monarchic tremors of the revolutionary cult than sanctioned moments where the cult of the nation-state is celebrated and elevated. In other words, the violent desires that effervescence draws upon are ordered and transformed into socially useful forces through the permanence of the totemic nexus of relations, a technique of the social body which ensures the channelling of violent energies; the state, like the totem, is an arbitrary marker, one which, as Georges Balandier suggests, is "only *postulated* to make primeval violence seem like a form of primitive energy ... society is shaped in accordance with its use of this energy. Violence is converted into 'creative violence' ... order and violence are linked by a complex and ambivalent relationship" (Balandier 1986, p.500). Effervescence ensures that instincts are not directed at the state, and are tamed and pacified while raising the totem to new heights.

If one closely examines Durkheimian effervescence it becomes increasingly clear that the moral unity that moments of such collective effervescence unleash function as a pinnacle of the individual's effacement in the group. This effacement however, does not push him into contact with the forces of non-form and radical negativity, but rather produces a rational and pragmatic citizen driven by his duties to the state and occupied only with the larger interests of the group. Effervescent self-dissolution, as Stoekl remarks, foregrounds not the individual who has been cast into the abyss, but the reasonable and moral agent whose sacredness and personhood lie in his co-extensiveness with the greater moral community, its conscious, conscience and collective destiny:

[T]he person derives from the group a communal energy that is nothing other than a reflection of his capacity for logical, moral and autonomous action. The frenzied cultist twisting in an orgiastic dance, who is possessed by *mana* and has seemingly lost all personhood, is, in his modern, fully self-conscious avatar, the independent thinker who makes rational judgments for the good of society – Durkheim himself, in other words. The cult of the person is inseparable from both responsibility (or subservience) to the community and free judgment (Stoekl 1992, p.32)

Subservience to society and steadfast devotion to its continuous socio-religious renovation function as the essence of Durkheim's moral individual who participates in the unified system of beliefs and practice that solidify the moral community into a church. In the midst of the tautologies that constitute Durkheim's social and religious plans, the actor is forced to construct himself between the despair of freedom and the abolition and repression of particularity. The micro-fascistic desire for order, authority and discipline is set in opposition to the anarchic impulse to surpass Being itself. Authority, anomie and anarchy form a libidinal, psychic and social gradient. Totalitarianism privileges homogeneity and considers individuals expendable. Durkheim's republicanism affirms the sacredness of the person but nevertheless insists that such sacredness can only take hold in the larger ensemble of the group. More importantly, the Durkheimian project is defined by utility. The member of the group, his ritual and religious life, the social bonds he creates with the other and his sacred personhood are understood purely in terms of their usefulness to the group enterprise and the preservation of the social. Durkheim merely reconfigures the imperative: "the categorical imperative of the moral conscience is assuming the following form: *Make yourself usefully fulfil a determinate function*" (Durkheim 1947, p.43).

Beyond the universe of the utilitarian project lies a useless excess; negativity, violence, rivalry, expenditure, agnostic exchange, the unbridled and terrifying Dionysian forces of nature in their full exuberance, the transgression of the taboo, the will to non-subjugation, the refusal to serve, the death drive, melancholia, suicide and the will to annihilation itself. Whether heroic and heretic or alienated and hollowed by hopelessness, these phenomena resist positivism. They prove, as Jules Monnerot argued, that social facts are not things. The totem therefore illustrates the paradoxical political economy of religious life: negativity must be temporarily unleashed only to be recuperated and ordered by the totem to which one remains subservient. The totem furthermore reveals the paradox of the Durkheimian *homo duplex*, where, as Shilling explains "individuals must deny what is essential to their bodily selves in order to enter into the symbolic order of society, yet *need* this social order if they are both to survive and flourish" (Shilling 2005, p.212). In essence, collective effervescence simulates or flirts with the negative, only to disavow it through the suturing effects of symbolic life which remain firmly in place during moments of collective exaltation. Effervescence is thus not a road back to Eden, if Eden be understood as an anomic regime of pre-political, pre-social and pre-symbolic relations. On the contrary, the ontological identification of the clan member, the social and the totem that congeals in the midst of the circulation of social *mana* proves that the effervescent body in excess can only explode under the watchful eye of the totem or state-formation that foments the explosion itself. It was, after all, the members of the clan who erected the totem, revealing how the violent nature of desire is encoded in symbolic life as opposed to threatening it. The Durkheimian and Lacanian symbolic orders are hence more complementary than often assumed in so far as "The super-ego is fucking articulated as an imperative – *Come (Jouis)*"! (Lacan 1990b, p.52).

Society does not function here as an external agent that comes up against the individual, but rather as that which dwells within the autonomous individual. The totem reminds us that there is no boundary between psyche and society, that there is no real outside; one is constituted as an individual through, to use Stoekl's phrase, the totem act. Effervescent desire is impossible; it is not polymorphously perverse, boundless or flourishing in plenum; it serves the totem, the state formation and the Big Other of the social, a Big Other born in the psyche and body of the clan member, a Big Other whom the clan member wants to be swallowed by. The state knows that the transgression upholds the law. Effervescent desire appears as nothing more than a narcissistic and paranoiac demand issued to an object that has already been interjected into the constitution of the clan. The circulation and seeming end-lessness of social energies are nothing more than a surplus to be recuperated by the totem. The site of *jouissance* remains a negative space, hollowed out around the totemic structure, where, "the dialectical relationship between desire and the Law causes our desire to flare up only in relation to the Law, through which it becomes the desire for Death" (Lacan 1990a, p.83), the desire to enter into pure immanence with the matrix of totem/social/clan. The totem is, however, always ambivalent. It is precisely this that creates the narcissistic specularity in the dialogue with the totem or, rather, the pseudo-dialogue with the totem as an inverted model of the ego. The clan member sends his desire up to the symbolic regime but the totem does not respond, yet offers an image of reciprocity in perpetuating stable social relations. It is the totem's lack of response, coupled with the cyclical churning and accumulation of social energies, that produces the seasonal repetition of the effervescent festival where the totem is again asked to recuperate the clan member as surplus value; the eternal return of the clan member's simultaneous thirst for recognition and annihilation in his becoming-totem. The individual body is transcended, the descent into animality is mediated by the intervention of the totem; neither human, nor beastly, the totemic body incarnates the social. The sacred is, hence, the experience of being devoured by a symbolic regime that is constructed and imagined by the clan member and projected as this inverted form of the ego. Durkheim lacked a theory of ideology, but the *dispositif* of the totem may provide a basis for its development.

The Durkheimian categorical imperative is actually "Send up your desire to the totem *so you may* make yourself usefully fulfil a determinate function". With health renewed, the totemic social body, recharged by the energy of exalted symbolic life, may now return to the Sunday of the profane, newly prepared to exercise its political and moral duties. But energies wane on Sundays and although Durkheim pleaded for effervescent continuity even in times of peace, there appears to be no practical means to perpetuate the energetic charge of the assembly in moments of slackening and routine.

Energies may equally wane during the effervescent rite itself. As institutional and symbolic life becomes less persuasive the effervescent charge is less potent. In other words, the impotence of state formations and symbolic codes coupled with the inscription of effervescence into regulated periods of times (calendars) radically reduces one's capacity to be thoroughly intoxicated. The effervescent assemblies that Durkheim studied and envisaged for the future were not spontaneous eruptions of revolutionary desire but state or clan sanctioned affairs that, by virtue of their civic and legislated orientation, inevitably fail to produce profound states of exaltation.

The sacred could not simply erupt at any moment and the effervescent encounter could not unfold from within the folds of the profane. The dualism had to be upheld at all costs as "the sacred and the profane are always and everywhere conceived by the human intellect as separate genera, as two worlds with nothing in common" (Durkheim 1995, p.36). However, the strict separation of these genera was, from a Durkheimian perspective, not to be maintained on theological or ontological grounds. Rather, the sacred should never touch the profane so that the moral transcendence of the social would rest protected from any possible transgression. Passage between the two worlds, moreover, could only transpire when liminal flight paradoxically upheld the duality of the two: just as the transgression is hostile to the social, the profane is hostile to the sacred.

Douglas' celebrated indictment of Durkheim, however, attests to the way in which the effervescent assembly itself may be a source of pure somnambulism, how it may in fact participate in the ennui of the profane. Douglas also argues that Durkheim, like Mauss in his analysis of the gift, may have been mystified by the *mana* he sought to decrypt:

The idea that cults stimulate emotion is not very convincing. Have you ever fallen asleep during mass? It is important to note how such an idea runs contrary to the methodological principles elaborated by Durkheim. Social facts must be explained by social facts. ... Durkheim breaks with his rule when comes to depend upon the vitality of the sacred, of the emotional excitement inspired by grand assemblies ... it is more useful to follow Durkheim in his lessons and not in his practice and reject functional explanations based on censured emotions which maintain the system. (Douglas, 1999, p.56)

If Durkheim was indeed mystified by the social energies that he described in the *Elementary*

forms, such a mystification cannot simply be explained by any betrayal of the sociological method. Durkheim was prescribing effervescence to a civilisation where the simple joy of being with one another had given way to fragmented subjectivities and fragmentary politics. But Douglas is nonetheless correct to claim that Durkheim's dramatic rendering of the opening of collective passions and his depiction of the society conscious-of-itself as the platform for temporal transcendence and inward transformation points to something beyond the closed universe of social facts.

The dark spot displaced
Effervescence and fascism

So did Durkheim "think the unthinkable" and how do we account for his relative inattention to potential for various misappropriations of the effervescent crowd? A range of thinkers from Monnerot to Descombes have exploded the semblances between Durkheimian effervescence and fascism, a connection further problematised by the correspondence between Mauss and Ranulf. In Durkheim's defence, Shilling also suggests that in alluding to the ambiguity of the sacred and the existence of both ecstatic fervour and sorrow-ridden piacular rites, the life-bringing and the death-dealing, Durkheim was also theorising the ambivalence of effervescent action, an essential ambivalence that was illustrated by Nazi rallies and Nazism's genocidal destruction during the Second World War (Shilling 2005, p.203). Following Robertson Smith, Durkheim does propose that "religious forces are of two kinds" (Durkheim 1995, p.412), and that the "evil powers that result from and symbolise" piacular rites push societies members "to give witness to their sadness, distress, or anger through expressive actions. It demands crying, lamenting and wounding oneself and others as a matter of duty" (Durkheim 1995, p.415). But the tragic purging of suffering and even the ritual violence inflicted on the self and expiatory victims simply do not satisfactorily account for the energies unleashed at Nuremberg and their sustained presence in acts of genocidal destruction, where tragedy, mourning, sorrow and grief are entirely absent.

The distinction between the piacular and the ecstatic does little to account for Nazi rites and fascist spectacle. The problem here, as Graham remarks, is that "the test case against an automatic embrace of effervescence is Nazism" and, as he continues, the Durkheimian model "fails to differentiate bad effervescence from good" (Graham 2007, p.35).

Albeit context-bound, the decline of the Durkheimian school was partially caused by the radical disconnect between socialist optimism, its utopian reveries and the harsh realities of the Third Republic in its final years. An irreconcilable chasm formed between the moral crusade that was sociology and a social that was bereft of moral nerve (Munich). Mired in prescriptive idealism the Durkheimians responded to the crisis with a series of sociological correctives, a series of proposals concerning the Ought to Be that remained too detached from the *être* itself to be dialectically compelling. The elementary forms were helpless theoretical postulates when placed besides the thralls of national regression and the various models of social cohesion that the Durkheimians had once arduously proposed were the ossified residues of a different time. By 1938 Durkheimian logic appeared hopelessly out of touch and Durkheim's error may have been to conflate an imaginary *sui generic* social with a society to come.

Or Durkheim simply believed in society too much. His perhaps naive trust and faith in the inherent goodness of social morality undoubtedly blinded him to the possibility of Nazism, fascism and violent nationalism. Durkheim was convinced of the liberating dependence that society offered, a real and conditional freedom that was born of one's submission to the social, a freedom that was greater than any metaphysical rhapsody on absolute freedom or ceaseless transgression, and, as Bauman remarked, in Durkheim's lifetime:

The "liberating dependence" was yet to show its other ugly, pugnacious, totalitarian face and at the time Durkheim eulogised on the benignity of society's embrace he could do it with a clear conscience, having romantic dreams and bohemian practices for sole opponents. Society could still be trusted to promote morality, to guard the cause of goodness against evil. An unanswering loyalty to the great and intelligent force of society could still be viewed as the best guarantee of the happy result of the moral crusade. It was difficult, if at all possible, to discern Big Brother's self-promotional propaganda, in the casting of "blind, unthinkable physical forces" as the target and prospective casualty of the battle and the only adversary to be vanquished and trammelled. Nothing as yet had disturbed the harmony between "coercive social facts" and theorizing the ennobling impact of the society that produced them. (Bauman 2005, p.372)

While potentially unconvincing to us post-moderns to whom apocalypse, catastrophe, genocide, ethnic cleansing and violent nationalism figure among the many spectral banalities of a ubiquitous political pornography, Durkheim's historical moment shielded him from such possibilities and "it would not be just to lay the blame at Durkheim's door" (Bauman 2005, p.372).

Durkheim's larger historical moment, to which the conditions of his own thought were transparent, simply prevented him from envisaging the excesses to come. They also fostered within him a certain myopia that prevented him from thoroughly engaging the excesses of colonialism in his own epoch. Within the historical womb of the Third Republic Durkheim also developed the consciousness of a moral crusader. Durkheim's steadfast belief in the better moral judgement of the individual, his blind faith in the intelligent forces of the social, behind which he never ceased to rally, oriented his thought in one direction. On some level, even to entertain the thought of a possible perversion of the social would have been a signal of Durkheim's loss of faith, the sign of an inner moral crisis that would sacrifice the cause of the sociological revolution that was taking shape before his very eyes.

Hence, effervescence was always already good. It could not be otherwise. To think the unthinkable would have meant losing one's nerve and betraying the Third Republic to which Durkheim felt only gratitude after Dreyfus' rehabilitation. The historical conditions of the Third Republic established the possibility of Durkheim's thought that was further nourished by unyielding sociological-socialist fervour and an unshakeable faith in society's innate moral goodness. He could not think the unthinkable nor see into the future. His greatest shortcoming was therefore not intellectual in nature, but rested rather in his inability to systematically think through the problem of evil and, in a more mundane sense, accept that not all individuals defer to their better moral judgment. Durkheim's limitations were the limitations of the moment, the limitations of the Durkheimian sociological spirit itself.

But he was, at the same time, certainly not opposed to the ecstatic. Effervescence is neutral. It is neither fascist nor socialist in nature but a socio-physiological fact. Contagion simply "is" and the Nazis were by no means the first to use fire in group rituals. However, while it is not inherently useful or inherently dangerous, it can, nevertheless, be used politically in both revolutionary religions that oppose tyranny and by tyrants themselves. As a socio-physiological fact it is therefore not effervescence itself that should be judged, but the ideological and semiotic scaffolding that functions simultaneously as the trigger, the *raison d'être* and the stage for effervescent rite. The phobia of circulating social energies is, thus, a phobia of the semiotic regimes that find such energies ferociously attached to them.

On one hand, the totem quells the rise of internal energies that cannot be mastered by consciousness. On the other hand the totem can inspire those energies to overflow to hitherto unforeseen points of frenzy that capitalise on a disdain for other groups and are channelled into various forms of aggression against them. But the outcome of the process is ultimately decided by the contents of the totem itself, contents that are less visceral or ecstatic than ideological (involved in the distortion of consciousness). The sign may embolden solidarity and refortify agonising individual subjectivity but it may also naturalise instinct as culture or bring instinct to trample culture.

Unlike the advocates of communicative reason such as Habermas, Durkheim did not deem the ecstatic to be a regressive or intrinsically dangerous force closely tied to barbarism. And he certainly did not consider the plane of effervescence to be non-communicative or incommunicative. Rather, he understood that effervescence and ecstasy as well as discipline, order and restraint, were not necessarily totalitarian forms: therein is found one of Durkheim's greatest contributions. The distance between socialism and national-socialism, between Durkheim's society and *Volk*, is vast and a series of dramatic steps need to be taken to bring one from one point to the other.

Post-anomie

By 1938 Mauss was probably not thinking about anomie. Although the expectations that the Republic had instilled in its citizens had been unfulfilled, no sense of infinity abounded in those dark days. Instead, the end of the 1930s resembled an ultra-anomie that would problematise or render inapplicable Durkheim's earlier observations. Moreover, it was difficult to speak of collective pathology in an age of fissure, atomisation and molecularisation. This is not to say, of course, that the collective national morality had dissolved, but that in 1938 one would have been hard pressed to locate a functional interpretive paradigm for this, a civilisation in decline. Mauss, for instance, did later admit that the concept of anomie had to be entirely reconceived: "To my uncle's great irritation, I found it too philosophical, too juridical, too moralistic, insufficiently concrete" (Fournier 2006, p.346). But anomie as a concept was not the sole problem. If sociology was indeed a moral science, what could it achieve in a universe divested of its moral core. Or rather, how could one ensure that its moralising could even be heard, let alone internalised?

Durkheim did not live to see Nuremberg or have the occasion to defend himself against the various accusations of totalitarianism that circulated throughout the 1930s and continued to cast a shadow over the Durkheimian enterprise. This burden would fall on Mauss who, according to Shilling's reading of his correspondence with Ranulf, noted that "Durkheim's theories can be applied to Nuremberg rallies as much as liberal-democratic forms of the 'cult of man'" (Shilling 2005, p.223). But a closer examination of Ranulf's correspondence with Mauss and his article on proto-fascist and crypto-fascist scholarly tendencies (where the aforementioned letters were reprinted) reveal no equivocation on Mauss' part, but instead bewilderment and horror and, as Strenski notes in this volume, Ranulf does little to make his case.

Like most Jewish intellectuals, Mauss was opposed to Munich and along with Simone Weil, Lucien Lévy-Bruhl, Emmanuel Berl and Andé Weil, he was also one of the signatories on the petition "We do not want war" circulated by André Delmas, a member of the *Syndicat*

National des Institeurs (Fournier 2006, p.331). But in this time of confusion, where it was not clear if the pro or the anti-Munich party was on the side of the good, even the Durkheimian legacy was questioned and inverted. Ranulf, a student of Mauss, would be among the first to directly pose the question of fascism and the Durkheimians. In his 1939 article, "Scholarly forerunners of fascism," he wrote:

Is not the rise of fascism an event which, in all logic, Durkheim ought to have welcomed as that salvation from individualism for which he had been trying rather gropingly to prepare the way? In all logic, undoubtedly. But there are aspects of fascism that would probably have seemed unacceptable to Durkheim – as they do to at least some of his followers – and that might perhaps induce a reconsideration of the whole view of nineteenth-century individualism as a thing to be deprecated. The longed-for new solidarity may well, when it at last materialized, have appeared to be worse than the evils which it was expected to remedy. (Ranulf 1939, pp.31–32)

Marcel Mauss would go on to spend much of the late 1930s defending the legacy of his uncle against the appropriations of the neither left nor right sensibility, and with great pain attempted to clarify the significance of collective representation, effervescence, totemism and the corporation. Ranulf cited sections from Mauss' letters to him; here we witness Mauss's shock at the resurgence of "primitivism" and the "orgiastic" that typified the sacred horror of the new political spectacles; "neither he nor [the Durkheimians] could have predicted that . . . great modern societies, having more or less emerged from the Middle Ages, could be as suggestible as Australians are to their dances, could be set spinning like children playing ring around the rosy" (Ranulf 1939, p32). In 1939 he would conclude that the crisis was "a great tragedy for us" and "too strong a verification of things we had pointed out and proof that we ought to have expected such a verification to come about through evil rather than through good" (Ranulf 1939, p.32).

Yet the 1930s were a time of flourishing for French ethnology and Mauss laboured on, devoting himself to the "extension and development of research" (Fournier 2006, pp. 318–321). Fournier also notes that Mauss' intellectual production in the late 1930s consisted of "papers he delivered, one in London and the other at

Copenhagen . . . Mauss discussed the history of the idea of 'person,' the 'idea of the self'" (Fournier 2006, pp. 323). In the opening paragraph of these papers, entitled "A category of the human spirit: the notion of the person, that of the self" (1938), Mauss problematises the self not just as a phenomenological category, but as a category assumed to contain within it an inextricable moral kernel:

It's a question of more or less explaining to you that one of the categories of the human spirit, – one of these ideas that we believe to be innate – has slowly been born across long centuries and across numerous vicissitudes, such that it is still even today, floating, delicate and precious and in need of further elaboration. This is the idea of the "person", the idea of the "self". Everyone finds it natural, precisely at the foundation of his consciousness, everyone is equipped at the foundation with the morality that is deduced from it. It is a question of replacing this naive view of its history and of its actual value, with a more precise view. (Mauss 1950, p.333)

In classical Maussian manner, the articles, although limited in data, nonetheless functioned as an encyclopaedic tour de force touching on the notions of the self and the person from Aristotle to the Pueblo Indians, to the Indians of the American north-west, to Australia, China, India, the Christian person, the psychological structure of the person and beyond. Examining masks, masquerades and personae, as well as epistemological (self-knowledge), juridical/legal (rights/recognition), psychological (consciousness) and moral conceptions of the self (the duty and sacredness of the self), Mauss was intent on revealing the arbitrary nature of an array of acquired conceptions of selfhood. He concluded the article by again reposing the question of the self as an innately moral or sacred category:

Who knows if the "category" that everyone here believes to have a foundation can be further recognized as such? It is not formed for us, within us. Even its moral force – the sacred character of the human person – is called into question, not only in the Orient which has not arrived to the stage of our sciences, but even in the countries in which this principle is found. We have great benefits to defend, but with us can disappear the idea. Let's not moralize [about] the human though . . . it arrives slowly, across time, societies, their contracts, their changes, articulating itself through the most hazardous paths. And let us work to illustrate how we must be responsible, in perfecting it, in better articulating it. (Mauss 1950, p.362)

But Mauss was moralising, insisting that the cause of the sacredness of the person, one conferred upon him by virtue of his responsibility to the social, must not be abandoned in the dehumanising and depersonifying tumult of recent years. Mauss was not, like Foucault, interested in liquidating the concept of the person, the self and the human, as a vestige and product of deployments of power, discourse and the human and social sciences. On the contrary, he was struggling to retrieve the person as a moral agent from within the confines of the social (moral) sciences themselves. The self, a fragile achievement, had, like civilisation, taken centuries to complete, and while civilisation and the social may have been falling apart at the seams, the fundamental building block of the latter categories could not be sacrificed at any cost.

The person was relational, autonomous within himself, but dependent on and cognisant of Others. But this simple and primordial social fact had given way to the solipsistic enclosure of liberalism and its leisure pursuits and been thoroughly eroded by a series of political imbalances and social transformations that ate away at the moral (read social) tissue of the self. En route to give one of his lectures, Mauss too witnessed proof of his suspicions live: "on his way to Copenhagen, Mauss crossed Germany by train. Soustelle recounted: 'The train was constantly being shunted off onto a sidetrack. There were soldiers everywhere. It was clear Germany was preparing for war . . . that everything was about to lead us to catastrophe'" (Fournier 2006, p.326).

But faced with civilisation's violent regression and the overturning of all that he, his uncle and their colleagues had so arduously struggled to uphold, the late 1930s were for Mauss a time of melancholy. In 1939 Mauss, the social scientist, could not predict what was going to occur and unfortunately "there were too few of us for too many things and moreover, everything's sort of falling apart now and necessarily so" (Fournier 2006, p.332). Mauss retired in 1939. But, in the years immediately before and after, the Durkheimian school would suffer a series of blows. Fauconnet had already died in 1938, devastating the already frail team of *L'année sociologique*. In 1939 Lévy-Bruhl too died, followed by Abel Rey and Célestin Bouglé in 1940. Following the Occupation Mauss would also hear of the death of his close friend Marcel Granet.

Under Vichy, Mauss would sew a yellow star onto his coat and begin moving his books; he and his wife had been evicted and their large apartment was given to a German general. As Fournier recounts:

The Mausses moved into a tiny ground floor apartment at 2 rue de Porto-Riche in the 14th arrondissement. It was an "appalling slum" that quickly became "impracticable" because it was so cold, dark and dirty. His friends worried. The winter was harsh and "took its toll on [his] body . . . He recovered – a 'resurrection', according to his doctor – owing to 'the excellent reserves [his] system possessed". (Fournier 2006, p.345)

But his work suffered and became even more fragmentary than it already was. Although he had prepared one complete piece of work, "Instructions for a descriptive sociology", Mauss penned a couple pages here and there, but produced nothing of real substance. However, in 1942 he did manage to write some reflections on the crisis. The cause of contemporary disarray was egoism, isolation, and individualism:

This state of egoism, of absolute individualism, characterises the crisis and all of its effects and I reflect on the isolation of the individual. . . . The crisis is a state in which deregulated things are the rule and regulated things impossible. This is the moment where "nothing gels," where the world falls apart along with everybody . . . everything that is organic, at varying degrees of complexity, even the smallest of animal cells, is a composition that "gels" . . . the crisis' "un-gels" (Mauss 1942, in Fournier 1997, pp.770–771)

The rise of violence during the crisis was thus symptomatic of the breakdown of the social organism, its un-gelling and mass anomie or deregulation as rule.

Conclusion

A state of mutation

The articles collected in this issue tarry with the tropes, models and structures of feeling outlined by the Durkheimian school and attempt to reorient them historically and in light of our current moment. Ivan Strenski, Sue Stedman Jones and Mike Gane all seek to articulate a Durkheimian theory of violence, one that is, nevertheless, plagued with the tensions of the sociological project's rapport with its own moment. Jacques Plouin, on the contrary, argues against an overarching Durkheimian theory of violence in favour of a Durkheimian theory of constraint and coercion that itself betrays a certain rapport with violence. Moreover, one must also ask to what degree Durkheim's own sensitivities were shared with or imparted to those with whom he collaborated and those who followed in his lead. Dominique Guillo and Jean-Christophe Marcel further demonstrate how concerns with the violence of modern life in the city and certain Darwinian trends would also merge in the work of the other beacon of the Durkheimian school; Maurice Halbwachs. At stake is also what Alexander Riley has called the renegade Durkheimianism of the College of Sociology and in some sense, the work of Georges Bataille and Roger Caillois function as the Durkheimian return of Durkheim's repressed. My own article in this volume examines the trajectory from Durkheimian effervescence to Roger Caillois' theory of paroxysm and re-poses the question of war as the black festival of modernity. It should also be noted that these concerns do not disappear with the Second World War and, contrary to historicist perspectives, the Durkheimian tradition is not one that flourished only during the Third Republic and the inter-war years. As Stjepan Mestrovic demonstrates, Durkheimian frames can still be used to examine even the most troubling and non-theorisable manifestations of contemporary life, including torture. Alexander Riley pushes this line of inquiry even further and connects the Durkheimian tradition to the prophet of post-modernity, Jean Baudrillard, in his exploration of mass-mediated suicide. Finally, Ronjon Paul Datta theorises a political Durkheimianism bound in the theory of the sacred and invokes a new potential politics to come, charting novel directions in post-political theory.

In a current social and political landscape typified by, on the one hand, the contingent nature of all normative structures and on the other, the rise of violence across the globe, the Durkheimian desire to make gel merits the utmost imaginative and critical attention and a reappraisal of the fundamental tenets of Durkheim, his colleagues and those he influenced.

And while the hour for militant sociological prescription may have passed, in the Durkheimian tradition is still found a crucial nexus of concepts and methods that should certainly not be overlooked in the analysis of contemporary forms of barbarism, which may still be the symptoms of a larger historical malady.

While many a post-modern may deem the social, anomie, effervescence, solidarity, the symbolic and the sacrificial to be terms that circulate in an archaic universe (preferring themselves to be the grand arbiters of the nomadic, the joyously nihilistic, the bearers of rights without responsibility), one cannot deny their hermeneutic force and indeed their resonance in a too deterritorialised world characterised by the incessant search for precisely the normative social frames that Durkheim considered essential to liberty. But these new normative frames have manifested themselves in various non-Durkheimian forms that reveal the presence less of friendship and beauty than of the frenzied search for meaning and territories in the midst of global deregulation. Nationalism, fundamentalism, cultural essentialism, xenophobia, loss, the denial of the existence of innocent suffering, phobia and fear characterise our new societies of risk which, for all of their playfulness, push everything to the brink and leave well-being teetering on a narrow precipice.

In a precarious balance between *nomos* and *anomos*, the social-symbolic and between the atomised are the reservoirs of violence that Durkheimian moralism sought to empty of their force. The Durkheimian tradition believed that it could annul violence and displace it by fashioning of a robust model of solidarity and erecting a state apparatus that was not only the reflection of collective consciousness but the arbiter of order. This order was authoritarian but the authority that it incarnated was welcomed as a force that guaranteed that the sacredness of personhood and the sacredness of a human body should never be violated. The person was intrinsically replete with value and an embodiment of values. However, institutional and moral mechanisms were required to protect such value; the state, the social, morality, discipline and the symbolic realm.

Since Durkheim's time these mechanisms have been deemed entirely contingent and among the greatest victories of the late twentieth century is the supposed destruction of symbolic orders and anything that claims absolute status. Yet in the wake of such destruction, in the wake of relativism, situational ethics and perspectivalism, a void has been produced. Durkheim's socialism and Mauss' anti-liberal liberality thus, in a strange twist of historical fate, appear conservative and reactionary in the fields of the post-modern and the hyper-modern, precisely because of their ardent belief in human betterment and absolutes; absolutes that were by no means static but were evolving while remaining loyal to the moral core of social life. With the evaporation of symbolic orders, one witnesses simultaneously the evaporation of those mechanisms that defended against violence in its multiple forms. The void is a place of suspension where a return to order is no longer possible, but civilisation appears both incapable and unwilling to produce new values to replace the ones it has so rigorously devalued. And in this space of void those reservoirs of violence stand prepared to spill over.

In his essay with Henri Beauchat on the seasonal variations in "Eskimo societies: a study in social morphology" (1904–1905), Mauss came upon a crucial discovery: social law "goes through successive and regular phases of increasing and decreasing intensity, rest and activity, expenditure and restoration." Because it did violence to consciousness, life in common was possible only if members of a group could "partly withdraw from it" (Mauss and Beauchat 1950, p.143).

What Mauss himself could not think of (and what we habitually confront) was a world where life in common and the rhythms of expenditure and restoration had given way to pure dispersion, one where it is not social law that does violence to consciousness but the absence of the social; un common life.

While anomie may be a pathology that no longer applies to the current crisis of civilisation (or its continuation), one which is at once economic and social, Duvignaud reminds us that anomie is the surging of the raging forces of negativity that should be followed in "lived anomic mutation" in hopes that such fulfillment of anomie will produce a new critical disposition and generate new concepts (Duvignaud 1986, pp.63–64). It cannot be denied that our current world is engaged in a process of accelerated mutation and is all too often characterised by violence. But "living and fulfilling anomie" in order to surpass it necessitates a strategy for confronting new forms of violence. This volume functions not as a polemic that advocates a return to Durkheimian order, but represents a modest attempt to rethink the Durkheimian strategy and its own internal prism of violence in light of contemporary mutations.

Durkheim's theory of violence

Mike Gane

Introduction

The fundamental contribution of Emile Durkheim to sociology is well known and unchallenged. His writings have provided a basic framework, methodology and empirical studies such as *Suicide* ([1897b] 1970) that are still essential texts today. But the way that his work has been interpreted has been to assimilate his writings to the conservative, functionalist tradition, and this has ignored his analysis of conflict and violence. In this chapter the principal aim is to elucidate his contribution to the understanding of violence, and this will be done by examining his writings on sanctions, on gender, on suicide and on war against his concept of humanity as *homo duplex*. It will examine Durkheim's attempt to formulate his theory of violence in his studies on education.

Mike Gane (b. 1943) was educated at Leicester University and the London School of Economics and currently is Professor Sociology at Loughborough University. He has written widely on Durkheim (his books include *On Durkheim's rules of sociological method*, Routledge, 1988, and the edited collection *The radical sociology of Durkheim and Mauss*, Routledge, 1993). His other interests have been in the origins of French sociology. His book *Auguste Comte* was published by Routledge in 2006 and in contemporary French social theory, his book *French social theory* was published by Sage in 2003. He has written a number of works on the writings of Jean Baudrillard. Email: M.J.Gane@lboro.ac.uk

Essential background and context

Durkheim (b. 1858) passed his baccalaureat in 1875 and 1876 when the new political regime of the Third Republic was beginning to settle into its republican formation. He came to maturity during the early years of the new regime as a student at the *Ecole normale supérieure* between 1879 and 1882. In the recently discovered lectures given as a school teacher at the *lycée* at Sens (1882–1884) he clearly reacted strongly against the legacy of the violence of the Paris Commune by arguing that communism and even socialism were in principle "immoral" (Durkheim 2004, p.260). He clearly worked towards a rapprochement with socialism soon after his Sens period by critically reconstructing Comte's sociology (he claimed that neither Hegel nor Marx had a direct influence on his thought), and seems to have adopted Comte's view that war would quickly disappear with social progression. He debated with socialists, acknowledging that pacifism, socialism and sociology were both profoundly indebted to Saint-Simon and Saint-Simonianism (Layne 1973, p.99). It is clear that by the 1890s he had adopted what Marcel Mauss identified as a position close to guild socialism and a pacificism close to that of Jean Jaurés (Layne 1973). In developing this line of sociological thinking Durkheim adumbrated a distinct conception of the causes of violence, one that embraced its manifestation in all the main social spheres and in all social types. The examination of the theory here will be set against an overview of his general view of the human condition as *homo duplex*, as set out in the short essay "*Le dualisme de la nature humaine et ses conditions sociales"* published in 1914.

Durkheim's essay, as many have pointed out, anticipates Freud and Elias but it strikingly starts with Comte's founding idea that sociology is a study of civilisation and the problem that if man makes civilisation "it is civilisation that has made man what he is" (Durkheim 1960, p.325). But into this problem Durkheim inserts in a particular way his own theory of the sacred and profane and, like Comte, puts religion at the heart of the sociology of civilisation. However in reconstructing sociology Durkheim changed the terms of the problem, the definition of religion and the conception of the individual (and thus the body–soul relation). But there is something of Comte here in the sense that Comte held that modern civilisation in the metaphysical state was out of balance with the needs of the individual human constitution itself – this would be rectified in the coming positive polity in which the balance would be restored. It is immediately apparent that Durkheim's conclusion is that this kind of balance will not be restored: "all the evidence compels us to expect our effort in the struggle between the two beings within us to increase with the growth of civilisation" (Durkheim 1960, p.339).

Homo duplex, social energy and social causation

The key idea of the 1914 essay is that the human sphere is not only marked by a dualism between the individual and the social, the body and soul, but that this is an antinomy. Durkheim argues that his *Elementary forms* (published in 1912) sought to look at this dualism from a scientific point of view by examining totemic religion in Australia, having found the dualism among one of the most primitive societies known. He concludes the essay by suggesting that this antinomy not only grows with civilisation but will in fact continue to develop.

Durkheim's essay in effect attempts to answer the question why the body and soul dualism is a universal one. He claims that it is found in all religions and is even more of a universal than the incest taboo. His answer, in section I of the article, is that the body is experienced as a sensory individual world of emotions and activities while the soul is impersonal and transcendent. Durkheim's argument is that this impersonal world is in fact the world of the collectivity, and it is through the media of language, concepts and thought that the world of the collectivity is maintained and communicated. Society is a being in its own right, *sui generis*. It has a logic, and above all it contains moral forces, energies of its own. So there is the individual body of the individual on the one hand and the exterior forces of the social on the other. This articulation is uneven, and indeed conflictual. On the one hand, the individual has to make important sacrifices since society can only exist if it "penetrates" individual consciences and practices while, on the other, the individual depends on the social in terms of intellectual resources, moral values and energies.

In section III of the article (section II is a critique of other explanations), Durkheim introduces more explicitly the notions of sacred and profane and specifically the thesis that the antinomy – body and soul – is "only a particular case of this division". He says that in *Elementary forms* he has demonstrated that the sacred was identified as collective ideals borne along by a specific energy creative of a *ton vitale* in the individual. These ideals can exist only when embodied by signs and symbols and they permit individuals to commune in unison. The sacred sphere is divided off from the profane in rituals by acts of radical separation. Thus religion produces a dynamogenic influence in the individual. Even in the individual the introjected social sphere of the sacred retains its specific character and is respected as such. The essay ends with the observation that society can always be seen to make its own specific demands on the individual, and in so doing sets up a more or less painful tension. Against the spontaneous flows of individual consciousness the social demands willed attention and this does violence against some of our most tyrannical inclinations. Thus, between the individual and the social there is no immediate spontaneous harmony, and the dualism will remain a constant, even growing feature of civilisation.

The publication of Durkheim's early lectures of 1882–1884 (Durkheim 2004) allows us to resolve some of the fundamental issues of his intellectual development.[1] The lectures can be read as a critique of the limits of pure philosophy as a means for assessing and resolving the problem of social integration in France (Gross, in Durkheim 2004, p.7). His early writings suggest that he worked to arrive at a position that would avoid the errors of the Commune on the one hand, and individualist liberalism (and anarchism, which took a turn into terrorism in the Third Republic in the years 1892–1894), on the other hand: a position that formed the basis of his famous intervention in the Dreyfus affair (1894–1906).[2] Many commentators have seen Durkheim's position here as a valuable move beyond the confines of liberal political theory (Parsons), while other have found that the absence of a theory of political parties constitutes the blind spot of Durkheimian sociology (Lukes). Clearly it is both. From the mid-1890s Durkheim was working in close association with Marcel Mauss (b. 1872). In the division of labour between them Mauss was more closely involved in political practice. The phase of socialism that developed in western Europe (particularly 1876–1890) after the Commune, revealed, Mauss later remarked, a variety of practical developments of a new kind that left behind the heroic and utopian age of theory (Marx and Proudhon). Only from an existing nation, said Mauss, can the transition be conceived as an internal progression of an organic type. There is, however, some debate over whether Mauss rejected the conception of *homo duplex* (see Richman 2002, p.149), or whether he tried to build on and add to the basic idea (Schlanger 2006). Mauss seemed to want to develop Durkheim's notion of *homo duplex*, but he did this in a way that did not confront the philosophers head-on. The long running dispute about reason and pure rationality, on the one hand, and social determinants, on the other, produced on Mauss's part some ingenious interventions. His early concern with bodily gestures, indicated in his 1909 thesis on prayer (Mauss 2004) continued throughout his career with essays on techniques of the body and technology (Mauss 2004, p.26). He held that from *homo duplex* it was possible to think of *homme total*, and of thinking not only with the brain but with the fingers (Karsenti 1997; Schlanger 2006). But this was a move away from Durkheim's general theory of social energy and violence towards structural anthropology, on the one hand, and political journalism, on the other (Mauss, 1997).

The primary aim of the project that Durkheim and Mauss developed was not, however, directly political. It was to ensure the implantation of sociology in the universities as a reputable discipline with a pivotal role to play in the identification of the normal forms of the emerging institutional structures of modern societies (Clarke 1973, pp.162–195). It was not to establish or guide a political movement or party. Durkheim stood at a distance from politics, even

the social and moral crisis of the Dreyfus Affair in which he played a large part, did not change his attitude. Even during the war, he was among those who put no hope in the so-called internationally organised working class. He therefore remained uncommitted – he "sympathised" ... with the socialists, with Jaurès, with socialism. But he never gave himself to it said Mauss (in Durkheim 1962, pp.34–35).

Durkheim held that class solidarity would not solve the problem of the nature of the *patrie* (Layne 1973). What he gave himself to was the development of sociology, conceived as a discipline that would be a science capable of resolving questions previously framed within ideologies.

One of the striking developments of Durkheim's burgeoning sociology of the 1890s was his consistent use of the idea of social energy as a causal principle. In the *Division of labour* ([1893] 1964) Durkheim defines repressive sanction as a "reaction of passionate feeling, graduated in intensity, which society exerts through the mediation of an organised body over those of its members who have violated certain rules of conduct" (Durkheim ([1893] 1964, p.52). In discussing this emotion Durkheim presents an early version of his *homo duplex* theory (([1893] 1964, p.61). But what is interesting is the explanation of the way social energy, passion, is created and notably how its effect in producing crime is "an entirely mechanical reaction . . . from passionate emotion, for the most part unthinking" (p. 62). Punishments do not arise from intellectual theories of justice alone, but from the various gradations of the intensities of emotional reactions to violations of social norms.

Education and punishment

Durkheim developed his theory as his researches grew more extensive. He began by suggesting that the more primitive the society was the more likely it was to have repressive sanctions. In his early lectures on moral education (Durkheim, 1973a), for example, he argued that there was a plague of violent punishment in the schools of the Middle Ages and the lash remained in constant use in schools up until the eighteenth century. He later revised this view completely. After researching his lectures on educational thought in France (Durkheim 1977) he describes the thesis of the violent mediaeval colleges as simply a legend. He had discovered that these educational communities remained essentially democratic and these forms "never have very harsh disciplinary regimes" because "he who is today judged may tomorrow become the judge" (Durkheim 1977, pp.155–7). The new analysis suggested that the turn towards a more oppressive disciplinary regime began at the end of the sixteenth century, just at the moment when the schools and colleges in France became centralised and radically isolated from the outside community.

Durkheim faced up to the issue of punishment as a practical issue for teachers in his pedagogy classes. Between the offence and the punishment, he observed, there is a hidden continuity, for they are not "two heterogeneous things coupled artificially" (Durkheim 1973a, p.179). It is because this link is misunderstood that erroneous theories of punishment arise. One such theory sees punishment as expiation or atonement another sees punishment primarily as a way of intimidating or inhibiting further offences. From a pedagogical point of view, however, he argued, the problem concerns the teacher's capacity to neutralise the demoralising effects of an infringement of group norms. The effectiveness of punishment should be judged primarily by how far it contributes to the solidarity of the group as a whole, since certain kinds of punishment can contribute to the creation of further immoral acts (Durkheim 1973a, p.199). Even so, once applied punishment seems to lose something of its power. A reign of terror is, in the end, a very weak system of sanctions often driven to extremes by its own ineffectiveness. There is also a contradiction in the resort to corporal punishment in advanced societies as it involves an attack on the dignity of the individual, a dignity increasingly valued and fostered in modern societies. Durkheim always rejected any reductionism. In his lectures on

Moral education he asks "What use has a rite observed to the letter if the spirit of it is no longer felt? . . . Discipline can train mechanically; but it cannot educate, since it produces no inner effects" (Durkheim 1973a, p.202).

Gender and religion

His theory of gender also went through a notable shift as it developed through his writings of the 1890s. The fundamental idea was that it is through the unequal involvement of men, women and children in the cult that social (and individual) differences are produced, and these have consequences in turn for the body and for psychological development. *Homo duplex* is not a single category, as it were, but a complex universal structure, participation in which varies across a lifetime and according to social group (such as gender or race). This progressive or regressive participation is also affected by degrees of development of civilisation: "the woman of past days was not at all the weak creature that she has become with the progress of morality" (Durkheim ([1893] 1964, p.57). With the introduction of the sacred/profane problematic in the 1890s Durkheim began to add to this view an analysis of ambivalent relationships to blood in primitive society. In his 1898 article on the incest taboo he wrote:

[S]ince the feminine sex alone served to perpetuate the totem, the blood of the woman seemed much closer in relationship with the divine substance than that of man; as a result, it is probable that it also acquired a higher religious value, which naturally communicated to the woman herself and placed her completely apart. (Durkheim 1963, p.90)

Faced with the connection between women and evil powers Durkheim noted that what had happened was that after time "the primitive . . . had a choice between these two interpretations: he had to see in the woman either a dangerous magician or a born priestess" and he concludes "[t]he inferior situation that she occupied in the public life hardly permits us to accept the second hypothesis; the first imposes itself" (p.92). He goes on to give various examples in which there are either positive or negative attitudes to blood, and note in primitive societies "the extreme ambiguity found there of the notion of the

Film still from *Pink Floyd: The wall* (1982), directed by Alan Parker. MGM/United Artistsakg-images/Alan Parker

divine" (p.96). This thesis provided the framework for a theory, worked out in the *Elementary forms*, not just of the origin of the sacred in the effervescent collective gathering but also of scapegoating, for women, he suggested, had become minor subjects, stigmatised by a radical otherness; outsiders against whom effervescent violence could be unleashed (see Gane 1983).

If we return to Durkheim's article on *homo duplex* we can see that it presents something of an oversimplification of the theses in *Elementary forms* in two ways. Firstly, the expression in the essay that perhaps needs great attention is that the body and soul are "only a particular case" of the division of the sacred and profane. In the *Elementary forms* Durkheim goes to great lengths to show that the primary elements are the energies created in effervescent assemblies: the forces created and recreated, the dynamogenic forces that create the sacred (good and evil) are also represented in the body as the individualised part that is held sacred (a small, even infinitesimal in simple societies), and to which the representations of the soul correspond. Secondly, when Durkheim referred to the fact that society makes its own specific demands on the individual and in so doing sets up a "more or less painful tension", he could also have said that when conflicts arise between groups or societies, energies can be released that give rise to forms of violence that can unleash extreme levels of physical torture. These, he argued, cannot be explained except in terms of the social types involved (and complex involvements of types) and the degree to which levels of control can be created nationally and internationally to prohibit and effectively punish infringements of its codes. Today, as the debate between Lukes (2006) and Levey (2007) around the US government resort to torture reveals, the cult of humanity is far from having been irreversibly established.

Suicide

Durkheim developed this basic idea in his study
Suicide ([1897b] 1970), where such intensities are
realised in violent actions against the self. In
attempting to establish the significance of sociological interpretations Durkheim looks specifically at the determinants of rates of suicide.
Stephen Turner has noted that "the novel
feature of Durkheim's treatment of suicide is
neither the thesis of social determination, which
was conventional, [and nor] the actual explanation ... but the specific statistical reasoning he
uses and the way he interprets his results ... to
produce a genuinely novel result" (Turner 1996,
p.335). In the earlier and well-known work of
Morselli analysis stopped with the demonstration of regularity between two variables.
Durkheim's own strategy was to examine "relations between rates in which perfectly equivalent
rank-orderings at some level of aggregation
can be discovered ... [indeed] he uses the
term 'law' to describe these relationships,
and these relationships alone" (Turner 1996,
p.367). Thus, Durkheim was not interested
in simple statistical relationships. What he
looked for was the parallelism of rankings
between the substantive series he analysed:
"concomitant variation". Turner has examined
some of the efforts Durkheim must have gone to
in order to produce a demonstration of these
parallelisms. With reference, for instance, to
Table XIX (Durkheim [1897b] 1970, p.164)
which compares suicides and educational levels
in Italy, Turner notes:

It would be hard to imagine what sort of hypothesis would
attempt to relate suicide rates for a given period to illiteracy
rates for a later period ... it is not easy to find series that
match this nicely with one another, and whatever search
procedure Durkheim or his helpers employed to find this
particular match, it must have been quite involved.

Similar tables can be found in Morselli but they
would have had to have been reworked from the
original official statistics in order to be available
in Durkheim's different form (Turner 1996,
p.370). For Turner the "'theoretical' achievement of *Suicide* is the construction of a synthetic
explanation which reduced a number of highly
diverse relationships to a few basic social forces,
each of which can be illustrated by a table with a

few perfect or near perfect parallelisms" (Turner
1996, p.374). These social forces are the energies
that manifest themselves in specific forms of
suicide, read by Durkheim as the causes of
violence against the self.

In *Suicide* Durkheim does not work with
conflicts that arise from the constitution of the
individual (conflict of drives, instincts in a
Freudian manner), but in relation to the social
forces theorised as currents and flows of energy,
conceived as social causes. His morphological
classification suggests the fundamental forms of
suicide are always associated, not with specific
means of committing suicide, but with certain
highly specific emotional states: egoistic suicide
is performed with apathetic emotional detachment, altruistic suicide performed with calm
resolve and anomic suicide with agitated irritation and disgust (Durkheim [1897b] 1970,
p.293). More complex forms are discussed
subsequently as combinations of these fundamental ones. Analytically he finds a major
division between morphology and aetiology,
which lies between the actual forms of the act
itself and the social causes of suicide. Then there
is a subdivision concerning what he calls the
emotional character of the performance of the
suicide (apathetic/energetic) and the means of
committing suicide (hanging, drowning, shoot-
ing). The important discovery of the absence of a
causal link between the latter and suicide itself is
reported dramatically: "intimately related as
these two elements of a single act seem, they are
actually independent of each other. At least
there are only external relations of juxtaposition
between them. For while both depend on social
causes, the social conditions expressed by them
are widely different" (Durkheim ([1897b] 1970,
p.293). Durkheim here presents one of the
crucial conclusions of the study, and yet it is
passed over in a couple of paragraphs.

His illustrations of suicide types are drawn
from real historical accounts,and from novels
(by Lamartine, Goethe and Chateaubriand).
What he produced is sometimes called the
psychological forms of suicide and the account
is dominated by a theatricalisation of mood
or attitude resulting from the way that the
fundamental energy of the "resolve" of the
impulsion is composed and acted out. The
characteristic mood of egoistic suicide, for
example, is suggested by the specific reflective

detachment of the individual from social groups: its mood is meditative, intellectual and ironic and there is often an element of self-analysis reflecting the emptiness of existence. Egoistic suicide has two main variations. The first is a lofty, pure, melancholic, dreamy form where pain can be a feature of the suicide. Such a suicide is the businessman "who goes to an isolated forest to die of hunger. During an agony of almost three weeks he ... kept a diary"; or another who "asphyxiates himself ... and jots down his observations bit by bit" or someone who "builds a complicated apparatus to accomplish his own death without having his blood stain the floor" (Durkheim [1897b] 1970, p.281). The second egoistic type is characterised by indifference and scepticism (here the victim minimises the pain of the suicide). Durkheim examines Epicurus's view that one should live as long as it is interesting to be alive and, "as sensual pleasure is a very slight link to attach men to life, he exhorted them always to be ready to leave it, at the least stimulus of circumstance. In this case philosophic, dream melancholy is replaced by sceptical, disillusioned matter-of-factness, which becomes especially prominent at the final hour" (Durkheim [1897b] 1970, p.282). The victim here "makes no long preparations" and only wishes to "terminate a thenceforth meaningless existence". The act itself is thus performed "without hate or anger" and the victim "assigns himself the single task of satisfying his personal needs" (Durkheim [1897b] 1970, p.282).

The characteristic mood of altruistic suicide is, by contrast, energetic, active and often full of affirmative emotion. "Altruistic suicide ... involves a certain expenditure of energy, since its source is a violent emotion" (Durkheim [1897b] 1970, p.283): "the individual kills himself at the command of his conscience ... thus, the dominant note of his act is the serene conviction derived from the feeling of duty accomplished; the deaths of Cato and of Commander Beaurepaire are historic types" (Durkheim [1897b] 1970, p.283). There are three forms of the altruistic suicide: it can be obligatory, optional or another form that he calls acute (where "the individual kills himself purely for the joy of sacrifice" (Durkheim [1897b] 1970, p.223). The sacrificial form can be an affirmation of a unity with a deity or a

sombre form of appeasement to a deity: the victim "has a goal but one outside this life, which henceforth seems merely an obstacle" ([1897b] 1970, p.225): an officer says: "I have just hung myself, had lost consciousness, the rope broke ... My new preparations are complete, I shall start again shortly but shall smoke a pipe first; the last I hope" (Durkheim [1897b] 1970, p.284). Yet if

there is no resemblance between the religious fervour of the fanatic who hurls himself joyously beneath the chariot of his idol, that of the monk overcome by acedia, or the remorse of the criminal who puts an end to his days to expiate his crime. Yet beneath these superficially different appearances, the essential features of the phenomenon are the same. (Durkheim [1897b] 1970, p.283)

The anomic suicide is characterised by a mood of anger and disappointment, pain and disillusionment. There is blame and recrimination, and it is this form which is associated with the combination homicide-suicide, murder of someone accused of being the origin of personal suffering. The emotions are anguished: life is full of sharp conflicts. Instances include disappointment in love (such as Goethe's *Werther*) and disillusionment after the failure of a project. There is also a form in which after a long struggle the individual "lapses into a sort of melancholy resembling somewhat that of the intellectual egoist but without its languorous charm' but where 'the dominating note is a more or less irritated disgust with life" (Durkheim 1970, p.286).

Durkheim's method, then, is to examine very carefully the energies, the dynamogenics of the causal process. From a theoretical point of view the study of suicide and his observations that anomic and egoistic suicides increase with civilisation provide a reference point for Durkheim's conclusion in his article on *homo duplex* – especially on the problem of the regulation of the appetites (and desire) – but in this case it is not the tyranny of the social that is the cause of the problem; rather, it is an energy deficit.

Family and state

Durkheim's theoretical sociology, however, did not shy away from the issues of the nature of the modern state and political power. Durkheim's argument suggests that social theorists are often mistaken in thinking that the state is either a purely repressive machine or that the purely political division of powers can deliver political and social liberty in the fullest sense. For Durkheim (1992, p.64) the Spencerian thesis that freedom is freedom from the state ignores the fact that it is the state "that has rescued the child from family tyranny [and] the citizen from feudal groups and later from communal groups." Indeed, Durkheim (1992, p.64) argued the state must not limit itself to the administration of "prohibitive justice . . . [it] must deploy energies equal to those for which it has to provide a counterbalance". Against the political illusion of power, for example, as found in Montesquieu, Durkheim tried to show that liberty is based on a particular form of the total social division of power: the state "must even permeate all those secondary groups of family, trade and professional association, Church, regional areas, and so on" (Durkheim, 1992, p.64). Lamanna suggests that Durkheim's analysis of the family reveals how "[t]he tension between spouse and kin as heirs reflects the historic struggle of the conjugal family to emancipate itself from kin dominance" (Lamanna 2002, p.91). This historic struggle, one that is still in progress even in modern societies, is central to Durkheim's grand narrative of the movement from societies based on mechanical solidarity to those based on organic solidarity. It is also the narrative of the modern state that increasingly intervenes in favour of freely chosen marriage contracts and against violence used by kin to enforce family "honour".

Types of society and types of power

The central theoretical issue here was addressed in his attempt to reconstruct the theses of *The division of labour* ([1893] 1964) in an article of 1900 called "Two laws of penal evolution" (Durkheim, [1888] 1978, pp.153–180). Durkheim criticised Spencer for thinking that the degree of absoluteness of governmental power is related to the number of functions it undertakes. But he worked towards a very Spencerian

formulation: "the more or less absolute character of the government is not an inherent characteristic of any given social type" (Durkheim, [1888] 1978, p.157). Durkheim presents an account of French society that is diametrically opposed to that of Marx: "seventeenth-century France and nineteenth-century France belong to the same type" (Durkheim [1888] 1978, p.157). To think there has been a change of type is to mistake a conjunctural event in the society (revolution) with its fundamental structure, since absolutism arises, not from the constituent features of a social form, but from "individual, transitory and contingent conditions" in social evolution (Durkheim [1888] 1978, p.157). In principle, the form of state is never a fundamental constitutive feature of any social type.

Both Durkheim and Mauss were influenced by the Comtean view that war was incompatible with the advancement of industrial society. Both believed it impossible that there could really be deep seated causes of war between advanced nations – by which they meant France, Britain and Germany. The diplomatic activities of these nations were democratic, not divorced from popular control. In the run up to the 1914–1918 war, therefore, Mauss in particular contrasted the political maturity of these nations against the autocratic and feudal regimes of eastern Europe, particularly Russia. His view was that German ambitions lay eastwards and the western nations would not be drawn in. When the war broke out Mauss enlisted immediately, abandoning his pacificist stance. Durkheim again turned to his theory of social abnormalities. The state can become too strong and develop its own pathological dimensions and capacities. In his pamphlet "'Germany above all' German mentality and war" (Durkheim 1915) he critiqued the ideas of the German political philosopher Heinrich von Treitschke, ideas that he took to be representative of the mentality that had brought war to Europe in 1914. He was careful to say that he was not analysing the causes of war, only examining one of the manifestations of a condition of social pathology (Durkheim 1915, p.46). Durkheim contrasted the democratic idea in which there is continuity between government and people with Treitschke's thesis that there is a radical antagonism between state and civil society. This latter idea requires a state power capable of enforcing mechanical obedience from its citizens, whose first duty was to obey its dictates. Its leaders are possessed of enormous ambition and unwavering determination, and with personalities that have "something harsh, caustic, and more or less detestable" about them (Durkheim 1915, pp. 30–34). These states flouted international law and conventions, and their idea of war pushed the development of military technologies which were almost "exempt from the laws of gravity . . . [t]hey seem to transport us into an unreal world, where nothing can any longer resist the will of man" (Durkheim p.46). Where there is a shift towards the concentration of power in the state, as occurs in wartime, the structures protecting individual values are weakened. In wartime there is to be expected not only an increase in altruistic suicide, most commonly associated with military discipline (Durkheim [1897b] 1970, pp.228–30), but also an increase in civil homicides since the individual as such is less protected in moral value when social energies return to reinforce group solidarity (Durkheim 1992, p.110–120).

Conclusion: towards a theory of energy and violence

The theme that emerges in Durkheim's first lectures in sociology is that although we can talk of society and the individual there are many types of society and many types of individual. He very specifically critiques Comte (Comte 1975, II, p.83): "Despite Pascal's famous formulation, which Comte wrongly revives, humanity cannot be compared to a solitary man who has lived all these past centuries and still survives. Rather it resembles an immense family" (Durkheim, opening lecture, [1888] 1978, p.53). There are different social species and the role of institutions change according to the overall social structure. Durkheim's basic framework was developed very early on. In the earlier social species religion exhibits a strong, even tyrannical *conscience collective*, infringements of which are harshly and violently punished. Christianity represents a

world historical turning point in that it raises humanity in the scale of things and reduces matter to the profane – the disenchantment of the world (Durkheim 1973a). Eventually the civic religion of humanity presents a structure in which infringements against the individual are taken much more seriously and punished. But against this framework there is a universal unifying idea of *homo duplex*: society creates and is itself a creation of social energies. And under certain conditions this involves violence. Indeed it is possible, then, to find in Durkheim a general theory of violence. It was stated in *Moral education*:

When two populations, two groups of people having an unequal culture, come into continuous contact with one another, certain feelings develop that prompt the more cultured group or that which deems itself such – to do violence to the other. This is currently the case in colonies and countries of all kinds where representatives of European civilisations find themselves involved with underdeveloped peoples. Although it is useless and involves many dangers those who abandon themselves to it, exposing themselves to formidable reprisals, this violence almost inevitably breaks out. Hence that kind of bloody foolhardiness that seizes the explorer in connection with races he deems inferior. The superiority that he arrogates produces a veritable intoxication of self, a sort of megalomania, which goes to the worst extremes, and the source of which is not difficult to fathom. We have seen, in fact, that the individual controls himself, only if he feels himself controlled, only if he confronts moral forces which he respects and on which he dare not encroach. Where this is not the case, he knows no limit and extends himself without measure or bounds. As soon as the only moral forces with which he has anything to do are depreciated in his eyes – from the moment when, because of the inferiority he imputes to them, he sees in them no authority requiring his deference – they cannot perform this moderating function. Consequently, nothing restrains him; he overflows in violence, quite like the tyrant whom nothing can resist. This violence is a game with him, a spectacle in which he indulges himself, a way of demonstrating that superiority he sees in himself. (Durkheim 1973a, p.193).

Thus, it is possible to see that although it appears that Durkheim is a radical relativist in his framing of sociological analysis, there is an element that remains constant throughout his theorising and his research. It is surprising that this is not better known and understood.

Notes

1. Durkheim's *Sens* lecture course of 1882–1884 clearly outlines the body–soul duality, which forms the basis of the course: "nothing happens in the body that doesn't find its echo in the soul and vice versa" (Durkheim 2004, p.51). The *Sens* lectures have an evolutionary framework for the individual and the social, and the basic (Cartesian) assumptions about body and soul are already in place. It was a very short step to formulate the idea that the representation of God varies with social type, that God represents society.

2. Durkheim (1969). On the significance of this article see Richard Bellamy (1992, pp. 74–104).

Durkheimism: a model for external constraint without a theory of violence

Jacques Plouin

Introduction: a model in which violence occupies a problematic place

Durkheim's theoretical work is often regarded as being uninterested in social struggles and hence ill-equipped as a tool for understanding violence, which is most frequently associated with an excessive use of force but, like activities that exceed norms in general, can have a symbolic or moral dimension. Thus, thinking on violence does not initially seem to be a constituent of the concept of society traditionally associated with Durkheim and that is found, for example, in *The division of labour in society* (Durkheim 1986), in which collective life is underpinned by cooperation and solidarity. But this reference to solidarity is not enough to explain the absence of a general theory of violence. Comte, from whom Durkheim's solidarity inherits a great deal, incorporates a theory of violence into his law of the three states of human progress by inserting between the theological first stage and the positive third stage a metaphysical stage that is logically the period of dissolution, social destruction and revolution. However, Durkheim rejects this structuring of historical evolution in terms of a concept of progress, which he considers illusory, perhaps avoiding a mechanism for the general interpretation of violence in societies.

The author is at the Centre d'Epistémologie et d'Ergologie Comparatives, Université de Provence and is Lecturer in Social Sciences at the Institut d'Études Politiques, Paris. His research interests include social theory, the epistemology of social science, Durkheimism, social norms, the sociology of science and domestication theory.
Email: Jacques.plouin@sciences-po.org; j_plouin@hotmail.com

The singularity of Durkheim's situation must be emphasised, for in the history of political thought since the birth of the modern state and the civil and religious wars that accompanied it, the production of a general theory of violence seems to be almost a corollary of any social theory. The modern political thought of today often remains grounded in a discussion of Hobbes' concept of the war of all against all. Meanwhile, Marx strives to theorise violence through alienation, exploitation or the class struggle in an analysis of society in which the very concept of social history is systematically structured by conflict and hence by forms of violence, which may be more or less latent or expressed, between social groups. Here we have a general theory of violence in the sense that, through the medium of social conflict, violence is a technical force that is structuring the reality of the social.

For Weber, too, violence is a crucial dimension of the social world. The great matrix of his analysis of social action is the pair formed by rationality and its opposite, irrationality. In this model violence can always find expression because the irrational may erupt at any moment. Thus, Weber's political concepts hinge on the idea of domination, a submission of the will that, even when it is accepted, is always a kind of violence that we can join Bourdieu in describing as symbolic. Moreover domination requires forms of repression that the state, for example, claims to use legitimately and in a rational and controlled way, but which is always in danger of turning into violence.

Should we conclude from this that violence represents a blind spot in the Durkheimian model in so far as it is not the subject of a general theory? Should we conclude that the model is ill-suited to understanding or explaining violent phenomena because when social regularities are taken into account violence is solely a matter of residues of irrationality whose evaluation is always subjective? Such a hypothesis would place us in a position where, even if Durkheim's work notes the existence violence, of conflicts between groups and individuals, this violence has no real sociological significance. Such a hypothesis would also expose Durkheimism to certain criticisms of a theoretical order, because in postulating that phenomena are residues one always runs the risk of missing the rationality that passes through them, and also of a social order, because in claiming to base society on solidarity one always runs the risk of masking the reality of violence that is part of collective life.

However, there is a way of looking at Durkheim's work in which these criticisms perhaps miss their target. While it does not include a systematic theory of violence in the usual sense of a general system of interpretation or explanation, in practice Durkheim's model gives a central place to the very similar concept of constraint or coercion, which in his work characterises the action of society on individuals. While this social constraint does not seem to influence the way in which the moderns generally understand violence, it must nevertheless be noted that, at an abstract level, social constraint can be analysed as violence done to the individual nature of individuals. Relations between groups or individuals may be little affected by violence, but violence has a kind of avatar in the forces exerted by society on individuals, as in the case of suicide, whose exclusively sociological nature Durkheim showed (Durkheim 1993b, p.2). But if the violence of the social on the individual is the only violence that can be understood, does providing no more than a slightly less euphemised version of the solidarist vision of society really constitute a response to the above criticisms?

The problem for Durkheimians is thus to assess whether the loss that results from abandoning the old modern project of producing a general theory of violence is balanced or indeed recompensed a hundredfold by the theoretical gains to be made.

In contrasting the absence of a theory of violence in Durkheim's work with the importance the model gives to constraint, our intellectual technology will be theoretical reading – a craft distinct both from historical commentary and epistemological analysis. The aim is to read Durkheim as a theoretical resource that can be drawn on, in particular when an investigation is losing its grip and we are forced to redefine our initial concepts, reinvent the terms of problems, adapt observation protocols, modify measuring techniques and so on. Scientific reading is never the simple gathering of information but is always also continuing professional development in reasoning, whose logical dimension as a craft or conceptual design is clearly emphasised here. From this point of view, the founders of any scientific domain have a special, unique place because they are the primitive matrix in which a new grammar of reasoning emerged, using components foreign to it.

A theoretical reading of a founder thus has three important characteristics: first, it is always a rereading, since in doing geology, for example, one is always an heir to Lyell, even if we have not read what he wrote we always reread on the basis of presuppositions that must sometimes be deconstructed for new concepts to be invented (theory is a neo-ancient practice). Second, theoretical reading is by nature intertextual and is relatively unconcerned with academic dissection and overly rigid periodisation. In so far as theory seeks to forge resources for reasoning, it is crucial to use intersecting readings to identify or to create similarities that are pertinent to the exploration one is undertaking. Lastly, and most importantly, theoretical reading is selective in the sense that, when exploring Galileo's writings, for example, physicists are unlikely to adopt the idea of circular movement, which is present in the master's work but which they will leave to one side. A selective theoretical reading of Durkheim will at the minimum distinguish between the Durkheimian model or matrix of sociological reasoning and the complete, historically situated oeuvre of the individual officially known as Emile Durkheim. Thus our theoretical exploration of violence in Durkheim's work will be primarily based on *Rules*, in which the model plays a larger part than in *The division of labour in society* or *The elementary forms of religious life* (Durkheim 1998), where the concept of society used is one which, like Galileo's circular movement, we shall leave to one side.

Violence as a symptom of the social

Constraint or coercion play such a central theoretical role in Durkheim's eyes that, in the second preface to *Rules*, he notes that the social fact, as he defines it, consists "of ways of acting or thinking or feeling which can be recognised by their particularity of being able to exert a coercive influence over individual consciences" (Durkheim 1993a, p.xx), but we must at once make clear that the coercive influence of the social is simply a sign of recognition, an element of social symptomatology. For Durkheim this coercive influence becomes manifest when individuals resist a social fact, such as the duty to keep a promise or those inherent in their role as sister or friend. So there can be no theory of coercion, since it is an individual manifestation, imbued with ungraspable subjectivity, which must be refined if the social dimension of the observed phenomenon is to be identified. In other words coercion, even when understood as a euphemisation of violence, has no constituent or theoretical role because it is one of the phenomena to be described. The sociologist's task is then to use coercion as a working tool. This approach to coercion can be related to the provisional definition, an important tool of the Durkheimian model, which supports the work of investigation in seeking to establish theories and theses, but is not itself a theory. Its aim is to enable the identification of external signs to which analysis will be applied.

So the importance Durkheim gives to coercion does not correspond to a unified theory of coercion, which would make it into a structuring aspect of the social, since coercion serves only to distinguish one social effect from others. In a note accompanying the passage cited, Durkheim adds:

Indeed the coercive power we attribute to the social fact is such a small aspect of the whole that it may appear quite opposite in nature. For, while institutions impose on us, at the same time we want to have them; they compel us and we love them; they constrain us and we are gratified by their functioning and constraint itself. The moralists have often noted this antithesis between the two notions of good and duty, which express two different, but equally real aspects of moral life. There are perhaps no collective practices that do not exert this dual function over us, which is moreover contradictory only in appearance. If we have not defined them by this special attachment, at once interested and disinterested, it is simply because it does not manifest itself through easily perceptible external signs. Good has something more internal, more private about it than duty, and so less graspable, (Durkheim 1993a, p.xx).

Coercion being, according to Durkheim, more visible than enjoyment or pleasure, it is thus privileged solely because it enables an easier and more effective identification of the social. One is more visibly a social being when one does violence to oneself, when one makes an effort over oneself than when, for example, one enjoys a conversation. At the theoretical level the two are strictly and precisely equivalent, but their individual expressions differ and offer the sociologist different handles, which remain merely external. As a first diagnostic tool, social violence cannot thus be the subject of a general theory because it is not the whole of the social fact, but only its visible part. At best we might speak of a heuristic or weak theory of coercion as detectability of the social, because on this point, as Durkheimism well understood, is a model of methodological relativity: violence has no meaning a priori and is identified as a tool or method of observation solely in terms of its effects. So Durkheim's precept could be as follows: seek out forms or expressions of coercion or social violence and you will find social facts and underlying regularities to study, but these will have nothing quintessentially violent about them since, whether we resist or seek them out, they are phenomena that occur whether one wills them or not.

The second preface thus provides a valuable clarification, giving us a comparatively easy tool to manipulate in the form of coercion. However, two criticisms of this approach can be made. Firstly, it is hard to believe that the answer to the initial problem; the question of whether violence has any meaning in Durkheim's model beyond that of subjective evaluation, could be that its meaning is exclusively methodological and thus exclusive to sociologists. We should also note another criticism. One might ask whether, through this instrumentalisation of violence,

Durkheim is really answering the criticisms made on the publication of *Rules* (and sometimes still today) concerning the place of coercion in his model. These criticisms often involve what Durkheim regards as obvious in the passage under consideration and that we have expressed in the phrase "whether one wills them or not", in which educated common sense sees a negation of the autonomy of individuals and an undue claim to interpret human behaviour in the register of natural facts. It seems we need to deepen our theoretical exploration.

Sociological externalism

Durkheim comments on his definition of the social fact, describing it as strictly instrumental, but it must be observed that some passages of *Rules* still raise difficulties. The chapter "Rules for the explanation of social facts" ends with the following statement: "The rules that we have just set out would, on the contrary make it possible to develop a sociology that sees a sense of discipline, founded in reason and truth, as the essential condition of all life in common" (Durkheim 1993a, p.124). First remark: with such a foundation "in reason and truth" we have left all strictly instrumental or relativist frameworks behind. Next we might ask how Durkheim can maintain that coercion is only a symptom of the social while regarding the sense of discipline, which supposes the internalisation or individualisation of constraints through habituation, training or education, as the essential condition for any life in common (and for the personality compatible with such life).

The answer to this question seems to lie in the definition of the social fact given by Durkheim at the end of the first chapter of *Rules*: "A social fact is any way of acting, whether fixed or not, capable of exerting an external constraint over the individual; or which is general over the whole of a given society while having an existence of its own, independent of its individual manifestations" (Durkheim 1993a, p.14).

The definition of the social fact establishes a sociological externalism. Within this framework traditional notions of the individual as an autonomous centre of action, or of society as either association or totality, are suspended and rendered useless from a theoretical point of view:

they are primarily tools arising out of practice and, as such, can only be objects of the investigation as opposed to its tools or general principles.

The term externalism is taken from the philosophy of mind or linguistic philosophy, where it refers to the postulate that the (mental or linguistic) phenomena studied occur not in the minds of individuals but outside them, in the structures formed by their exchanges (see Auroux 1998; Descombes 1995; Esfeld 2004). This is the schema that a theoretical reading enables us to identify in the work of Durkheim, whose definition of the social fact posits that it acts on the individual from the outside and has its own existence independent of individual manifestations. Since a strict positivist or relativist cannot hypothesise the ultimate nature of the social, look for fundamental principles of practice or pose questions on the origins of society, we will not waste time speculating on what might lie underneath social facts. The main thing for now is to have a graspable, fertile canvas, such as the concept of natural selection that formerly acted in the identification of genetic processes.

Durkheim's model is often described as holistic or collectivist, but the definition of the social fact invalidates these labels. True, society features in the definition. But we must then ask whether the concepts of society and the social fact are operating on the same level in it. From a logical point of view it is surprising that a model said to privilege society over the individual should, in defining the social fact, start by supposing the existence of society. A backwards reading of the first chapter of *Rules* sheds light on this deceptive appearance of a petitio principii. The chapter identifies human societies as heterogeneous collections in which biological, psychological and sociological phenomena are found intertwined, the latter being, as a result, simply one category among other societal phenomena that are more or less generalised in a society. Society and social facts do not exist on the same logical level: the latter are events, the former is an open or ecological environment. To avoid losing sight of externalism, we will postulate that there are two heterogeneous concepts of society in Durkheim's work, one ecological and the other organicist or holistic, which we must leave aside as metaphysical in so far as it is a response to philosophical questions on the substrate or origin of social facts.

Consequently, if by collective we meant only a fact's property of being more or less general in a given human population, it would be no less sociological for all that. It is its external character that is the theoretical property of the social fact and that makes it the subject of a theory in the strong sense in which, if the distribution of a social fact can vary to the point that it could, hypothetically, be either realised universally or revealed by one person alone, it cannot, invariably, constantly and rigidly be other than external or independent of its individual manifestation. Sociological externalism must therefore be very clearly distinguished from sociological realism: there is no logical equivalence between the counter-intuitive statement, unknown until the late-nineteenth century, that social facts are purely and simply external to individuals (even if the notion of individual has to be reconceptualised on that basis) and the old idea, upheld by Durkheim himself in *Rules* and *Forms*, that it is society itself that is external to individuals.

The logical core of the definition of the social fact is thus not society, either as an association of individuals or as an organic whole. From a theoretical point of view the social fact is not "social" in nature, but external (in social facts sociology does not study something that has metaphysically happened to naturally distinct individuals but something that has archaeologically happened to an already social environment of prehuman primates in which archipelagos of individuality surface). Already we can ratchet up the argument: from this point in the analysis we can call pointless, doubtful and false any interpretation that sees holism, totalism or collectivism as the core of the Durkheimian model. We shall content ourselves with the view that these labels reflect methodological individualism's attempts to impose its own terms on a debate that the theoretician gains nothing by entering anyway.

Mechanical and psychological constraints

The sociological property of the social fact, systematically present in its definition, is externality: true, constraint is there too, but it is described as "external". In choosing to approach Durkheim's work as an externalist tool kit, we must here perform a semantic reversal and substantiate externality in order to use it as the base for our understanding of the social and to understand the idea of constraint in a relativist way. The social fact is constraining in a mechanical sense. It is because it is external that it is constraining and not the other way round, as in the individualist view that sees social behaviour as the projection or realisation of intentions or motives developed in the inner conscience.

There is constraint in the mechanical sense when two extrinsic realities exert a force on each other in a given frame of reference or context. One of the most important rules in *Rules* is to explain a social fact in relation to its social setting or context (Durkheim 1993a), anticipating Wittgenstein's thesis that the criteria for success or failure in following a rule have meaning only in relation to a social context (Wittgenstein 2005). The relativity involved here does not thus consist in maintaining that everything is of equal value in absolute terms but that, in a way that is not trivial because it leads to empirical enquiry, everything is of equal value in a given context.

We can use this to refine the concepts employed by Durkheim: in practice, though they may be congruent, contextualist relativism must not follow methodological individualism in positing a concept of the individual that can be understood as a centre of action or a closed entity. When we are talking about social constraint exerted on an individual, what we call individual has nothing substantial about it; as Durkheim ventured to maintain, the constraint is not that of society in general exerted over the individual in particular, but the interaction of social facts, roles, norms and so on. This is manifested in the dilemmas of which individuals are the arena (there is a dilemma when an individual no longer has control over the staging of his existence as a fluid movement from one role to another). This Durkheimism is a little more abstract than usual, but it enables important gains to be made at the theoretical level.

While at first coercion served primarily to identify social facts that were more salient than the rest, external constraint now becomes the theoretical property that defines the grammar of sociological reasoning. Seen through this logical matrix, individuals are born into environments

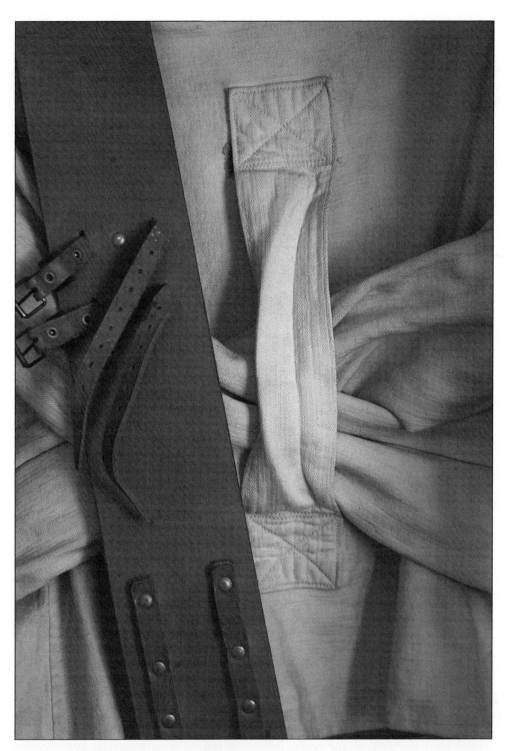

Detail of Straightjacket Exhibition (2007). Sainte Anne Hospital Museum, Paris, France. Agence France-Presse/Joel Saget

that are already social, where, in addition to natural processes that are more or less open to domestication, they find obligations, roles, expectations, desires and requirements that are not of their doing (more precisely, they find contents, but they can also invent some of those: what they do not invent or make is normativity itself, the fact that social facts have social value). We must then distinguish between two understandings of constraint: one relativist or mechanical, linked to the theoretical domain in the strong or systemic sense and concerning only relations between mutually external realities, and the other of a psychological order, which covers individual manifestations of the social and can be used to identify their effects (sociologists are not psychologists but, as Durkheim notes, they need a psychological culture as support).

This distinction between the two forms of constraint is indispensable to obtaining a rigorous image of externalism. However, it is often ignored, as in the following analysis by Dubet:

> While the theory of constraint conceives of action as an internalisation of the social, that of externality calls for a radical separation of "inside" and "outside" for reasons that have more to do with the project of positive sociology itself than with anthropological plausibility. Paradoxically, this position, which most strongly embodies Durkheim's "sociologism", leads him to concede a great deal to psychology and individual conscience; ... madness, sex and the psychic dispositions of individuals are granted a far greater autonomy than that that might be required by a rigorous "sociologism". (Dubet 1997, p.211)

Let us first observe that the idea of referring a scientific model to anthropological plausibility is a dead end to be avoided at all costs: it presupposes the logical error of measuring the tools of sociological enquiry against extra-sociological criteria; the idea of anthropological or any other form of plausibility implying a recourse to preconceptions external to the scientific jurisdiction of the social sciences.

Sociological externalism is not the addition of a theory of constraint to a theory of externality. The social fact is an external constraint, with no gaps: it is not a thing that is first external and then goes on to produce constraints. Constraint is the immediate corollary of the externality of the social fact in the mechanical sense in which two bodies exert a constraint on each other. In distinguishing

between externality and constraint Dubet presupposes the existence of an absolute individual nature troubled by its relation to externality: from an individualist point of view, individuals, usually defined by self-awareness or a relationship to rationality, are arbitrarily posited as existing fundamentally in relation to themselves. The individualist grammar converges with the teleological grammar of Aristotelian physics, in which natural states contrast with violent movements.

Secondly we shall note that, from a relativist point of view we cannot suppose the existence of a "radical separation of 'inside' and 'outside'". Any spatio-temporal zone is always an inside or an outside relative to a given frame of reference (the fact that, aside from certain experiments, human consciousness posits or experiences itself as a closed totality does nothing to prove the contrary). In the externalist model externality does not have internality as its opposite: it has no opposite; just as the mechanism has no goal as its opposite, since it is a theoretical grammar that excludes the possibility of a goal, which only upholders of teleology believe must be included.

The mechanist interpretation reveals the congruence of a number of theses advanced by Durkheim. His critique of the autonomy of individuals is thus a critique of the very concept of internality, which is the prenotion leading us to imagine that we act according to motives of an internal nature. The suggestion that social facts act from the outside in no way requires a substantial internality for individuals: mechanist reasoning simply rejects the possibility of a scientific use of the concept of internality, whether in the context of things (against pre-Renaissance physics), living beings (against the biology that preceded Bernard and Darwin) or human primates (against methodological individualism). External constraint is thus not violence by the social against individuals since the latter have no inner nature of their own.

From this mechanist perspective we understand why Durkheim sees constraint in the psychological sense as a good diagnostic tool: desire or pleasure can be related to a form of behavioural inertia, resistance to an obligation can be coded as a friction or change of direction in the sense of Galileo's definition of movement according to which "movement is movement and operates as movement as long as it is in relation to things that do not have it; but for all those things that also have it, it does not operate, it is as though it were not" (Galileo 1992, p.228). To act according to one's wishes is to share the movement of a social norm.

The reference to mechanism must be specified immediately in order to avoid the traditional misunderstandings. It is imperative to stand up to the philosophical vulgate according to which mechanism cannot constitute a model for the analysis of human actions on the grounds that they have an intrinsically axiological dimension. In dialectical sparring this problem turns into a canonical opposition of facts and values. Such a distinction presupposes that the mechanism recognises facts of nature while values relate to a special regime of reality that is absolutely irreducible to the former. But it has nothing on its side but the power of the underlying prejudices that it deploys. Without entering the thicket of this dialectic, we shall note and follow Durkheim's rejection of the distinction between facts and values on the grounds that it is metaphysical and not made for sociological enquiry. "Judgements of value and judgements of reality" thus states that

to explain value judgements there is no need either to reduce them to reality judgements by doing away with the notion of value, or to relate them to some faculty whereby man enters into relation with a transcendent world. Value does come from the relationship of things to different aspects of the ideal; but the ideal is not an escape to a mysterious beyond; it is in and of nature. Clear thought has a hold on it as on the rest of the physical and moral universe. (Durkheim 1995, p.137)

In this proposition, the immediate content of the concepts at stake matters less than the hold they offer to sociological reasoning: the distinction between fact and value is thus pertinent only in a conceptual grammar in which a choice has been made to begin with their opposition.

Our understanding of the real, virtual or actual is always in relation to a grammar or conceptual matrix on the basis of which we define the criteria for what is real: splitting the real into facts and values or norms has nothing of the fact about it. It is a way of organising the real to render it graspable to practices that are not at all scientific (the latter are, in fact, fairly rare and costly). At the level of theoretical debate there is no sense in asking whether this or that conceptual grammar corresponds or not to the facts, precisely because it is the grammar that

makes it possible to determine what constitutes a fact. Durkheim recommends adopting a different language from that of the philosophers or social theoreticians, who seem to believe that before practicing sociological theory one must wonder at length about what the relations between facts and values should be, as conditions of the theory.

Durkheim's implicit approach is to start by looking for what the enquiry can grasp. This is not a dialectical opposition but an tool for identification constructed in such a way that the distinction is meaningless: the concept of a social fact is the concept of norms, of practices (Durkheim says, ways of doing, being and thinking) identified in such a way that they behave like any other type of real event (notably, presenting regularities such as those that can be revealed by statistics). Norms are facts like any other and social constraint should not be regarded as a special essence. The sociology of sciences, notably starting with Schaffer, Shapin and Latour, has pursued this Durkheimian rejection of the opposition of facts and norms, moving the distinction from the status of a principle of enquiry to that of historical object to be described empirically: the distinction between facts and norms is a practice for organising the real that should be explored in the same way as any other social practice.

Disentangling Durkheim's writing to distinguish the model from the work

Before proceeding any further we need to return to the fact that the mechanist portrait of constraint results from an ostensibly selective reading of Durkheim: his writing is more tangled, sometimes combining both mechanical and psychological understandings of constraint in the same passage:

No doubt we are making constraint into the characteristic of any social fact. Only this constraint does not result from a more or less clever machinery, intended to prevent men from seeing the traps in which they have caught themselves. It simply arises because individuals find themselves in the presence of a force that dominates them and to which they bow; but this is a natural force. It does not derive from a conventional arrangement added in its entirety to reality by human will; it comes out of the entrails of reality itself; it is the necessary product of given causes. And to lead individuals to submit to it willingly, no artifice is required; it is enough to make individuals aware of their state of natural dependency and inferiority – whether they create an emotional and symbolic representation of it through religion or manage to shape an appropriate, clear notion of it through science. As the superiority of society over them is not simply physical, but intellectual and moral, it has nothing to fear from free examination, as long as this is properly used. By showing men how much richer, more complex and more durable is the social being than the individual, reflective thought cannot fail to reveal to them the intelligible reasons for the subordination demanded of them and the feelings of attachment and respect that habit has fixed in their hearts. (Durkheim 1993a, pp.121–122).

This passage is typical of the difficulties to be raised in order to formulate a rigorously socio-logical externalism, for in it we find both registers of constraint at work, one mechanist and the other psychological, in which constraint is sub-mission to an individual (here society as a whole).

On the one hand this passage is authentically mechanist. The notion of constraint is expressed in the language of physical forces. Just as, being a thing, the social fact is a social thing, so, being a mechanism, constraint is a social mechanism. In distinguishing external constraint from machin-ery, Durkheim is careful to prevent any error of interpretation: a mechanism is not the anthro-pological projection of an artificialism that would make the social into a machine built to serve human domination. Here the mechanist reason-ing is coherent, legitimately referring to nature in order to posit the autonomy of causal series that are independent of any intentionality and at the same time to discount teleological explanations, of which contract theories, for example, are a variant. Social or sociological constraint is not social or interpersonal domination – which is why there is no systemic theory of social violence.

On the other hand, however, this passage reveals a degree of inconsistency in the handing of the concept of constraint. True, Durkheim begins by defining constraint in a mechanist and naturalist way, but a considerable part of the paragraph raises certain problems. For Durk-heim surreptitiously shifts from the description of a mechanism to an apology for submission to society. In so doing he confuses the making of theoretical tools with a search for what Boltanski and Thévenot have called a "superior principle of order", that serves not to describe but to

justify forms of collective life (Boltanski and Thévenot 1991). The problematic nature of this passage can clearly be felt in the presupposition of a "state of natural dependency and inferior-ity", a concept that is in contradiction with the fact that the notions of dependency and infer-iority have only relative, contextual and norma-tive meaning.

Durkheim breaks with externalism when he ventures a discussion of the motives – however universal or general – for which individuals act socially. Either we have a social relation to society or the social is simply that by virtue of which there is one relation rather than another. The latter alternative is clearly mechanist and more congruent with naturalism. However, it is obvious that Durkheim regularly tends to express himself in the terms of the former, notably in the passages where he considers the foundation of our relation to society. Here Durkheim shifts from the language of naturalist exploration, which defines social facts as the constraint to which some resistance is made, hence as obliga-tions, to a philosophical, moral or political justification of these obligations. Instead of confining himself to observing sociological reg-ularities he seeks to give them a basis and to understand their legitimacy, when this is the most social of objects that should, therefore, be the object of enquiry rather than its foundation. Sociological realism, which led Durkheim to reify society in the form of a super-individual, clearly relates to this paralogism of hierarchical relations in which any phenomenon of obligation, obedi-ence or submission results from the delegation of an underlying structure of obligation, obedience or submission to someone or something.

A theoretical reading of Durkheim is thus sometimes similar to a Durkheimian critique of Durkheim. But such a critique is indispensable since, where the question of constraint and coercion is concerned, the difficulties he enters into are not the result of accidents or simple errors of inattention: they are linked to a tension inherent in the problem he is dealing with. The absence of a theory of social violence must be well understood. We should not conclude that the Durkheimian model has no unified or structuring view of violence because this would be subjective and science is objective. Durkhei-mism rejects internality and free will, but this does not make it a form of behaviourism: if coercion is a heuristic diagnostic tool, this is because violence as such has a meaning at the level of practices in so far as it corresponds to the violation of a norm – for example, violence done to an individual is an assault on the sacredness of his or her person. So violence is neither irrational nor subjective; it is the indication that a norm is being resisted, since individuals and groups are sensitive to the violation of norms that drive or structure them (in the sense of the terms used here, for example, not all human societies regard all human individuals as human persons).

The plurality of norms and violence

In making coercion a symptom of social norms, the Durkheimian model pre-empts some of Canguilhem's theses on the norms of life (Canguilhem 1984) and notably those that do not see health and sickness in opposition along the lines of being and non-being, but as two norms of life that are conflictual and perceived differentially. We can translate this into sociological reasoning to suggest that manifestations of violence are the mechanical result of conflicts of norms in a society. From there one can suggest that, just as there can be no general theory of sickness, since sickness has meaning only in the relationship of an individual to his surroundings, so there is no general theory or unifiable principle of violence, because violence has meaning only in the relationship of norms to their normative context.

So the apprehension of violence is thus a twofold function of one's frame of reference. On the one hand, the frame of reference is that of the ecological context of norms; on the other, it is that of the very enquiry whose characteristics are crystallised in the provisional definitions one adopts at the outset. Assuming that what we usually call a society is the frame of reference in which social facts can be grasped, it becomes crucial to break with the sometimes organicist dimension of Durkheim's work. For organicism leads us to understand the social as a unified totality and to make violence a residue of irrationality or subjectivity. However, as we have just noted, in order to have a functioning theoretical model we must be able to think in terms of conflicts of norms.

Paradoxically, we can protect the Durkheimian model from the holistic vision that feeds Durkheim's work using the chapter of *Rules* where organicism seems to shatter most clearly. This is the chapter on the distinction between the normal and the pathological, which has always had a bad press. Today it is criticised for its attempt to structure the social on the basis of a metaphor taken from life, while some are shocked that the normal should be an indicator of social health (normality?). We should also recall that when the book was first published this chapter caused a scandal because it was thought that the assertion that crime was normal constituted its moral justification. But such readings are truncated and ignore the fact that Durkheim's concepts of the pathological and of crime lie at the core of an authentically relativist theory whose main aim is to identify social dynamics in an absence of absolute referents (such as those that a general theory of violence claims to provide, for example). In this perspective, where there are no absolute markers beyond effective and efficient norms, the only solution is to seek to adopt the point of view of a norm for which the pathological is simply that which counters its affirmation. This perspective may seem strange, but the theoretical landscape is overturned when we restore social facts to their position of empirical plurality and comprehend them within a relativist framework.

If Durkheim regards crime as a normal phenomenon, this is not because everything is of equal value, but because everything is of equal value in a given context. According to Durkheim crime is mechanically required to happen very regularly due to the heterogeneous diversity of individuals, since a human population is made up of individuals who are too diverse and heterogeneous to permit the behaviour of each to conform to a social norm (Durkheim 1993a, Ch. 3): violations of norms are thus a mechanical phenomenon. From a strictly externalist viewpoint we should add that we cannot argue as though the norms were ranged opposite full, complete individuals: the diversity of individuals is that of the norms that constitute them as such. We can shift perspective again with a sociological translation of Canguilhem's proposition concerning life: outside one particular norm we find other, equally particular norms. So crime supposes an environment composed of a multiplicity of norms whose contradictory affirmation it also supposes. Once we abandon the organic or unified concept of society there are no operations that can reduce, recuperate or rationalise the untamed, heterogeneous multiplicity of social norms. Durkheim suggests this himself in considering the dynamics or evolution of societies in terms of the actions of founders of a religion or spiritual movement:

[i]t can happen that crime itself plays a useful role in this evolution. . . . For so many times it is simply an anticipation of the morality to come, a movement towards what will be! According to Athenian law, Socrates was a criminal and his sentence was entirely just. . . . The case of Socrates is not isolated; it reoccurs periodically throughout history. The freedom of thought we now enjoy might never have been proclaimed if the rules that forbade it had not been violated before being officially repealed. However, at that time, this violation was a crime, since it was an offence against feelings that were still very much alive in most minds. (Durkheim 1993a, p.71).

From a strictly relativist point of view, this passage is an attempt to use the normal and the pathological to understand human societies as ecosystems woven from heterogeneous norms coexisting in intertwined plurality, some of which will be in conflict in precisely the manner identified by Canguilhem in relation to health and sickness, their meaning as norms dependent on normative relations in a given ecological context. If we adhere to this point of view (and choose to ignore others maintained by Durkheim himself), we can advance the hypothesis that his theoretical model functions far better without a concept of society. For in the passage cited we are dealing with a plurality of heterogeneous and contradicting norms – which does not make much sense if we understand society as a holistic totality or a living being – where confrontation between them produces violence and all forms of violence are revealed as violations of a norm. All we need from an externalist – and thus mechanist and relativist – point of view is to take coexisting norms or external social facts as our theoretical basis. So, without further presuppositions – without, in other words, constructing a general theory of violence – we then see the mechanical appearance among the phenomena to be observed and described, of situations of violence from which

specific enquiries can then disengage a meaning that can only be contextual.

Conclusion

A general theory of violence means viewing social reality by means of an interpretative schema that gives meaning to violence a priori, but which always ultimately proves to privilege one norm of interpretation to the exclusion of others. The (vain) ambition of achieving an overview is probably the reason why the traditional debate of the moderns on violence often turns on questions of rationality and irrationality. However, this conceptual duality disguises the unity of an approach that consists in approaching the social from a single, reductive point of view because the category of rationality-irrationality is one of the norms employed by certain individuals and groups who use it as an ethnocentric tool for the political regulation of a society that resists their grasp.

In other words, a general theory of violence can lead to forms of symbolic violence by pre-empting the meaning of all possible violence. When, on the contrary, we settle for seeing violence as a predictable indication of normative tensions, we are saying very little – extremely little, almost nothing – but at the same time opening up a boundless landscape of possible enquiries, for which we have far more powerful cartographic tools than contract-based theories or the straitjacket of rationality.

So the absence of a general theory of violence is not a deficiency in Durkheim's work but a theoretical gain. It is the corollary of an externalist model in which the external constraint of social facts on individuals is the only property appropriate to the practice of sociological theory. Externalism is also a theory of sociological relativity, whose importance lies in enabling us to consider norms in their empirical plurality within a robust mechanist framework but without involving a stage of ideal-typical generalisation. The rationality-irrationality schema cannot thus be used to understand social practices or individual actions in sociological terms. As this plurality is irreducible, there can be no theory of violence, since violence is one of the effects of the local coexistence of norms and is part of the object to be described.

While deflating attempts to regard violence as a phenomenon originating in the social, and social critique in opposition to sociological theory, the Durkheimian analytics of constraint also permits an open understanding of violence in the framework of practical enquiry. Because the model rejects the possibility of a general, unified or systemic theory of violence it is constructed so that no form of violence can slip its grasp, and it is doubtless this that enabled Durkheim to use the empirical analysis of a phenomenon so apparently statistically minor as suicide to identify anomie as an unusual form of violence suffered by individuals lacking regulation – regulation that individualist precepts would tend to posit as violence done to the nature of the individual (Durkheim 1993b).

The aim of a theoretical reading is to reveal the fertile matrix of the writings. In a sense, this exploration of violence revealed its prize fairly early on; most of our analysis has served to clarify the conditions for use of a Durkheimian rule that were not formulated by Durkheim but that may be useful to new enquiries: "seek out forms or expressions of coercion or social violence and you will find social facts and underlying regularities to study".

Durkheim, the question of violence and the Paris Commune of 1871

Susan Stedman Jones

About suffering they were never wrong,
The Old Masters; how well they understood
Its human position. W.H. Auden "Musée des Beaux Arts"

The intellectual and political milieu in which Durkheim was educated as a philosopher and in which he went on to develop his social science began with the Franco-Prussian war of 1870–1871, the Siege of Paris and the Commune; it ended with the First World War of 1914–1918. He entered the *École normale* in 1879 and he died in 1917, reputedly with a broken heart through the loss of his son André, together with so many of his young students, in the First World War. Although, war, insurrection and international conflict constituted the opening moments of the Third Republic in which he lived, Durkheim's works cannot be characterised, in those simplified divisions of social theory, as a type of conflict theory. At first sight there would appear to be little reference to conflict or violence in his writings. Is the subject of violence really absent or is it so neglected that his writings are no longer relevant for us? More deeply, does he even acknowledge violence? There is a widespread view, even among Durkheimian scholars, that he does not.

Susan Stedman Jones's first degree was in philosophy and she then studied postgraduate anthropology, both at University College, London. She completed a PhD in philosophy "From Kant to Durkheim". She was formerly Convenor of the Philosophy of Social Sciences course at Goldsmiths College, London University, and now pursues independent research, dividing her time between London and Paris. She is a member of the British Centre for Durkheimian Studies, University of Oxford and is on the editorial board of Durkheimian Studies/ *Etudes durkheimiennes*. Recent publications include: *Durkheim reconsidered* Cambridge: Polity (2001); "Truth and social relations: Durkheim and the critique of pragmatism" Durkheimian Studies/*Etudes durkheimiennes* (2004); "From varieties to elementary forms: William James and Emile Durkheim on religious life" *Journal of Classical Sociology* (2003) and "Functionalism of mind and functionalism of society; the concept of conscience and Durkheim's *Division of social labour*" Durkheimian Studies/*Etudes durkheimiennes* (2007). Email: suestedman@ googlemail.com

I will argue that his theory was developed, at least in part, as a response to the above violence. In general it can be said that he has a negative view of what violence can achieve. His espousal of humanism, which he held to be the developing morality of the age, meant that Durkheim denied the any positive value to violence and held that respect for human life was the supreme value of contemporary morality (Durkheim, 1909). In arguing that his thinking was influenced by the events at the beginning of the Third Republic, I will stress the importance of the Commune of 1871. This strongly marked the development of socialist thought and its effect was such that the leaders of democratic socialism, Jaurès and Malon, renounced violence as a means or as a strategy for social transformation. The great suffering of the French proletariat in the Commune and its failure to achieve its political aims was a turning point in the understanding of violence. However, although Durkheim does not extol violence as a means of developing social change, this does not mean that he neglects it or the questions that large-scale violence poses for social theory. I have maintained that the

Commune lead to the questions that were fundamental to his theory (Stedman Jones 2001a). We will see, for example, that this includes the way in which society is understood. The concept of the organic nature of society was raised during the Commune. Although, of course, there were other sources for this, this conception of the nature of society was supported by the Communards, who opposed it to bourgeois egoism. It is interesting that organicism is still widely regarded as central to a conservative view of society in many student texts in sociology.

I will maintain that Durkheim does have a theory of violence. It goes beyond the definition of violence as the exertion of force so as to injure or abuse. He has a wider conceptualisation of violence than the concept of intentional injury, or verbal and emotional abuse towards others and extends towards characterising a society that denies freedom as violent. In so doing, his discussion goes beyond debates as to whether violence is inherent in human nature and makes the question of violence a social question. The idea that it is society, rather than human nature, which causes the *malheurs* of the people, was a result of socialist thinking (Dittmar 2008, p.125). These considerations are important for the contemporary significance of his theory, for however bloody the catastrophes in France at the time were, they were only a prelude to the twentieth century as the bloodiest and most violent century in human history so far, in which 191 million people lost their lives (World Health Organization 2002). Given the wars and terrorism that surround us, violence seems a major feature of life in the twenty-first century.

We must firstly address what is meant by a theory of violence. The latter could mean a theory that stresses the utility of violence in stimulating change and development. The revolutionary left, anarchism and certain forms of Marxism maintain the utility of violence in stimulating change and development. Durkheim does not support this and thus would not support Engels, who held violence to be the accelerator of economic development (Arendt 1969). Further, a theory of violence might be one that puts violence centre stage in human life and holds that we are by nature aggressive creatures who are dominated by a territorial imperative. We will see below that he has distinct criticisms of such biological theorising about the social. A

theory of violence could be one that puts violence at the heart of society, such that it is involved in the very constitution of the social. Durkheim criticised Hobbes for his view that the individual is naturally resistant to social life and can only accept it through force; he rejects Hobbes's view that the object of society is to "contain and constrict the individual" (Durkheim 1895, p.120, trans. p.142). He certainly does not share the view of Sorel, Pareto or Franz Fanon, who glorify violence for violence's sake (Arendt 1969, p.65). As we will see, he rejects George Sorel's glorification of violence as an expression of the natural "upsurge of an '*élan vital*'" of proletarian power. And if by a theory of violence is meant transgressive action, the social realisation of Bataille's Acéphale, then we do not find this in Durkheim either. Unlike Bataille, he would not see violent transgression as necessarily liberative. "One must not lose one's reason and approve of a violent movement simply because it was violent" (Durkheim 1905, p.288).

If, however, we look at those thinkers who are concerned with violence and who doubt that it could constitute a progressive force, then we get closer to the Durkheimian position. So Arendt, who acknowledged that violence may have a short term instrumentality in dramatising grievances, held that it neither promotes causes, history, revolution, progress, nor reaction (Arendt 1969, p.79). For Walter Benjamin, a critical approach to violence is primary "The task of a critique of violence can be summarized as that of expounding its relation with law and justice" (Benjamin 1921, p.132). Vittorio Bufacci outlines two concepts of violence. He defines a minimalist conception of as an intentional act of excessive or destructive force. In contrast, the comprehensive conception covers a violence of rights, including a long list of human needs (Bufacci 2005). I will argue that the whole of Durkheim's oeuvre in dealing with *le mal*, which characterises the condition of modern society, is a theory of violence in the comprehensive conception outlined by Bufacci.

However, the lack of explicit reference to violence makes his works feel like *Hamlet* without the Prince of Denmark. Violence is rarely mentioned as such, but its ghost is there. Given this absence, violence can be seen as a counterfactual of his theory: the great themes of

Durkheimian thought are a warning about what might happen if we don't educate, if we don't address and challenge the forces that undermine solidarity and altruism or the passionate power of the collective consciousness and mitigate its possibly destructive tendencies and help orientate it towards the interests of humanity (Durkheim 1895, p.74, transl. p.104). But more forcefully, the account of the causes of violence, of violence as an expression of a greater and deeper evil, is fundamental to his thought, just as is the implied critique of violence in his study of solidarity. The conclusion of his thought is that violence does not generate solidarity or humanistic tolerance. We should then differentiate between a description of violence and a theory of violence; Durkheim's works are short on the former while they are long on the latter.

The important initial question is the definition of violence that must precede any account of a theory of violence. The World Health Organization (WHO) defined violence as "the intentional use of physical force or power threatened or actual, against oneself, another person, or against a group or a community, that either results in or has a high likelihood of resulting in injury, death, psychological harm, maldevelopment or deprivation". There are three subcategories: self-directed violence, interpersonal violence and community violence. To extend this definition we see that beyond violence to the body there can be violence to the self and to the totality of society. Durkheim addresses the causes of these and outlines the social conditions which could prevent such violence. In the analysis of significant areas of Durkheim's thought that follows, I will show that he does have a theory of both internal and external violence. This is evident in his studies of the causes of social pathology, beginning in 1893 with the constraining and anomic division of labour. This sets the terms of his radical definition of violence as more than simply a physical attack. Violence is a sign of a deeper malaise. The malaise of contemporary society is a concern that is constant throughout his work.

Of course violence, like sexuality, at a superficial level is a physical act. However, as he points out, the sexual act is far from being merely a physical action (Durkheim 1903, vol. II: p.504). It is an act to which moral or immoral values are ascribed; and it is the social significance of acts of violence that are of concern to Durkheim. We see this in his study of sacrifice, suicide, punishment and of the collective consciousness in passionate assembly. Violence is sign or a symbol that indicates something about the milieu in which it occurs and of the agents and agencies that employ it. He deals with violence both at the macro and micro level. I will show that, at the micro level, Durkheim has a dialectic of action which, in its relation to thought, moves from the rationality of the *conscience claire* through the levels of conscience to the darker impulses of unconscious passions. Acknowledgment of this aspect of his thinking is obscured by the dominant contemporary interpretations of his thought, and by the neglect of his theory of action and his theory of conscience as well as its philosophical significance (Stedman Jones 2001a).

But firstly I address first the question whether Durkheim even acknowledges violence. At one level the social world of his writings is free from pogroms, domestic violence, war and terror. It sometimes seems to represent an agreeable state of positive solidarity. This may represent the optimism of contemporary socialist thought that had an "optimistic view of social becoming" (Charle 1994, p.147) Later in this chapter I suggest that there is a historical reason for his advocating the social and its benefits. Initially, however, I must first address first the question of whether Durkheim even acknowledges violence.

The acknowledgment of violence in the works of Durkheim

This question is part of that stale old problem whether Durkheim acknowledges conflict. Bottomore claims that Durkheim emphasises solidarity, rather than conflict, through his neglect or his rejection of the significance of class conflict (Bottomore 1984, p.107). This is quite wrong. In his *De la division du travail social* (hereafter called *La division*) a central form of society where solidarity has not been developed is the constraining division of labour. He characterises this as the "war of the classes" in the original table of contents (Durkheim 1893, p.415). His recognition of this is hampered by the unjustifiable exclusion of this from the 1984 translation of *La division*. Further, "constraint" (*contrainte*) is translated as "forced". But it is clear that constraint means "all forms of inequality in 'the external conditions of struggle'" (Durkheim 1893, p.415). The malaise of contemporary society is identified as inequality (Durkheim 1893, p.373, transl. p.314). And more profoundly he identifies "real constraint" as that state where even struggle is impossible "(p.371, transl. p.313). He follows the philosopher Charles Renouvier (his "educator") in this. In his *Science de la morale* (1869) Renouvier defines *constrainte* as indicating the conflictual nature of society, which is in a "state of war" – that is where freedom does not exist (Renouvier 1869 vol. I p.332), where injustice and inequality reign and reciprocal rights and duties are not established. It is no accident that in the conclusion of *La division*, Durkheim argues "Our first duty now is to make a morality for ourselves" (Durkheim 1893, p.406, transl. p.340), and that the task of modern society is "a work of justice" (Durkheim 1893, p.381 transl. p.313).

The question of justice is central to the critique of society: for Durkheim, class domination and economic inequality are unjust: "If a class of society is obliged, in order to live, to accept any price for its services, while the other due to its own resources can avoid this ... the second has an unjust domination of the first" (Durkhim 1893, p.378, transl. p.319). To achieve real consent in work contracts, the parties of the contract must be "in equal external conditions" (Durkhim 1893, p.377, transl. p.318). Constraint must be entirely absent. And constraint is not just the "direct use of violence", but also is found in "indirect violence" that "also suppresses liberty" (Durkhim 1893, p.376, transl. p.317). So for Durkheim, violence characterises constraining social relations.

The acknowledgment of violence is central to his study of punishment in *La division* in his study of mechanical solidarity. He describes what occurs when a cherished belief is threatened. We react emotionally "with more or less violence" (Durkheim 1893, p.65, transl. p.53). These "violent emotions" are "forces" used when personal feelings are in danger (Durkheim 1893, p.66, transl. p.54). These are central "to

the strong states of the conscience commune" which "cannot tolerate contradiction" (Durkheim 1893, p.67, transl. p.54). It would appear that what we now call cognitive dissonance is part of Durkheim's explanation of violence. He argues that primary among the causes that provoke a violent reaction is "the representation of a contrary state", for this attacks the "the overall coherence (*l'intégralité*) of our conscience" (Durkheim 1893, p.64, transl. p.53). When we are dealing abstract ideas the region concerned is the "more elevated and superficial of conscience". But when we are dealing with a belief that "is dear to us", then a deeper emotional reaction is engendered, which can be violent. The antagonism between adversaries can be attenuated by "a general sympathy", but this must be stronger than the antagonism so that both parties renounce the struggle. He identifies the "reciprocal tolerance" that terminated the wars of religion as being of this nature (Durkheim 1893, p.66, transl. p.54).

But what of the violence of history: does Durkheim acknowledge violence in the historical process? The French revolution of 1789 and its Terror were etched on the consciousness of nineteenth century France. Both liberals and conservatives condemned the violence of the Terror; and 1789 was seen as a revolution that ran out of control. Durkheim does not share the views of either conservative or liberal opinion. Indeed, he honours St Simon for his acknowledgement that the French revolution "definitely ruined" the *Ancien Regime*, and brought about a new system which was in line with 'the new order of things'" (Durkheim 1900, p.115, transl. p.6). We cannot immediately conclude that this constitutes a justification for the violence of the Terror for Durkheim. But it was one of the most significantly violent moments of French history and we find Durkheim agreeing with the father of French socialism, not only about the historical importance of the revolution itself, but also of its importance in ushering in a new set of social relations. He calls the French Revolution one of the "creative eras" of history (Durkheim 1890, p.224, transl. p.41) He repeats this judgement in *Les formes élémentaires de la vie réligieuse* where he holds that the French Revolution, together with the Crusades, was one of the historical moments of creative effervescence (Durkheim 1912, p.301, transl.

p.213). Such periods were a ferment of new ideas and a passionate assertion of ideals and of beliefs that pass into action; they are moments of social and historical change. In another context, we find him arguing that the Franco-Prussian war was the stimulus to the redevelopment of the science of society. The collapse of the imperial regime of Napoleon III posed the question of social organisation, for what replaced it must be founded "in the nature of things" (Durkheim 1912, p.123, transl. p.112). Indeed the effect of the war of 1870–1871 was to lead to an intellectual re-awakening (Durkheim 1912 p.122 transl. p.112).

The point is that Durkheim is not justifying violence per se, but identifying a violent period as a social fact of the greatest importance. It is the social fact that he is concerned with. His idea of social fact must be taken into account when evaluating whether Durkheim has a theory of violence. "All maladies are facts" (Durkheim 1905, p.288). The milieu, the historical and social context and the beliefs and ideals that feed people's actions and struggles must be taken into account when describing violence. In his critique of revolutionary syndicalism, Durkheim argues that Lagardelle's Marxist materialism leads him to neglect "the factor of consciousness" and that it was the new aspirations forged in the French revolution that made it the beginning of French socialism (Durkheim 1905, p.289).

However, although Durkheim acknowledges violence he does not espouse theories that seem to justify violence as a means of social development or even give it a positive role. Indeed he quite explicitly opposes theories that do so.

Durkheim's critique of theories that justify violence: revolutionary socialism, social Darwinism and political absolutism

It is clear that for Durkheim there is a connection between theories, mentalities and action. Theories can foster violent ideologies which can encourage action. This is clear in his *L'Allemagne au dessus de tous*. "Those disconcerting actions . . . have their origin in ideas and feelings . . . Here there is a whole mental and moral system, constituted with war as its goal which, during peace, remains in the back of consciousnesses" (Durkheim 1915, p.13). The significance of the criticism of such a theory for Durkheim is not simply to undermine its theoretical rationale, but also to undermine subsequent justifications of action based on the theory. We see this in his critique of Marxism, Darwinism and political absolutism.

We have seen that, like Marx, he criticises the brutalising of human nature by economic factors "one cannot remain indifferent to such a degradation of human nature" (Durkheim 1893, p.363, transl. p.307). And like Marx he stresses the conflictual nature of the economic system encouraged by political economy. We see this in his critique of Spencer's account of interest as the dominant force that drives economic systems and thus exchange. "Where interest alone rules, since nothing comes to rein in egoism, then . . . . each self finds itself on a war footing and any truce in that eternal conflict is short lived" (Durkheim 1893, p.181, transl. p.152). However, he has a quite different evaluation of conflict than that which is found in Marxism. Durkheim does not see conflict as means of provoking change. This assumption is central to the Marxist model of revolution, which in turn involves a theory of economic determination, a particular logic of history and a model of power. All these are challenged by Durkheim.

Marx may not have envisaged the violence of his subsequent followers and violence per se may be an unintended consequence of the theoretical insights of Marxism. However, it is clear that the Marxist model of historical development, and what it thereby permits in the hands of its followers, lies behind some of the great atrocities in the twentieth century. For the WHO, beside the First and Second World Wars, two of the most catastrophic events were the Stalinist Terror and the Chinese Great Leap Forward of 1958–1960. Together with Pol Pot's genocide these share a common intellectual background. All have as an ideological justification the development of the necessary and inevitable laws of history. It is clear that revolutionary groups can set themselves up as the purported agents of history and thus as the fulfilment of necessary laws by eradicating useless or outmoded classes. The Marxist model of conflict as generating change towards a classless society operates in a model of development where the end justifies the means. This is precisely what Durkheim objected to in the political absolutism of Treitschke, who extolled the principle that the end justifies the means as a political rationale (Durkheim 1915, p.46).

Durkheim rejects both the logic of both historicism and materialism, which are central to the doctrine of historical materialism. This, together with the "Marxist theory of value, the iron law of wages and the pre-eminence of conflict" are "disputable and out of date hypotheses ... which compromise the idea of socialism" (Durkheim 1899, p.36, transl. p.50). He repudiates the logic of the base–superstructure model that is central to Marxist explanation and change and to its logic of power. There is no economic foundation that is uniquely and objectively determining, for the economic is always interpenetrated by values, which are matters of opinion, established by the demands of moral consciences and which vary socially and historically (Durkheim 1908 vol. I, p.221, transl. p.231). He rejects materialist monism for making life the simple epiphenomena of physical forces and which denies the "heterogeneity of things" (Durkheim 1903, p.1, 124, transl. p.177).

The Marxist law of history "pretends to be the key to history" (Durkheim 1897a, p.252, transl. p.172) yet provides no methodological series and its purported facts are incapable of "empirical representations" (Durkheim 1897a, p.248, transl. p.170). "The Marxist hypothesis is not only not proved, but it is contrary to the facts which can be established". Scientific socialism requires "a complete system of society" stretching from the past into the future, but Durkheim denies that "a system of such extent can be scientifically constructed" (Durkheim 1897c, p.242, transl. p.136). For Durkheim, revolutionary socialism is logically tied to the doctrine of historical materialism: if this is false then so is the logic of revolution (Durkheim 1897a, p.249, transl. p.170). So he suggests that socialism and revolutionary destruction do not imply each other – is this not a route to the development of a new Middle Ages? (Durkheim 1928, p.286). Societies do not have to be overthrown to establish socialism (Durkheim 1905, p.292). His critique of Marxism, together

with its Hegelian logic of history, means that if there is no necessary historical law with a dialectical momentum then its progressive development cannot be fostered by the implementation of conflict. So without these intellectual supports a positive gloss on class violence is difficult to sustain. Thus Durkheim, who recognises the "sad conflict of classes", does not believe class conflict is the motor of progressive development. Class war is not central to the definition of socialism for him (Durkheim, 1928a, p.53, transl. p.58).

Stalin and Mao were able to operate with absolute power. As we will see, this, for Durkheim, is characterised by the lack of any countervailing force that moderates the implementation of power (Durkheim 1901, p.246, transl. p.23). He presciently warns of the dangers of democratic centralism: "One can foresee that what gives rise to such a power is the unification [reunion] of all the directing functions of the state in one and the same hand" (Durkheim 1901, p.247, transl. p.23). Further, a significant aspect of the violence and destruction caused by both Stalin and Mao was the belief that human beings were expendable in the passage to socialism. As we have seen, this is part of the logic of the ends justifying the means. Tied to this is the belief that Stalin shared with Mao, namely that society was a *tabula rasa* that could be re-made from scratch given a superior will and sufficient ruthlessness (Buruma 2004, p.5). Durkheim argued, on the contrary, that the aim of revolutionary socialism for a *tabula rasa* on which to construct the future was impossible (Durkheim 1928, p.160, transl. p.171).

For Durkheim, on the contrary "if individual life is not worth something, however little this might be, the rest is worthless, and the evil is without remedy" (Durkheim 1887, vol. I. p.330). The human being must be "a touchstone" whereby good is distinguished from evil (Durkheim 1898a, p.264, transl. p.246). Marxism ignores questions of justice, which for Durkheim are central to the critique of society and of human action. He identified with the values of humanism. "The human being is the "sacred thing" (Durkheim 1989, p.265, transl. p.246). From this a conception of moral violence can be developed. Moral violence is where human beings are treated without respect and with abuse and cruelty. The values of humanism were rejected as bourgeois individualism by Marxism.

This belief in the value of the human being is also central to the idea of human right. For Durkheim the sphere of individual rights grows through history (Durkheim 1950, p.103, transl. p.69). And in relation to the question of human rights and the state human rights are above those of the state. The Drèyfus affair made this clear. Jean Jaurès, in his famous *Les preuves* (1898), showed that the question of rights and individual liberty were central to socialism and not simply a question of bourgeois ideology (Durkheim 1898, p.7). Durkheim rejected the idea of a '*Raison d'état*' in *L'individualisme et les intellectuels*. "There can be no reason of state which could justify an attack against the person, when the rights of the person are above the state" (Durkheim 1898, p. 265, transl. p.246). The idea of a raison d'état had been invoked by the enemies of Drèyfus and it was a supreme law for the Action Française (Weber 1962, p.45).

So it is no surprise that Durkheim rejected the claims of revolutionary syndicalism and with it the arguments of George Sorel. He was a supporter of revolutionary syndicalism for a while before his alliance with French fascism and the Action Française. It is not surprising that both Lenin and Mussolini admired him! Sorel admired the violent strikes of revolutionary syndicalism and held that the entry of anarchists into syndicalism was important for the development of social war. His apocalyptic vision of politics envisaged heroic violence as releasing an energy that overcomes decadence. In his "On violence" he claims, "Proletarian violence not only makes the future revolution certain, but it seems also to be the only means by which the European nations – at present stupefied by humanism – can recover their former energy" (Durkheim 1908, p.107). His attack on rationalism and humanism, and particularly on the intellectuals who espouse them must surely have had Durkheim in view. While he held Durkheim to be the theoretician of conservative democracy, it is significant that neither Durkheim nor his friend Jaurès went on to support fascism, as did Sorel. "Parliamentary socialists make such great efforts to persuade the public that they have the souls of sensitive shepherds, that their hearts are over flowing with good feeling, and

that they have only one passion – hatred of violence" (Sorel 1908, p.119).

Durkheim believed neither that violence would overcome decadence nor that social war through violent strikes is a form of heroic moral action. "The destructive revolution that is advocated" would be worse that than if war broke out between France and Germany which would be "the end of everything". To destroy society was to destroy civilisation:

Man's intelligence should precisely have as its overriding [goal the] taming and the muzzling of these blind forces, instead of letting them wreak destruction. I am quite aware that when people speak of destroying existing societies, they intend to reconstruct them. But these are the fantasies of children. One cannot in this way rebuild collective life; once our social organisation is destroyed, centuries of history will be required to rebuild another. In the intervening period there will be a new Middle Ages. ... It will not be the sun of new society that will rise ... we will enter a new period of darkness. Instead of hastening the advent of that period, it is necessary to employ all our intelligence so as to forestall it. ... And to do that we must avoid ... acts of destruction that suspend the course of social life and civilisation. (Durkheim 1905, p.286)

As I write we face a rise in biologically determinist accounts of human behaviour, inspired by the discovery of the genome. In certain hands Darwinism has been revived, together with reductive and biological explanations of all aspects of human action. These are no longer be couched in terms of zoological aggression or the biological imperative; instead the concept of the hardwiring of our genetic inheritance is commonly used. The reductive logic is the same, however. The force of Durkheim's arguments against Darwinism and social Darwinism are still significant today, for they show that history, culture and, indeed, any freedom of consciousness transcends Darwinism. And, while this may not be intended, the survival of the fittest in terms of strength and force may not be far from view, morally and politically. In Durkheim's day Social Darwinism was eagerly embraced by fascism, in the Action Française. Indeed, we see it in the thoughts of Nietzsche, which are echoed today in the anti-humanism of post-structuralism. Nietzsche attacks pity and altruism: the "overcoming of pity" is among "the nobler virtues" (Nietzsche 1888, cited in Richardson 2004, p.18). "In the concept of the *good* human one sides with all that is weak, sick, failed, suffering of itself, with all that ought to perish, that crosses the law of selection" (Nietzsche 1888, cited in Richardson 2004, p.142). "Nothing", says Arendt, "could be more dangerous than the tradition of organic thought in political matters by which power and violence are interpreted in biological terms. ... For violence here is justified in terms of creativity. These life philosophies see creation and destruction as two sides of the natural process (Arendt 1969, p.75). Durkheim dealt with such types of theorising by challenging the adequacy of these accounts of history, of human consciousness, action and race.

Firstly he explicitly denies Spencer's point that sociology is dependant on biology (Durkheim, 1885, vol. I, p.346). Against this biological reductionism, Durkheim argues that the social world has a reality *sui generis* which is irreducible to the biological. It is the development of "psychic life" that differentiates human beings from the animals (Durkheim 1893, p.338, transl. p.284). The concept of the psychic indicates the presence of mind and of conscious cognitive experience. Central to the psychic is the freedom of mind. "The history of the human mind is the history of free thought itself" (Durkheim, 1897b, p.430, transl. p.375). His clearest arguments against biologism are presented in his 1898 article *Répresentations individuelles et representations collective*, where he opposes Huxley and physiologically reductive accounts of mental activity. He stresses the independence of "psychic facts" from brain cells and calls those theories "which reduce conscience to be no more than epiphenomena of physical life" a form of "intellectual nihilism" (Durkheim 1898a, p.22, transl. p.29). The mind is not a mere epiphenomenon; the evidence for the *sui generis* functions of the mind lies in its capacity for judgement, which is relatively autonomous of physiology. The representations which constitute the mind (Durkheim 1898a, p.31, transl. p.17), are irreducible to the biological. His philosophical support for this line of reasoning are Boutroux, Renouvier and before them Kant and Schopenhauer. Durkheim extends this relative autonomy of the representational nature of the mind to society: social life consists in "collective representations". Through this he argues for the specific autonomy of the sphere of the cultural

and historical, and thereby the distinct nature of different social and historical epochs. We can see that this diversity of representations is hard to explain on a reductive, biologically determinist model.

Durkheim challenges Social Darwinist theories of race and of the role of instinct in evolutionary development. In *La division* he argues that racial theorising is socially and historically inaccurate; since there are no new races, racial theorising is undermined (Durkheim 1893, p.296, transl. p.250). How can the concept of race explain the huge developments in history and culture? Purported explanations in terms of our hereditary physiology must confront both history and the division of labour. Heredity, he argues, can transmit only general and simple aptitudes, whereas activities are becoming more complex and specialised. Thus our biological inheritance becomes less and less determining as work becomes specialised. Further, he challenges Social Darwinism on its use of the instinct. Human intelligence is quite distinct from the instinct of animals. "The progress of conscience is in inverse proportion to that of instinct" (Durkheim 1893, p.338, transl. p.284). He challenges the use made of Darwin by incipient French fascism and opposes their argument that instinct and force should be allowed full expression to preserve the purity of the race. The Action Française argued that heredity is the biological basis of race, and argued for war that, as an expression of force, was a good in itself.

Durkheim also challenged Social Darwinism's view of history. Although he admits that a struggle for existence is manifest in history, any conclusions drawn from this must confront social and historical facts and the division of labour. The view that the survival of the fittest dominates the historical process is used to justify force and violence as necessary and useful tools in weeding out the weak and eugenic limitations on the evolutionary development of the race. Such views are, for Durkheim, historically inaccurate. Firstly, they imply that egoism was the starting point of humanity and thus that altruism was only a later development. This is contrary to the facts of society and history, for Durkheim. The "authority of this hypothesis" is that it appears to be a "logical consequence of the principles of Darwinism". In the name of the "dogma of vital competition and natural selection" a dismal picture of primitive humanity is painted where conflict over food is the sole occupation. "Nothing is less scientific". The hypotheses of Darwin must be used with "even more reserve and caution than in the other sciences". Secondly, it abstracts "the essential element of moral life, that is, the moderating influence that society exerts over its members and which tempers and neutralises the brutal action of the struggle for life and of selection. Wherever there are societies there is altruism, because there is solidarity" (Durkheim 1893, p.174, transl. p.144). As evidence for this he cites the practices of the ancient Gaul who would not survive the chief of his clan, and the ancient Celt in choosing death to free his compatriots from yet another mouth to feed (Durkheim 1893, p.175, transl. p.145). Thirdly, in social terms the primitive state of mind is so dominated by the collective consciousness that egoism, which is associated with the later historical sphere of the personal, shows little development. So the moral use of Darwinism ignores solidarity and altruism (Durkheim 1893 p.174, transl. p.144). Similarly it ignores the cooperative nature of human labour, as does political economy, which views exchange as an activity that puts people on a "war footing".

In *L'Allemagne au-dessus de tous* (Durkheim 1915), he challenged political absolutism which views war as a means of aggrandisement of the state. Treitschke viewed the state as an absolute, as above international law, civil society and morality. He advocates freeing the power of the state from all limitations and argues that war is an instrument of its will (Durkheim 1915, p.20). For Durkheim, absolutist power is characterised by a lack of reciprocal or bilateral relations: it is defined by the unilateral nature of relations (Durkheim 1901, p.246, transl. p.223). "That which makes power more or less absolute is the more or less radical absence of any countervailing force that is systematically organised with the intention of moderating that power" (Durkheim 1901 p.247, transl. p.223). Against this Durkheim argues for the relativity of sovereignty and for the internal limitations of state power. His argument for intermediate institutions between the state and the individual supports this, as do his arguments for democracy and the importance of human rights which,

for Durkheim, are growing through history (1950, p.93, transl. p.57).

Furthermore, this internal limitation must be complemented by an external limitation on the power of states through containment by other powers within the terms of international laws. And whereas for Durkheim the object of morality is "to realise humanity and to liberate it from servitudes . . . to render it more loving and fraternal" (Durkheim 1915, p.45), in this form of political absolutism, morality is only for the "little people". Treitschke utters "not a word on humanity" or the states' duty towards these people (Durkheim 1915, p.44).

Such are Durkheim's critique of theories which in some way justify violence or force. But does he have a theory of what violence is? His study of suicide can give us a clue and in turn offers the possibility of a solution; we find here a theory of the hope and meaning that social life should offer. There is not only a conception of coherent, expressive and satisfied action but also of the finitude and limitation that the latter requires. The milieu and social life must be viewed as part of the solution to violent action.

Suicide and violence against the self

Suicide is the ultimate act of violence against the self. Durkheim, in arguing for the social causes of acts of self-destruction, demonstrates the importance of society in maintaining people's will to live and constructive human action. Here we find a micro-theory of action and of its connection with society which is telling for an account of violence. The theory that lies behind *Le suicide* is that it is solidarity that preserves us. This reveals a socialist interest in society as the forum for the development and maintenance of human life. "It is the action of society which raises in us feelings of sympathy and solidarity which inclines us towards others" (Durkheim 1897b, p.226, transl. p.211). The more detached we are from society the more likely suicide is. "In a vital and coherent society there is from all to each and from each to all a continual exchange of ideas and feelings and there is a kind of mutual moral assistance, which makes the individual, instead of instead of being reduced to its own

La maudite (the cursed year, 1871). Lithograph by Honoré Daumier (1808–1879), published in Le Charivari, 1 January 1872. akg-images Sue Stedman Jones

force, participate in the collective energy which stimulates their own when it is exhausted" (Durkheim 1897b, p.224, transl. p.210).

So the suicide rate is evidence of "an alarming moral misery" (Durkheim 1897b, p.445, transl. p.387). It is through failure of the communication of consciences, central to a vital society that morbidity in the will to live arises. "In these conditions does not the will to live become weakened?" (Durkheim 1897b, p.282, transl. p.253). An invisible world is expressed in these communicative relations, which affects at a profound level our will to live. In *l'éducation morale* he discusses the concept of an energy that is attached to life.

To live, we must face up to multiple necessities with a limited amount of vital energies ... [this] is necessarily limited by the sum total of forces which we have at out disposition, and the respective importance of ends pursued. All life is thus a complex equilibrium, whose diverse elements limit one another and this equilibrium cannot be broken without producing suffering and illness. (Durkheim 1925, p.34, transl. p.39)

So for Durkheim "this tendency to suicide has its source in the moral constitution of groups" (Durkheim 1897b p.343, transl. p.305). What is it about the moral constitution of groups that gives rise to suicide? The central theme of *Le division*, the relationship between individual personality and social solidarity, reappears in *Le suicide*. It is in the relation between forms of individuation and solidarity that the causes of suicide in its egoistic and altruistic forms must be found. Anomic suicide postulates a breakdown in the overall coherence of relatedness and thus in "the regulating action" of society; the anomic state of society "weakens the will to live" (Durkheim 1897b, p.282, transl. p.253). Egoistic suicide occurs when "the individual self affirms itself [*le moi individuel s'affirme*] with excess in face the social self and at the expense of it"; this results in an "unbounded individuation" (Durkheim 1897b, p.223, transl. p.209). We no longer have the courage to live, that is, to act and to struggle, when we only have ourselves as the objective of action: "all our efforts are finally destined to lose themselves in nothingness (*le néant*)" (Durkheim 1897b, p.225, transl. p.210).

Altruistic suicide expresses a contrary state: here there is an insufficient individuation. Here individuals cannot make their own milieu, which is unique to themselves (Durkheim 1897b, p.238, transl. p.238). There is too much "impersonality" (Durkheim 1897b, p.243, transl. p.225) and the individual is deprived of reality. When the individual personality starts to grow, an under-

standing of the right to life is the first thing to be developed (Durkheim 1897b, p.237, transl. p.220). This is only suspended in exceptional circumstances, in war, for example. For altruistic suicide the individual must be completely absorbed by the group, and this in turn must have "a compacted and continuous mass". For this reason he held that altruistic suicide would be rare in modern society (Durkheim 1897b, p.246, transl. p.228).

Contemporary suicide bombings can be interpreted as a perverse form of altruistic suicide, when coupled with the terror tactic of group murder. Although he did not live to see this scourge of modern life, nevertheless Durkheim's analysis throws light on the nature of terror groups and those who join them. For him, those who join must suffer from insufficient individuation: they have not developed enough of a life for themselves and thus have little personal development; consequently the group overwhelms them through its "massive cohesion" and "compacted" nature (Durkheim 1897b, p.237, transl. p.220). So while with egoistic suicide there is too much individuation, here there is too little, so that here the self (*le moi*) "does not belong to itself" and it " merges with something other than itself" and where the goal of action is situated outside of itself, that is, in one of the groups of which it a part". He labels this type of suicide "obligatory altruistic suicide" (Durkheim 1897b, p.238, transl. p.221).

Central to his concept of anomic suicide is the notion that it involves the overturning of habits (Durkheim 1897b, p.322, transl. p.285) and concerns the breaking of the equilibrium of individuals with their milieu (Durkheim 1897b p.326, transl. p.288). He uses the concept of tendency, which is central to a theory of action and to the concept of the habitual. A tendency is central to satisfied action; in dissatisfied action the tendency atrophies; thus the will to live, which "is only a result of all the others", is also weakened (Durkheim 1897b, p.272, transl. p.246). Satisfied action is balanced action; it is impossible where ends are inaccessible because they are infinite; this leads to a state of perpetual discontent (Durkheim 1897b, p.274, transl. p.248). Fatalist suicide occurs when there are no possibilities for the exercise of human power and therefore of will. Here the tendencies of action, and most importantly of will, are blocked.

For Durkheim, limitations are central to effort and hope; passions lack restraint in anomic suicide (Durkheim 1897b, p.288, transl. p.258). All who support the dogma that material prosperity is the coefficient of industrial success fail to recognise this; this is true of both political economy and economic materialism. The apotheosis of the dogma of material prosperity leads to limitless desires that translates into rates of anomic suicide (Durkheim 1897b, p.284, transl. p.255). The theories that "celebrate this instability" are "the passion for infinity" as "a mark of moral distinction" and "the doctrine of progress, the most rapid possible" (Durkheim 1897b, p.287, transl. p.257).

The doctrine of continuous progress based on the enjoyment of new and more intense pleasures is destructive of the real conditions of effective action in human beings. The will to live is part of the tendencies of action and disappears when the conditions of effective and realised action (satisfied action) are damaged. He shows that action, habit and pleasure are connected. So he offers a micro-theory of action that is important for understanding his account of action and his rejection of the doctrine of progress. Happiness is relative (which Comte recognised [(Durkheim 1893, p.231, transl. p.195]); it does not increase with progress. For Durkheim happiness, like pleasure, disappears as it is repeated: continuous repetition makes happiness disappear, for it becomes unconscious. "The needs of the mind are periodic, like the psychic functions to which they correspond" (Durkheim 1897b p.234, transl. p 197). Absolute continuity, which is the denial of periodicity, requires that we have new pleasures and new excitements. Discontinuous repetition, on the other hand, which involves the habitual, is at well-spaced intervals; it is thus felt and the expense of energy is repaired. If, on the contrary, there is repetition without interruption, then each function is exhausted and individuals become unhappy [*douleureuse*]. Healthy action thus requires habits that are characterised by periodicity: this leads to feeling of well being. The pathological continuous need for excitement, which leads to a vacuum (*vide*) opening up that needs to be filled, is replaced by the feeling of well-being. So Durkheim argues that there is a need for stability in our enjoyments (*jouissance*) and the regularity of our pleasures: it is on this

limiting and discontinuous condition that life maintains itself.

At the centre of this human world is the logic of need. A "complete need" Durkheim argues, requires two terms: a tension of will and a definite object. However with "incorrigible malcontents", this process is "half representative" (Durkheim 1897b p.235, transl. p.198). Here the object is in the imagination, "an intimate poetry", instead of being an effective "movement of the will". It does not take us out of ourselves and is merely "an internal agitation" (Durkheim 1893 p,235, transl. p.198). Effective action, where the objects of will are realised in action, goes from inside to outside. In contrast to this, in ineffective, unsatisfied action, the energy is blocked halfway. This frustrates tendencies, which require that action achieves its goals. That is, there is a movement implied in all action (whether of needs or of an ideal) that is realised in a new state.

The concept of hope is central to Durkheim's account of action and thus of suicide. "If men have learned to hope, they have formed the habit of orientating to the future and there to find compensation for their present suffering" (Durkheim 1893, p.225, transl. p.190). Hope plays a part in the instinct for conservation: its loss is associated with the loss of energy whereby life loses its attraction (Durkheim 1897b, p.225, transl. p.190). Hope alone is not, however, a sufficient explanation of preferring life to death, for we learn to hope and to have a will to live only in a social milieu. The coherence and continuity of this is central to viable human life: it is this that gives the terms and limits of action. "If our efforts lead to nothing lasting, why should we labour in vain?" (Durkheim 1887, vol. I, p.329). Meaningful action is central to a happy life. This is part and parcel of Durkheim's critique of civilisation through its rate of suicide (Durkheim 1893, p.226, transl. p.191). And the conception of action and its goals is central to this. Goals should be achievable and proximate; "an inaccessible end ... leads to permanent discontentment" (Durkheim 1897b, p.274, transl. p.248).

The unconscious, the energy of action and education

In *Les règles* he argues that "the tendency to suicide varies like the tendency to instruction".

But whereas instruction reaches "only the most superficial regions of conscience; on the contrary our instinct for conservation is one of our most fundamental tendencies" (Durkheim 1895, p.131, transl. p.152). Durkheim has a theory of the unconscious which is important for his theory of suicide and thus of violence. It is found in the concept of unconscious representation and the concept of the obscure that he relates to both representation and conscience. "Outside of (*en dehors de*) clear representations, in the midst of which the scientist operates, there are the obscure ones which are linked to tendencies (*tendances*)" (Durkheim 1893, p.331, transl. p.278). He argues that the understanding "is only the culminating and thus the most superficial part of conscience" and is not the seat of psychic life (Durkheim 1893. p.267n, transl. p.225). This conception of the obscure connects to Renouvier, for whom conscience occurs in degrees stemming from the obscure to its clearest form in free thinking and reflection. And the obscure relates to the unconscious: there are unconscious representations (Renouvier, 1875, vol. II, p.310).

So Durkheim argues that we have to recognise the profound depths (*les dessous profonds*) of psychic life which are only reached with difficulty (Durkheim 1897b, p.351, transl. p.311). In *La division* he argues "Every strong state of conscience is a source of life; it is a factor of our general vitality. Consequently everything which tends to weaken it diminishes and depresses us" (Durkheim 1893, p.64, transl. p.53). The unconscious is crucial to his argument about suicide and thus violence against the self and about coherent action in general. It is in the psychic depths that lie the passions, habits and tendencies that make up the substratum of each conscience. It is at this level that certain fundamental tendencies exist. So the disposition to sacrifice one's life "is an active tendency" (Durkheim 1897b, p.320, transl. p.284). The point is that "that which is diffuse, obscure, unknowable escapes our action" (Durkheim 1950, p.121). Nevertheless, a deep impulse to assert physical strength can be educated and controlled by the reflective power of understanding. Only in this way will change at the social and individual level be brought about. "All these obscure feelings are by nature diffuse, all acquired habits are resistant to change

precisely because they are obscure" (Durkheim 1950, p.117).

The elucidation of the unconscious urges brings us to the question of education and what it deals with – the power of action. Action, for Durkheim, relates to nature of force. He stresses its inner and psychic nature (Durkheim 1912, p.599, transl. p.422). In the first instance it has a reflexive foundation in conscience and in the second, it is developed and expanded through social cooperation. It is clear that force has an immediate connection with will, energy, the elan of action; it goes from inside to outside. This reflexive foundation for the power of action in consciousness is important for the study of violence, for it firstly distinguishes power from physical strength and secondly distinguishes between power and violence. Arendt regrets the equation of power with violence (Arendt 1969, p.52). For her, like Durkheim, power is the ability to act and to act in concert and must be distinguished from strength and force.

So in the broadest sense Durkheim's concept of force denotes the energy of action which, when compounded in a whole, constitutes social power. But what should we do with this power? Durkheim suggests a thought experiment.

Imagine a being liberated from all external limitation, a despot more absolute even than those of which history speaks, a despot that no exterior power [*puissance*] contains or regulates. By definition the desires of such a being are irresistible. Would we say that he is all powerful? Certainly not, for he himself cannot resist them. They are masters of him as of everything else. He submits to them, he does not dominate them. In a word, when our tendencies are freed from all bounds [*mésure*], when nothing restricts them, they become tyrannical, and their first slave is the person who feels them. (Durkheim 1925, p.38, transl. p.44).

In *L'education morale* (Durkheim 1925) he deals with moral forces, with this energy and power, in terms of the education of the young child. In educational terms the central question is, what to do with this energy? How can it be converted into successful and constructive agency, which realises autonomy and self-mastery? He outlines the spirit of discipline as one of the primary forces of the moral life: "That faculty of containing our tendencies, of resisting ourselves, which we acquire in the school of moral discipline, is the indispensable condition for the appearance of a reflective and personal will"

(Durkheim 1925. p.42, transl. p.49). It is central to effective action and indeed to happiness. The will needs accessible and close ends for coherent action to be possible. Unhappiness comes with ends that are infinitely out of reach which are thus unrealisable. The spirit of discipline, as well as attachment and autonomy are primary forces of the moral life. Discipline is central to effective action and indeed to happiness. The child must learn that "happiness does not grow without limits, with power, knowledge or wealth" (Durkheim 1925 p.43, transl. p.49).

There is a doctrine of limitation in Durkheim's account of social action. In *Les règles* he argues that "the goal of humanity recedes into infinity" when determinate goals are given and terms of action not set and which thereby "escape all limitation" (Durkheim 1895 p.74, transl. p.104). So, accompanying this account of effective social action is a micro-logic of effective action. This involves the idea of moral limits, which are an aspect of moral authority (Durkheim 1925, p.31, transl. p.35).The goal of moral education must be to cultivate restraint, *"une faculté d'arrêt"*, as Durkheim puts it (Durkheim 1925, p.40, transl. p.46), which allows the containment and limitation of desires and passions. The impatience with any limitation is the "appetite for the infinite" (Durkheim 1925, p.31, transl. p.35). So health consists in moderate activity. "It implies the harmonious development of all the functions, and these can only develop harmoniously on the condition of moderating one another, that is, containing one another within certain limits, beyond which illness (*maladie*) begins and pleasure ceases" (Durkheim. 1893, p.216, transl. p.183). There is an interesting consideration here. The leader of *Action Francaise*, Charles Maurras, attacked the idea of a man of reason and the idea of an equilibrium between the elements of its nature, which he associated with decadence and democracy. Against this, he argued for the dominance of will: the elements of our nature should be ordered by and through will, which brings around virility and health (Weber 1962, p.26). In *La division*, Durkheim argues, "Conscience, like the organism, is system of functions which balance one another" (Durkheim 1893, p.217, transl. p.183).

By the time he wrote *L'Allemagne au-dessus de tout* he was aware of the will to power and its disastrous consequences in the context of an absolutist view of the state. The theories of Treitschke advocate the power of the state free from all limitation which uses war as an instrument of its will (Durkheim 1915, p.20). Here we find a morbid mentality that suffers from a "hypertrophy" of the will, that is a "mania of willing" (*manie de vouloir*) and "a morbid inflation". In contrast "the normal and healthy will" knows how to accept the necessary limitation of the milieu; to liberate themselves from this a (*vide*) vacuum must be created, which means to place itself beyond the conditions of life itself" (Durkheim 1915, p.84). The will to power is central to such absolutist conceptions of sovereignty.

His conception of successful action involves a conception of power and self mastery, which in turn require a theory of limitation. He identifies optimism with limitation and pessimism with a lack of limits. He notes "the correlation of sadness with the feeling of the infinite" (Durkheim 1968, vol. II, p.309). This concerns effective action and the use of energy and power. "In reality all absolute power (*puissance*) is the synonym for impotence (*impuissance*)" (Durkheim 1968, vol. 2 p 309). Limitation is central to will: "The mastery of will presupposes above all the limitation of need" (Durkheim 1968, vol. II, p.309). He invokes limitation as the condition of knowledge; the principle of the finite has implications for action, energy and optimism in a favourable milieu. So he talks of *le mal de l'infini*. Finite is opposed to absolutism, infinity and the doctrine of progress for the philosopher who most influenced him – Charles Renouvier (1864, p.244). So for Durkheim hope, limitation (Durkheim 1925, p.35, transl. p.40), the constructive use of energy, and containment by the milieu, which avoids both "the cult of the self" and "the feeling of the infinite" (Durkheim 1925, p.61, transl. p.72) are central to positive action. A limitation of power is central to a healthy will and thus of the will to live. In contrast the illusion of power makes us believe that we are independent of others. So financial crises, both negative and positive, entail a rupture of equilibrium and push the individual to voluntary death. The individual is weakened by extreme disturbances of wealth and poverty.

This doctrine of limitation and of the finite seems to oppose Durkheim to Bataille and his concept of transgression and through this to Foucault's idea of the limit experience. I have argued (Stedman Jones 2001b) this is a misunderstanding in one important sense. The historical moments of effervescence are transgressive for Durkheim in the sense that the old is overthrown and new ideas and beliefs are generated. They are thus important sources of the new and creative energy in society, as Durkheim claimed for the French Revolution and the Crusades. Of course, he would not support Bataille's idea of transgressive excess with its dark nihilism as a permanent force in society. Both Foucault and Bataille can be challenged on the question of how illimitation and transgressive action, in all forms, can establish a viable society.

The totality of moral rules forms around each man a kind of ideal barrier, at whose feet the wave of human passions come to die without being able to go further. And precisely because of this containment, it becomes possible to satisfy them. But if at any time this barrier weakens, then human forces which up to then contained, will pour tumultuously through the breach; once released they can no longer find the limit where they stop. (Durkheim 1925, pp.36–37, transl. p.42)

Solidarity is central to society for Durkheim, but how does unrestrained transgression generate solidarity, rather than a war of all against all?

Solidarity

Durkheim's lifelong preoccupation with solidarity shows his concern with the conditions which provide durable bonds between people. He focuses on the positive nature of the bonds of attachment that tie us to one another and cement communities. The central theme of his thought is that positive relatedness is the great prophylactic against violence. It is clear that a breakdown of solidarity or its inadequate development can be a substantial cause of violence. Whilst the concept of solidarity is more evident in his early work especially in his *La division*, the theme is not abandoned in his later study of the sacred and of religion in general. The sacred is a great source of solidarity, for through representations of the sacred people are drawn together and form relations through it. This remains a key meaning of solidarity. It is fundamental to what he means by society and it is the object of

sociology: "The study of solidarity thus rises from sociology" (Durkheim 1893, p.31, transl. p.67). As "one of the conditions of existence of society" (Durkheim 1893, p.394, transl. p.332), it is fundamental to the possibility of society. As such it is a "social fact of the first rank" (Durkheim 1893, p.31, transl. p.67).

Solidarity for Durkheim is "a disposition of our psychic life" (Durkheim 1893, p.31, transl. p.67); it is a condition of our psychic life to be related one to another. This may be the reason Durkheim insists that "solidarity comes from within and not from outside" (1886, p.212). "There is a deep internal sense/state of attachment which is associated with *conscience*. There exists a solidarity which comes from a certain number of states of conscience which are common to all the members of the same society" (Durkheim. 1893, p.78, transl. p.109).

But if solidarity is the prophylactic against violence, what type of solidarity is possible for the modern world? Durkheim contrasts two distinct types of society that are accessed by two distinct types of sanction found in legal relations – the repressive and restitutive. These correspond to different forms of solidarity, the mechanical and the organic. It is interesting to note that both of these are forms of positive or real solidarity; that is they "lead wills towards common ends" (Durkheim 1893, p.85, transl. p.116). Negative solidarity links things to persons, not persons to persons (Durkheim 1893, p.84, transl. p.115). It is interesting to note that Durkheim's use of positive solidarity corresponds to Renouvier's use of the term in his *Science de la morale*. He talks of a "positive contract" where an object of communal interest is found and that gives a "common end" (Renouvier 1869 vol. I, p.63).

Organic solidarity presupposes the division of labour and characterises the type of relatedness in the modern world where economic and social differentiation are the rule. Since the division of labour brings together different functions, it can be seen to be a source of solidarity. Nevertheless, it is important to note that for Durkheim the division of labour only produces organic solidarity if it is spontaneous. And "by spontaneity is meant the absence not simply of explicit and definite violence, but of everything which hinders the free unfolding of the social force which everyone carries within themselves (Durkheim 1893, p.370, transl. p.312). Further, perfect spontaneity "is "only a consequence ... of absolute equality in the external conditions of struggle" (Durkheim 1893, p.371, transl. p.313).

He criticises Spencer and political economy generally for focusing only on the economic interest of exchange. Durkheim holds that consciousness is interpenetrated in a profound way by the relations that spring from the division of labour. In Spencer's vision of exchange, where interest alone determines action, "consciences are only superficially in contact; they neither penetrate each other nor do they adhere" (Durkheim 1893, p.181, transl. p.203). As we have seen, he argues that if "interest is the only ruling force" then individuals are "in a state of war with every other" (Durkheim 1893, p.181, transl. p.204). Spencer does not acknowledge that the division of labour establishes

a social and moral order *sui generis*. If the division of labour produces solidarity, it is not only because it makes each individual an agent of exchange (*échangiste*), as the economists say, it is because it creates amongst men an entire system of rights and duties which link them together in a durable way. (Durkheim 1893, p.402, transl. p.406)

The bedrock of this is the interpenetration of consciences. Outwardly "two beings are mutually dependent because they are each incomplete". But internally, he argues, the image of one "who completes us becomes inseparable from ours ... It thus becomes an integral and permanent part of our conscience". There can be "no solidarity between others and us unless the image of others unites itself with ours". So he offers a supplementary explanation of solidarity in terms of the internal economy of the psyche: in the exchange of differentiated services we internalise the image of that being which is different from us and thus which completes us, and thus becomes inseparable from ourselves. This association becomes a "permanent integrated part of our conscience" (Durkheim 1893, p.25, transl. p.61).

So it is clear that solidarity has both an epistemic and affective dimension. It is a deep internal state of attachment. The affective aspect is the feeling of bonding and belonging, where the feeling of attachment is evident. Solidarity is to do with bonding. "Men cannot live together without acknowledging and consequently making mutual sacrifices, without tying themselves one to another with strong durable bonds (*liens*). Every society is a moral society" (Durkheim 1893, p.207, transl. p.228). These links and relations, in other words, have to be strong and durable. This attachment must be embedded in a whole network of beliefs and practices that are institutional. It is clear, then, that positive relatedness found in both micro-solidarity and macro-solidarity is a barrier against violence.

However, group solidarity could lead to violence against others by a group with a strong sense of internal solidarity. We find this with the Mafia and with groups with strong ethnic identities who can operate with an exclusive solidarity against others. This is a most common form of violence in the twentieth and twenty-first century. Durkheim was unwilling to admit a tension between solidarity and morality in *La division*, and indeed criticised Renouvier for holding that solidarity could also be a source of corruption (Durkheim 1893 1st edn, p.10). However it is clear, as his thought developed, that solidarity to a group is no longer satisfactory per se. The Drèyfus affair underlines the importance of human rights and moral individualism. "Man has become a god for man. ... And since each of us incarnates something of humanity, each individual conscience contains something divine and thus finds itself marked with a character which renders it sacred and inviolable to others. Therein lies all individualism" (Durkheim 1898a, p.272, transl. p.252). So solidarity must gradually be developed beyond the group to cover wider spheres of society, and this in turn means progressively reaching out to all of humanity, and the dynamic of this is the individual held as sacred.

Historical moments: the Third Republic and reflections on violence

I have looked at Durkheim's critiques of theories of violence, his study of suicide and of solidarity. He deals with the conditions that could inhibit or foster the development of violence. Nevertheless, he appears to be at pains to differentiate the social per se from violence. Why is this? Durkheim's developing science cannot be disassociated from his time and from the socialist interest in the social and republican politics of fraternity. We have seen Sorel sneering at French democratic socialists for their hatred of violence. Together with the contemporary leaders of democratic socialism, Jaurès and Malon, but unlike the Marxist Guesde, we have seen that Durkheim did not see violence as viable means for developing social change. Indeed we have seen him claim that the syndicalist exhortation to violence would lead to a period of darkness. There were further considerations; the fragility of the Republic which for many years after 1871 was constantly under threat and the revolutionary method that could provoke a *coup d'état* from the right (Renouvier 1879), which Durkheim also feared (Bourgin 1942, p.76).

We must look to history and the early events of the Third Republic to understand this. I suggest that the Commune of 1871 was a significant event for understanding Durkheim's approach to violence. Although never explicitly mentions the Commune of 1871 (as far as I am aware), he does argue that the Commune is not merely an "archaic institution destined to disappear with history", but the "cornerstone of society" (Durkheim 1893, p.xxxv, transl. p.xliv). He holds it will provide "a communal solidarity" that will prevent the law of the strongest from dominating industrial and commercial relations (Durkheim 1893, pp.xii, transl. p.xxxix). This is a significant statement politically, given the events at the beginning of the Third Republic that strongly marked the development of political thought and the development of social theory.

But how was Durkheim connected to this period? His maternal grandfather survived both the siege of Paris and the Commune. Durkheim was a supporter of Gambetta (Filloux 1977, p.12), who was viewed as "dangerous extremist" for his sympathy to the Commune (Chastenet 1952, p.19). Gambetta organised the amnesty for the surviving Communards, and forced it through the Chamber in 1880 (Jellinek 1937, p.384). As I have shown, many of the issues raised by the Commune entered into the theoretical questions of Durkheim's sociology (Stedman Jones 2001a, p.54). We can see this in his account of the organic nature of society, his study of solidarity and egalitarianism, the role of

associations – especially as intermediate between the individuals and the state; his study of socialism and the state as free, rational and democratic and as respecting human rights. However, to extol the Commune as such in the context of developing his new science would have been to associate society with violence, which would have been detrimental to the development of interest in the new science of society and to the fostering of democratic socialism. For the memories of the Commune hung heavy over these early years; the French people never wanted to be exposed again to such horror (Réclus 1945, p.23). And it was held to retard what it proposed to develop: the social question and socialism (Chastenet 1952, p.30). It is for this reason, I suggest, that Durkheim, through his aim of both developing his science of society and fostering democratic socialism (Filloux, 1977), was at pains to differentiate society from the violent, and socialism from revolutionary violence.

The Paris Commune of 1871

For Louise Michel, the Paris Commune of 1871 changed "the axis of human societies" (Michel 1898, p.13). This extraordinary episode of only a few months duration, is the subject of rich and ongoing research. Although it has been claimed by Marxism as the first stage of the proletarian revolution, it can be separated neither from the Franco–Prussian war and the siege of Paris which followed it, nor from the exasperation of the working class at the Empire that had brought this war upon them. The republicanism of the Parisian working class was seen as concerned with order as opposed to the chaos the Empire had led them into (Lissagaray 1876, p.471). Their patriotism turned against the Provisional Government with its royalist majority, then in Versailles, which brokered a "shameful" peace with the Prussians. So on 18 March 1871, when Thiers tried to retake the canons and arms of the National Guard in Paris, the Parisian population rose up. They arranged elections on the following day to elect a Commune – as part of a republic of free and democratic communes (echoing the republicanism of 1789), independent of the Assembly in Versailles. Its republicanism had developed in opposition to both the Empire and the real possibility of the return of the monarchy. An added factor was that of Paris against the provinces, who "detested Paris", although this was unknown to the Parisian working class (Malon 1871, p.58).This anti-Parisian sentiment had, as a central idea, a bourgeois belief in the dissolution of the social organism. On the contrary, the ideas of solidarity (that they opposed to bourgeois "egoism") and the reciprocity of rights and duties in a republic were central to the thinking of the Commune (Malon 1871, p.50).

Despite the attempt of the leaders of the Commune, elected on 26 March, to bring about a pacific and legalistic solution and wanting to avoid violence, the sporadic retaliatory violence of the crowds may well have provoked the reaction of Thiers. As a former minister of Louis Philippe, he had wanted to crush the 1848 Parisian uprising, and was now leading a legalist and royalist Assembly. He organised the repression without conciliation or negotiation. Recent scholarship on the Commune said the bloody week that followed was "the most deadly and destructive few days in the history of Paris, the most ferocious outbreak of civil violence in Europe between the French Revolution of 1798 and the Bolshevik Revolution of 1917" (Tombs 1999, p.10). Jackson says that 25,000 were killed – more than died in the Franco–Prussian war and certainly many more than worked for the Commune (Jackson 2008). For significant partisans of the Commune the number is higher. Louise Michel said the official list of the number of victims was 3,000, but she estimated that 100,000 was nearer the truth (Michel 1898, p.14). Benoit Malon estimates that there were 37,000 dead as a result of the conflict, 50,000 died slowly from subsequent privations and thousands more went into exile (Malon 1871, p.523). Both Malon and Michel, through their participation in the Commune, were in exile for many years. The important effect of this was not just the huge number of socialists who were killed; it was the decimation of the Parisian working class and their work; Paris became an industrial desert (Malon 1871, p.521). Further, since it was French soldiers who undertook the barbarism involved in the repression of the Commune, the whole episode was seen as a civil war.

It has been questioned whether the Commune was the dawn or the dusk of socialist politics in France. It would appear to be both. The judgement of Lenin that this was the first stage of the proletarian revolution was endorsed by Jellinek (1937, p.15). However, the Marxist–Leninist view, stressing the centrality of class conflict and the need for authoritarian party direction, was not accepted by most Communards. They respected legitimate property rights and saw socialism as the progressive replacement of capitalism by the association of workers in cooperatives. The leaders insisted that the Commune should be "the triumph of science, work, liberty and order" (Tombs 1999, p.215). The Marxist–Leninist view was not accepted for many years by the French left in general. Jaurés did not take the Commune as the blueprint for future action, although he praised their struggle for reconciliation through justice (Tombs 1999, p.202). Although the Marxist account prevailed for a while, the Commune led to the abandonment of revolutionary tactics among most European socialists. Indeed, the testimony of French history since 1789 to 1830, 1848 and 1871 did not support the unequivocal success of revolution as a means of social transformation; on the contrary, it appeared to strengthen the forces of reaction in post-revolutionary retaliation. For Renouvier the revolutions in French history had effectively served the interests of the bourgeoisie (Renouvier 1872 vol. II, p.3). So the Commune formed "the ultimate exorcism" of the violence that had been an inseparable part of French public life since the end of the eighteenth century. "With Paris in flames ... the French revolution bade farewell to history" (Furet 1992, p.506).

So, while it may have been the dusk of a certain kind of Blanquist revolutionary socialism, it was the dawn of new thinking about politics and society that Durkheim's sociology was heir to. This extraordinary period was regarded as a tragic failure, despite the carnage and suffering that was largely borne by the working class. However, it generated many important social and political questions. It provided a major contribution to this period of social questioning and it fed into the "*vouloir politique et moral*" of the *École normale* of Durkheim's day.

Conclusion

We have seen that, while Durkheim offers no positive account of the role of violence in the constitution of the social or in constructive social change, his whole oeuvre can be seen to offer a theory of violence in the comprehensive sense. Throughout his work he offers insights into the causes and conditions of violence. We have seen in his study of the micro-logic of human emotional reaction an account of the causes of violence in the repudiation of difference by the type of conscience collective found in mechanical solidarity. This can offer an understanding of radical Islamic terrorism, for its roots lie in societies that have not developed an advanced division of labour, democracy or human rights. But Durkheim's thought offers insight into those conditions that can prevent violence. I have shown this through an examination of his study of suicide, of solidarity and of moral education, with its stress on the importance of moral rules and of limitation. The latter are not repressive for Durkheim, but are considered as the key to a greater self-mastery. These theoretical developments were brought about, at least partly, in response to one of the most violent and destructive episodes of nineteenth-century France. These reflections are not without significance today. Nelson Mandela held that violence thrives in the absence of democracy, respect for human rights and good governance (WHO 2002). Durkheim would agree.

Durkheimian sociology, biology and the theory of social conflict

Jean-Christophe Marcel and Dominique Guillo

Durkheim is often rightly presented by intellectual historians as a proponent of the idea that social phenomena cannot be explained by individual dispositions of biological origin (Mucchielli 1998). However, this thesis is frequently interpreted by commentators as a rejection of biology in general, and of the explanatory power of the laws of heredity in particular. Such interpretations treat Durkheim's frequent references to the life sciences in his early works as strategic concessions to the biologically influenced mood of the times, to which they regard Durkheim's thought as intrinsically contradictory (Mucchielli 1998).

However, such a reading confuses two theses, thereby failing to grasp the underlying coherence and complexity of Durkheim's references to the biology of his day. In reality Durkheim does forcefully state, in a now famous phrase, that social facts must be explained in terms of other social facts. But this thesis in no way implies that individual behaviour and dispositions should be explained solely by social facts and that biological facts have no causal power in this domain. On the contrary, if we take it literally, the homogeneity of cause and effect on which the justification of the autonomy of sociology is based, must also be valid for other kinds of phenomena: just as social facts cannot be explained by individual phenomena, so individual phenomena cannot be explained, directly at least, by social phenomena.[1]

A consideration of Durkheim's use of biology can thus make his work easier to understand on the condition that we do not look at it from a contemporary viewpoint which, in resorting to general categories such as biologism, naturalism or biologically influenced language, reduces his use of biology to naturalist reductionism. In short, by taking seriously Durkheim's references to the biology of his day and the thinkers who drew on it, notably Comte, and regarding these references not as meaningless or strategic concessions but as a real conceptual anchor, we can hope to reveal certain important aspects of the theoretical framework developed by Durkheim.

There are many pitfalls here, notably because Durkheim sets out his views in a field of biological concepts that are certainly very precise, but also very different from those of today, despite a similarity of terms and doctrinal references, with Darwinism figuring most prominently among them. This conceptual field proposes a very particular view of society seen as an "organisation, in other

Dominique Guillo is a researcher in sociology at the Centre National de la Recherche Scientifique (GEMASS, UMR 8598). He works on the relationship between the social and life sciences from a historical and theoretical perspective and on links between humans and animals. His publications include *Les figures de l'organisation. Sciences de la vie et sciences sociales au XIXème siècle*, Paris, PUF, 2003 and *Des chiens et des humains*, Paris, Le Pommier, 2009.
Email: dominiqueguillo@yahoo.fr
Jean-Christophe Marcel is a lecturer in sociology at the University of Paris-Sorbonne and researcher at the GEMASS (UMR, 8598). He works on the history of early twentieth-century French sociology. His publications include *Le durkheimisme dans l'entre-deux guerres*, Paris, PUF, 2001 and, co-edited with Philippe Steiner, François Simiand's *Critique sociologique de l'économie*, Paris, PUF, 2006.
Email: Jean-Christophe.Marcel@paris-sorbonne.fr

words a material form able to perform a certain number of vital functions" (Guillo 2006, p.516). This results in a theory of different types of societies distinguished by a variable degree of differentiation, itself based on the morphological criterion of the greater or lesser psychological and material density of the society. Thus, the passage from the famous society of mechanical solidarity to the group in organic solidarity unfolds as a modification of the society's form under the effects of the division of labour and differentiation (Guillo 2006, p.516)

Furthermore, far from being just a passing fad in an early work, this conception seems to have had a posterity in the Durkheimian programme, notably in the economic sociology best represented by Maurice Halbwachs and François Simiand, the similarities and mutual influence of whose work is well known (Marcel 2001), and more particularly in the way that both understand economic development and the role played by social classes in its evolution. Halbwachs and Simiand understand the march of civilisation as a series of actions that society carries out on its substrate (its population and their settlement in a space) in order to adapt to transformations in its environment. In this struggle for existence the social classes and the way that they come into contact play a crucial part. The arrival of urban civilisation seems not to have been of benefit to all and the social classes show different types of organisation, more or less developed according to their greater or lesser dependence on nature or, what comes to the same thing, their greater or lesser proximity to whatever represents the essence of social life at any given time. However, in this struggle for existence each class has its own function, which binds it to all the others, and in the collective consciousness this solidarity supposes, the place of animosity and conflict is not sufficient to undermine the social order. So one could reasonably read Halbwachs' theory of society's distribution around a central focus and Simiand's theory of economic action as continuations of Durkheim's morphological theory and the Darwinian paradigm found in it.

It is important to recall this affiliation both to understand the complex relations between the emerging social sciences and social Darwinism and to shed light on what today's commentators regard as a surprising rejection of Marxism – and indeed of all forms of revolutionary socialism – by the Durkheimians (on the links between Durkheim and socialism see Filloux 1977, and, more recently, Fournier 2007). It thus offers a theoretical element for understanding why there is no real consideration of collective revolutionary violence in Durkheimian sociology.

Durkheim's theory of the evolution of societies: the development of types of social organisation

Durkheim's references to the biological theory of evolution, like those of the sociologists whom he abundantly cites, notably Comte, Spencer and Espinas, refer to a clearly delineated current of thought in the life sciences. Indeed, from the start of *De la division du travail social* (Durkheim 1893, p.3) Durkheim explicitly locates his views in the tradition of research carried out in comparative anatomy and embryology by Karl Ernst von Baer and Henri Milne-Edwards. Adopting themes and hypotheses that were very widespread in the final third of the century, Durkheim thus notes: "it has been known, indeed, since the work of Wolff, von Baer and Milne-Edwards, that the law of the division of labour applies to organisms as to societies". The division of labour, he adds, must therefore be regarded "no longer as simply a social institution ... but as a phenomenon of general biology whose preconditions must, it seems, be sought in the essential properties of organised matter" (Durkheim 1893, pp.3–4).

These words from the book's introduction bring into sharp relief the investigative area and specific concepts Durkheim uses to formulate the problems that he intends to solve and the solutions he proposes that are unfortunately, blurred to our contemporary eyes by the categories we use to read borrowings from the life sciences during this period. In choosing the theme of the division of labour and associating it with the biology of von Baer and Milne-Edwards, to whom he adds the ideas of the naturalist Edmond Perrier (a reader of Espinas, given to general philosophical meditations on living things), from the outset Durkheim places the question of the definition of social science and its object of study in the much more general framework of the laws of evolution and the development of organisms. This way of conceiving of sociology is precisely that of Comte, Spencer and Espinas, three authors whose importance for Durkheim is well known, at least in his early works. Despite their clear differences, not only regarding sociological theory but also concerning the interpretation of their conceptual sources in biology, these three authors locate their work in the same field of notions that came to occupy an important, not to say dominant place, in debates around the constitution of social science at the time when Durkheim was setting out on his career.

So, if biology seemed so attractive to many philosophers and sociologists, it was because a vast field of shared thought, a vast cosmology constructed in the mid-century through the extension of a triptych of notions initially taken from comparative anatomy and embryology – organisation, classification and development – governed the philosophical space in which the thinkers intending to link the life sciences and the social sciences were formulating their sociological models. This field of concepts, this cosmology, thus constituted the field of thought in which Durkheim formulated his first explorations and explanatory models (on all these points see Guillo 2003).

Society as an organisation

First of all, in accordance with the central idea of this tradition of thought, Durkheim describes society using the concept of organisation, as revealed by the subtitle of the first edition of *The division of labour in society* and the omnipresence of the word throughout the book (this book itself constituting a "study on the organisation of higher societies"). So, for Durkheim, society must be seen as an organisation, in other words, in accordance with the received meaning of this notion in biology, as a form, a structure able to perform certain functions. Basing his work on the concept of organisation meant adopting the model of the living body that prevailed in the life sciences before the emergence of experimental physiology. In the theoretical framework shaped by this essentially morphological concept,

knowledge of the functioning of organisms, in other words, physiology, remained dependent on anatomy or the comparison and systematic classification of different species of living forms (known as comparative anatomy since Cuvier's earliest work in the late eighteenth century). In the absence of conceptual tools and factual data that might permit the experimental analysis of living things – such as knowledge of the constituents of tissues and biochemical exchanges, the conceptualisation of the cell as an elementary physiological unit of the living body or the modelling of organisms as self-regulating systems of biochemical exchange – the physiology that developed around the concept of organisation was thus necessarily speculative (see Balan 1979). It could not constitute a space of autonomous scientific questioning in which a productive trade of ideas and facts could take place and remained thus closely bound to an idealist morphology. This conceptualisation, which was not necessarily linked to the concept of organisation but to the usage made of it in this particular context, despite what was stated on the surface of the language, always governed it, whether closely or at a distance. Thus the theoretical and empirical gaps in this physiology were filled by clearly metaphysical notions, such as the *Bildungskraft* mentioned by von Baer, and extremely abstract and speculative models, such as the mechanics of development proposed by Spencer or, more importantly for our concerns here, analogies with society, the most famous of which produced the concept of the division of physiological labour proposed by Henri Milne-Edwards (1851).

The biological philosophies of organisation thus unfolded in a conceptual field very different from that of the experimental physiology that gradually emerged out of the work of Claude Bernard in 1860. With this physiology the medical concept of the organism as a self-regulating system of exchanges and biochemical interactions replaced the anatomical concept of organisation in the life sciences. Although the sociologists of the last third of the century, and Durkheim foremost among them, frequently used the word organism, their thinking was undeniably linked to the concept of organisation (symptomatically, Spencer notes that "the only point in common that he recognises between the two kinds of organism is their organisation and the principles that regulate it" (Spencer 1878, p.192). On this point we refer to Guillo 2003.) Unlike his contemporaries, in his epistemology Durkheim undeniably does make good use of recent developments in Bernard's physiology. In particular, the meaning he gives to the notion of the function in his most theoretical passages certainly owes far more to this conception of living things than to that of comparative anatomy and embryology. But these far-reaching developments, which are moreover expressed in a language free of any reference to biology (as shown by Boudon 1994, p.262), are used locally, in his early writings, in the context of an underlying notional field that remains classically centred on the concept of organisation, as witnessed by the quantity of morphological vocabulary and theme of the form in Durkheim's thought on the nature and development of societies.

The body of society, social classes and organisation: morphology in Halbwachs' work

If it is useful to consider Durkheim's intellectual influence on his collaborators we can say that Halbwachs undoubtedly retains the primary role of morphology in the genesis and conformation of social facts and develops an understanding of society as a structured organisation in space. His objects of study (including the expropriations in Paris, social class and collective memory), centres of interest – notably demography, which examines the "body of society" – and the tools he uses – primarily statistics – make him very aware of the question of form. We have moreover suggested that in his work all socially defined knowledge is based from the outset on a primary collective representation that is related to a material form of the group (Marcel 2004, 2007). So social life is reducible to a collective survival instinct that society instils in its members, based on the stable spatial images that individuals have of groups and which enable these groups to organise in order to work for their own preservation; or in other words to adapt to their material and human surroundings

(Marcel 2008). From this point of view the concept of a way of life (*genre de vie*), linking the establishment of human beings on the ground to manners and mentalities is a first step in understanding how this adaptation functions (a "way of life" is defined by Halbwachs as "a set of customs, beliefs and ways of being, resulting from the habitual occupations of men and their mode of establishment").

Thus, for Halbwachs, in any activity developed by a group, the group becomes aware of its body and adapts its organisation to the possibilities it perceives, "just as individuals need to perceive body and space to retain their balance" (Halbwachs [1938c] 1970, pp.12–13). But this awareness occurs differently according to the functions occupied by groups in society. In the case of social classes, the function can be understood through the role they occupy in the production process and their resulting share of revenue. This revenue defines standards of living and the aspirations that crystallise once the group becomes set in a material form:

Indeed, just as the members of the same class associate with each other and go to each other's houses, we can say that to each class there corresponds a part of the space, comprising all the premises that class inhabits, a spatial ensemble that is ill-defined in the class members' minds, but which is nonetheless a reality. In the past, more so no doubt than today, this would have been supplemented by more or less public places – shops, theatres, promenades, parks and gardens, resorts and hotels – where they were more likely to meet men of their own class than others. At any rate, still today there are regions and cities that are clearly characterised in this way, wealthy towns, neighbourhoods and streets, working-class towns, suburbs and neighbourhoods. . . . There are rich people . . . and poor people who have never ventured into rich neighbourhoods. The classes have at least a tendency to separate from each other in space. Facts of this type are closely linked to economic life, making it easier to understand. For they are the result of a diversity of living standards. In each group, needs, tastes and manners tend to become uniform, at a level that is no longer the same when one moves from one group to another. (Halbwachs [1938c] 1970, p. 50)

The classes are particularly active groupings in the organisation of society since their function controls the economic development that underlies the process of civilisation:

Thus agriculture, industry and trade depend on the movements that transform and renew the social classes.

What are classes, to the economist, but groups of buyers that go to this or that set of shops, just as the crowds flowing into a theatre divide into two great currents at the doors, one requiring boxes or seats in the stalls and the other destined for the upper levels and the balconies. These groups have contours, the currents have direction and form: it is by studying them closely that we are better able to discover the nature and degree of economic activity in a society" (Halbwachs 1938a, p.51).

From this point of view we can understand social classes as taxonomies of social types which, in combining morphological and economic principles, make it possible to grasp the organisation of an entire society working to preserve itself in its material and human environment. It is in this light that we should understand the creation of new roads in Paris under the Second Empire: the arrival and direction of roads does not artificially determine the movement of the population, but "always meets definite needs of both kinds. The city was transformed in the way and at the time that trends in the population required it", and not solely through the action of some sovereign or planner such as Haussman. (Halbwachs 1928, pp.167–168). The needs and "natural trends of the groups scattered across the city" (p.269) result from a growth in their population and are an expression of the effort they are willing to make to adapt to their surroundings. Their particular relationship to their neighbourhood rules out any a priori decision concerning the direction in which human traffic should move. The expropriations translate trends and needs among populations that are entirely concerned with their own preservation in the environment in which they have settled.

Classification of types of social and individual organisations: return to Durkheim

The dominance of the morphological approach based on comparative anatomy and embryology in the thought of Durkheim and his heirs can also be seen in their closely linked conceptions of the classification of social and individual types on the one hand, and the principles governing their evolution on the other. The views Durkheim develops on these points link him to the

constellation of approaches which, in the late nineteenth century, began to congeal under the label, social Darwinism. This label might suggest that the biological paradigm adopted by these sociologists was a Darwinian model in the contemporary sense; in other words, a model based on competition between individuals,[2] seen as entrepreneurs seeking to maximise the number of their descendants and constrained by the cost of appropriating limited resources. Displaced by analogy into the social domain, such a model would provide a competitive image of society and the social classes more closely related to the model emerging in neoclassical economics than to a Comtian spontaneous consensus. However, we should not misunderstand the concepts of the life sciences of the time and the way they were understood. In reality, like the great majority of sociologists, philosophers and biologists of his time, Durkheim read and interpreted Darwin's theses within the very different conceptual framework of comparative anatomy and embryology. Unlike the Darwinian paradigm as it is understood today, this framework was fundamentally ordered, as noted above, around the idea of collective or individual organisation, which produces an image of living things – and by analogy, societies – that were intrinsically harmonious and static, noticeably different from a model whose starting point is the dynamics of competition between individuals. In the paradigm of organisation, the diversity of living things is understood in terms of typology, a classification that places types of organisation in a linear hierarchy, graduated according to the quantifiable morphological criterion of their degree of internal differentiation. The movement of evolution was then conceptualised as a projection through time of the scale obtained using this morphological criterion. This does not mean that sociology based on the paradigm of organisation paid no attention to inter-individual conflict and competition but simply that in this model they were not the primary constituent principles of society.

So, in accordance with the central principles of the philosophies of organisation rooted in comparative anatomy and embryology, whose main aim was to identify the laws of life through a systemic comparison and classification of their forms, Durkheim gives a central place to taxonomy. And like the scientists who inspired him, he constructed his classification of social types using the morphological criterion of the "degree of composition" or, put another way, of the internal differentiation of the organisation (Durkheim 1895, pp.174–179). The real meaning and weight of the biological concepts that Durkheim was using are revealed much more clearly in Chapter IV (Durkheim 1895) generally little cited or commented, than in Chapter III on the "Rules relative to distinguishing the normal and the pathological"), which, according to him, realise and reveal the degree of the division of labour.[3] This characteristic being, as Durkheim explicitly says, "of a morphological order, we could call *social morphology* that aspect of sociology whose task is to constitute and classify social types" (Durkheim 1895, p.174 (Durkheim's emphasis). We can show that this classificatory schema is adopted by his successors to distinguish between the different groups in a single society.

Armed with this criterion, Durkheim establishes a "complete scale of social types" (Durkheim1895, p.176). It begins with the "horde" (Durkheim 1893, p.149), a "society that is perfectly simple or has a single segment" (Durkheim 1893, p.179). When hordes get together they form clans, whose association creates "segmentary societies" (Durkheim 1893, p.150), which themselves combine to form "poly-segmentary societies" (Durkheim 1895, p.177). Citing the naturalist Edmond Perrier, whose views are in the direct tradition of von Baer and Milne-Edwards, Durkheim notes that these societies obey the same principle of organisation as "colonial" animals, which "are formed of similar segments, arranged either in irregular masses, or in linear series" (Durkheim 1893, p.167). As elements of segmentary organisation, the individuals that make up these societies are united by a kind of solidarity that Durkheim calls, as we know, mechanical. Moving up the "scale of social types", segmentary forms give way to "the organised type" (Durkheim 1893, p.161) characterised by organic solidarity. Segments gradually disappear as organs specialising in ever greater numbers of defined, differentiated and interdependent tasks take shape. Again drawing on Perrier, Durkheim notes that the same tendency towards differentiation in structure and activities is apparent as one moves up the animal scale (1893, p. 361).

Social classes: a predominant social type in developed organisations

Taking these views on organisation and its evolution a little further, the pre-eminence of social classes in modern societies can be understood as a product of the most highly differentiated structure. Such an approach is clearly apparent in the work of the Durkheimians. Thus, for Simiand, the way of life and distribution of expenditure: "a certain set of habits for the use of these revenues, notably the nature and categories of expenditure and the proportion of the various categories of expenditure" (Simiand 1930, p.446) are indicators of a class consciousness that underpins collective aspirations to this or that way of life and resistance to this or that change. Moreover, social classes are defined in the terms that are most important for social organisation in each society. Here we find the identifying criterion of the taxonomies:

Generally speaking, classes form in relation to those aspects most valued in a society, which confer consideration, power, authority and the means of life and action, whether real or regarded as such" (Simiand 1930, p.442).

It is, then, in economic terms that the role and place of classes in the hierarchy of a society based on complex exchange can be assessed:

It seems to us a major, evident fact, little open to dispute, that the economic fact proper, with a distinct existence and highly differentiated character, is a relatively recent fact of human societies, unlike other categories of social phenomena. ... In no society other than our western, modern and above all contemporary societies has the economic fact appeared at once so clearly and distinctly constituted and so important. (Simiand 1930, pp.582–583).

In other words, the social classes are social types rooted in the most extreme division of labour in existence. In the economic sociology of complex societies, Simiand regards the emergence of this type as requiring a particular economic mentality, whose influence can be gauged by the impetus it gives to the economic dynamic, itself reducible to the society's way of adapting to its environment and regulating the struggle for life. Characterised by a series of economic cycles comprising alternating phases of recession and expansion, this dynamic arises out of the coexisting actions of workers and those of entrepreneurs. This coexistence leads to growth in wealth and revenues (Marcel 2001).

Individual types, social types and the evolution of societies

In Durkheimian thought the paradigm of organisation is also used to understand the laws underlying individual behaviour. Although Durkheim stresses that the laws of social organisation are independent of those governing "individual organisation" and cannot be deduced from them, he still regards it as necessary that each type of individual on the scale of forming societies be well defined. Drawing on the anthropology of his day, a discipline explicitly located as an extension of zoology and using the concepts of comparative anatomy and embryology, Durkheim describes the scale of individual types as being parallel to that of social types. Like the latter, it is graduated according to complexity of organisation, in this case, of the body. Thus, Durkheim says, we can note "the growing homogeneity" of organic characteristics "as we go back towards the origins" of humanity, the most "primitive" human types (Durkheim1893, p.104. Durkheim is using Gustave Le Bon here). "On the contrary, among civilised peoples, two individuals can be told apart at first glance, without the need for previous training" (Durkheim1893, p.104). As in the work of von Baer and Milne-Edwards, external differentiation is the consequence of an internal differentiation of bodies that, as they grow in complexity, also grow in specificity and become increasingly different from each other. In particular, the organs that perform the functions that Durkheim, with many of the biologists on whom he bases his work, judges to be superior – the higher cerebral functions – are, in his view, less developed and differentiated in "the savage" than in "civilised man" (Durkheim 1893, p.149).

So Durkheim expounds his views on man and society within a cosmology rooted in the thought of Comte and Spencer and based on the concept of organisation. For Durkheim the scale of social types is the last section of a much greater scale, a chain along which all organic beings are arranged side by side. Graduated by complexity of organisation, this scale starts with basic, unsophisticated protoplasm, the simplest of living things. So begins the zoological series, which ends with the types on the scale of human beings. This is followed by the scale of social organisations, with segmentary societies, the real "social protoplasms" (Durkheim 1893, p.149) at the bottom and, at the top, the most "composed" and "differentiated" human societies, in the form of the western societies in which the division of labour is most extreme.

The development of types of social and individual organisation

Differentiation and non-linear development of social types

As noted above, we must still explain the evolution of social types and individuals. Like the scientists and philosophers on whose work he drew, in a second stage Durkheim projects these two scales into time, presenting them as substrata of the necessary process of "development" or "evolution". The gradual differentiation of society through the division of labour is thus a "law of history" (Durkheim 1893, p.112, footnote) which governs the development of all existing societies and the succession of different types or species of societies throughout human history. Like Spencer and Perrier, Durkheim adds that this law of development should not be understood as an "ascendant linear series" (see, for example, Durkheim 1893, pp.282–283), a succession of stages that each empirical society is bound to pass through from one end to the other. Contrary to Comte's assertion, development in practice or, to put it another way, the actual succession of social types is not linear. In reality, like living things, each society starts from a simple seed and differentiates throughout its existence, more rapidly and strongly the higher the type of species to which it belongs; more succinctly, ontogenesis reproduces a shortened version of phylogenesis. Durkheim notes that, in accordance with the principle of transformism, as the evolution of individuals through gradual transformation is passed on to their descendants, each society generally takes differentiation a little further than the one it grew out of. Thus over time, society by society, the average type of societies of the same stock shifts, gradually evolves and develops through greater differentiation (see, for example, Durkheim 1893, pp.282–283). This differentiation is at once both internal and external: internal because the average type acquires more differences; external to the extent that, by gaining more specific properties in this way, the different types emerging from the same initial stock gradually diverge from each other.

Adopting very precisely the arguments used by von Baer, Milne-Edwards and Spencer to criticise the biologists of the first third of the nineteenth century – on whose work Comte had based his thought – Durkheim notes that the actual development of human societies, like that of living species, forms an ever more complex tree, with the differentiation of an initial single trunk into ever-diverging branches. In this sense the classification of actual societies as it appears in this tree structure can no longer be exactly superimposed on the scale of social types. The former is not a direct, immediate realisation of the latter.

However, although the regulatory power of the scale of social types over the actual development of societies is somewhat indirect and refracted, in Durkheim's work, as in that of the biologists he draws on, it remains the modal principle underlying the development of all societies. Although regression is possible, each society tends to differentiate throughout its existence and overall average types tend to progress towards ever higher, more differentiated forms, even if the organisations, whose specific properties grow in number, are increasingly different from each other. Durkheim notes, "We can say of a type that it is *above* another when it has begun by having the *form* of the latter and has left it behind. This is certainly because it belongs to a *higher* branch" (Durkheim 1893, pp.112–113, footnote [our emphasis]). On this point see also Durkheim 1895, p.113. So for Durkheim the scale of social types still transcends the actual development of societies. In a parallel way the scale of individual human types provides the basis for their development through time. For Durkheim the history of humanity is thus a necessary modal development towards types of "social organisations" (societies) and "individual organisations" (human bodies as the substrate of faculties) whose structure and functions are ever more differentiated. Within this framework the notions of organisation, as a more or less differentiated form, development, as a process of internal and external differentiation, and classification, as a distribution tree differentiated into constantly diverging branches, which can be read modally as a scale of social types graduated by degrees of internal differentiation, have reciprocal meanings. Chronological position, location on the hierarchical scale and degree of differentiation are three aspects of a single phenomenon: being earlier means "being inferior" and having a less differentiated organisation. These three meanings are covered by a single phrase: the "degree of development".

Social classes as an illustration of uneven development

For Halbwachs this criterion also undoubtedly makes it possible to gauge the distinction between those social types constituted by social classes. In this light the type of the peasant farmer, which he depicts as more wild because less separate from nature, can be seen as a sort of survival of an earlier type, less developed than the rest. For him the peasant classes bear the marks of a bygone world and are part of the world of "things":

Attachment to the soil, to their land (hence the name "peasant" [from the French *pays*; Transl.]), certainly seems to be the fundamental motive explaining why they do not want to leave the little corner where they were born, where they have taken root and where their family has lived since a time that seems to them immemorial. (Halbwachs [1938b] 1964, p.65)

They are viscerally attached to the land to which their group identity is bound, and because their group has remained the guardian of a bygone world, not merging with the rest of the population, their collective life is based a dual awareness of being at once slightly separate and a centre of tradition. Occupying land which is, to some extent, part of them and of the group itself reinforces their sense of the immutability of life above and beyond the passing generations. Thus "The life of the peasant group is profoundly and completely engaged with nature. Hence it has a particular flavour and bitterness, a greater degree of spontaneity, primitive impulse and even savagery. ... It is a collective life at once very strong and very simple, or very simplified" (Halbwachs [1938b] 1964, p.79).

Correspondingly, this simpler, more primitive life minimises social life, understood as the ability to get together, to make space for collective life and allow shared desires and aspirations to develop. For peasant farmers tend not to want to leave their village or their land, are tempted to turn in on themselves and can keep on working the land for a low income, in sometimes appalling conditions. Peasant farmers live in isolation and are not concerned with the well-being of any but their own family: "Harshness and selfishness, individualism from top to bottom. They are thrifty, frugal. ... They do not worry about the others. There is no natural tendency to get together in the name of shared interests, even among the inhabitants of a single village or region" (Halbwachs [1938b] 1964, p.81). Their life is thus more instinctive because less marked by a collective spirit, insofar as this spirit keeps the more "natural" or "savage", animal instincts at bay.

This instinctive life can be explained by the extreme isolation of their houses and the lack of order and organisation in their distribution, due to the fact that each has been built as the centre of the family farm. So a village is not seen as a unit, with the result that it retains "an *inorganic and disorganised* appearance [our emphasis], expressing, if not the isolation and independence of the peasants, at least the relinquishing of social ties in rural groups" (Halbwachs [1912] 1970, p.43). This disorder is due to the peasant mentality, as peasants do not think of their houses as distinct from the rest of their property. "So collective awareness among such groups is much more diffuse" (Halbwachs [1912] 1970, p.42).

So we should doubtless understand that where civilisation is at work, in the march towards Durkheim's society of organic solidarity, as long as the collective spirit is still present alongside the trend towards individualisation, a group consciousness can be created that is more powerful because less hindered by the instinctual life. This is why peasant farmers are to some extent excluded from the march towards a different civilisation and the least integrated

into the social world, in other words, the world of complex collective representations.

Causes of social and individual development: the role of the struggle for life

The struggle for life and the development of species

Within the framework of the paradigm of organisation, we still need to explain how the dynamic of development is reflected in the static and, in itself, timeless scale of social types. In other words, we need to identify the forces that cause the inevitable development of organised bodies through their gradual differentiation. Such is the aim of what is known, following Spencer, as "transcendent physiology"; in other words the science of the principles governing the different developmental processes observable in nature (see for example Spencer 1898). In the conceptual field within which Durkheim expresses his views, two competing causes are traditionally proposed: on the one hand direct adaptation of the Lamarckian type and, on the other, natural selection or, in Spencer's phrase, "the survival of the fittest".

In the first case, the development of individual or social types of organisation is seen as a consequence of the hereditary transmission of adaptive modifications that directly affect living bodies throughout their existence. The mechanical balances that constitute these bodies are said to be continually modified and adjusted under the effects of forces emanating from the environment. Passed on to the offspring, these adaptive modifications accumulate with the passing generations, thus leading, in the long term, to the formation of types of species whose complex organisation is increasingly balanced and adapted to the physical forces exerted by the environment, which are themselves increasingly complex.

In the second explanatory mechanism, development derives from the disappearance of types with certain properties that render them insufficiently adapted to the requirements of the environment in which they live. In this framework differences of organisation are not seen as products of direct adaptation but as

Esthétique Assédic: l'oeuvre. Flickr/Arnaud Elfort and Guillaume Schaller

distinctive hereditary characteristics regularly produced by other causes. Those that prove advantageous spread and multiply with the passing generations, while those that are disadvantageous lead to the disappearance of the stock or lineages that bear them. In this struggle for life a complex division of labour, in other words an extreme internal differentiation of activity, brings undeniable advantages. Thus natural selection must necessarily lead to a modal differentiation of individuals and species.

In the energetic debates around this question, the different positions are distinguished primarily in terms of the weight given to one or other of these explanatory mechanisms. Spencer, for example, maintains that Lamarckian adaptation is more important. Durkheim meanwhile, in a famous passage in *The division of labour in society*, which is by far his most overt reference to Darwin, conversely asserts that the inevitable law of the development of species and social types has its main cause in the "struggle for life" advanced by Darwin in his explanation of the "divergence of characteristics": for Durkheim, "if labour is further divided", if societies tend to differentiate, at the level of both functions and structures, this is because "as the societies become more voluminous and dense . . .

the struggle for life within them becomes fiercer" (Durkheim 1893, p.248. The other citations in this paragraph are taken from 1893, book II, chapter II).

Halbwachs then takes up this theme, using it in a very particular way. In his view the shift from a rural to an urban life style, in making social life more complex, can be reduced to this intensification of the struggle for life. In the countryside collective life is at once very strong and very simplified. Occupations and events are more limited because there is little separation between working life and family life. Differences and conflict create bigger gulfs, so there is a greater degree of spontaneity, primitive impulse and savagery. On the other hand, opportunities for clashes are fewer. In urban society, "not only are the places where working life unfolds separated and usually at some distance in space from the houses that provide the material setting for domestic life, but also the time allotted to these two modes of existence are clearly distinct and do not intrude on each other" (Halbwachs 1930, pp.505–506). In these two spheres of life people connect with each other more quickly and a greater diversity of situations of different durations are concentrated into a single moment. In towns and cities the pace of social life is more intense while at the same time it is fragmented by dispersal in space. As a result there is less savagery and collective representations are more complex and fluid. At the same time, we understand that, if social life is more differentiated, it is more complex and more bound up with society or, put another way, less bound to the "naturalness" that supposes a simpler way of living. Here again, a morphological criterion provides the means for grasping this dichotomy.

Collective life in town is more intense in so far as it is held in a network of paths on which traffic is more intense than anywhere else. The result is a mixing of collective representations that means that social groupings are more likely to dissolve here than they do elsewhere. In the economic world we see that the various professions gain self-awareness when they are arranged in particular areas of space, such as shopping streets or those given over to particular trades. Yet, at the same time, proximity with others higher up on the social ladder gives individuals a hierarchical image of bodies and

reminds them of their comparative poverty. Thus, there are more opportunities for each to feel a collective spirit that is more powerful than elsewhere, linked to the apparently boundless mass of people, but also, and in parallel, they are more likely to feel extremely isolated, as will be seen in the case of manual labourers. Bad luck, difficulties and career disappointments "occur more frequently in a more complex society, in which individual situations change more often and more quickly, where the pace of life is faster and individuals are more likely to find themselves poorly adapted to their environment" (Halbwachs 1938a, p.13). In modern, more individualistic societies, individuals are left to themselves and so, for example, they are more vulnerable to suicide because life becomes more complicated. The rise in the suicide rate is the product of stable trends, the consequence of this greater or lesser degree of complexity, the substitution of urban ways of life for their rural equivalents, which should be understood as the process by which one mode of social regulation takes over from another. It is the counterpart of a "necessary complication that is the necessary condition of a richer, more intense social life" (Halbwachs 1938a, pp.13–14). For Simiand this complication increases with the growth of economic competition and its ever more important place in the life of the society, as we shall see below.

Differentiation and inequalities in economic and social functions

To explain the mechanism by which the struggle for life is intensified, Durkheim began by noting that when the segmentary type disappears, in other words, when societies that were formerly separate come into continuous contact, the number and intensity of relations between individuals increases, as does the volume of the new society that forms (Durkheim 1893, pp.248–259). This increase in the density and volume of societies – as societies develop and grow, like the higher organisms, they include a greater number of individual constituent units – brings with it an intensification of competition, of the struggle for life. Durkheim notes that as "Darwin has rightly observed ... the competition between two organisms is the fiercer the more similar they are. Having the same needs and pursuing the same goals, they constantly find themselves rivals" (Durkheim 1893, p.248). Correspondingly, this competition "is soothed" when individuals are different: they can then live in the same territory in greater numbers. "Men are subject to the same law" (Durkheim 1893, p.249): when social groups enter into continuous contact, when the barriers separating them are removed, "it is inevitable that similar organs", in other words similar professions, "affect each other, struggle with each other and seek to replace each other" (Durkheim 1893, p.252). Durkheim observes that, as Darwin suggests, this increased competition necessarily leads to differentiation, giving rise "to dissimilar varieties that diverge further and further" (Durkheim 1893, p.259), for only the variation generated by differentiation allows supernumerary individuals to exist by escaping competition. "However this substitution occurs" within societies, the struggle

can only result in some progress along the path of specialisation. For on the one hand, the segmentary organ that triumphs, so to speak, can perform the much greater task that now falls to it only by a greater specialisation and division of labour and on the other, the vanquished can maintain themselves only by concentrating on one part of the total function they have hitherto fulfilled. The small business owner becomes a foreman, the small shopkeeper becomes an employee, and so on. (Durkheim 1893, p.252)

So the internal and external differentiation of societies and the division of labour are "a result of the struggle for life". They are a necessary consequence of the intensification of competition provoked by the "increase in the volume and moral and material density of societies".

It was probably this result that guided Halbwachs's thinking on the status of the middle and working classes. In an article on the middle classes he explicitly states that this grouping is bound to grow since it comprises the personnel necessary to the functioning of trade, industry and administration (Halbwachs 1939). When these organs (Halbwachs himself uses this word) expand, the group increases in number and also in its power to act. But how can a single term be found to cover a set of individuals who are otherwise very different (such as artisans and

civil servants)? The answer is to look explicitly at their function and the stage of development that it reflects.

The members of the middle classes carry out a technical activity that supposes a practical knowledge of rules that are applied with certainty, since technical knowledge comprises a corpus of precepts and rules devised so that they can be uniformly applied in most cases. Technical knowledge goes with the exercise of a subordinate function: transmitting orders given by the bourgeoisie to the workers or, more generally, to those who will carry them out:

Alone in society (like the peasant), the manual labourer performs his work directly on inanimate matter, with which he is consequently in daily contact. Through the fact of their work, all other members of the society are brought into contact with men or with human substance, whether they carry out liberal professions, are shopkeepers or even employees. Some give the impetus, orders or advice while others draft and transmit them, making sure that they are carried out and monitoring the results. Only manual labourers are confined to receiving orders or instructions and, when they carry them out, act only on matter rather than men. (Halbwachs [1912] 1970, p.75)

When the function of the bourgeoisie is to ensure that life in society is adapted to the ends of that society, to innovate by inventing new rules that are better adapted to the new demands (for example, a judge who must rule in cases that figure little or not at all in the penal code or an entrepreneur launching a new product on the market), the application of technical knowledge supposes the introduction of general, fixed rules in a social mode that has become unstable. It brings uniformity where there was only movement and difference. From this point of view, it supposes the exercise of a subordinate function which "is different from the function seen in all its fullness" (Halbwachs 1939, p.45): if the procedures are not applied, the decisions cannot be applied. But without a prior decision being made, technical knowledge is useless. This leads to a situation conferring intermediate prestige for, unlike manual workers who work exclusively with matter, the work of employees and artisans involves human relations (for example, when artisans sells to their customers, as Halbwachs earlier suggests) but remains constrained (this artisan must set his selling price according to market rules set by the major entrepreneurs).

Manual workers and subservience to matter

So the victorious segmentary organ can be assimilated to the bourgeoisie, who delegate executive functions to the other classes. After the middle classes, manual workers thus appear as the vanquished in the struggle for life, whereas the peasants, as we have seen, embody a type that is less evolved. For, "Gathered in the mines or in teams around machines, manual workers are groups subject to discipline. They carry out orders, but do not give them" (Halbwachs [1938b] 1964, p.132).

Manual workers do not control "the progress and pace" of their work (Halbwachs [1938b] 1964, p.135). More than this, Halbwachs adds, in our western societies "the law of work and regular, uninterrupted, sometimes intense activity, which obliges men to go push themselves to the limit, has become ever more dominant" (Halbwachs [1938b] 1964, p.146). In industrial premises, "the worker loses part of his personality" (Halbwachs [1938b] 1964, p.175), to the point where, generally speaking, the manual workforce does not choose the available tasks so much as it adapts to them. As a result the heredity of parents becomes important and those who have done a job for a long time are reluctant to change:[4]

For there is little doubt that all the activities of manual workers are based on human instincts and dispositions. Sharp senses, sure movements, strong nerves, muscular strength, ingenuity, agility, these are all active, tangible faculties that seem to us to develop simply from tendencies that are part of human nature, and were present there in an embryonic state before manifesting themselves in work. (Halbwachs [1938b] 1964, p.142)

So the distinctive features of the psychology of manual workers are also to be found among the least delicate and developed social types:

A cast of mind that turns serious early, developing as it does in isolation, thought at once slower and rougher, sensibility blunted and repressed; a greater appearance of nonchalance, perhaps, their seriousness having spent itself in work that obliges their minds to leave the social circle entirely;

less sociability combined with more solidarity, in other words a certain detachment in relation to society and its customs. (Halbwachs [1912] 1970, p.76)

In a word, manual workers form a group maintained by their condition below a certain level of sociality because they are subjugated by the matter with which they work:

Work obliges them, for the greater part of the day, to remain in contact with inert matter, with malleable, fragile substances ... hard, resistant substances ... dangerous substances, dirty substances. ... As a result the industrial labourer is isolated from the world for most of the time, unlike other agents of economic life, traders, employees, foremen, cashiers and so on, whose work brings them into contact with people and does not oblige them to leave human groups behind. (Halbwachs [1938b] 1964, p.142).

When they gather in groups as part of their work, manual workers combine "their physical strength and movements". This cooperation is an element of their technical knowledge, so that the relationships it establishes are mechanical and "involve neither thought nor feeling" (Halbwachs [1938b] 1964, p.142). It is undoubtedly no exaggeration to suggest that, from this point of view, deprived of the cognitive, psychological and social resources that would make them into a fully developed social organisation, manual workers cannot attain an awareness of themselves and others comparable to that of the bourgeoisie. The environment of the latter, on the other hand, has enabled them to acquire the qualities necessary to adapt rules and general laws to their own conditions, but these qualities are rare, and this sets them apart from the rest.

Just as society mercilessly eliminates its lame ducks by driving them to suicide in order to adapt to the conditions of a more complicated life in which the struggle for life is more intense (Halbwachs 1930), so it ejects "an entire class of men destined for manual work, has succeeded in making tools to wield tools" (Halbwachs [1912] 1970, p.75). This obstacle that the struggle for life imposes on manual workers in the movement from nature to culture could be said to offer a paradoxical explanation of those workers' very strong attachment to their work, the desire to devote most of their time to their efforts and the distress that fills them when faced with the question of how to use their leisure time (Halbwachs [1938b] 1964).

But, as Durkheim had already said, the social stratification resulting from the struggle for life in modern societies "is a gentler outcome. For it means that rivals are not obliged to eliminate each other, but can coexist side by side" (Durkheim 1893, p.253). This interpretation of natural selection highlights the roots of Durkheim's thought and that of the biologists he drew on in the paradigm of organisation, ultimately grounded in a static morphology in which conflict and competition cannot appear as first principles of the logic governing individuals – individual organisations – and societies – social organisations. In this sense the social Darwinism of Durkheim and the Durkheimians, like that of most thinkers of the day, is not Darwinian (Guillo 2003). For in a truly Darwinian framework natural selection is not a necessary operator of internal differentiation in societies and individuals, still less the principle of development mechanically and inevitably moving towards growing organisational complexity. Furthermore, as commentators have shown, Darwinian thought marks a break with philosophies that regard the development of life as necessarily orientated towards the formation of ever more complex organisations. Darwin replaced this image ultimately founded on the static morphology of the scale of beings with that of contingent history, produced by competition between individuals, in which chance occupies the prime place and any hierarchy of beings is relative and reversible (on these points see, for example, Balan 1979; Mayr [1982] 1989).

To sum up, in the philosophies of organisation, competition can be more or less directly understood only against a background integrity necessary to all societies, which in turn supposes a minimal degree of harmony.

The history of humanity as a necessary mechanical development of types of social organisation

The necessity of development and "collective reason"

In accordance with the conceptual field in which Durkheim was developing his sociological ideas in his early writings, he presents the development of human social groups as a development of types or species of social organisation. Mechanically caused by increases in the volume and density of the society, development is a necessary process of internal and external differentiation of structure and functions: human groups from the same original stock have gradually and continually diverged into a multiplicity of groups which, as they gained internal specificities at their own pace and became more different from each other, created a tree of distinct types. Despite their divergence, a progression can be seen in the development of human societies, measurable by the degree of their division of labour, in other words, the degree to which the organisation shows internal differentiation. The development of humanity thus necessarily moves towards the formation of social and individual organisations that are ever more differentiated in their structure and activities: in this scenario history as an endless succession of contingent phenomena obeying random causality can have no more than a residual place.

While this kind of development may involve confrontation, there cannot be any major conflict likely to threaten the overall equilibrium. For during their development into complementary social types, the victorious and vanquished social classes come to depend on each other more and more and it is in their interests to maintain the social order. In short the vanquished seem to consent to and indeed be content with the situation that the bourgeoisie works to arrange for them.

This idea is best illustrated in the thought of the convinced socialist Simiand. As we have sought to show elsewhere, for Simiand the movement of civilisation is characterised by a series of economic cycles of alternating phases of recession and expansion. This succession of phases, resulting from the coexisting actions of workers and entrepreneurs, gives rise to the growth of wealth and incomes (Marcel 2001). The acceleration of economic development results from reactions on either side and variations in the quantity of money in circulation. This result is not individually intended, Simian explains, nor is it sought by people going about their everyday activities. These social movements and kinds of behaviour are brought about "by a sort of life instinct favourable to the development of the group, though without the full awareness of individuals or ... more precisely, by a collective reasoning that is better and more effectively applied to major realities" (Simiand 1932, vol. 2, p.518).

The development of the group and consequently, we might say, the development of groups, since, while the resulting theory of social action does not deny the existence of confrontation, in accordance with Durkheim's Darwinian reading of the development of social types, rules out the possibility of its resolution through generalised political violence. The alternation of cycles could be said to result from the sublimation of the struggle for life into antagonism in the market for goods and services. In the existing conditions of a developed economic system, the actions of workers and entrepreneurs combine to produce alternating cycles understood as progress in the march towards civilisation. These actions can be split into two categories: those relating to monetary gain, whose elements can always be expressed monetarily, and those related to services provided in exchange for profit, which are psychologically quantified as a greater or lesser degree of effort. They are always collective in nature and their relative force explains the succession of economic cycles (see Marcel 2001, pp.117–118; for more details, Gislain and Steiner 1995, pp.90–91). The variations in prices and wages that result from these movements affect the groups' perception of their place in the social arena but always express the efforts they make to adapt together to the situation in which the society as a whole is evolving.

In this sense, though they take the lion's share for themselves, the bourgeoisie nevertheless work for the common good, since they are the driving force behind the evolution through which the society seeks to perpetuate itself. So there is no reason to diagnose their inevitable decline a priori, still less to call for its destitution through revolutionary action.

The upper class as the driving force of history?

Among the collective representations and characteristic aspirations of the upper class we find a sense of duty and responsibility, noted for example by Halbwachs:

As members of a higher class, it seems to them like bourgeoisie *noblesse oblige*. And they want to prove to others that they are worthy to belong to this class. Hence the bourgeois concern with respectability, which requires them to act according to the rules of the morality usual in their circles, where it is accepted that man must do all he can to increase his wealth, but in accordance with the customs and traditions underpinning the prestige of the class itself. (Halbwachs[1938b] 1964, pp.118–119).

Thus, against a background of traditional morality, the bourgeoisie has developed qualities that have enabled it to adapt to the new conditions of life in society. What the bourgeoisie characteristic of modern capitalist society best expresses is a set of collective representations that have come out of the new economic regime and that all those concerned believe they must obey, in other words a new social environment. Among the motivations that emerge from these representations we find a preoccupation with wealth and its endless growth: "the duty to enrich oneself, not to enjoy more property than one will consume, but to have the means to make oneself even richer: such is the new duty that underlies capitalist morality like a categorical imperative" (Halbwachs [1938b] 1964, p.97). Citing Schumpeter and Weber, Halbwachs explains that this motive generates a perpetual tension, a continuous effort of will and energy.

For all that, what best characterises the mentality of this social class, following on from the "qualities mentioned above, is the spirit of struggle and competition, alongside which notions we find individualism and liberalism". Competition has become the law of production and sales. The greater intensity and complexity of the struggle for life in the economic sphere, notably with the general introduction of credit, is explained by its increasingly dominant role in the life of the society. This results in "realistic" and "selfish" dispositions that appear as "a necessary reaction and, more importantly, a weapon in the struggle for life and above all for profits" (Halbwachs [1938b] 1964, p.103). In a word, the spirit of enterprise, which assumes a spirit of expansion, renewal and transformation, is the best means of adapting human society to the laws governing the social environment, and which also supposes a sense of collective responsibility.

As we can see, competition is in some sense a driving force of history here. But it remains understood in the context of a theory of collective representations, which itself sits within the non-agonistic framework that is the paradigm of organisation.

In Simiand's work the bourgeois classes are the prime motor of general economic evolution. They start businesses, they are the captains of industry and other magnates who provide the conditions for altering economic phases. Assuming management roles, taking the risk of launching new products and setting up commercial and financial operations, in short employing economic means, they have an eminently social role linked to collective ends: "undertaking all the economic action that best corresponds to the identified goal" (Simiand 1930, p.417). In the last resort this means making a profit to develop an enterprise a little more. This function is imbued with great responsibility, since is has ever more general importance in a complex exchange society.

The action of the bourgeoisie makes exchange possible and through it the establishment of valuations in the form of prices. By making it possible to create wealth and attribute it through exchange, the bourgeoisie ensures that "the economic value of things" has "a certain recognised correspondence to a human need" (Simiand 1930, p.428). It can thus be said that, for Simiand, the upper class also possesses a socially constituted knowledge that is implemented through certain economic actions that are fundamental to the society as a whole. Entrepreneurs make predictions by "reasoning concerning multiple elements that cannot be known" and through "judgements for which no simple, automatic, material rule can be given" (Simiand 1930, p.58). In other words, in making predictions they try to get an idea of possible later developments in the market. Now these capacities are known to go beyond the domain of clear awareness, being more a matter of social instinct. It is thus logical to assume that they develop best in the supporting social environment of the bourgeois class, at the heart of the collective life in societies characterised by complex exchange.[5]

Among the actions flowing on from this we find the fundamental economic role of helping the economic system to move from its present stage to a future stage by creating an inflow of money through borrowing and credit. This is, Simiand explains, "A process that consists in realising sums drawn on this future in advance. ... In other words during these phases, without having thought it through or even always understood it, human society discovers and practises the fundamental, effective means of enrichment that is, strictly speaking, capitalising on the future" (Simiand 1932, vol. 2, p.519)

Borrowing makes it possible to give an impetus to the anticipatory realisation of riches to come, thereby constituting the prime means available to human beings to develop their activity and ensure its future results by increasing their property and wealth. Prices and wages are collective representations based on collectively produced evaluations. They are eminently complex signals that must be decoded and that imply the constitution of "a social belief and faith" created by the bourgeois class, for which the currency is the vector (Marcel and Steiner 2006, p.214). So the bourgeoisie are the principle possessors of a "knowledge" that enables them to best express the society's social instinct by anticipating the future;[6] in other words they are the prime embodiment of the "collective reasoning" governing economic progress, which is reducible to an evolved form of the struggle for life.

So the social hierarchy is understood as being in the order of things, the result of a sort of movement of history through which society expresses its perfection and increasingly frees itself from nature by organising and inflecting the struggle for life. In this general movement each class works to preserve itself, with an idea of its place in the whole and of what will be best for its preservation. But this effort is always understood to be complementary with the actions of the other groups. Simiand's conception earned him harsh criticism from his socialist friends, shocked by the fatalism of the theory of the economic cycle its and logic of nonintervention. For example, in 1933 the socialist Georges Boris denounced "the doctrinal irresponsibility" of the theory of progress through the alternation of long waves or "fundamental pulsations" that are "the manifestation of a permanent biological law that governs our society" (in Frobert 2000, p.181). Perhaps we should see the persistent presence of the paradigm of organisation among the Durkheimians as one explanation of the gap between their activism as citizens and their beliefs as theoreticians. There are undoubtedly elements here that can help us understand why Durkheim insisted on regarding historical materialism as so "crude and so simplistic" as to be unscientific (Durkheim 1998, p.71) and why his collaborators always remained impervious to Guesdism, although some – including Simiand and Halbwachs – were committed political activists.

Our focus here is on is the general conceptual field within which Durkheim set out his early ideas. This is not to suggest that his theory and sociological arguments are entirely contained in these general propositions: on the contrary, his theories of norms, law and collective beliefs and his epistemology of functions have their own logic independent of the concepts mentioned here and can be easily expressed in a different language, without reference to biology.

Conclusion

In referring the life sciences to theorise the social, Durkheim gives a particular meaning and status to the mechanism of the struggle for life. In agreement with most of the sociologists who were employing this concept in the same period, his understanding of this mechanism is based on a representation of society – and living things – as fundamentally organised, developing through a necessary process of increasing complication that encounters no real barriers. In this framework the norm is a harmony of functions and structures within society; discord is pathological. We should not be misled by the reference to the struggle for life. For Durkheim the agonistic dimension of life in society is systematically repressed on a more fundamental conceptual level in which society is understood as an entity characterised by its plenitude and the consensus of its parts, including individuals.

The conception of society as a particular type of organisation with social classes seems to have persisted in sociology in the approach of some of Durkheim's successors who see the undeniable part played in society by conflict, violence and death as consequences of the adaptive march of groups towards greater perfection, and not as a constituent principle of society. From this perspective no form of conflict, from the dialectics of struggle to creative violence or, indeed, competition, has any fundamental place in relationships of coexistence in which each has a reciprocal role to play. While, in this framework, evolution may leave some by the wayside so that society can perpetuate itself or, in other words, so that social ties persist, revolutionary violence and capitalist competition can only be understood as regressions to a more primitive and savage life, less engaged in sociality.

This singular way of understanding conflict may perhaps shed light on the deep aversion of this group of intellectuals to Marxist-inspired revolutionary ideology, which they always regarded as unscientific, just as it also undoubtedly explains the terrible shock – the total denial of intellectual, scientific and other beliefs – which had been for them of the rise of totalitarianism and the outbreak of the Second World War.

Notes

1. Durkheim is so clearly and sharply aware of the need to separate these two theses that he delegates the task of studying the way that "organico-psychic" (Durkheim 1893) and social causalities merge to form individual consciousnesses to a special science – which he calls "socio-psychology" (Durkheim 1893, p.341). Using this distinction Durkheim was also able to maintain, without contradiction, that phenomena of individual consciousness can broadly obey the laws of biological heredity – although less and less so as the division of labour develops – while strongly refuting explanations of social facts such as crime in terms of biological dispositions. On all these points see Guillo (2006).

2. We refer here to the version of the theory of natural selection given by Ernst Mayr (Mayr 2001, pp.126–128). Mayr believes that it is individuals who reproduce and thus it is they who are in

competition with each other in the selective dynamic of life. It should be noted, however, that in the last 40 years or so there have been fairly lively debates in evolutionary biology concerning the real target of selection and whether the entity at the centre of biological evolution is a gene, cell, organism or social group (Dawkins 1976; Sober 1984; Sober and Wilson, 1998; Williams 1966). Some biologists have thus maintained that natural selection is ultimately governed by competition between genes rather than groups or individuals (Dawkins 1976; Williams 1966). Whatever the case, the main thing for us here is to note that Darwinism is based on the idea of competition for reproduction – or replication in the case of genes – between certain entities in a population, whatever these entities may be. This idea is a very long way from what was called Darwinism in the nineteenth century, even if it is clearly present in Darwin's work (see Gayon, 1992: Mayr 2001).

3. Whether they locate causal priority at the level of functions, in other words, activities, or the structure or forms, the philosophies of organisation always draw on the idea of a close correspondence between the two. Although here Durkheim sees activities or functions as pre-eminent in determining the structure of societies, his thought remains dominated by their differentiation, adjustment and division of functions, as his vocabulary suggests.

4. As can be seen, the theme of biological heredity is still found in the work of the Durkheimians. In Durkheim's work – as we mentioned in our introduction – this theme does not contradict the idea of the radical epistemological autonomy of the social in relation to the psychological and biological. The advantage of a return to the biological sources used by Durkheim and those who continued his work is thus to bring out this important aspect of their thought.

5. This also doubtless explains why Simiand's work offers no real theory of the middle class. The 30th class of the second year of his *Cours d'economie politique* devoted to this question offers more of an enumeration than a real definition, as Halbwachs rightly observes (Halbwachs 1939, p.33). The place of the middle classes in the movement of economic cycles is not in fact clearly identifiable.

6. Although from a different perspective, Steiner shows that the question of anticipation lies at the heart of the functioning of life in society in the religious sociology of Mauss as much as in the economic sociology of Simiand. In an effort to explain this convergence of viewpoints, he subtly identifies two branches deriving from a research programme drawn up by Durkheim (Steiner, 2005).

"Change only for the benefit of society as a whole": pragmatism, knowledge and regimes of violence

Ivan Strenski

Durkheim, the pragmatist?

Almost everything we read about Durkheim would indicate that he and his followers were not only temperamentally averse to violence, but that these aversions grew out of a deeply entrenched view of the world and human nature. Durkheim's Third Republic liberalism was conceived as an alternative both to the authoritarian militarism of the right and the revolutionary radicalism of the left. They stood against the Bonapartists and partisans of the "man on a horse" of the reactionary French right and against the Communards, Anarchists and radical Syndicalists of the left. In short, the Durkheimians were repelled by the programmes of violent, extra-parliamentary social change that populated this period of French history. Disorderly as parliamentary governance systems were, nothing matched the absurdity of self-proclaimed tribunes of order. On the one hand, General Boulanger, like the risable "man on a horse", was shamed into silence by being caught *in flagrante delicto*. On the other hand, Georges Sorel, the bard of Marxist revolutionary violence, was preaching the pseudo-Catholic myth of the general strike.[1] Furthermore, no mention of violence in Durkheim's world can pass over Durkheim's role in the First World War as both patriotic promoter of the French war effort and critic of the German militarist philosopher, Heinrich Treitschke

Ivan Strenski is a Holstein Family and Community Distinguished Professor of Religious Studies at the University of California, Riverside. Recent publications on Durkheimian themes include *Durkheim and the Jews of France*, *Contesting sacrifice* (Chicago University Press), *Theology and the first theory of sacrifice* (Brill), and *The new Durkheim* (New Brunswick: Rutgers University Press, 2006), *Émile Durkheim*, an anthology of critical articles (Ashgate) *Dumont on religion: key thinkers in religious studies* (Equinox, 2008) and in press, *When God plays politics: radical interrogations of religion, power and politics* (Blackwell).
Email: echomax1@verizon.net

(Lukes 1972). Of more specialised interest to the guild of sociologists is Randall Collins' attempt to take on a subject broader even than that of the present volume of essays – the Durkheimian contribution to conflict theory (Collins 1988).

Suicides, schoolmasters, sacrifices, empires and regimes of violence

Once one delves beyond these well-known and clear-cut cases, a far more interesting inquiry becomes possible – namely, that there may be no general answer to the question of the relation of Durkheimian thought to violence. Indeed, it seems to make more sense to speak of the relation of Durkheimian thought to varieties of forms of violence – to violences, so to speak. This is particularly so for the Foucauldian question that tends to lurk behind such inquiries about knowledge and violence these days in the humanities: notably, how is Durkheimian knowledge, in Foucault's sense, implicated in regimes of power or violence?

I shall argue in this chapter that Durkheimian knowledge shows a range of possible relationships to power, violence and their associates. If any common thread can be found in these cases it is that the Durkheimians are constantly weighing the matter of how to live in a real world of concrete possibilities. This is why Marcel Mauss characterised Durkheim's attitude as that of someone who "desired change only for the benefit of society as a whole" (Lukes 1972, p. 322, citing Mauss's introduction to *Socialism* in Durkheim, 1962, p. 34). In such a world, they seem guided, appropriately enough, by an adage from Voltaire's *Dictionnaire philosophique* that "the perfect is the enemy of the good". Though it is clear in this sense that Durkheim and his circle were ideologically predisposed to liberalism, it more accurately reflects their state of mind to call them pragmatists than ideologues. I am not unaware that pragmatism itself can be just another sort of ideology, but in the sense I see it working in the case of Durkheim, pragmatism seems more a rule of thumb for muddling through, dictated by what I would call the concern to keep society and, thus, the whole, alive and well. This is also why Lukes echoes Durkheim's dire warnings about a possible world war: " how could it be possible that tomorrow man should wish the destruction of society and the advent of barbarism? Man was man because he had a social life; how could he want to destroy society? ... To destroy society was to destroy a civilization" (Lukes 1972, p.543). Thus, the Durkheimians would concur with another adage, namely that "ideologues believe that if something is right, it has to work, even if it doesn't work". Above all, the Durkheimians wanted things to work. In this sense, the ideal of things working for the sake of social development determined their choices more than any particular vision of what things ought to be. I realise all this may seem passé, if not downright naive, but I hope that by the end of this chapter I will have convinced readers that the Durkheimians were the kinds of muddling through pragmatists that I claim them to be, rather than thinkers transfixed by an ideal.

To this end, we ought to take a close look at a number of cases where violence can be said to arise somewhat more obliquely or subtly in connection with Durkheimian knowledge. Consider the implications that might flow for the use of social constraint or institutionalised violence from Durkheim's *Suicide*. Durkheim's great work has not been the subject of a Foucauldian challenge, although it might well be – and will in this chapter. Is there any way that Durkheimian knowledge itself contributes a kind of violence of its own to the phenomenon of suicide – in particular for the tools of social control that will reduce the numbers of such suicides, even perhaps to the extent of promoting the violent suppression of suicides? Similarly, what Foucauldian critique might be made of Durkheim's theories of education, especially as they involve staples of Foucauldian theory such as personal discipline and punishment? Was his well-known commitment to discipline so great that he might have approved harsh methods of restraint in the schools? Conspicuous as well in the Durkheimian oeuvre is the quantity (and quality) of attention devoted to the frequently violent subject of sacrifice. What does Durkheimian knowledge reveal of itself in this instance?

Moving to another potential area in which violence and domination might well be close to the surface of things, we might focus on the residual evolutionism of Durkheim's views of social development dating from *The division of labour* to *The elementary forms of the religious life*. Here, Durkheim's belief in the fact that there are things we should call primitive or elementary might suggest evidence of his sympathy – whether expressed or not – for the colonial policies of the Third Republic that also relied on designating certain communities as "primitive" and therefore in need of the "civilising" intrusion into their midst of European imperial powers.

The direction of any inquiry has been dictated by the critique of liberalism initiated by Michel Foucault and carried forward by those like Talal Asad (2003, Ch. 6). These thinkers raise the question of how the knowledge we call Durkheimian thought has conspired – wittingly or otherwise – to further regimes of domination and violence. In terms of their worthiness for Foucauldian ethical reproach, regimes of domination may range from those of relatively insignificant moral pertinence, such as in relatively mild modes of social control, to those deserving stout moral rebuke for their perpetration of regimes of severely dehumanising domination. In this attention to the imperative of personal dignity and liberation, Foucault anticipates the full-blown ethical work that emerged later in his studies on human sexuality and the care of the self, in part sketched out in his "On the genealogy of ethics: an overview of work in progress" (Foucault 1984, pp. 231–232; Hoy 1986, pp.16, 227–240).

However, there is a second source for our knowledge of these things at the periphery of the consciousness of most students of Durkheim. Here, I speak of those areas where Durkheimian knowledge ought to be better known for its possible influence upon the formation of regimes of power and violence, but where, shamefully, it is not. I refer in particular to those areas of the world that generally fall outside the purview of what are considered normal concerns for American sociologists. For example, although Durkheimian knowledge has been an agent in shaping regimes of control and constraint and for some thinkers, with regard to violence in nations such as Japan or Turkey, little is know about the details of such influence. This chapter is devoted to considering some of these ways that Durkheimian knowledge may be complicit in regimes of power or violence and, in doing so, to drawing some conclusions about the general relation of Durkheimian thought to violence that organises this volume.

The myth of institutional violence

Another way I have tried to focus this discussion is to concentrate upon what I would call real violence. In this sense, I am taking a page from Durkheim's book by being careful to distinguish some of the things we casually call violence from other things that, unpalatable or morally repugnant though they may be, are not violent in the strictest sense of the term. Durkheim would be puzzled, and perhaps rightly so, of the prolific usage of the term "institutional violence". Durkheim was much too sensitive to the qualitative difference brought about in human affair by regimes of actual violence from those of, say, mere injustice, to confuse the two. That was one reason why he believed that progressive social change was to be preferred over (violent) revolution. Here it is well worth rehearsing Lukes's argument summed up in quoting Durkheim's contemporaries like Marcel Mauss and Hubert Bourgin, respectively. Said Mauss in relation to Durkheim's attitude to class struggle,

Durkheim was "deeply opposed to war whether of classes or of nations; he desired change only for the benefit of society as a whole and not for any of its parts". Furthermore, when it came to revolutionary violence, Durkheim was dismissive, seeing it "as more theatrical than serious" (Lukes 1972, p.322, citing Mauss's introduction to *Socialism*). Moreover, perhaps with Bonapartism in mind, Durkheim was more than a little acquainted with the notion of institutionalised violence. This is partly due to the fact that he added greatly to our conception of institutionalisation – of a socially constructed or sanctioned state of affairs. But institutional violence and institutionalised violence are different beasts.

In this way, Durkheim was like George Orwell whose "Politics and the English language" warns us of how careless or heedless political speech is often bedevilled by bad habits:

Modern English, especially written English, is full of bad habits which spread by imitation and which can be avoided if one is willing to make the necessary effort. If one gets rid of these habits one can think more clearly, and to think clearly is a necessary first step toward political regeneration. (Orwell 1956, p.355)

I think one of our more egregious bad habits in talking about violence comes to us in the locution, institutional violence. I take exception to the use of this phrase, not because I (or Durkheim) think institutions cannot violate human rights, or because I think institutions cannot act violently. Institutions can certainly be guilty of such crimes. I take exception to the phrase institutional violence because I think it fosters one of those bad habits of which Orwell wrote. It is a stealthy way of insinuating that there are only at most quantitative differences between conflicts that involve physical means and those that lack them. Thus, there is only at most a quantitative difference between, by way of example, being blindsided by an underhanded parliamentary manoeuvre in a faculty meeting and being blindsided on the football field, between a high-tech lynching before a Senate committee and a high-tech lynching from a cottonwood tree, between a covenant that excludes me from owning a house in a given neighbourhood and being physically dragged from my home and so on.

To be sure, in both kinds of cases, the actuality of injustice is just as real. That is not my point in arguing for recognising a certain difference. What I do claim is that the locution institutional violence is finally just a rhetorical device. It broadens the sense of violence to suggest that the use of physical means in conflicts does not qualitatively change the register and kind of those conflicts. Its purpose may well then be silently to authorise and condone the use of physical force to overturn such instances of institutional violence. In this way of thinking, both institutional violence and physical violence are violence and thus they are beasts of the same species. Therefore, it would make no difference as to how one remedies institutional violence – whether by military force, on the one hand, or by persuasion, legislation and other means, on the other.

As such, discourse informed by language such as institutional violence loses a certain logical edge. "Violence" marks so much of what is out there in the world that it fails to stand out against anything that might contrast with it. When so much can be called violent, how little it all begins to matter. But such a loss of logical edge is perhaps more than sufficiently compensated for because institutional violence has an emotive edge for those who wield it. Institutional violence is a rhetorical device fit for use in a struggle.

Consider by contrast the similar-looking term, institutionalised violence. War might be said to be an example of violence that has been regularised by being institutionalised – by being shaped by certain conventions, social arrangements and the like. There is no confusion here about how the term violence is understood. The main effort is to call attention to how the use of force or other means of physical agency have taken on or been given the forms of institutions. Durkheim's studies of suicide would as well be another example of precisely the same sort of institutionalised violence. Here, Durkheim classically dwelt upon identifying the social determinants of suicides that might vary concomitantly with membership in various sorts of religious communities.

In reality, though, aside from its rhetorical sense, the use of "violence" in the term institutional violence is, I would submit, really no different in meaning to "injustice". Using the term violence adds a charge to discourse employing it and thus aids the causes pursued in connection with it. Institutional violence is a metaphor, albeit an unacknowledged one. The term violence in the term institutional violence sprawls out broadly to include more than would most often be included in the simple term, violence. From a Durkheimian sociological point of view there are excellent reasons to insist on avoiding the use the term violence in the broad way embodied in such terms as institutional violence.

Durkheim believed that conflicts change – often dramatically, and thus qualitatively – when physical violence, or what I call real violence, breaks out. Because the introduction of violence into disputes changed the very kind of social reality in question, Durkheim believed that opting for the violent alternative in social change courted enormous risks. In 1905, during an exchange with Hubert Lagardelle, the theorist of revolutionary syndicalism, Durkheim warned that if violence were introduced into a dispute, it could have effects far beyond what would seem the immediate result of such action: "we must avoid acts of destruction that suspend the course of social life and civilisation" (cited in Lukes, 1972, p.544), lest in doing so we plunge our world back into an age of "darkness" (Durkheim 1905, p.423). There thus exists a world of difference between our metaphorical and physical ways of being violated. Being an embodied and material being matters; just as the difference between being blindsided by an underhanded parliamentary manoeuvre or rules in a faculty meeting and being blindsided on the football field and so on matters. Discrimination may deprive me of life options, but, although this may be cold comfort, it does not necessarily deprive me of my life. This insight lies at the heart of the genius of Gandhi and Martin Luther King, Jr. They not only recognised, from a pragmatic point of view alone, during violent physical conflict, that their forces would be outgunned and disadvantaged. They also recognised that once a conflict becomes physically violent it can spiral out of control and thus degenerate into chaos that leads to endless unmanageable recriminations to even the score. It becomes our greatest human nightmare – a real "war of all against all". Furthermore, one thing Durkheim surely feared was the suspension of social constraints. Like Durkheim, Gandhi and King knew about struggle and knew how explosive real violence was. So they might see in Durkheim someone who considered that resorting to violence was to abandon oneself "blindly to one's emotions" (Lukes 1972, p.544, citing Durkheim 1905). But it was not just loving kindness that made non-violence their tactic of choice: it was also a profound insight into the qualitative difference between physical violence and other institutional or moral forms of violence that guided them. If, then, one believes, as I do, that it makes sense to distinguish between physical uses of power and force – violence as such – and those uses of power which do not and therefore, which are non-violent, then it makes sense to reject the locution, institutional violence.

Moreover, taking these differences into consideration reinforces the claim that Durkheim was the kind of anti-ideological pragmatist that I perceive him to be. His objection to violent revolution as a method of social change was pragmatic, not ideological – it was about what seemed most likely to work, not about an ideal. Durkheim believed that violent revolution simply did not *work* as well as progressive social change. For one thing, it tended to be counter-productive since it was likely to provoke a "reaction" generating perhaps even greater repressive forces than before (Lukes 1972, p.323, citing Hubert Bourgin's *Le socialism universitaire* (1942). Theoretically speaking, of course, one might be able to refer to cases where violent revolution could succeed. Possibilities are endless. Durkheim simply felt that as far as he knew, that the evidence pointed away from prospects of success in revolutionary change.

There are those who nonetheless may suggest that an explicit threat to violence may itself be classed as fully violent, or further that the implicit threats to violence sometimes embedded into the structure of institutions are likewise fully violent and thus provide cases against my argument – even though neither are violent in the physical sense I have considered. To such objections, some ready counter arguments are available. Firstly, the promise of violence – which is what a threat to violence essentially is – is not the same as the actuality of violence. Threats are made typically to intimidate or bluff an opponent and in so doing to

avoid real violence. Threats are the tactics employed by bullies, people who often are the best at bluffing and the worst at engaging in real physical violence. Winning by not having to fire a shot is always better than the alternative of a real exchange of fire. Nothing is risked if one's opponent surrenders to threat.

In the heat of battle, however, much can go wrong. Control may slip from the hands of the superior combatants and accidents may occur. Once real violence is unleashed the risk of disorder is immediately increased, purely by virtue of the fact that physical control of a situation is so complex. The bully bearing down on me might be surprised by the concealed weapon I pull from a place he has simply failed to consider. As anyone knows who has ever actually tried to build a house from plans, plant a garden by the book or perform an surgical operation following precise procedures, physical reality simply contains too many variables over which one could have perfect knowledge. There are simply too many a slip twixt cup and lip.

Similarly, the same objection can be levelled against those who would equate the violence embedded in institutions with the violence dealt out by institutions. Promise, prospect, possibility, capacity and such, whether located in individuals or institutions, differ just as much from actuality whatever their location. A prisoner may be intimidated by the menacing threat of sexual violence to their person that is well known to be implicit in the prevailing conditions of our penal institutions. But who would mistake such a sinister atmosphere of sexual violence for actual rape? Reality still makes a difference.

Knowledge/power to prevent suicide

Given, then, that we want to address situations of such real violence, where can we see Durkheimian knowledge actually aiding and abetting prominent regimes of control smacking of violence? Consider, firstly, the case of suicide and the social controls – even violent ones – that emerge in Durkheim's approach to suicide. One could wager that it would be hard to whip up the kind of moral condemnation of social mechanisms for controlling suicides that readers of

Foucault's study of mental asylums or prisons would be prepared to bring to those topics. In the latter, Foucault brilliantly demonstrates how a supposedly humane and well-intentioned device as the Panopticon introduces into the regime of prison punishment the radical dehumanisation of the inmates. By means of its deprivation of privacy, the Panopticon's constant surveillance strips perhaps the last shred of dignity left to those under its care. Here indeed is something to inspire Foucauldian moral protest. Yet I submit that one needs to put the harder question of whether critics of social control, such as in the cases in which Foucault has rightly won a reputation, really are ready to commit themselves to the general elimination of all such regimes of domination and control, or only some? Suicide, for example?

Durkheim's answer would, I believe, vary with the circumstances. Having said that, in the end it would be governed by the practical principle of whether or not social flourishing was enhanced in the process. To begin, one answer would be attempts to submit suicide to a regime of social control, given that one might conceive suicide, or at least a broad range of it, as a social malignancy, in part because it might, for example, weaken the morale of others to go on and persist through life's inevitable struggles. In that case, would suicide not call for the application of Durkheimian regimes of social constraints or controls – no matter how the application of these might compromise freedom of choice in the matter of taking one's own life?

One might counter this argument with the idea that relief of unbearable or devastating pain by means of regulated methods of suicide for the terminally ill should be encouraged for the sake of greater social solidarity. Knowing that one will not be required to suffer untreatable pain in a terminal condition may very well reassure people of the existence of an overall reasonable concern for their welfare, even if that means euthanasia. Such a reassurance would undoubtedly strengthen the social bonds of trust. One will not be left to suffer excruciating pain unto death.

At the other extreme are suicides that may rightly be gathered under the rubric of malignancies, such as suicides resulting from fits of depression. In this instance, what one might see as erratic suicides or suicide done out of mistaken motives represent cases of individuals

doing invalid harm to themselves. By doing so, they are also harming the social whole by treating life and death issues lightly or by doing something of such import for no good reason, despite the range of criteria governing what one counts as good.

The strongest implications of the meaning of Durkheim's work on suicide ought to be seen in the context of an entire oeuvre that argues for pragmatic methods of strengthening society and social bonds. In the case of suicide, Durkheimian thinking urges that everything, from face-to-face dissuasion to active, even violent intervention to prevent persons from doing harm to themselves ought to be undertaken. Durkheimian societism urges us to resist any actions that further the killing of society as it were, even if only piecemeal by means of the individual suicide done for no good reason.

His advocacy of social controls on such unreasonable suicides would seem then to challenge any Foucauldian reluctance to pull the levers of such mechanisms because they might constrict human freedom. For example, where is evidence of the contrary – namely that Foucault was eager to pull the levers of social control on individuals? Instead, a reading of Foucault as tribune of freedom shows us someone reluctant to invoke external social controls at all. Thus, as Michael Walzer keenly observes, it is true that in Foucault's resistance to domination he does not accuse some "dictator or a party or a state that shapes the character of disciplinary institutions". Yet Foucault "is focused instead on what he thinks of as the 'micro-fascism' of everyday life" (Walzer 1986, p.63). For some, this makes Foucault not only an anarchist, but more, a nihilist. This is particularly true in light of his thoughts regarding codes of conduct in which he "gives us no reason to expect that these will be any better than the ones we now live with. Nor, for that matter; does he give us any way of knowing what 'better' might mean" (Walzer 1986, p.61).

Both too tender and too tough about school discipline?

As an indictment of Durkheim's attitude to violence, Lewis Coser's influential essay,

"Durkheim's conservatism and its implications for his sociological theory" may come as close as we can get to conventional wisdom on the subject. Coser gave Durkheim's critics ample opportunity to ridicule his idealism or naivety about human nature. His attack on Durkheim's idealism implicates him as a rather soft-headed dreamer:

> We cannot reproach Durkheim for lacking the gift of prophecy, but we might reproach him for not having grasped the irreducible facts of power so glaringly obvious in the living past of his own age. If he had had the tough-minded detachment of Marx or a Weber, his contribution might have been of value to the understanding of an era which was in crucial ways different from his own. As it was, his tender-minded attachment to the institutions of Republican France proved to be a fatal handicap. (Coser 1960, p.222)

Coser takes this assault on Durkheim's supposed tender-mindedness deeper into the treacherous domain of religious and ethnic self-hatred. Coser knows well the story of Durkheim's rejection of Judaism and Jewishiness. He adds to this a lesson on the costs turning away from the historical lessons of Durkheim's Jewish origin: "This man, the son of a people who has suffered from religious persecution perhaps more than any other Western people, never allowed knowledge of these events to intrude into his thinking when he constructed his system (Coser 1960, pp.224–225). Foolish Durkheim should have known better, but he "never allowed knowledge" of his Jewishness to intrude into his world. Part of the cost of suppressing this part of his origins was thus to misread the entire social world in so far as it had to do with the real world of power, politics and violence. Thus, in a vain attempt to assimilate to secular French gentile society, Durkheim blocked out a more rounded and realistic understanding of social reality than we get with his tender-minded idealistic liberalism. We would have all been better served, not to mention the improvement to Durkheimian political theory, had he welcomed the lessons of Jewish historical identity.

But, Coser is seemingly unable to leave matters rest at this point. To him something profoundly ironic results from Durkheim's failure to face up to his Jewishness and to his subsequently tender-minded attachment to the institutions of Republican France, with an abstract, liberal (and dare one say, gentile) nationalism. The result is that Durkheim reveals himself to be a far more repressive figure than the liberalism of the Third Republic would seem to promise. Coser essentially suggests that perhaps an honest embrace of Durkheim's natural identity, with its realistic grasp of politics, power and violence, might have produced another result. What Coser seems to have in mind is that Durkheim appears to have struck a bargain for assimilation – namely to over-subscribe to the values of the Third Republic and its radical commitment to a highly regimented, national educational policy. Coser believes this side of Durkheim emerges in a surprising place, namely in his thoughts on educational policy, embodying Durkheim's conservative pessimism about human nature that leads him to embrace strict regimes of punishment in the schools.

Here, Durkheim proposes a model national schoolmaster as a stern advocate of strict classroom discipline, all in the service of the noble goal of national renewal after the French defeat to the Prussians in 1871. In a posthumously published piece Durkheim espouses a view on the nature of education that will strike Coser as harsh for its top-down character. Durkheim asserts that the goal of "education is to superimpose upon the individual, non-social being that we are at birth an entirely new being. Education must lead us to go beyond our initial nature: it is upon this condition that the child will become a man" (Giddens 1986, p.183). The child born into a society characterised by an advanced state of the division of labour will be expected to show many of the unruly aspects of the individualism produced by this level of social development. Thus, in order that the child may succeed in this highly advanced world, discipline will have to be learnt from a young age. This child will need to "learn to keep his natural selfishness within bounds, to subordinate himself to higher ends, to submit his desires to the domination of the will and to place appropriate limitations upon them. The child must apply his mind intensively" (Giddens 1986, p.183). However, Durkheim is quick to admit that the same discipline would be required of the schoolmaster. But this would not lessen the intensity of classroom regimes of punishment. Durkheim thus will require of the instructor an equal level of self-discipline in order to model the social ideal to the child. Indeed, teachers will need to approach priests in their degree of self-mastery and secular sanctity:

Just as the priest is the interpreter of his god, the teacher is the interpreter of the great moral ideas of his time and his country. Let him be attached to those ideas, let him feel all their greatness and the authority inherent in them and of which he is aware cannot fail to communicate itself to his person and to everything that emanates from him. (Giddens 1986, p.185)

Thus, far from the tender-minded idealist, Durkheim here reveals himself then as an ideological enforcer of a policy of national discipline to be realised in school.

Citing the educational psychologist Jean Piaget, Coser claims that "Durkheim's general conception of the need for social constraint" caused him to seek severely to "curb the wickedness of biological propensity" in students and thus to a "view on education fundamentally at variance with most modern [that is, 1960s] thinking, leaving no place for the idea of cooperation between children or between teacher and pupils. Durkheim conceived the schoolmaster as a kind of priest who acted as an intermediary between society and the child" (Coser 1960, p.228). As a result, everything depended on the schoolmaster and the moral rules were seen as a kind of revelation which the priest of society reveals to the child.

Revealed thus as a kind of secular priest of the secular Third Republic, according to Coser, Durkheim made no secret of the need for strict discipline and punishment in education. Citing from Durkheim's *Evolution of educational thought*, Coser notes that Durkheim says of discipline in the schools: "Life is not all play; the child must prepare himself for pain and effort and it would therefore be a disaster if he were allowed to think that everything can be done as a game" (Coser 1960, p.228). Denouncing the pleasure principle inherent in the notion of play, Durkheim effectively provides further ammunition to Coser: "Nothing is more false and deceptive than the Epicurean conception of education, the conception of a Montaigne, for example, whereby human beings can be educated through play, without any motivation

save the attraction of pleasure" (Giddens 1986, p.183).

According to Coser, Durkheim's sociology of education is a "sociology of educational constraints". It is a fundamentally violent system designed to contain potential classroom violence. As if anticipating all that Michel Foucault was to write only a few years later in *Discipline and punish* or *Madness and civilization*, Coser previews their common themes of the often violent unintended consequences of self-styled liberal or enlightened regimes of correction or therapy (Foucault 1965, 1979). Durkheim may have thought himself the model enlightened, high-minded liberal of the Third Republic, but his harsh policies for discipline and punishment in the schools seem hardly tender-minded.

For Durkheimian theory, the end result is that it never faced up to its own violent demands upon people, preferring instead to dwell on the sweeter functions of integration, consensus and shared values, morality and religion. But in the process of failing to face up to the reality of the violence perpetrated by his own liberalism, Durkheim in effect set himself up to promote it, as we have seen in Coser's arguments. Despite his well known objections to the German militarism articulated by Treitschke, his distaste for the anarcho-syndicalist violence of his day or his preference of gradualist social reform instead of (certainly bloody) revolution, Durkheim seems at ease with the suppressed violence attending his own liberalism. In Coser's view, when put up against the other giants of sociological theory such as Weber and Marx, Durkheim cannot match them for their across-the-board frank realism about the pervasive violence of human affairs, whether intended or not. For Weber or Marx, Coser suggests "struggle, conflict and contention defined the state as a human group" (Coser 1960, pp.220–221). For Durkheim, by contrast, one finds either the blindness we have just noted or a lack of "reference to the authoritative enforcement of will". In terms of politics, Coser feels that Durkheim gives us "a curiously abstract and intellectualistic conception of the state" (Coser 1960, pp.220–221). Even regarding that jewel in the crown of Durkheimian theory – religion – Coser claims that it "never occurred to Durkheim that religion may serve as a means

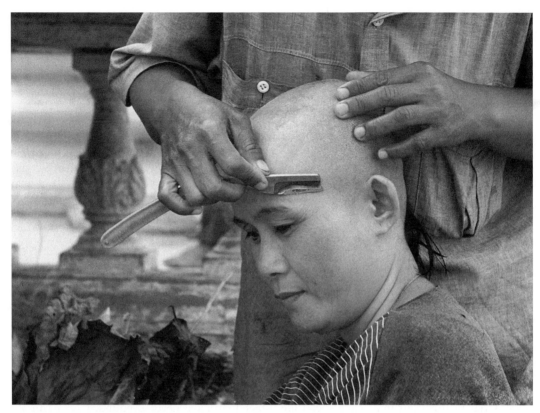

A Cambodian woman has her head shaved at Dang Ke pagoda, Phnom Penh, 2 June, 1999, giving her hair as an offering to fulfil a promise for prayers answered by Buddha. Agence France-Presse /Rob Elliott

of legitimising and glorifying acts which would not have been perpetrated in good conscience had such legitimation not been available" (Coser 1960, p.225). Thus, instead of a full-blooded appreciation of real life as it was lived, with its violence and politics, Durkheim either preferred the way of the removed philosophical thinker, or the *deracineé* enforcer of the hypocritical norms of secular liberal education. Coser does not leave us with a pretty picture of Durkheim or Durkheimian theory.

One might be tempted to dismiss Durkheim's perplexing mix of tender mindedness and tough mindedness as determined by the peculiarities of the problems of discipline and control among schoolchildren. After all, as any school teacher these days well knows, maintaining classroom order, especially in our inner city schools, is a major problem for achieving effective instruction and education. In light then of our own realities of gang culture, school shootings or the weaponised classroom, it is Coser's hope for a cooperative – dare one say progressive? – pedagogy may seem dangerously naive. Furthermore, Coser's own idealism that informs his criticism of Durkheim's frank admission of the need for classroom discipline smacks of its origins in the 1960s and thus of its being an artefact of that era's youth culture or the free school movement. Just who comes out looking more tender-minded in this comparison of Coser and Durkheim, I need not say. What should be said, nonetheless, is that the case of discipline and violence in schools might be a special rather than a paradigmatic case in approaching the issue of Durkheim and violence and especially given the ambivalence one finds there. This is why we might well look elsewhere in Durkheim's life and writings to see if the pattern of rationalising tough mindedness repeats itself.

Too tender and too tough about sacrifice?

Another conspicuous domain where this deceptive pattern of hidden violence seems to reappear is Durkheimian theory of sacrifice. Here one finds at least two ways in which the Durkheimians repress full admission of violence and thus fail to take responsibility for it. First, while the reported facts of sacrifice in Durkheimian literature very often include frank and explicit reports of the rite as a violent affair, where blood and guts are spilled in quantity, the Durkheimians do not leave sacrifice there; they seem to make excuses for it. Nor do they indict sacrifice for being violent scapegoating in the way that René Girard has over the course of an entire career (Girard 1977, 1986, 1987). Sacrifice is not a pretty sight, but an often murderous deed, which the Durkheimians tend to play down.

The horror, anguish and pain of sacrificial violence – especially for the victim – is suppressed by having our attention drawn to the Durkheimian social function of the sacrifice. The Durkheimians claim that sacrifice fulfils a whole series of functions that make social life possible. In 1898 Durkheim noted that "family relations started by being an essentially religious bond; punishment, contract, gift, hommage are derived from the expiatory, contractual, communal, noble sacrifice" (Durkheim 1980, p.54). Moreover, up until his final days, Durkheim maintained the view that morality required sacrifice: "There is no moral act that does not imply a sacrifice, for, as Kant has shown, the law of duty cannot be obeyed without humiliating our individual, or, as he calls it, our 'empirical' sensitivity" (Durkheim 1960, p.328). But his appeals to morality notwithstanding, when we consider the plight of the victim, instead of suppressing it as the Durkheimians do, we can see how they seem to have anaesthetised our moral sensibilities. It is as if the Durkheimians say of sacrifice: "Well, yes, sacrifice is a terrible violent act, but since it serves useful social function, we may play down its violent aspects".

The entire sacrificial rite is thus sanitised of ethical consideration for the plight of the sacrificial victim by deflecting attention from its violence to the social functions performed in the process. In their classic, normative statement of the Durkheimian theory of sacrifice, Henri Hubert and Marcel Mauss say the normal kind of sacrifice was one in which a victim was placed between the person offering or sponsoring the sacrifice and the "god" or being to whom the sacrifice was being made. The substitution of the victim for the sponsor or sacrificer was made so that the sponsor of sacrificer would not have to offer themselves. Hubert and Mauss offer what one might call a prudent person's way of offering sacrifice by offering a victim in their stead. One saves oneself by offering another in sacrifice. As Henri Hubert and Marcel Mauss say in *Sacrifice: its nature and functions:*

> In any sacrifice there is an act of abnegation since the *sacrifier* deprives himself and gives. . . . But this abnegation and submission are not without their selfish aspect. The *sacrifier* gives up something of himself but does not give up himself. Prudently, he sets himself aside. . . . Disinterestedness is mingled with self-interest. (Hubert and Mauss 1964, p.100)

A painful social truth thus emerges from Hubert and Mauss's meditation on sacrifice, despite the fact they have never expounded on it. In the same way that one cannot absolutely escape the crunch of victimisation in ritual sacrifice, so too one cannot escape the lamentable need for human victimisation in civic contexts, despite an effort to minimise it. We are all, alternatively givers and takers. The world, whether religious and ritual or social and civic, is so arranged that it cannot be otherwise. There is no religion without marking boundaries between sacred and profane, pure and impure. Ambivalence about identity notwithstanding, there is no society that fails to mark boundaries between us and them, between who we are and who we are not, between others and selves. In both cases, Hubert and Mauss felt that sacrifice functioned to mark the boundaries essential to life, whether this be religious or social life and whether or not they dwelt on the costs involved.

The ambiguity of the Durkheimians, deliberate or not, aside, their suppression of the more distasteful features of sacrifice is perhaps typical of a mentality at home in the early twentieth-century civic spiritedness. At any rate, its singularity comes out more clearly when we contrast it to a succeeding generation of

Durkheimians who sought to take their work further in the 1930s. Here the notorious figure of Georges Bataille deserves mention in any discussion of sacrifice, not to speak of the relation of Durkheim to violence.

What sets Bataille apart from the original Durkheimian mentality is his refusal to play down the violence meted out to the sacrificial victim. Rather, he exalts in it. Bataille also never suggests that such violence is redeemed by the social function served by sacrifice. Violence is, in and of itself, something to be celebrated, according to Bataille. Thus, far from suppressing the perversity of sacrifice as unbridled self-destruction and violence, Bataille flings it in the face of the bourgeoisie. Embracing Sade, Bataille finds cruelty a virtue that emerges right in the heart of ritual animal sacrifice. While Georges Bataille believes, like the Durkheimians, that sacrifice serves a key social function, there is little indication that he wishes to suppress anything about it. For him, sacrifice functions to help bourgeois humanist culture to transcend itself by ascending beyond its limits all the way to the sacred. Sacrificial violence was for him a kind of desirable or good evil in this respect. It vapourised bourgeois self-assurance in the ultimacy of the profane individualist consciousness. In engaging in bloody sacrifice, we open ourselves to the transgressive power embodied in acts of ritual violence. Bataille wants such experiences of blood sacrifice to be fraught with anguish for the participants, so that in that way they would feel the mental horror that is sure to come in knowing that we are to die (Letvin 1990, pp.74–75). It is a "limited experience of death", our own rendered possible by the contemplation of the most violent and transgressive acts (Letvin 1990, p.111).

We may tentatively conclude, then, from these the examples of Durkheim's respective pedagogical and sacrificial theories that violence features in surprisingly challenging ways in Durkheimian thought. The problems arise both from how violence is intentionally conceived by them, but also, and perhaps more interestingly, by the unintentional implications of their thinking about violence and its suppression. Can suppression be excused because it is needed for practical social flourishing? Is it naive to believe that society is possible without sacrifice and thus a degree of vicitimisation?

Durkheimian sociological knowledge as knowledge for imperialists?

Given the present vogue for post-colonial studies, another area where Durkheimian knowledge seems vulnerable to suspicion about facilitating regimes of power and violence is in their personal and intellectual role in the effort of Third Republic colonialism. Since Durkheim is silent about colonialism we are left to sift through circumstantial evidence for some sort of connection between Durkheimian knowledge and French colonial power. Consider the following scenario: the years 1893–1914 encompass both the high-water mark of the French colonial effort and also the most intense period of intellectual vitality of the Durkheimian group. During that period the political party closest to the Durkheimians, both in actual membership and moderate liberal, bourgeois and anti-clerical ideology (the *Parti radical*), was in the vanguard of promoting French imperialism. Strange though it may seem, those forces pressing the colonial effort forward in the end of the ninteenth century spanned the entire ideological spectrum in France (Andrew and Kanya-Forstner 1971, p.120). Much of the broad support for the colonial enterprise to do with the cultural imperialism of France was achieved in its commitment to its *mission civilisatrice* (Andrew and Kanya-Forstner 1971, p.127). Having said that, competition between the Great Powers and patriotism stimulated an equal, if not greater measure of support for imperial adventures. French struggles with Great Britain over Egypt, Indo-China and West Africa, or with Imperial Germany over dominance in North Africa, typified perhaps by the Agadir Crisis in 1911, give a sense of the competitive atmosphere among the Great Powers over colonial hegemony before the First World War. Even on the left, those socialists closest to the Durkheimians, Albert Thomas, with whom Henri Hubert had worked during the First World War on the creation of what would become the International Labour Federation, or Jean Jaurés, the great leader of the French socialists and Durkheim's classmate at the *Ecole normale*, were avid proponents of a socialist colonialism. Even in Germany the liberal democratic socialist, Edouard Bernstein, whom many

French socialists held in high regard, embraced a revisionist socialism favouring colonisation as a way of protecting the "uncivilised" from the advance of less enlightened European powers (Hovde 1928, p.590). To them, colonialism was something of a proletarian duty that "civilised" nations needed to embrace in order to aid in the development of uncivilised peoples and to protect them from the ravages of capitalism that would otherwise assail them (Hovde 1928, pp.580–581). The Durkheimians, with their modified evolutionist perspective on the relation of the world's cultures to one another, would not find the sentiments of their political kin strange or perhaps even objectionable. All these considerations then show that much of what made up the spirit of, at least leftish, colonialism was not foreign to Durkheimian ways of thinking. More than that I am not able to say. The evidence is coincidental and if there be a touch of guilt by association it will need to be kept in abeyance until more can be known. However, if we address the related matter of the possible involvement of Durkheimian knowledge in political regimes, we have much more to go on. Two cases stand out: western European fascism and Turkish corporatism.

Fascism and the Durkheimian corporate state: regimes of violence?

Scholarly forerunner of fascism?

Finally, perhaps at that end of the spectrum where violence has notoriously been celebrated, we know that even in the 1930s critics of Durkheim like Svend Ranulf indicted Durkheimian collectivism for providing the seeds of fascist statism (Ranulf 1939). To what degree did Durkheimian thought provide legitimacy for the suppression of dissent, for the regimentation of social order and for a regime of social order that revelled in its use of physical force or violence? If we are to believe Lukes, as we ought to, and consider the course of modern German history, the answer is, not at all. What evidence is there that any Nazi executive considered Durkheim's teachings or that they used him to obtain a blueprint for any formation of the Nazi state? The Nazis were quite capable

on their own of providing their own ideological underpinnings. Even if we consider France and French fascism, we cannot plausibly blame Durkheimian knowledge for causing Vichy integrism, collectivism and traditionalism. Furthermore, even following Foucault's genealogical approach, can we say that it conditioned Vichy fascism (Foucault 1984, p.104)? Vichy fascism could be (and was) conceived aside from any sort of Durkheimian societism.

Given the rich and explicit sources of conservative anti-individualist French fascist thinking, the ideas of de Maistre or Bonald made Vichy epistemologically conceivable. To my knowledge, Durkheim was never able to achieve this. This is not even to bring in Durkheim's well-known defence of individualism during the Dreyfus Affair, his philosophical position on the left of French Hegelianism and neo-critical neo-Kantianism, all of which are major sources of French liberal thought (Strenski 1989). As we will see below, it is highly significant that thinkers who actually knew the Durkheimians came to quite different conclusions about their political tendencies than those of Ranulf. It is true that Marcel Mauss admitted that the Durkheimians, in their readiness to learn the value of myth, ritual and religion from "primitive" cultures, underestimated the way that ritual, for example, would be adapted by fascist regimes to stoke political passions and identity (Lukes 1972, p.338f n71). But again, it is one thing to point out impressionistic similarities in the shapes of theoretical positions and quite another thing to substantiate the causal and even conditioning influence of Durkheimian knowledge upon fascist regimes of violence. The Nazis knew an enormous amount about ritual and myth, thanks to the extensive work of German Romantic scholarship. They had no need, nor did they show any need, for the studies of the "elementary forms" of Australian aboriginal religion undertaken by a French Jew to legitimise anything they did (Mosse 1964; Poliakov 1974; Stern 1961).

This remark might just as well serve to introduce the final part of my extended argument because it was a Turkish thinker, the jurist and legal scholar, Hüseyin Nail Kubalı, who wrote his doctoral dissertation for the Faculty of Law in Paris on the contributions of Durkheimian thought to liberal ideas of the state (Kubalı 1936). Unlike Ranulf, Kubalı engages Durkheim substantially rather than impressionistically. Ranulf sums up the results of his article in a telling way:

> The gist of the preceding survey is to show that both these groups of sociologists [Toennies, Comte and Durkheim] have – for the most part unintentionally and unconsciously – served *to prepare the soil for fascism* by their propagation of the view that the society in which they were living was headed for disaster because of its individualism and liberalism and that a new social solidarity was badly needed. (Ranulf 1939, pp.33–34, my emphasis)

This is unadulterated rubbish. Most critics have treated Ranulf far too gently. Perhaps, after nearly 70 years, it is time to take off the gloves? So, here let me address some issues.

To start with the matter of material influence in cases such as the abetting of evil regimes is something I take very seriously. That is why I have chastised those like David Chidester for tracking down obscure and remote figures in the study of religion for their allegedly responsibility for legitimising South Africa's apartheid regime, but totally ignoring the massive theological justifications given it by the Dutch Reformed Church or even those academics directly responsible for the official policy (Chidester 1996; Strenski 1995, 1998b, 1998c). There is similarly a world of difference in according responsibility for the Nazi hatred of Jews between the admittedly anti-Semitic Luther and the Nazi *Religionsforscher* (religion researcher) that were given the task of dredging up typically forgotten remarks by Luther for use in the propaganda of the Nazi era – and this after the fact that the Lutheran church historically did not propagate Luther's hatred of Jews. It took the determined work of a Nazi archivist and scholar to dig up the citations from Luther long after they had been sent down the memory hole of embarrassing religious history (Strenski 1995). So when the real villains escape and the easy targets are skewered one gets a little impatient with the moral posturing of those laying claim to great exposés.

In this vein, Ranulf never cites a single instance of any fascist who ever claims to have been so influenced by Durkheim. Instead Ranulf indulges in a kind of impressionistic exercise. That is, he states that one result of the Nazis following of Durkheim's lead was giving the group a certain priority in human affairs. Durkheim was thus, according to him, a "scholarly forerunner of fascism". One wonders why Ranulf failed to consider Moses or Jesus in this light while he was at it. After all, they both had plenty to say about the sacredness of human community. Ranulf does not understand that a critique of individualism can be many things, including a critique of egoism or a selfish utilitarian individualism, as was made by both Durkheim and Jesus. We know how committed Durkheim was to a renovation of liberalism that opened individualism to the social whole from his defence of Dreyfus (Durkheim 1975). There is thus no evidence any such fascist "soil" having been prepared by Durkheim, as Ranulf claims.

Scholarly forerunner of Kemalism?

Not unlike this critique of Durkheimian sociological knowledge as facilitating fascist power is the critque by those who have looked farther afield beyond the boundaries of Europe to its easternmost region, Turkey. In this instance there is substantial evidence of the contribution of Durkheimian knowledge to what has been claimed the fascist power of the corporate state established by Kemal Atatürk. What draws one to this case is that we know that Durkheimian thought directly influenced the formation of the plans for a corporate state by Atatürk. Unlike the alleged relation of Durkheimian thought to western European fascism (á la Ranulf), we are not relying on impressionism, coincidence or formal homologies between Durkheimian knowledge and fascist power. Turkey's corporatism owes direct, explicit and substantial debts to Durkheimian thought, especially as articulated in Durkheim's *The division of labour* and *Professional ethics and civic morals* (Durkheim 1957). Thus, my analysis discards weak readings of Foucault's genealogical approach – interpretations that steer clear of the causal implications of Foucault's approach to the relation of knowledge to power. The issues at hand are those social praxis and not literary analysis. We are not engaged in some sort of hunt for a camel in the clouds. The issues here turn out to be well informed by historical knowledge, unlike many such investigations. There are some real facts available upon which to make historical judgments about influence and causality. We thus find it important to note that Durkheim's ideas about corporations, especially secondary or mediating institutions, were embraced by the influential "young Turk" Ziya Gökalp in the formation of the corporate state planned for the republic by Mustafa Kemal (Parla and Davison 2004; Kubalı 1936; Strenski 2006b). In this sense, the more we focus on precise issues of the nature of the particular Kemalist corporatism to hand, we discern that such a programme for social reconstruction is not really thinkable outside the narrowly solidarist conceptions of society taught by Durkheim. A garden variety sort of organic conception of society would simply not do.

Durkheim: Kemal Atatürk's state philosopher?

While the connection between Durkheimian sociology and colonialism is speculative and his link with western European fascism lacking in material support, no other European thinker was more enthusiastically appropriated by Turkish republican intellectuals than Durkheim. In their attempts to articulate a vision of a modern Turkish nation-state, Durkheim gave them a theoretical blueprint for social reconstruction. But given the dubious reputation of Mustafa Kemal Atatürk's authoritarianism – some even use the term Kemalism to mean a Turkish form of fascism – Durkheim's connection with this regime raises precisely the kinds of questions Foucault has inspired about the connection between knowledge and power. In particular, it is the corporatist political regime that Atatürk sought to set up under the guidance of the Durkheimian corporatist thought that is found in *The division of labour* and *Professional ethics and civic morals* that bears the brunt of such questioning. In this newly born Turkey, the Foucauldian question must be whether it is fair to see Durkheimian social theory as a kind of scholarly forerunner of Kemalism and thus of Turkish fascist corporatism? Further, was Durkheimian corporatism actually operationalised from the blueprints provided in his works, so that he became an actual perpetrator of fascist or fascist-tending corporatism, such as that which some scholars have identified at periods in

Kemalist Turkey's history (Parla and Davison 2004, pp.13, 265ff; Ranulf 1939)?

For Durkheim's part there is no doubt that he meant his meditations on the subjects treated in the works mentioned for practical application. No matter how sketchy Durkheim's plans in *The division of labour in society* and *Professional ethics* may have been, they were intended to guide the reconstruction of societies in the modern age. Charting a middle path between Marxist class-based visions, liberal individualism and fascist corporatist schemes, Durkheim sought to articulate a future shape of society. Resisting the charge that either Durkheim or Atatürk were fascists in any salient sense, recent commentators claim that both men actually laid out the outlines of what has been called a solidarist as opposed to a fascist corporatism (Parla and Davison 2004, p.12). This is not to deny that in the hands of certain segments of the Kemalist party and regime a fascist reading was given to the solidarist scheme of social organisation (Parla and Davison 2004, pp.244, 246, 255–266). But Durkheim's illustration of the corporate society and the original Kemalist plan were solidarist as opposed to fascist. It was an illustration of desiderata for the reconstruction of modern society that called primarily for a harmonious assembly of professional or occupational groupings, independent of the state apparatus (Hawkins 1994). This was no call for a militarised or regimented society.

The charge that Durkheimian corporatism was fascist in nature, then, echoes the related charges of the Swedish sociologist, Svend Ranulf, that Durkheimian societism was guilty of being a "scholarly forerunner" of west European fascism (Lukes 1972, pp.338–371; Ranulf 1939). A similar linkage has been suggested between Durkheimian social thought and fascist versions of Kemalist corporatism (Birtek 1991; Davison 1998, pp.95–99; Heyd 1950, pp.55–57). Moreover, these charges that Durkheimian knowledge facilitated Turkish power – fascism – have been deemed particularly credible in large part because the leading ideologist of Turkish nationalism, Ziya Gökalp (1875–1924), was a devoted Durkheimian and primarily responsible for introducing Durkheimian thought into modern Turkey. Thus, the logic of this connection runs as follows: since Gökalp was the key theorist behind Kemalism, and Kemalism stood for fascist corporatism, we should conclude that Durkheimian knowledge participated in theorising and intellectually legitimising fascist power in the form of a political order (Parla and Davison 2004). The main question that needs to be analysed is the justice of the charges that Durkheimian knowledge – either as interpreted by Gökalp, or as directly conveyed by Durkheim – could in practice be linked to fascist corporatism.

Durkheimian solidarist corporatism and civil society

Aside from any of these or other considerations, one reason for doubting the justice of the characterisation of Turkish Durkheimianism as fascist corporatism, at the very least, is the place of Durkheim's corporatist thought as articulated in *The division of labour* and *professional ethics and civic morals* in theorising the diametrically opposed political social formation known widely as civil society. Taking Durkheimian thought along this opposite political axis, other commentators have seen *Professional ethics and civic morals* as anti-totalitarian in its articulation of the social conditions standing in the way of such staples of the fascist programme, namely statism (Emirbayer 1996a, 1996b, 2003; Kumar 1993). The Durkheim of *Professional ethics* articulates the view that nothing less than the "associational relations of civil life" – lies between the state, the capitalist economy and the individual, "the intermediate domains of social life", as stated by Mustafa Emirbayer (1996b, p.112).

In a work of the same genre, Emirbayer believes that Durkheim's *Evolution of educational thought* celebrates the way pedagogical theories of the humanists, along with the break-up of monolithic Christianity produced, a "'movement toward individualism and differentiation'" (Emirbayer 1996a, p.273 citing Durkheim 1977, p.171). Emirbayer celebrates precisely the anti-statist features of Durkheim's thought; the rise of free thought and the cult of the individual: those movements that "emboldened rising social groups to press their right to deviate from existing beliefs" (Emirbayer 1996a, p.273). J. M. Hawkins, a long-time student of

Durkheim and politics, also brings highlights the way the Durkheim of *Professional ethics* emphasises the nature of occupational and professional groups as a means not only to discipline an unruly egoism but also to clear a political and moral space independent of the state in which individuals could be nurtured in default of the weakening of family ties in industrial society (Hawkins 1994, pp.474–476). Although he never demonises the state, neither does Durkheim indulge a mystique of the state (Davy 1950, p.xxxix). Rather, he seeks to "devise intermediaries between individuals and the rest of society. ... The state must have a relation to the nation without being absorbed in it and therefore they must not be in immediate contact. The only means of preventing a lesser force from falling within the orbit of a stronger is to intercalate between the two, some resistant bodies which will temper the action that has the greater force" (Durkheim 1957, p.101). Again, the question of justifying these characterisations of Durkheimian thinking about professional and occupational groups as facilitating the creation and sustenance of civil society must be addressed.

Continuing on my concern with real violence, in light of the real intellectual causes of various regimes of violence, we need finally to ask how Durkheim was read by the Turks. We do not want to repeat the errors of a Ranulf by remaining solely at the textual level. We need to inquire about the actual influence of Durkheim's solidarist corporatism in Turkey, not how the abstract schemes laid out in his writing might seem to be similar to other schemes in Turkish politics. Thus, while these theoretical discussions of Durkheimian corporatism make for interesting analyses of Durkheimian texts, they are of no assistance in considering whether or not the anti-fascist principles of civil society were ever either implemented in the way the fascist ones are claimed to have been, or even whether these more liberal readings of Durkheim attracted any practical following in Turkey. Is the liberal or solidarist reading of Durkheim's corporatism nothing more than a hopeful idea without any actual application to the real Turkish state? In the present discussion, I shall argue that besides the Durkheimian thought of Ziya Gökalp and those in Kemalist Turkey leaning in the direction of fascist corporate society are those who read Durkheim (or at least certain texts of Durkheim) to support a notion of solidarist corporatism typical of civil society proponents. The thought of Hüseyin Nail Kubalı and his publication in Kemalist Turkey of Durkheim's *Leçons de sociologie physique des moeurs et du droit*, in particular, demonstrates that, at least in highly placed quarters of the Turkish Durkheimian intelligentsia and political leadership, an anti-fascist re-appropriation of Durkheimian thought was well under way.

Hüseyin Nail Kubalı and Turkish Durkheimian liberalism

Hüseyin Nail Kubalı provides continuity as well as a deepening understanding of what a Durkheimian corporate construction of a democratic culture would entail. In 1936, Kubalı wrote his doctoral dissertation on the Durkheimians and their contributions to the idea of the state compared with those of the French right wing, accused by the likes of a Ranulf of forming the intellectual basis for fascism. Kubalı's thesis, *L'idée de l'état chez les précurseurs de l'école sociologique français* (1936), refutes such claims. It sought to compare the theories of the state of those thinkers commonly cited as precursors of Durkheimian sociological thought with what was actually said by the Durkheimians. Kubalı's thesis epitomises the work of a man who would later stand up for the rule of law and for the independence of the social groups making up civil society when such values were not altogether favoured by the regime. In the contemporary Turkey of the mid-1930's, Kubalı laments the way the governmental administration takes "initiative" and exercises 'extensive use of ... general power'" in political affairs, "where stability takes precedence over any other considerations" (Kubalı 1936, pp.304, 305). Kubalı specifically celebrates Montesquieu's notion of what would become Durkheimian mediating institutions – his "judicious conception of intermediary bodies – to which the Durkheimian School attaches such capital importance" (Kubalı 1936, p.256). Citing Georges Gurvitch, a contemporary French sociologist independent of the Durkheimian camp, Kubalı affirms the "particular value and importance for

today" of the Saint-Simonian ideas of juridical pluralism whereby "'different juridical orders limit themselves reciprocally in their independent collaboration on the basis of equality in national life as well as internationally'" (Gurvitch 1931, p.14; Kubalı 1936, p.262).

With regards to statism, Kubalı argues that the statisms of the eighteenth and nineteenth centuries must be distinguished, both from each other and from Durkheimian thought, however indebted the Durkheimians may be to any of the thinkers one might call "statist". Kubalı's analysis has the effect of defending the statist thinkers of the eighteenth century. He concludes that the statism of the Enlightenment was "conceived to safeguard the individual", much as he might have thought the interventionist actions of the US federal government were to be in ending racial discrimination (Kubalı 1936, p.255). Kubalı asserts it was this kind of statism that was "transmitted to the Durkheimian School" (Kubalı 1936, p.256). Of the nineteenth century statists, Kubalı paints a picture of irrationalism and mystagoguery. They were concerned with hierarchy and submission, seeking a return to a static order reminiscent of the European Middle Ages (Kubalı 1936, p.259). In the end, Kubalı concludes that despite the debts Durkheimian thought had to the nineteenth century past, it "took an independent attitude" toward politics. Seeking to disengage Durkheimian thought from politics completely, Kubalı takes a pragmatic view of politics. Durkheimian sociology should not be used to support any ultimate "'metaphysical' or ideological 'system', but should be seen to be sociology and nothing but" (Kubalı 1936, p.265).

Thus, when we look closely at a case where Durkheimian social thought is explicitly adopted for the purposes of social reconstruction, we find that it aids the forces of moderation and democratic empowerment, rather than what most would recognise as a real regime of violence, the extreme right-wing of Kemalism.

Concluding remarks

To conclude, I hope that I have shown how careful we need to be in leaping from some sort of knowledge to a regime of power or violence. This is true whether one is positing an actual, causal link, as I have sought to do, or whether one is citing what a genealogy in the sprit of Foucault would do in referring to that "which conditions, limits and institutionalises discursive formations" (Foucault 1984, p.104). I think we can do much more than Foucault and his followers are prepared to do. I believe that in sifting through the several cases we might expect to find definite positive links between Durkheimian knowledge and various regimes of violence. I have turned up a wide range of relatively conclusive and inconclusive results. There is simply too much that we do not and cannot know even though there are some cases, such as that of modern Turkey, where we can know a great deal. For example, in the case of a link between Durkheimian Third Republic liberalism and the burst of colonial activity sponsored by Durkheimians' liberal fellow-travellers in the *Parti radical*, we find tantalising hints of a possible connection Durkheimian thought might have had with the facilitation of the French imperial enterprise at the end of the nineteenth century. But there is simply not enough evidence to go very far with this probe. Perhaps thinkers of a different stripe might attempt some sort of Foucauldian genealogy here? These efforts can quickly degenerate into little better than hunting down camels in clouds, especially since we both lack the knowledge and prospects of ever finding any, with respect to Durkheim's facilitation of fascism, as claimed by Svend Ranulf. The Swedish scholar's brand of inquiry – "guilt by analogy" – his own version of seeing camels in clouds – is little better than a smear tactic, since it tars the reputations of thinkers without employing a methodology capable of achieving a conviction. I, at least, want to know about real influences of Durkheimian knowledge upon the formation of real fascism and not whether one might see a fascist camel in a Durkheimian cloud – even if it is packaged as a fashionable Foucauldian genealogy. More intriguing are the questions raised about the implications of Durkheimian attitudes toward classroom discipline (and punishment) and the fate of the sacrificial victim. There, one could at least make a case that Durkheis had

blind areas in his vision – blind as to the actual efficacy, for example, of the harsh regimes of discipline that he felt were required for maintaining social flourishing. Indeed, Durkheim's notoriously rebellious nephew, Marcel Mauss, and his complaints about his uncle's excessively strict regimen tell us at least something about the wisdom of the degree of Durkheim's devotion to discipline (Clifford 1988). But, if alongside the case of school discipline we put Durkheim's possible attitudes toward suicide, then we can at least see how Durkheim's concern for the integrity of the social whole has served him as a guide through difficult terrain. After all, life is hard and is not to be treated as trifling. Perhaps being a little harder on the young, like intervening even forcefully with a potential suicide, is not such a bad thing after all. Again, an overriding practical concern to enable social flourishing seems to mark Durkheim's attitudes.

Harder to rationalise, however, is the Durkheimian neglect of the fate of the mediating sacrificial victim. We might pause to ponder the relative insensitivity to its/his/her fate by the Durkheimians. I have written about this as a symptom of Durkheim's bourgeois mentality and still feel that critics of the Durkheimians here, including René Girard, have at least a case to make against their apparent insensitivity to what otherwise might be called scapegoating (Strenski 1998a). Yet, as unattractive as this lack of attention for the victim is in Durkheimian thought, I suggest we must return to what I have claimed is something of an overall principle guiding Durkheimian thinking, namely their pursuit of "change only for the benefit of society as a whole"; their hard-headed, tough-minded and thus practical concern for human flourishing. We would all like to believe the brighter view that society is possible without sacrifice, including without the victimisation of any individual or group. Without committing myself to such a view, what if society is not possible without sacrifice? What next? One answer is that the Durkheimians, in their insensitivity, look a lot more practical and ultimately humane in their commitment to doing what is necessary for human flourishing.

Note

1. Here readers will benefit from discussion of the Durkheimian relation to Marx, Georges Sorel and the revolutionary violence of anarchy-syndicalism, as so admirably treated by Josep Llobera or John Stanley. One might also look at Durkheim's preference for progressive change over (violent) revolution which has been well-exposed by Steven Lukes some decades ago.

Festival, vacation, war: Roger Caillois and the politics of paroxysm

S. Romi Mukherjee

Introduction: from effervescence to paroxysm

The oeuvre of Roger Caillois casts a long shadow over both French literary and intellectual history. A mandarin of sorts, Caillois's concerns traversed the worlds of literature, philosophy, comparative mythology, mineralogy, zoology and sociology. A student of both Marcel Mauss and Georges Dumézil and a one-time frequenter of both René Daumal's mystico-surrealist group *Le Grand Jeu* and Surrealist circles themselves, he was at once a graduate of the prestigious *Ecole normale supérieure*, a student of the history of religions and a member of the avant-garde. Moreover, in the highly charged political context of 1930s France, his studies in meta-political mytho-politics cast him as a nonconformist, while the equivocation, provocation and severity of his early works equally positioned him in the interstices of the burgeoning *ni gauche, ni droite*, which searched for new paradigms for thinking the political. Caillois, like many of his generation, was traumatised by the fall, in 1937, of Leon Blum and the Popular Front, elected earlier in 1936, reproaching them for their inability to both wield the pontifical power and *mana* of Saint-Just and transform themselves into an effective combat unit. Democracy simply had no authority. A classical anti-authoritarian revolution would thus be futile; it was necessary to revolt in the name of a greater authority.

Caillois was therefore typical of a generation of disabused militant intellectuals who

S. Romi Mukherjee teaches political theory and the history of religions at the *Institut d'Études Politiques de Paris* and the University of Chicago Paris Center. He is also Secretary-General of the *French Society of Durkheimian Studies*. Email: romi.mukherjee@sciences-po.org

extended the political into the mystical and engaged the sacred and sacred power as the only authentic foundations for the political. Understanding religious affectivity to be the most potent of sensations, he theorised political life as a religious, spiritual and sacred construct, a participation in the mythic and the channelled and directed unleashing of the orgiastic and the ecstatic. Like many other anti-modern reactionaries, revolutionaries and revelationists, Caillois attempted to unveil a new horizon of political and social theory rooted firmly in the affective and the instinctual and did so in the interstices of religion and politics, from where, as Sternhell has noted, emerged one of the most fatal critiques of democracy, socialism, liberalism, positivism and Marxism: the liberal heresy (Sternhell 1995, p.214).

In 1937 these universes would all collide in the decidedly post-Durkheimian experiment that was the *Collège de Sociologie* (1937–1939). Co-founded by Caillois, Georges Bataille, Jules Monnerot and Michel Leiris, the *Collège* understood itself to be conducting Durkheimian and Maussian sociology while perverting and transforming it through uneasy interpolations of, among others, Nietzsche, Dumézil, Sorel, Pareto and Baudelaire. By *Collège*, they understood a sect, an order or a secret society rather than a liberal institution. By sacred, they understood the vertiginous limit-experiences of attraction and repulsion that function as the harbingers for the desublimation of negativity and the effacement of bourgeois utilitarianism. By sociology, they understood the study of the manifestations of the sacred in society, but also the active spreading of sacred contagion into the social. The members of the *Collège* refused to wait for the Third Republic's envisaged rational-socialist utopia to take form. They were not of the generation of Dreyfus and, unlike Durkheim and his collaborators, did not feel the slightest amount of gratitude towards the Republic and nor enchantment with its utopian dreams. They were not Jewish defenders of the secular society but lapsed Catholics who had come of age in the ashes (Caillois, in fact, was raised in the post-war rubble of Reims) of the Great War.[1] What emerged was a Durkheimianism against itself, a Durkheimianism reforged as a critique of the Third Republic the centrist-leftism that Durkheim and his colleagues ceaselessly defended. The rules of sociological method could no longer be strictly applied as the object and the stakes of sociology had shifted: the sociology of the sacred was now a sacred sociology. It was against this backdrop that Caillois and his interlocutors began rethinking the political question in terms of a spiritual crisis, divirilisation, devitalisation and ill-health.

Due in part to the influence of evolutionism and biologism as well as to the throngs of mutilated soldiers on Paris streets, interwar France was occupied with the larger question of social health. The body in question also reflected a shifting set of social and epistemological conditions and collapsed the distinction between the external and material origins of power and the isolated body that is acted upon by power. Rather, the political and bodily were considered to be necessarily entwined. This is the site of what Kam Shapiro calls political somatics, a reciprocal chiasma where "not only are politics somatically invested but somatics are politically invested" (Shapiro 2003, p.2). The somatic is the ground of total social fact where health, politics, ritual, ethics and excess all collide and collude. The political somatic is the point of dialectical mirroring where the isolated physical body refracts and reflects upon the abstract social body; a point where ideological production thrives through both discipline and fantasy; where symbolic life is inscribed upon the body and respectively generated and challenged by it.

The Durkheimian socialist body was a robust and vibrant form constituted by holism, integrity and responsibility. The smooth dialectic of the individual will and the collective will was further assured by a morality that emerged from bodily feeling, galvanizing the individual with the social and its symbolic order:

In other words, the human body conceals in its depth a sacred principle that erupts onto the surface in particular circumstances. This principle is not different in kind from the one that gives the totem its religious character. (Durkheim 1995, p.138)

In locating the body at the centre of the nexus of the social-sacred-symbolic, Durkheim suggested that health was not simply a physiological category but a condition deeply embedded in the vitality of social, economic and representational orders.[2] But as the inter-war years progressed and the ambiance shifted from what Winock and Azéma (1976) call *L'âge d'or* (1880–1918) to *Le decline et la chute* (1919–1940), the Durkheimian body was also recoded, if not entirely superseded. While the Durkheimian somatic order was regenerated by moments of collective effervescence by 1938, Caillois was calling for total paroxysm.

Caillois was gesturing towards a visceral political ontology that underscored the interaction between the social, the bodily and the natural. Far from being purely anthropocentric, such a political ontology sought to realign social and political practices with the excesses of physical and natural life, both spaces of radical non-linguistic negativity. In other words, social and political processes, as embodied, could never fully resolve the antinomies of the *homo duplex* and were themselves equally torn in two; the social duplex and the political duplex obeyed the same laws of energy flow as nature and the human body, where energy is cyclically accumulated and expended. Social harmony is corporal in the human organism in so far as it can only be maintained through occasional periods of dissolution, release and purging. It is governed by the same principles of tension, discharge, equilibrium and seizure that guide the body. Between the rhythms of accumulation and expenditure lies an interval, a moment of stasis and meta-death. Collective meta-death was located in the mass desublimation that was the festival.

As a paroxysm that ensured future equilibrium, the bodies that entangled themselves during the festival revealed that the body itself is not political, but rather that politics is bodily. The question posed by the various theorists of festival in the 1930s was whether civilisation's preservation and stability depended not only on the tempering of appetites, but also on the regular revenge of these appetites on civilisation itself. But this is always a matter of degree: as a spatial, temporal, bodily and psychic event the festival finds itself spread along a continuum between the reinforcement of society and the symbolic order and pure subversion: a continuum that traverses the spectrum between effervescence and paroxysm.

The trajectory from Durkheim's 1914 model of effervescence to Caillois' 1938 theory of festival as paroxysm is a radical crescendo from salve to seizure, from champagne giddiness to beer brawls, from the pleasure of being with others to unstoppable agôn. This projected mutation of the social body was, more importantly, a passage from the useful and the preservative/conservative (temporary formlessness in the service of form) to the useless and the destructive. Socialist Eros was besieged by nonconformist Thanatos (the overdetermination of the annihilation of all form, the cleansing and spiritual dimensions of violence). Effervescence served to parry the shocks of civilisation and ward off the grip of anomie. Caillois' paroxysm, on the contrary, was a shock to the system that further demonstrated that as the 1930s wore on the social body required a more violent convulsion to be thrust out of torpor. And within this miasma of bodies and political somatics the festival functioned as both a prescription and an object of nostalgia and wistful lament. Insisting on the continuum between the archaic and the modern, Caillois struggled with the question of festival's disappearance from modern life. The interwar years would come to close with Caillois' fatal question: is war the black festival of modernity?

The social against society

Between 1938 and 1939 Caillois devoted himself to composing what would be the culmination of the Durkheimian tradition, the Dumézilian world-view and everything in between, a culmination that, in many ways, would function as

something of a crescendo. According to Claudine Frank, Caillois' *L'homme et le sacré* (1939) was less an attempt to systematise and synthesise the various strands of the Durkheimian theory of the sacred, than "an osmotic or theoretical absorption of the greatest post-Enlightenment residual of all", the sacred (Frank 1991, p.366). However, *L'Homme et le sacré* also signalled a definitive end to Durkheimian and Republican optimism. In 1938 Caillois not only apprehended the failure of the Enlightenment project but was forced to be reconciled with a civilisation that had nothing left to offer and a social that loomed only as a shadow and fetish. What was left and what was inevitable was war. But Caillois' strategy was not purely reactionary. While harkening back to the archaic and the foregone vibrancy of the Saturnalia, he understood that was too late for any return to the past. The waning of civilisation and the perceived untenability of Enlightenment ideals, nonetheless, produced the possibility of an overcoming that would necessitate the surpassing of hitherto naturalised epistemological, social and bodily categories that were too readily taken for granted. Society was growing old and weary; the oscillation between the sacred and the profane had to be rendered more dynamic, explosive and cutting.

Phlegmatic and incapable of being moved, the social had become a black hole of non-sacred and non-ecstatic, anomic depersonalisation; the *ordo rerum* of concentration and dispersion had simply been effaced by a purely homogenised order of things that did not tolerate the introduction of alterity. The Durkheimian dialectic of the effervescent and the orderly, of the ecstatic and the mundane, had thus been trampled by the established disorder of democratic regimes, frivolity in the face of the apocalypse and the vacation as vacancy; there was indeed "nothing durable, nothing solid, *no basis*" (Hollier 1995, p.9). Durkheimian appeals to the social and effervescent longings were of little help; all was razed, empty.

Hence, Caillois, the sociologist-diagnostician of civilisation, had to outbid Durkheimian sociology and politics itself and in rethinking the maladies of the social body he radically revised Durkheim's theory of effervescence. Caillois would push Durkheim to his limit and amplify the effervescent overflowing that the Republican moralist had once associated with *la fête républicaine.* In the waning days of the Republic Caillois' vision of the festival would not be a simple aggregation of social energies or champagne folly, but an epileptic seizure that would overcome Durkheim as well. Caillois was not simply interested in the social, but mad for the social in the same way that others were mad for God (Hollier, 1995, p.7), in the same way that others are mad for what exceeds and will always exceed them; the mad non-conformist, disdainful of the mass, longing for the social while eternally proclaiming his own anarchic/elitist singularity, was forced to go beyond the divisions erected between sociology, the sacred and the political.

The virtues of licence

At the College of Sociology on 2 May 1939 Caillois presented his "Theory of the festival", a chapter from the forthcoming *L'homme et le sacré*. He gained much from his rapport with Jean Marx, who had originally demonstrated the importance of festivals as well as the mythical status of kings and heroes in the constitution and conservation of France (Felgine 1994, p.99). The text remains a landmark and is readily acknowledged as a pioneering study of the festive, the carnivalesque and the ecstatic. Its force lies in its rendition of the festival as not simply a rite or event but as a psychic and political somatic site where total social facts articulate themselves. In other words, as François-André Isambert suggests, Caillois' study signifies "the passage from an image to a theory of the festival" (Isambert 1982, p.126).

The first outline of the theory, "*Fêtes ou la vertu de la license*", had appeared in *Verve* in the winter of 1938. The political somatic question was ultimately an issue of *vir*ility and *vir*tue that were synonymous with social cohesion. The apogee of cohesion, the foundation for health, was experienced not only in the suspension of the real but in the suspension of parliamentary democracy itself. Caillois denounced the bourgeois logic of accumulation and calculation and their political twins, the parliamentary paradigm and juridical reason. Underneath capitalist cultures of life (dieting, health, fitness, staying young, hoarding resources and time and so on), underneath the logic of accumulation and underneath religious doctrines of salvation and

immortality resides a paradox. According to Caillois, social, psychic, capitalist and religious paradigms of preservation are all actually models of decay that disavow the life force. Following Nietzsche's "yes", Caillois insists that vitality depends on explosiveness and wanes when constrained by consistency and accumulative logic. In other words, the body does not profit from conserving energies, but from expending and accumulating anew:

Excess takes place at the moment of regeneration ... in a critical phase, where the existence of society and the world vacillates and must be recreated by the influx of young and excessive vigour. (Caillois 1992, p.47)

The late 1930s represented just such a critical phase and Caillois, then all of 25 years old, was determined that society should not vacillate towards increased listlessness but regenerate itself with a shot of the virile that would, in inflicting excess, reveal the way to cosmic and collective cohesion. Society's energetic surplus demands licence, not more goods. The fecundation of the universe is an orgiastic act where humans, like the gods, must expend something of their vitality in the name of future prosperity. The crisis of civilisation was partially the result of a psycho-social error: a society comprised of paradigms that conserved without creating or re-creating. Extinction and entropy were the inevitable consequences of the life-preserving instinct, one that failed to recognise that the essence of the life force was embedded in the shivaic call to ritualised moments of creative destruction. In such moments society disavows its nature and in attempting to technologically master the universe, it disobeys the natural trajectory of expenditure to which it is inextricably bound. Social bodies must resolve the accumulation of tension; their inability to do so results in a fatal abundance.

Paroxysm and transgression

By 1939 the hallowed days of Durkheimian effervescence were long gone and many began to ask "Is another invasion possible"? (Weber 1994, p.248). The relief with which the French greeted the Munich Accords in September 1938 soon gave way to trembling. Caillois would come to reframe the virtues of licence in explicitly somatic terms. The festival was a paroxysm of the social body, the necessary seizure that would render it capable of withstanding the seizures of modernity through ritual purging/creation; epilepsy as imperative. In its clinical derivation, a paroxysm is a spasm or convulsion that afflicts the organism or body; it is a break or rupture in bodily equilibrium and regulatory functioning, a sudden seism in the constitution of life-preserving forces. A paroxysm is a moment where the body finds itself in excess or hyperbole. For instance, epilepsy, stroke and infantile gratification disorder are all grouped under the rubric of a paroxysmal attack.[3] Paroxysmal attacks, albeit violent, nonetheless purge the body and serve to restore it to equilibrium:

In its most complete form, in fact, the festival must be defined as the paroxysm of society, which it simultaneously purifies and renews. It is its culmination not simply from a religious point of view but also from an economic point of view. ... Festivals appear everywhere, no matter how differently they are pictured and whether altogether in one season or spread out during the course of the year to fulfil a similar function. They constitute a break in the obligation to work, a deliverance from the limitations and constraints of the human condition: it is the moment in which myth and dream are lived. One exists in a time and in a condition in which one's obligation is to use things up and spend oneself. Motives of acquisition are no longer acceptable; one must waste and everyone outdoes the other in his squandering of gold, his provisions, his sexual or muscular energy. (Caillois 1939, p.301)

The paroxysm is a break, a suspension and the ascent of a mythical space of ritualised inversion and total potlatch (economic, bodily and discursive). It is not a challenge to reason or an infraction of the law of the father but rather the natural corollary of all systems that aspire towards coherence, a corollary that Caillois understood modernity to disavow. It is the hyperbolic introduction of dissymmetry into stability (Laserra 1992, p.206). Hence, it breaks the processes of natural regulation that the body suffers; the paroxysm is the climactic interval that precedes the reintroduction of homeostasis and bodily regulation. In this interval is found not only the asymmetric but also the improbable. Any given system's survival depends on its capacity to withstand and integrate such improbability, which for Caillois meant the sacred of transgression, disorder, the uncon-

scious, the fantastic, the excessive, the demonic and the monstrous. The paroxysm is the infliction of vertigo into homeostatic orders that are all too sure of themselves. Through the symbolic actualisation of violence, it exorcises the violence that civilisation itself performs on consciousness; between civilisation and barbarism lies the paroxysmic eruption of the festival.

A rapprochement with the turbulence of the natural, the festival calls into question democracy and capitalism, the very foundations of civilisation, and thus functions as a critical threshold that dismantles the vectors of constancy, will, preservation and the human project only to recreate them anew. In other words, the will to accumulate and conserve are lodged in the impasse of civilisation; accountability, exchange and the desire for permanence negate the will to explosion, the catastrophic impulse that constitutes our common substrate with nature (that cannot, of course, be held accountable). The frustrations of instrumental reason and the human as tool can only be reduced with prodigality. I cease to be an object when I cease to be a subjectivity objectivised in market economies; I cease to be an object when I become something other than human, something wrested from the conditions of nature, its undulations and constraints. I am no longer exchangeable or bound by contractual relations. Therefore, unlike the inner workings of effervescence, the paroxysm does not construct a subject through whom the social speaks; it is not the world that speaks through me in the paroxysmic moment as the construction of the "I" and society itself overcome. Agency (the political agency of the individual or that of the transcendent social's interdictions) is simply eschewed and replaced by a zero-state. The sacred of transgression, paradoxically, liquidates all dualisms within its confines. We cannot ascribe to chaos the same parameters of agency with which we would embody the human. Therefore, it is not simply question of pinning expenditure against utility or transgression against taboo; inside the sacred of transgression these abstractions are surpassed. In other words, following Caillois, there is something non-human about the festival, something that fundamentally dissolves or purports to dissolve the physical, semiotic, economic and intellectual scaffolding of Being. And it is this that is often referred to as the sacred.

For all of its non-intrumentalism, the paroxysm is functional not because of its capacity to regenerate coherence but because, in forcing collision between society and the improbable or the negative, it injects alterity into the universe, an irresolvable tension that can only serve to create value. The paroxysm is a protest against the perceived spiritual stasis of democratic regimes, the metaphysical stasis of too much coherence that arises from the supposed resolution of contradiction that these states announce. The end of history, as a definitive end to contradiction, therefore produces a vigourless coherence that has forsaken the art of tension. The paroxysmic therefore illustrates how value emerges from states of antagonism and therefore also protests against the homogenising field of capitalism and the liberal lack of restraint that prefer consensus at all costs, absorption and facile third ways. In the early moments of what we now call late capitalism, Caillois was concerned about how democracy produced its own unending festival, but one that was stripped of the force of the sacred/profane binary and recuperated. The call for paroxysm is a plea for agôn in the social, a plea for dissonance against a field of absolute relativism and homogenised difference. The Cailloisian lexicon of rigour, severity, orthodoxy and paroxysm is part and parcel of a larger theoretical enterprise that operates as a virulent riposte against modernity's attempts to absorb all antagonism, to level the contradictions and roughness that are the necessary components of the regeneration of value and values.

The inexorability of the sacred and the profane, of the paroxysm and civilisation, are rhetorical means of deploying difference, alterity and untenable contradiction into a homogenising social field; the sacred as negativity, as radical heterogeneity. The non-human nature of the festival as paroxysm is a radical challenge to social slackening and to the world of reified exchange. It is the rebirth of monsters or the festive that becomes a monster within a society that needs to be scared; a trauma that heals.

Urzeit: once upon a time

It is the calculus of excess that ensures the ultimate success of the festival and its revitalising force (Caillois 1939, p.284). Excess does not comprehend democracy and is uneasy with accord, negotiations and order, but it is not autonomous from them either. In returning order to disorder, a differentiating consciousness to a consciousness that apprehends the cohesive melding substance of the primeval, the festival subverts the artificial axes that form quotidian life. Order and accumulation are also the accumulations of waste. And the body and consciousness that differentiate and engage in a ceaseless taxonomy of the world and sensation also wear down. The social body and the social psyche too must dispose of waste:

> The very health of the human body requires the regular evacuation of its impurities . . . in the end age weakens and paralyzes the body. In the same way, nature passes through a cycle of growth and decline. Social institutions seem not to be exempt from this alternation. They too must be periodically regenerated and purified of the poisonous wastes that represent the harmful part left behind by every act performed for the good of the community and this involves some pollution of the one who assumes responsibility for this regeneration. (Caillois 1939, p.284)

Following Caillois, civilisation's malaise emerges from its incapacity to eliminate and recognise the waste that an ordered world produces; social processes leave behind dangerous residues with every policy, pact and parliament; residues that, like sins, must be expiated. The negativity of the social must be ritually confronted and the dark spot that haunts every moment of daily life (impinging death, violence, trauma, faeces, urine, guilt, the crimes of our ancestors, the tragic, anxiety) has to be expelled.

Moreover, sociologists and anthropologists from Robert Hertz to Mary Douglas have demonstrated the analogy between waste, abjection and sin and how processes of expiation serve to re-establish and recalibrate social order (Douglas 1966; Hertz 1909). However, the paradigm is not simply organic or bodily. Following Goya, reason produces monsters, just as democracy is constantly flanked by the totalitarian urge, the anarchist insurrection and the socialist desire. In other words, any given epistemological, bodily, or political system, must find a means of confronting that which exceeds and outbids it. Residues of the negative are not individual affairs or solely ensconced in the atomised and agonized psyche; negativity is a social phenomenon that touches directly on the natural dimensions of human life that civilisation pushes against. Embracing negativity and sin in order to expiate them also entails a return to the primeval, primordial chaos and non-differentiation.

The elimination of the slag that every organism accumulates in its functioning, the annual liquidation of sins and the expulsion of the old year are not enough. They serve only to bury a crumbling and encrusted past that has had its day and that must give way to a virgin world whose advent the festival is destined to hasten. Prohibitions have proven powerless to maintain the integrity of nature and society so there is all the more reason that these prohibitions cannot make nature and society as young as they used to be. Nothing in rules makes them capable of reviving this integrity. It is necessary to invoke the creative power of the gods and go back to the beginning of the world, turning to the forces that transformed chaos into cosmos (Caillois 1939, p.285).

Reform of the system thus proves useless when the system has had its day. In 1939 it was too late; the entire political apparatus, its juridical frames, normative reasoning and assumptions had to be desecrated through the violent union with the sacred, which is "essentially negative" (Caillois 1939, p.283). The prohibition, the law and the various ethical and social contracts that found liberal-democratic systems, for Caillois, simply allude to the existence of the negative on the outside, but remain circumscribed within the limit of bourgeois reason. Simultaneously, the waste of the inside that forms internal negativity is not expiated or engaged. Any society that is thus understood as a simple legal aggregation that defines its citizens in strictly juridical terms while potentially procuring various rights for its members, refuses the super-contractual bond that it and its members share with nature. The social contract refuses integrity and constructs a subjectivity that is unappeased, unpurged, ageing and encrusting, unable to be born again.

Yet it should be emphasised that the scholarly category of the primeval is always a secondary ideological code, an explanation that comes after the fact and one that is replete with a series of political and metaphysical implications that Caillois failed to notice. As Isambert rightly

notes, the scholarly recoding of the leitmotif of festival/regeneration/the primeval itself constructs mythical narratives of a pre-sociological point of origin that precedes the fall into modernity; the primeval is "the myth of the myth of primordial chaos" (Isambert 1982, p.133). Modernity's crises are thus turned into narratives in the pseudo-theological frames of fall, decline, decay and impending apocalypse. On the one hand, the primeval is a scholarly myth used to account for the mythic temporal frame of the festival, the return to primordial chaos. On the other hand, the status of the myth of origins in scholarly accounts betrays a series of other real anxieties that are inherently associated with the perceived threat of the Other or others. This projection ultimately has no real meaning but erects a hierarchical temporal mytheme that contrasts a pure point of essence with an impure point of corruption. If the primeval is the One in so far it is a state of pure undifferentiated chaos, then the decline is the multiple and the differentiated. A series of perverse political, racial, biological and hierarchical meta-narratives may be easily developed here. Eternity, whether configured as point of origin or point of demise, often has a series of pernicious intellectual consequences; the rage for reconciliation and a rage against those deemed irreconcilable.

But unlike in the writings of his mentor Dumézil and unlike Eliade's post-war *Myth of the Eternal Return* (where Eliade also admits his own debt to Caillois' work), Caillois' primeval was not a point of biological, spiritual or metaphysical authenticity but was formed as a discursive mechanism with which to acerbically criticise the inevitable implosion of the myth of progress, positivism and the Republic. The critique of the present necessarily requires the construction of a messianic future or a past Golden Age. In both cases, one is nostalgic for what has never been experienced; nostalgic for an elsewhere. What the mythic and messianic forms of critique thus overlook is simply the necessity of the critique of things themselves, the way they are.

In contrast, the primeval is purely virtual and the "festival presents itself, in fact, as an *actualization* of the early stages of universe" (Caillois 1939, p.285). But while one may be tempted to think of this as an actualisation of a simulation, an imagined enactment of group fantasy it is not merely the mimesis of an empty event. Rather, in a variation on Deleuze (who would reject the category of the possible as a philosophically coherent notion) one could posit that both the actual and the virtual are both real in so far as they can both be registered on the plane of sensation and that the virtual is, more importantly, the very condition for the actual. The virtual is potentiality revealed in empirical facts and hence, as Deleuze writes, what we call the noumenal character of the presents finds itself "constituted by the relations of virtual coexistence between levels of a pure past, each present being no more than the actualisation or realisation of one of these levels" (Deleuze 2001, p.83). Therefore, both the *sui generis* and external nature of social facts (as things that simply are) are not necessarily divorced from the play of the actual and the virtual and, in Caillois' neo/post-Durkheimianism, the social fact may be apprehended by the science of sociology, but the laws that it follows are of phenomenon (and Durkheim was always something of a neo-Kantian). The festival demonstrates the dynamic intersection of potentiality and things and also that of the phenomenal and the socio-material. And while Deleuze may not have thinking about festivals, his theses on the virtual have significance in this context; he also suggests that "the virtual must be defined as strictly part of the real object – as though the object had one part of itself in the virtual into which it plunged *as though* into an objective dimension" (Deleuze 2001, p.209, my emphasis). The primeval is, perhaps, the spatial and temporal representation of this as the ritualised becoming of the virtual into the real; the primeval was both a time out of time and a space out of space but nonetheless, real. However, reformulating in a more fantastic manner Henri Hubert's theses in his 1909, *Etude sommaire de la representation du temps dans la religion et la magie*, Caillois goes on to suggests that the primeval is, in fact, a neo-Kantian transcendental space:

It is simultaneously set at the beginning and outside of evolution . . . it is no less the present or the future than the past; "it is a state as well as a period". . . . Basically, the mythical time is the origin of the other and continually emerges in it, producing everything disconcerting or inexplicable that arises there. The supernatural is constantly lurking behind what one can perceive and it tends to manifest itself through this medium. The primordial age is described with remarkable unanimity in the most diverse regions. It is the place of metamorphoses, of all miracles. Nothing was yet stabilised, no rules had been pronounced, no forms yet fixed. Things that have become impossible since then, at that time, were possible. Objects moved of their own accord, canoes flew on breezes, men turned into animals and vice versa. Instead of growing old and dying they shed their skins. The whole world was plastic, fluid and inexhaustible. Crops grew spontaneously and flesh grew back on animals as soon as it was cut off. . . . Order cannot, in fact, adapt to the simultaneous existence of all possibilities or the absence of all rules. The world then experiences insurmountable limitations that confined each species inside its proper being and prevented its getting out. Everything was immobilised and what was prohibited was established so that the new organisation and law would not be disturbed. Last, death was introduced into the world . . . with death, cosmos has emerged from chaos. The era of disorder is over, natural history begins, the rule of normal causality is instituted. Unbounded creative activity is succeeded by the vigilance required to keep the created universe in good order. (Caillois 1939, pp.285–286)

The Great Time, also a "Great Space" (Caillois 1939, p.288), is a temporal and psychic configuration of the obverse of civilisation; it is a space of unrestrained becoming, mutation, reversibility, metamorphoses and the fantastic. Caillois' prose, alternating between historical sociological and myth itself, opposes the world of possibility to the world of finitude. The latter is embedded in the nexus of labour/death/time/thingness, which forecloses the unlimited becomings of the primordial age that were buoyed by a thirst for exuberance, surplus, plenum, and more life. In the transition from chaos to cosmos we move from men becoming-animal to men killing animals, from play to dead labour, from cyclical time to linear time and from regular regeneration to a life organised around the moment of its finality. And in these passages, the former term, the space of myth and its festive ritualisation, is effaced and forgotten. Caillois' theory of the festival, on the contrary, asserts that such forgetting poses a social and epistemological danger in so far as the virtual potentiality of the subterranean and the primordial is precisely the precondition for order. That is, the mythic and the festive are necessary frames that are, on one hand, dialectically bound to order, and on the other hand, within and without it in so far they are at once thinkable, but thought as offences to closed order, virtually inscribed in what they exceed.

The supposed transcendence of the sacred and its imagined transcendent nature remain still circumscribed in social conditions of knowledge that thinks an outside from within the inside. No longer lodged in the tensor of festive chaos and order, modern democracies are neither formed nor unformed but are instead somnambulistic, suspended and drifting.

The festival is, hence, the imaginary flight to the outside from within, a ritualisation of chaos becoming cosmos and the paroxysm's waning into detumescence. Within the interval, in this virtual space of unlimited creativity, becoming allows its participants to resolve the dialectic of the individual and the social through a series of virtual performative identifications (becoming animal, becoming hero, becoming sovereign), which serve to exculpate guilt, settle psychic debts and exorcise the anxieties of finitude; "actors mime the deeds and gestures of the hero. They wear masks that identify them with this half-man, half animal" (Caillois 1939, p.289). Temporal and spatial liminality correspond to bodily and identitatarian liminality and these becomings also mirror the never-ending becoming of the universe; it is only at that time that we are wrested from the alienation and reification of modernity and the tragic *entre-deux* of civilisation. All will begin again in the nascent rising of the instant itself.

The regeneration of time is simultaneously the cathartic purging of the dark spot of a human life headed for death; the festival is an alchemical space where the finitude is overcome through social effusion and the theatrical simulation of unconstrained becoming; a real purging as opposed to the ruse of immortality and infinity that characterises the functioning of the market. Ultimately, the festival is the simulation of the psychical, bodily, intellectual fantasy of totality that demonstrates how both order and its paroxysm are artificially cordoned off and closed. But although it is artificial, the acting-out of impossible totality, the simulation of *plenum* is by no means a regression, but rather the only means of not falling prey to atomisation, where individuals replace singularities and difference without difference replaces the alterity introduced by the heterogeneity of the sacred and its paroxysmic agôn.

For Caillois civilisation and really-existing democracies were the point of origin for those

sinister fixed forms that hardened around the social body, an impermeable barrier that stultified vitality and the imaginary. The festival was a means of getting out and getting out begins with the revenge of all that is inadmissible.

However, what Caillois failed to properly underscore was how the mystique of transgression and the allure of the outside mask the fact that the festival remains a means of actually staying in. The co-dependency of order and disorder betray the impossibility of fulfilling the transgression; the refusal of the rule remains inscribed within the rule and the festival remains a manifestation of organicist functionalism and serves to only re-embolden the hardening of the social body in order. And Caillois' central concern was that civilisation had simply become too hard and that what was actually inadmissible was the putting into play of the virtual outside.

The right to abjection

Gandhi's clever manipulation of dress, language, milieu and social code allowed him to be readily perceived as a saviour of all that was low, base and indeed untouchable. In addition to his masterly anti-colonial semiotics, his political manoeuvring also mimed the inversions of the festive. In the Gorakhpur region in 1921, respectable upper-caste people ran the risk of being covered with excreta if they disobeyed Gandhi's commands. The Bakhtinian carnivalesque and the anti-colonial prophet of a liberatory recreation of time merged for one moment.

The festival is therefore not a strictly cosmic or epistemological theatre. Repressed bodily feelings are expressed through sexual licence and the frenzy of the orgiastic; political institutions and power are unmasked as potentially arbitrary constructs, mocked and sent up through satire, corrosive discourse, lewdness and abjection. It is the Rabelaisian plane of bodily fluids and the ribald. Social hierarchy implodes; castes, clans and social strata freely meld into one and class divisions may also be entirely reversed. The festival's capacity to symbolically invert existing social hierarchies and disrupt ossified power relations reveals the political stakes of the social body while also

The Aztec war god, Huitzilopochtli (1550). Coloured lithograph by Jules Desportes from the atlas by Diego Duran in *Historia de las Indias de Nueva Espana*.

serving paradoxically to re-entrench social hierarchy itself in the dual movement of conservation and regeneration.

In the paroxysm, however, purging is not simply a matter of bodily transgression and fluidity, but also an invitation to tear all totems down; those of the real political order and also the psychic order, of the super-ego; it is the locus of the devaluation of values where anything that claims absolute status must be exploded and a rite of reversibility that confounds normative frames of exchange, consumption, delimitation and form.

Form, the domain of the admissible, resists the mutability of the human, the initiatory passage and the frenzy of agonistic expenditure. Against form comes the universal confusion of the festival where "the order of the world is suspended"; "it is important to act against the rules. Everything must be done backwards. In the mythical era the course of time was reversed: One was born old and died a child" (Caillois 1939, p.293). But while the order of the world

may be suspended, the festival, in fact, inverts order and thus remains girded in its logic. It is a space of reversibility and one where corrosive criticism and sacrilege emerge from the same *dispositif*; the ever-increasing dissipation of coherence can be completed only through a total annihilation of all institutional life that depends on a full-on and impossible transgression of the rule; the rule is the absence of rules. However, while inevitably recuperated into the logic of inversion, the festival nonetheless ushers in a fleeting opening or clearing where new forms and values can be built.

Hence, the symbolic sacrifice of the king (the guardian of moderation and rules), the defilement of his body and the robbing of his coffers, open "a kind of efficacious power . . . the principle of disorder and excess that generates the ferment from which a new revived order will be born" (Caillois 1939, p.294). The crumbling of sovereign power is synonymous with the crumbling of kinship, clan and tribe; the real or symbolic death of the king allows the group to kill and eat the totemic animal, break the laws of exogamy and have sexual relations with the wives of the complementary clan (Caillois 1939, p.295). During the festival, a time of forbidden unions, classes and clans commingle along with family members. In the one recension of the Vedic creation myth, Prajapati has sexual relations with his daughter only to be shot down by the arrow of Rudra. Half of Prajapati's seed falls to the ground; during the re-enactment of the origins of the cosmos, myths of incest are ritualised as myths of creation. Sexual licence also extends to the now obligatory orgy; "the orgy of virility occasioned by the festival helps it perform its function simply be encouraging and reviving cosmic forces" (Caillois 1939, p.296). The orgy is the shattering of atomised subjectivity and isolated corporality. Moreover, it possesses a fecundating power and defies the law in so far as it problematises the social coding of man/woman and public/private and challenges the economic nexus of property, exchange and the division of labour. In orgiastic immediacy, bodies enter into formlessness, the non-temporal instant of ecstasy where there are neither rules, nor numbers, but only tactile flows and fluidity. Yet, in problematising social coding, the orgiastic re-establishes the presence of such codings as socially real while critically deconstructing them as unnatural. But the efficacy of the critical faculty of the orgiastic depends precisely on its capacity to carry over into the world of profane order and articulate itself.

Caillois also notes, however, that sexual excess is not the only means of turning the world upside down; "the result also comes from any other excess, any other debauchery" (Caillois 1939, p.296). To the ritual orgy must also be added the excesses of food, drink and discourse. Fertility is born of excess and monstrous ingestion (as opposed to routine and regulated replenishment) and is accompanied by "ruinous competitions for whoever forfeits the most" (Caillois 1939, p.297). He remains relatively silent about the excess of asceticism, but it too must be understood as a both a physical and symbolic inversion and form of potlatch.

During the festival one does not eat for subsistence or savour; the frenzy of potlatch also applies to how much can be ingested and how much alcohol can be consumed before passing out. In such gluttony the body is challenged and

physically sacrificed. Moreover, such a frenzy of ingestion also leads to the problems of digestion; corrosive political discourse is not always verbal and political satire has always depended upon a slippery syntax of burps, farts, saliva, odour, shit, piss and vomit. When in a position of social weakness, a position where your voice cannot be heard nor properly articulated, abjection functions as a convenient language for airing one's grievances; the rhetorical flourish of serious political debate can be equally matched by the non-serious force of throwing shit at the leader, pissing on his image, puking on the First Lady. When this fails one may try to catch him with his pants down or actually pull his pants down. In other words, gesture and matter are set free during the festival, which is "made up not simply of debauches of consumption involving the mouth or sex, but also debauches of expression involving words and deeds. Shouts, mockery, insults, the give-and-take of crude jokes" (Caillois 1939, p.298). Discourse, too, contains the potential for excess and the need to purge itself if its own slag, hitherto bound by normative regimes of signification and etiquette.

The low is permitted to ascend to the high. Untouchables become Brahmans and are worshipped by them. Semen is deposited in forbidden wombs. The slave is elevated to king, the king of chaos, while the real king himself is transformed into a pauper and his wife into a prostitute. In short, social organisation and the tripartite system falls apart as the duties and rules of conduct that constitute social division and organisation are forgotten. But within an instant, the return to normal:

Frenzy is succeeded by work, excess by respect. The *sacred as regulation*, that of prohibition, organises the creation won by the *sacred as infraction* and makes it last. One governs over the normal course of life, the other rules over its paroxysm. (Caillois 1939, p.301)

The profane does not necessarily set apart the sacred. Rather, it is the sacred that regulates the profane. Simultaneously, chiasmas exist and the paroxysm is a creative principle that does not oppose the life of work but surges from within it, revealing the quasi-transcendental dependency between paroxysm and normal life. The political efficacy of the festival is therefore paradoxical. On one hand, the emancipatory force accumulated within the Great Space can be carried over into quotidian life in forms of collective memory and anticipation; the fraternity of classes, the melding of bodies, the binding of clans are assumed to leave an indelible mark on the consciousness of participants that persists in the world of prohibition. Hence, although prohibitions and hierarchical relations are reconstituted in the universe of order they can be potentially rendered more supple after the festival. On the other hand, however, this occurs only through the very problematisation of the distinction between the sacred and the profane. While the sacred and the profane can be said to touch in so far as the chaos of the festival is fed into the constructions of cosmos, Caillois' real concern was the effacement of the distinction and its force in the continuous profane festival of modernity, a consumerist and ludic-liberal space where the risk, energy and vitality of the sacred of transgression had been absorbed and neutralised into an anomic modern *homo festivus*.

Yet Caillois may have been less radical than he imagined himself to be and, as Hollier correctly suggests, Caillois' theory of festival "would bring disorder itself into the principle of order, producing an order capable of disorder . . . reason has to account for its interdictions, for its limits; it has to take into account what it rejects and what rejects it" (Hollier, 1997, p.91). His vision was thus one of an epistemological plane that did not simply democratise the festive, but rather surpassed liberal reason and paradoxically integrated negativity while not scouring it of aura. Democracy must find a means of absorbing its negativity while not profaning it. More importantly, if it is unable to do so it risks being susceptible to the brute oscillation of incompatible terms which, in the case of governments, is that not of the sacred and the profane but war of and peace, democracy and totalitarianism. The radical alterity of the paroxysm is alone capable of surpassing the severity of these various concentrations and dispersions by envisioning, not a dialectical synthesis, but a super-term that may envelope both terms while refusing synthesis. The sacred, nonetheless, remains ambivalent. It is at once a hierarchical principle of alterity that opposes the lack of restraint of democracy and one that forces this profane to absorb all that exceeds it. It is rigid and supple, tumescent and detumescent. Caillois was plead-

ing for a modernity that would re-enter into the oscillations of the sacred of infraction and the sacred of regulation as opposed to disavowing their vertiginous play in the always already profane of bourgeois life, a world where "everything has to go on today just like it did yesterday and tomorrow just like today" (Caillois 1939, p.302). The latter, ironically, continues in the name of progress even though it has eliminated from its body all resistance, alternation and paroxysm. But one wonders if democracy could even withstand the paroxysm Caillois envisioned, one outside the universe of market exchange. One also wonders what would occur the day after the orgy: an essential political question. But the latter question is only essential in terms of the binary of the sacred and the profane and simply cannot be posed in the titillation of modernity's spectacle where there is no longer a morning after as festivals are no longer set apart. What Caillois was challenging was democracy's total immanence. And he, too, remained ambivalent, pleading for a return to festivals while simultaneously mourning their final departure from history; that is, democracy had not absorbed and globalised the festival, but replaced it with an impoverished replacement – the vacation.

Vacances: **August or the Sunday of the year**

On 11 June 1936 the Blum government tabled a bill granting every French worker, employee or apprentice, 15 days of paid vacation per year. Voting 536 to two, the Chamber of Deputies triumphantly decreed the victory of the right to do nothing. The Saturnalian rites of spring would slip into the summer sloth. And while the extreme right dreaded the democratisation of leisure, the law of 1936 was a measure to heal the endless cycle of strikes and looming political depression. The summer of 1936, the short-lived glory days of the Popular Front, was indeed a pause accentuated by the novelty of vacation, a simultaneously joyous and destabilising rupture. While workers cherished the escape from the subterranean life of the factory they were not sure how to be on vacation. Slumber needed to be honed and cultivated and multiple accounts describe the disorientation of the first days; it was necessary to habituate oneself to the shock of leisure.

Within the ranks of the Popular Front, there was also noted ambivalence; Léo Lagrange, a deputy from the north, was appointed as the new Secretary of Leisure and Sports, but, like Jean Zay, the Minister of Education, he envisioned a leisure and sports dedicated to the "improvement of the race . . . and to do this, he used methods pioneered by far more rabid racists in the Nazis' Strength through Joy leisure and sports organization" (Weber, 1994, p.160). But such rigorous training of the body bore little resemblance to the festive games of Granet's ancient Chinese civilisations, or to the play of agôn and *alea* that Caillois would later describe in *Les jeux et les hommes* (1958). In the end, however, "the state cared not a fig, it seems, for sports in general" and while "it was true that the taste for physical exercise counteracted the pull of drink and cards" (Weber, 1996, p.158), this taste, too, required discipline to develop. Furthermore, society and the profane were not entirely suspended during the summer of 1936 and, as Weber further remarks, not everybody took to the road on bicycles and tandems: "'we didn't dare think of it,' recalled a glass-worker of the Loir-et-Cher, but when the holidays materialised, he and his mates used the free time to earn a bit of cash helping to bring in the harvest. 'Between the garden and the fields, I had no time for boredom'" (Weber, 1996, p.157).

What Caillois further noticed was that the vacation functioned neither as a total break in work nor as a period of invigorating or paroxysmic inversion of social codes. What he saw was precisely a state of boredom, a new empty spleen to supplement the already sordid nature of spleen time. One could equally add here that vacations soon became occasions to flaunt newly acquired signs of wealth; tennis outfits, luggage and one's choice of region and beach recalibrated social divisions with the aid of the newly born leisure industry. But for Caillois, who was certainly not a Marxist, these concerns mattered little and moreover, the right of factory workers and the working class to rest a bit in the summer held no interest. His real enemy was the rising bourgeois leisure class (to whom he himself belonged) and bourgeois individualism *tout court*. Hence, with an air of aristocratic disdain and theoretical condescension, Caillois would claim that what had been

lost were the intensities of social energy that Durkheim had deemed so vital to society almost 20 years earlier. Cultivating the habit of boredom also meant forgetting the art of effervescence, dispelling the memories of solidarity and acclimating oneself to a new calculus of social energies that fluctuated not between the mundane and the explosive but between the mundane and the banal.

For Caillois, who had voted for Blum, the time of festivals officially ended in June 1936 and with it the possibility of corrosive politics. The crisis of vacation was that of a society that had lost its connection to natural rhythm, a body no longer spinning in the oscillations of the sacred and the profane, but rather "moving in the direction of uniformity, levelling and relaxation . . . the complexity of the social organism is less tolerant of the interruption of the ordinary course of life" (Caillois 1939, pp.301–302). On vacation, vacant and vacated, the social organism loses the natural complexity that hinges on the accumulation of tensions and their discharge. A reserve of energy is thus developed in the universe of vacations that serves to physically rehabilitate, but, following Caillois, does so through dissipating the social and betraying the alternations of the sacred and the profane. The period of relaxing is individualised and the alternation of work and vacation has replaced the ancient alternations of feasting and work, ecstasy and self-control and stability and frenzy (Caillois 1939, p.302). The vacation is therefore atomised leisure, a mandated withdrawal that cares little for the circulation of social energies and that understands health to be dependent on rest instead of excess. During the festival participants collectively fused and wrestled with their finitude, struggling with the nothingness and negativity that shadowed the body and psyche. On vacation one does nothing or, contrary to the prescriptive rites of the festive, one does what one desires. The crisis for Caillois may have been in fact spurred by a simple lack of ritualisation and he could hence only comprehend the vacation as the lack of vigour, a state of pure stasis interrupted only by the anxieties of searching for entertainment. But Caillois overlooked one family resemblance between festivals and vacations; in both activities, structures of power and social hierarchy remain unchanged if not reinforced. The beach is far removed from the centre of power as are the time out of time and the space out of space.

However, Caillois was undoubtedly using festival/vacation as a hermeneutic device to examine something much larger and in the 1940 post-script to the *Theory of festival*, published in the *Nouvelle Revue Française*, Caillois announced the original "death of the social", claiming that

a general effervescence is no longer possible.[4] The period of turbulence has become individualized. *The vacation* is the successor of festivals. Of course, this is still a time of expenditure and free activity when regular work is interrupted, but it is a phase of *relaxation* and not of *paroxysm*. The values are completely reversed because in one instance each one goes off on his own and in the other everyone comes together in the same place. The vacation (its name alone is indicative) seems to be an empty space, at least a slowing down of social activity. At the same time, the vacation is incapable of *overjoying* the individual ... the happiness it brings is primarily the result of a distraction and distancing from worries ... rather than communication with the group in its moment of exuberance and jubilation, it is further isolation. Consequently, vacation, unlike festival, constitutes not the flood stage of collective existence, but rather its low-water mark. From this point of view, vacations are characteristic of an extremely dissipated society in which no mediation remains between the passions of the individual and the State apparatus (Caillois 1940, p.302)

The violence that Durkheimian society performed on individual consciousness was softened by Mauss' Eskimo summer and the violence performed on the psyche during summer dispersion would be equally relieved through the period of orgiastic winter social concentration. But when men dispersed during the summer season, they never felt themselves to be entirely alone; socialisation may be a violent process but its ultimate value rests in the unshakeable womb that enwrapped the isolated individual. The acceleration of modernity performs a similar violence on consciousness, but without the support of the social. Turbulence therefore becomes individualised; in other words, it achieves no *telos* and has no means of expression. Individualised, it is never shared and agonizes the splintered consciousness, spiralling through vectors of victimisation, personal memory and narcissism.

As no catharsis, no collective overflowing of anxiety is available, one can only escape: whence

the logic of "got to get away", the "frantic secularization of festival" (Hollier, 1997, p.15), a logic that leaves anxieties intact and simply displaces them to the beach where we are made to believe they disappear. But sea, sex and sun, while feeling good, have no intrinsic psychical purging or paroxysmic capacities; they are among the many detours on the road to death. The problem of death, the capstone of the collective psyche can, on the contrary, only be confronted through the collective cathexis of the festival that does not defer, but *exhausts*. It exhausts, moreover, through overjoying as opposed to sleep: the vacation and the festival are flanked by two very different mornings after. Dilution, according to Caillois, appears as the stamp of the modern. The vacation does not truly cut the cord with the profane but simply superimposes prescribed catatonia and stakeless games (volleyball as opposed to potlatch) on a nice, happy and relaxed, (but never overjoyed or paroxysmic) petit-bourgeois individual. Happiness, in this context, appears as a figure of solipsism and not the social in which the imperative is the search for your own bliss – it is indeed everyone for themselves.

Dissipation also signals the end of active political passions, protest and the critique of power. It produces political impotence and does not, as in the case of festivals, ritually participate in forms of political inversion. Vacations are institutional respites designed to draw attention away from the real conditions of misfortune whereas in festivals these conditions are renegotiated, albeit temporally and often without lasting effect. Vacations are a means of escaping politics or rather deferring engagement with the political problem. The vacationer plays dead. In the summer of 1938, only weeks before the Munich Accord, the beaches were full and the thought of festivals neither seduced nor posed any real threat. From festival to vacation; from vacation to war.

However, what cannot be overlooked is the fact that, unlike the vacation, the space of the festival is a potential space of violence. The nature of this violence is polyvalent and occupies a series of unique registers. While the execution of criminals, scapegoats and kings has certainly functioned as a nodal point or lever for paroxysm, the festival is also a space of psychic and symbolic violence; the obliteration of civilisation and its purported renewal are inextricably bound to various axioms of creative destruction. Yet what is being decimated is not simply culture, time, history and the world, but also the very foundations of the human. In addition, from rites of passage to rites of competition such psychic violence is accentuated with dramatisations of aggression and lawlessness that are indeed mandated and sanctioned, but in the theatrics of the festive, there is a dark undercurrent that traverses the jubilation. While games have rules and orgies and are ritualised, it is difficult to speak of consensual violence at the moment of the recreation of the world. Energies can always spill over, just as champagne effervescence can mutate into drunken carnage – from giddiness to drunken warriors. Civilisation, a political somatic construct, may also suffer from the loss of mastery, breach its own limits, spill over and fall into paroxysm. A delicate calculus of energies, civilisation depends on the festival for its own preservation and hence, as Caillois painfully asked in 1940, "Is a society with no festivals not a society condemned to death"? (Caillois 1940, p.302). A new space of reflection thus presented itself for the sociologist of the sacred as well as a new set of conditions. As Hollier has noted, by 1940, Caillois had been carried off by Argentina Victoria Ocampo and "for this Luciferian, who was the very devil intellectually much more than physically, this war was a particularly long vacation . . . these five years in South America certainly warranted Caillois' going back over the last words of his 'theory of festival': it was not a vacation, it was war" (Caillois 1940, p.280).

The 1950 re-edition of *L'homme et le sacré* would not only contain a lengthy appendix on "*Guerre et sacré*", thrusting Caillois into the hitherto little explored domain of the sociology of war, but also a new concluding paragraph to the theory of festival:

So one must ask what brew of the same magnitude frees the individual's instincts, repressed by the requirements of organized existence and at the same time results in a sufficiently wide-ranging, *collective effervescence*.[5] And it seems that from the time strongly established States appeared (and more and more clearly as their structure asserts itself), the old alteration between feast and labour, ecstasy and self-control that periodically revived order out of chaos, wealth from prodigality, stability, from frenzy, has been replaced by an alternation of a completely different order and yet the only thing offering the modern world a nature an intensity that are comparable. This is the alternation between peace and war, prosperity and destruction of the results of prosperity, stable tranquillity and compulsory violence. (Caillois 1950, pp.302–303)

The semblances between war and festival are not purely formal, but substantive as well. The disappearance of the social oscillations between the sacred and profane result in the oscillation of nation-states at war and nation-states in preparation for war; the training exercise known as peace. The expenditures of the body, the potlatch between rival clans, mutates into the total mobilisation of the nation-state's resources and its men. The razing of civilisation and culture is no longer a symbolic or physical drama, but is rather dependant upon the complete devastation of the foe. War transforms ritual intoxication into the pre-delirium of battle, ritual orgies into rape, games into torture and sacrilege into the death of the other, the profaning of the other's body. Furthermore, the *mystique de guerre* is not simply a mystique of blood but equally the allure of camaraderie and the collective military life and it is also a liminal space replete with initiation rights, ritual and festive debauches and transgression, both on and off the battlefield.

Modernity is thus typified by its adherence to the interminable cycles of war and peace, a vertiginous wheel that effectively pushes the vertigos of the sacred and profane to their ultimate violent apogee. The vacillation of labour and ecstasy is effaced by pulsations of peace and war, labour and the labour of killing. War is a mobilisation of social energies that functions as an even more total social fact than the festival, in so far as the nature of mobilisation leaves no domain of social life, be it sacred or profane, untouched. It is the "paroxysm of existence of modern societies," which constitutes a "total phenomenon;" it destroys individual well-being, "interrupts happiness and the quarrels of lovers, the intrigues of the ambitious and the oeuvres pursued in silence by the artist, erudite, or inventor" . . . "it indistinctly ruins anxiety and placidness, nothing which exists in lack subsists, neither creation nor *jouissance* nor anxiety itself . . . war requires all energies" (Caillois 1988, pp.222–223). It interrupts precisely everything workers do not have time for, except, of course, when they are on vacation.

Nevertheless, the social is presented as a Janus-faced entity, regenerated through the mobilisations of either festival or war. In the latter, the ultimate taboo transgressed is the law that dictates that thou shalt not kill and the sanctioned inversions and excesses of the festival are hypostasised in the sanctioned annihilation of war. The expenditures of the body and consciousness are hypostasised into the expenditure of national resources and the population. According to Caillois, war is the most furious orgy, the ultimate paroxysm of political somatics. It cuts and suspends, recalibrating civilisation's march in an interminable cycle of before and after the war; the social body thus undulates between periods of limpidness and muscular contraction, which are only ephemerally relaxed in war through the release of instincts achieved in killing, the dark joy experienced in the supreme sacrilege: "like incest during the festival, death in war is an act of religious resonance" (Caillois 1988, p.226). The sacred act of war explodes not through ritual intoxication and the becoming-immanent of bodies through sexual licence, but rather through the lacerating immanence of death where the chasm between subject and object is obliterated with the terminus of life; an immanence achieved neither through the fury of exaltation nor through democracy, but through the fury that seizes the warrior who reclaims his instincts, previously buried deep within his heart by a lying civilisation (Caillois 1988).

In war the sacred, too, is double-sided and ambivalent, asking that all dare not only to die, but to kill as well, (Caillois 1988, p.223) a sacrament that gives and takes away. The impurities of peace are overcome by the pure *tremendum* of pure violence and war is baptism and ordination just as much as it is apotheosis (Caillois 1988, p.237)). In this tragic fecundation a new Earth is constructed through the battering of peoples, and political and social life – the nation-state itself – are re-erected upon the strewn bodies. Then nation-building; the gift of destruction is followed by the gift of reconstruction, rebuilding and various Marshall plans, which are not really free gifts at all as the offering serves only the disinterested material interest of the giver. Caillois exhorts repeatedly that festivals unite while wars fragment and shatter; what the festival opens is precisely what

war closes. An implacable showdown, war is endured; one pushes to the end, to death or victory. And in the oscillations of pre-war peace and post-war peace, civilisation is held hostage until the next total festival. At the end of the 1930s, with the time of the Saturnalia long past, the another festival would burst in forth in September with artillery and shelling.

But according to Caillois, the advent of war as the black festival of modernity does not signal a sudden rupture. Rather, the historical dialectic of the sacred and the festive has always been imbricated in a historical dialectic of war. In his 1963a study, *Bellone ou la pente de guerre*, he mytho-historically narrates the transition from festival to war in three successive stages corresponding to the evolution from primitive society to the nation-state. Presaging and also complicating some of Pierre Clastres' later theses, Caillois maintains that the paroxysm of primitive society "is necessarily that moment when the constitutive sub-groups come together in a period of official promiscuity. Conjoined and intermingled by festival, their members enter into the vertiginous world of the sacred, myths and dreams . . . In a society of this type, without a nation or state, war never exceeds the stage of ambushes, raids, plunder or revenge expeditions. It can never become a crucial concern and basically remains scattered and random event: that is to say, it does not exist. Such a society achieves its incandescence during and by means of the festival" (Caillois 1963a, pp.293–294).

Society against the state: festival against the state. Like Clastres (1974), Caillois imagines no pastoral paradise of the peaceful primitive. Primitive societies were violent, but such scattered violence did not function as society's total paroxysm and was deployed without and against the possibility of a monolithic state formation. Lacking a hierarchical top-down mechanism of identity, ideology and coercion, in primitive societies political life was a question of incandescence and hence was not organised around the accumulation of power, conquering, expansion or submission. Rather, it signified society's capacity to collectively experience occasional vertigo. Politics meant conjoining that which duration severs apart. The stateless society evades war by centrifugally dissolving its own violence within itself. Furthermore, in the incandescence of festival it produces a social aggregation that defies the political organisation (the hierarchy of seats of command) of the state apparatus. But, as Caillois further elaborates:

With the rise of hierarchy and the individualisation of power, as society becomes more complex and diversifies into specialised occupations – warriors, priests, blacksmiths, dancers, carpenters, healers, or other people with distinctive techniques founding their authority and determining their social role – a change takes place in the reciprocal prestations and the perfect equilibrium that governs the relations of complementary groups. Under these conditions the chief mainspring of the collective pact is no longer respect, but prestige, whether this involves initiatory brotherhoods or hereditary castes. . . . I would define these societies by suggesting that class distinctions create real barriers and divide opposing communities. Thus, war becomes the privilege – almost the monopoly – of an aristocracy, which reserves for itself the right to bear arms and whose members fight amongst themselves, just as they marry into their own ranks. This is the era of courtly war, which exists only in the hierarchal world and which opposes only people of equal rank, warriors by birth and destiny; the common people are merely their valets, auxiliaries or victims. At this stage, war is a game with strict rules. . . . Festival changed with society. It ceased to be a paroxysm of communing and became instead one of escalating rivalry in which leaders sought recognition of their own pre-eminence. (Caillois 1963b, p.294)

The deep past is mythically imagined as universe defined by anti-individualist holism, a universe before the advent of the caste system. And although Caillois had aided Georges Dumézil in his discovery of the Indo-European tripartite system, the social division of the priestly/kingly, the warrior and the agriculturalist, Caillois' narrative maintained that the absorption of festival into war was a mutation from the primeval state of harmonious solidarity and reciprocal exchange to rigid hierarchisation, a transition from holism to caste and class. Caste and class are synonymous with the rise of prestige and status and the devolution that Caillois describes should be read also as a critique of regimes of power that reinforce social stratification through the respective orders of signification and consumption, and secular individualist paradigms of status-mongering (a space of psychic accumulation). In other words, the *homo equalis* of democratic individualism, when fused with the *homo economicus* of capitalism, produces a caste system and new class of untouchables (not only the poor, but also the ugly, the obese and those

who can't dance) that not only shatters holism, respect and reciprocal exchange, but forces *homo festivus* to be reborn as *homo bellicosus*. Following Caillois' mythic narrative, social hierarchy escalates in synchrony with social complexity and complexity is synonymous with hyperindividualisation, specialisation and *techné*. On one hand, the various exchanges of the gift, of collective co-dependence and collective loss that animated the festival would be supplanted by the mad potlatch of the warrior class. On the other hand, the simultaneous dissipation of social bonds and the increasing segmentation of society into atomised and holistically unrelated sectors would dilute the political valence of the festival to become nothing more than an occasion to display power, as opposed to inviting its subversion.

However, in Caillois' nostalgia-soaked narrative of pure holism, during this transitional phase the thirst for pre-eminence and the delirium of escalating rivalry had not yet reached the level of total war and the festive had not been entirely effaced but simply reconfigured. As an interregnum between the return to chaos and the age of technological massacre festivals had lost their social significance but they nonetheless remained heavily ritualised; courtly war, albeit violent and agonistic, still maintained certain ritualised rules of decorum. The limit of potlatch, bloodshed; not the hurling of family heirlooms into the sea or the banquet, became the privileged mode of the festive. With this transposition the extravagant expenditures of the Kwakiutl were superseded by war that "itself is luxurious: it is the festival in which people risk their lives. However, it divides instead of uniting them and . . . it does not stand as society's pinnacle at all. In this transitional era, the high point is no longer festival, but it is not yet war" (Caillois 1963b, p.295).

This is the transition from the gift of wealth and the moral economy of shame and reciprocation to the gift of casualties and the counter-gift of more casualties in an economy of death that is beyond good and evil.

During the transitional era, the holism of the social gave way to the segmented stratification of society. In the final phase, however, society itself becomes absorbed into the armed totality of the nation. Caillois suggests that the rise of nation-state is contiguous with the advent of total war and the submission of the warrior-class to the larger mandates of the nation-state, defined at once by its psychic, cultural and geographical borders. Westphalia therefore precipitates the cycle of war and the birth of the state is, as Clastres warned, the destruction of society where violence can no longer be internally dissipated in social paroxysm, but must be directed outside of the borders of the state. Nation-states transform the warrior-class, girded by ritualistic codes of nobility and honour, into a monolithic military class entirely transparent to the mandates of national defence or expansion. The nation, like the body or the social, must also return itself to primordial chaos and the moment of its origin, but now, as Caillois comments, such a return is not simply an affair of a festive dramatisation:

In festivals . . . violence remained accidental; merely adding to the fertilising effervescence from which it sprang through excessive vitality and which it then raised to a feverish pitch. In war, however, violence is the object of systematic effort; it is mechanised and the deliberate goal of relentless hostility. *If the state is born of war, it returns the favour by producing war in turn. The two evolve together.* . . . Orgy and carnage, festival and war: two symmetrical phenomena that are both violent. They perform the same supreme function in two different contexts and hence share a similar capacity to fascinate – the first attracts and the second terrifies – depending whether the crisis is meant to fertilise or destroy, welcome or repulse. The path leading from festival to war merges with the evolution of technical progress and political organisation. Everything has a price: the current forms of war were developed in the very development of civilisation. And we have reached a point where the latter must quickly find a way of parrying this domestic danger, which feeds on the development of civilisation and threatens to destroy it. (Caillois 1963b, p.297, my emphases)

Societies without festivals are transparent to nation-states that have usurped society and the social, or rather socialised through militarisation. War is therefore the natural consequence of social atomisation and its corollaries; modern sovereignty and political organisation. The fatal choice is no longer that between civilisation or barbarism, as barbarism is the motor of civilisation and also its point of termination; civilisation against itself as technological mastery conspires in the return to animality. The choice, rather, is an impossible one; it is between the reconstruction of the social, the liquidation of bourgeois individualism, and gift exchange and civilisation's atomising processes, the socialisation of total war and the

gift of annihilation. In essence, if one pushes Caillois' conclusions to their limit (and in the direction of Carl Schmitt, whose concerns he shares), civilisation and particularly, democracy, must inevitably veer towards war, as it is the fate of nations, political bodies, to attain regular points of paroxysm; it is the fate of empires to desire continual expansions; post-festive nation-states are unable to dissolve their own negativity and thus, must direct it outwards through the total expenditure of war; and political regimes that search for consensus, as opposed to embroiling themselves in political agôn, can only engage such negativity at that fatal moment when the sovereign proclaims the failure of sanctions or the end of all negotiations: we will no longer negotiate.

Civilisation is suspended during the course of the endgame where it is not clear whether war is a continuation of politics or politics a continuation of war, where it is further unclear whether war is a paroxysm or a continuation of the spectacle. Had Caillois lived to witness current war processes, he might have added yet another term to the dialectic; the last phase may actually be one where the paroxysm of war does not replace the paroxysm of festival, but one where the paroxysm itself has disappeared.

At the end of the dialectic we are all passive spectators of war. In a static society, there is no alternation, no oscillation, no cutting. Instead, as Alliez and Negri claim, in a variation of Hobbes:

Peace and war: in its hypermodern imperial form, the conjunction of peace and war must be understood in accordance with a substitutive value that makes the two terms *absolutely contemporary with one another*, starting with the inversion both of their functions and of their "classical" relations. Once war signifies the regulation of constituted powers and the constitutive form of the new order, peace is merely a deceptive illusion fostering the power of disorder and its threat – *urbi et orbi* – against the security of the world. In the end, in this world without inside or outside, in which, with the global disintegration of living together ("internal peace"), the "commerce among nations" has thrown off the mask of external peace, everything happens as if peace and war were so tightly enmeshed that they no longer form anything but the two faces of a single membrane projected onto the planet. Peace, *in other words*, war. This is less a hypothesis than the common recognition of a hybrid identity that throws "the whole world" into a meta-politics in which peace no longer appears as anything other than *the continuation of war by other means*. A wholly relative alterity, that of a continuous police action exercised upon a globalised *polis* under the exceptional legislation of an *infinite war* – from which peace is deduced as the institution of a permanent state of exception. (Alliez and Negri 2003, p.109)

In such a wholly relative alterity, such a permanent state of exception, there can be no paroxysm but only the banality of war where things go on as they always did.

Postscript: *The Iliad*

In the summer of 1940, while Caillois fled the war to go on vacation, Simone Weil composed *The Iliad or the poem of force*. For Weil, force was neither the exertion of energy against an object nor the explosion of the virile and the vital. Rather, force was an impersonal flux that embodied an evil demiurge animating a universe that found itself forever at its mercy and prey to its whims. While force is employed by man, it is nonetheless that which "enslaves man, force before which Man's flesh shrinks away ... the human spirit is shown as modified by its relations with force ... to define force – it is that x that turns anybody who is subjected to it into a thing" (Weil 2003, p.3).

Force reifies human nature and does so by reducing the human to a corpse-making machine or a corpse himself. In the grip of "force", difference is apprehended only between that which has been killed and that which has not yet been killed. "Force" can infect a civilisation. It can take it as a prisoner and in its viral proliferation even co-opt the counter-"force" that struggles to ensure preservation. "Force" is an *ivresse*, a mania which only increases the appetite for more "force". Indifferent to the Earth, indifferent to itself, "force" begs to be abused, misused and inflicted. Excessive "force" breeds servitude to "force", an enslavement misconstrued as "paroxysm". The paroxysm of "force" is also war and it is war that "effaces all conceptions of purpose or goal", including even its own war aims. "It effaces the very notion of war's being brought to an end. To be outside a situation so violent as this is to find it inconceivable; to be inside it is to be unable to conceive its end". (Weil 2003, p.22)

As in the undulations of the festival, "force" can exceed itself and therein lies hidden the tragic nature of ecstasy, paroxysm and release. In the *Iliad*, "force is the sole hero", a blind and blinding protagonist that immolates all within its path without fail. In 1940, war may have indeed replaced the festival just as in the classical period "Roman gladiatorial fights took the place of tragedy". (Weil 2003, p.35)

The dilemma of force, the dilemma of the orgiastic, can only be resolved through a comprehension of its various intensities of diffusion and concentration, a quasi-mathematical calculus of incalculable social energies, political somatics and vitality, one typified by a distrust of force. The ecstatic waves of the social that form the mystical centre of Durkheim's vision are forever threatened by the fury of licence, disintegration and supra-abandon, which not only transgress normative codes and structures but menace the social itself. Becoming-animal may go beyond the simple donning of masks; it may also entail the dissolution of consciousness (the mark of the human) and in doing so suspend the ethical (the other mark of the human). Games can always get rough and the joy of the festive can always turn on itself to inhibit the other's pleasure or inflict pain on the other (sadism). Sadism is an attempt to incarnate authority, but as Hannah Arendt never ceased to remind us, authority is the responsibility for the world. (Arendt, 1993 p.189)

Notes

1. Frédéric Saumade also contends that among certain French intellectuals of Christian origin in the early twentieth century, one can easily detect in the overdetermination of eroticism, transgressive paganism and archaic sacrificial forms, a refusal of secular asceticism and rationalism and heretical tendencies. (Saumade, 2003, p.138).

2. This differs greatly from Nietzsche's ethics of the body. For Nietzsche the body existed in agôn with other bodies, each struggling to overcome *resentiment*, the instincts turned inwards, through mastery of the body's affects, rhythms and tendencies. Mastery, for Nietzsche, also meant mastery over pain. The Dionysian "yes" and its affirmation while mad and dancing were dependant upon such mastery, an asceticism of the spirit. Nietzsche's body in agôn was contrasted by Durkheim's body of reciprocation, mutual aid and cooperation.

3. The term paroxysm is derived from the Greek *paroxysmos*. The medical definition of paroxysm is: "1. the periodic increase or crisis in the progress of a disease; a sudden attack, a sudden re-appearance or increase in the intensity of symptoms; 2. A spasm, convulsive fit, or seizure; 3. A sudden usually uncontrollable bout of crying or laughter. (See *Gould's medical dictionary* 1935, p.999).

4. The original French reads: "L'effervescence générale n'est plus possible" (Hollier 1995, p. 691). Betsy Wing, however, translates the phrase as "A general ferment is no longer possible" (Hollier 1988, p.302). The term effervescence is generally used in French to refer to any state of excitation, effusion and intense activity. But, although this is a seemingly minor nuance of translation, there can be no doubt that Caillois reflecting on the modern counterpart to the festival and was thinking of Durkheim when the original postscript was written.

5. Once again, Betsy Wing translates effervescence as ferment (Hollier 1988, p.302), while the original French contains the word effervescence Caillois (1988, p.167). Here, however, there should be no question of Caillois' point of reference as he speaks of collective effervescence.

Durkheim's concept of *dérèglement* retranslated, Parsons's reading of Durkheim re-parsed: an examination of post-emotional displacement, scape-goating and responsibility at Abu Ghraib

Stjepan G. Mestrovic and Ryan Ashley Caldwell

The occasion of the 150th anniversary of Durkheim's birth provides an excellent opportunity to re-examine Durkheim's legacy in relation to law and its attendant concepts: justice, responsibility, crime and punishment. However, we note at the outset that Durkheim, the son of a rabbi as well one of sociology's founding fathers, understood sociology to be the science of morality, and the law as having its origins in religion. In his words, "morality is the indispensible minimum, that which is strictly necessary, the daily bread without which societies cannot live" (Durkheim [1893] 1984, p.13). Contemporary readers will be tempted to ask, "Whose morality?" The Durkheimian reply is that morality is a universal construct such that all moralities and religions are true in their own way so long as they preserve and promote societal and international integration. For example, Durkheim writes: "Fundamentally, then, there are no religions that are false. All are true after their own fashion: all fulfil given conditions of human existence, though in different ways. ... They fulfil the same needs, play the same role and proceed from the same causes" (Durkheim [1912] 1995, p.2).

We propose to limit this examination to one of his central concepts, anomie, and link it with his overall project to establish a science of morality. We will apply it to one of the defining episodes in recent history that is on par with the Dreyfus Affair, in which Durkheim participated, namely, the abuse at Abu Ghraib, a military detention centre in Iraq, as brought to public attention in 2004. We work within the overall framework that Durkheim offers a grand theory that is applicable universally as to how societies should function normally as well as how they function in anomic, pathological ways. We begin with the argument that the abuse at Abu Ghraib is best captured by Durkheim's original and contextual understanding of anomie, not subsequent or rival versions of this concept. His disciple, Paul Fauconnet (1928), published a complex treatise on responsibility that extends Durkheim's treatment of legal, moral and quasi-religious issues in *The division of labour in society* (Durkheim [1893] 1984). This analysis leads to the neglected and distinctively Durkheimian conclusion that society must "recognise collective responsibility for social conditions that create crime" (Cotterrell 1999, p.107). In other words, it is US society as a whole, not a handful of so-called rotten apples that are responsible for the abuse at Abu Ghraib and elsewhere in the war in Iraq, in much the same way as French society was responsible for

Stjepan G. Mestrovic is professor of sociology at Texas A&M University. He has published extensively on Durkheim and war crimes from Bosnia to Abu Ghraib and Iraq. His most recent books are *The trials of Abu Ghraib, Rules of engagement*, and *The "good soldier" on trial*.
Email: mestrovic@neo.tamu.edu

Ryan Ashley Caldwell is an assistant professor of sociology at Soka University of America in southern California. Her areas of research include social theory, culture, women's studies, applied ethics and issues of military accountability. Her recent publications include using social theory and gender to critically understand the war on terror, including the many power permutations involved. Mestrovic and Caldwell have extensive participant observation research experience at US military court martials.
Email: racaldwell@gmail.com

the anti-Semitism and other anomic conditions that led to the Dreyfus Affair, not just a handful of officers. While this conclusion will not come as a surprise to Durkheimian scholars, it is contrary to the popular perception that the abuse at Abu Ghraib is the result of the perverse actions of a few morally corrupt soldiers, while officers, civilian leaders and US society as a whole are exempt from responsibility.

Durkheim and Fauconnet both imply the controversial idea of collective responsibility. As May and Hoffman (1991) point out, collective responsibility has been used in reprehensible ways by the Nazis to scapegoat Jews and later by world opinion to blame all Germans for Nazism. On the other hand, they note that lawyers and governments routinely use collective responsibility to prosecute corporations and groups affiliated with some specific individuals, such as terrorists and this kind of behaviour is generally deemed to be socially acceptable. Similarly, Mannheim (2003, p.44) argues that "as Fauconnet has stressed, even after the disappearance of blood vengeance the collective element survived at least in the field of pecuniary co-responsibility of the group". One of our goals in this chapter is to distinguish between healthy and unhealthy, and integrative and dysfunctional collective responsibility. One of the keystones of Durkheim's entire system of thought is that the past cannot and should not be jettisoned entirely from modernity. Thus, punishment will always contain an element of passionate vengeance: "In the beginning, individuals took vengeance themselves; now it is society that avenges them" (Durkheim [1893] 1984, p.49). The creative tension in Durkheim's thought lies in discussing and understanding the difference between socially integrative and dysfunctional (anomic) vengeance (see Gruztpalk 2002).

The one and only synonym that Durkheim used for the concept of anomie is *dérèglement*, which literally means derangement. However, anomie has been and continues to be misunderstood as a condition of "normlessness". Does this discrepancy in understanding anomie as normlessness versus derangement matter? It matters from the vantage point of Durkheim's overall sociology, which holds that words and concepts are not the idiosyncratic creations of isolated individuals, but are the product of immense cooperation. Language is part of a system of collective representations that not only create meaning but promote social solidarity. In Durkheim's words ([1912] 1995, p.435), "language is fixed; it changes but slowly. ... It is common to all because it is the work of the community". The scientist "may innovate, of course, but his innovations always do a certain violence to established ways of thinking" (Durkheim [1912] 1995, p.435). Nowadays and in stark contrast to Durkheim's position, postmodern deconstruction of language and the notion of spin, namely, that any idea can be redescribed in any way that one chooses, have come to dominate academia (see Rorty 1989). We choose to follow the Durkheimian approach to language and truth, which would regard postmodernism as a historical instance of intellectual anomie.

Conceptualising the problem

The factual evidence for the presence of extreme social disorganisation and anomie comes from the US Government reports pertaining to Abu Ghraib as well as testimony from the courts-martial – which is described meticulously by Mestrovic (2007) and Caldwell and Mestrovic (2008) based upon eyewitness accounts of the trials – and includes, but is not limited to, the following points. There was a systemic lack of accountability. The filing system was disorganised. Government agencies and civilian contractors including the CIA operated outside established rules and procedures established by the Army Field Manual as well as the Geneva Conventions. Nobody was certain who was in charge of Abu Ghraib. The prison was overcrowded. There was no organised system for releasing prisoners. Soldiers failed to screen prisoners at the point where they were arrested as well as the point when they were brought to Abu Ghraib. No one screened the civilian contractors. New soldiers (but not entire units) were introduced to the personnel structure (a process that the Army calls cross-levelling). The army failed to adequately train military police and military intelligence in policing as well as interrogation procedures. The military police did not know what they or the military intelligence were not allowed to do. General

Taguba cited egregious lack of military discipline. There was intense pressure to obtain information from a population of prisoners that was not capable of providing the desired information. Soldiers were not trained in or familiar with the Geneva Conventions. Publicly, the US military upheld the Geneva Conventions while various attorneys for the White House opined that the Geneva Conventions did not wholly apply to the treatment of prisoners. General Taguba found poor paperwork and reporting procedures, along with a host of other facts that suggest extreme social chaos. For example, the supply officer at Abu Ghraib, Major David DiNenna, testified that he begged the Army for adequate water, food, toilets, light bulbs and generators and that his pleas fell on deaf ears. He testified in open court that he felt "abandoned" by the Army at Abu Ghraib (Mestrovic 2007, p.107). The documentation for all these facts is immense and consistent (see Danner 2004, Falk *et al.* 2006, Hersh 2004, Karpinski 2005, Strasser 2004, among many other books on Abu Ghraib, as well as two film documentaries, Rory Kennedy's "Ghosts of Abu Ghraib" and Errol Morris's "Standard Operating Procedure").

The characterisation of all these and other facts as anomic is practically non-existent in the literature. More important, the responsibility for the egregious disorganisation at Abu Ghraib was not pursued at the trials, in public discourse or scholarship even though a handful of soldiers were sent to prison for specific acts of abuse. Who was responsible for the lack of toilets, water, light bulbs, generators and bullets at Abu Ghraib? Who was responsible for the "poisoned social climate", in the words of General Fay, at Abu Ghraib, which in turn set the stage for the subsequent abuse? Despite the existence of the doctrine of command responsibility, which holds that military commanders are accountable via omission or commission for the behaviour of the subordinates, most of Major DiNenna's superiors in the chain of command were promoted, not punished. Durkheim (1893) held that as society progresses, the law changes in its emphasis from retribution to restitution. But neither retribution nor restitution characterise the Army's or US society's response to the failure to adequately supply, train, or prepare its soldiers.

As for applying social scientific concepts in the courtroom to make sense of the abuse at Abu Ghraib, Philip Zimbardo (2007) was an expert witness in Ivan Frederick's court martial where he used the "obedience to authority" paradigm and Mestrovic (2007) was an expert witness in the court martials of Javal Davis, Sabrina Harman and Lynndie England, where he used Durkheim's concept of anomie. Matt Taibbi captures the layperson's reaction to the injection of the sociological concept of anomie into legal discourse: "Mestrovic described Abu Ghraib as a 'state of anomie'. 'A what?' [Colonel] Pohl snapped, frowning. 'A state of anomie', the doctor repeated. Pohl shuddered and sipped his coffee, seeming to wonder whether such a word was even legal in Texas" (Taibbi 2005, p.48).

What is at stake here is the importance of Durkheim's legacy, not the desire to enter into a frivolous polemic with Zimbardo. In other words, which concept is better for understanding the abuse at Abu Ghraib, Durkheim's original concept of anomie or Zimbardo's obedience to authority paradigm? From Durkheim's and Fauconnet's point of view, if "obedience to authority" is the cause of the abuse, then the soldier bears the sole responsibility for disobeying an unlawful order. Indeed, Zimbardo (2007) exhorts soldiers to be heroes and to refuse to obey unlawful orders. The US military also lays the blame on the soldiers for failing to disobey an unlawful order, but the International Tribunal at The Hague invokes the doctrine of command responsibility, which holds military and civilian leaders as being the most responsible for acts of omission as well as commission (see Mestrovic 2008). Which approach is more just? This is an important legal and social issue which fails to invoke the Durkheimian project, even though Durkheim addressed precisely these sorts of sociological issues pertaining to law, justice and responsibility. As stated previously, the Durkheimian perspective places the ultimate burden of responsibility on the Army and society in general. Indeed, the military judge at the Abu Ghraib trials immediately grasped the import of Durkheim's perspective and rejected it, declaring several times, "The Army is not on trial here!" But from Durkheim's point of view, the Army was on trial, metaphorically speaking, at the Abu Ghraib court martials and the metaphorical "jury of one's peers" was the international community.

Fauconnet (1928) elaborates on Durkheim to argue that traditional societies regarded entire cities, regions, institutions and families – even livestock, pets and other animals – as being responsible for crimes and punished entire groups, not just individuals. Indeed, Durkheim did write that traditional societies:

[p]unish animals that have committed the act that is stigmatised or even inanimate things which have been its passive instrument. When the punishment is applied solely to people, it often extends well beyond the guilty person and strikes even the innocent – his wife, children or neighbours, etc. ... Nowadays, however, it is said that punishment has changed in nature. Society no longer punishes to avenge, but to defend itself. (Durkheim [1893] 1984, p.44)

Note the immediate relevance of Durkheim's theory to the fact that Afghan and Iraqi leaders respond immediately and negatively to the "collateral damage", that is, the deaths of women, children and livestock that sometimes occur when coalition forces target a specific person (for one example out of many, see Perlez 2008). Modern societies hold that individuals are solely responsible for their actions. However, the fine point of this discussion is that Fauconnet and Durkheim concluded that the traditional approach never disappears entirely from collective consciousness and is preferable to individualistic, "subjective", depictions of responsibility in modern law. Cotterrell quotes Fauconnet: "What is taken to be perfect responsibility is responsibility weakened and reduced to vanishing point" (Cotterrell 1999, p.107). The issue is extremely complex: modern societies seek to minimise collateral damage, but international law holds that the entire chain of command, not the particular soldier who killed innocents, is responsible. Our central point is that Fauconnet and Durkheim offer a vastly different understanding of what should have been the just and responsible reaction to the disorganisation as well as the abuse at Abu Ghraib compared to the actual response. We shall argue that Durkheim's grand theory leads one to regard the exclusive punishment of a handful of soldiers for the evils at Abu Ghraib as a form of scapegoating. In Durkheim's words, "We have remained true to the principle of the

talion, although we conceive of it in a more lofty sense than once we did" (Durkheim [1893] 1984, p.47). Nevertheless, for Durkheim, "punishment has remained an act of vengeance, at least in part" (p. 46).

We chose the abuse at Abu Ghraib as the vehicle for this discussion of anomie because it captured the collective imagination in the present era much as the Dreyfus Affair captured widespread attention in Durkheim's lifetime and because of the intimate knowledge we gained of the abusers as well as the abuse at Abu Ghraib through the participant-observation research we conducted in our roles working for the defence in three separate court martials that were held at Fort Hood, Texas, in the year 2005. In this brief study, we shall approach the abuse at Abu Ghraib in much the same way as Durkheim approached the topic of suicide vis-à-vis anomie: namely, suicide and the abuse at Abu Ghraib are vehicles for a much broader sociological discussion that involves the sociologies of knowledge, organisations, the military and culture. Numerous commentators on Durkheim's *Suicide* ([1897] 1983) seem to miss the obvious point that it is not a positivistic study of the phenomenon of suicide per se, but a study of the phenomena of "social currents" that compel individuals to engage in murderous thoughts as well as behaviour, against the self and others, ranging from the altruistic self-sacrifice of a soldier to various shades of deliberate versus accidental and unintentional violence.[1] Similarly, the violence at Abu Ghraib ranged from murder to verbal abuse and forcing naked, shackled Muslim men to wear panties on their heads and the abuse involved the misuse of culture (exploiting Muslim cultural beliefs regarding nudity, dogs, prayer and so on), psychic abuse (such as isolation) and a wide spectrum of social phenomena not usually regarded as abuse. Given the limitations of space, this chapter cannot serve as more than a sketch for such a Durkheimian approach to the abuse at Abu Ghraib.

Durkheim's overall sociology has been criticised for not paying sufficient attention to violence, despite the fact that every one of his books deals with violence in some form, ranging from a discussion of corporal punishment in *Moral education*, sacrifice and scapegoats in *The elementary forms of religious life* and to white-collar crimes in the business world in his *Professional ethics and civic morals* (see Mestrovic 1988). In fact, the idea of suffering is ubiquitous in all of Durkheim's studies, from his analyses of crime and suicide to religion and social solidarity. He held that it is possible only at the cost of the violence that society must inflict on the individual, as theorised by the concept of *homo duplex* or the dualism of human nature (Durkheim [1914] 1973).[2] One must distinguish between this "sanctifying power of sorrow" for the sake of social solidarity and the seemingly senseless suffering that results from anomie: "If anomie is an evil it is above all because society suffers through it" (Durkheim [1893] 1984, p.xxxv). For example, Durkheim's comment on the routine altruism expected of the soldier is directly relevant to understanding the abuse committed by US soldiers at Abu Ghraib:

Now, the first quality of a soldier is a sort of impersonality not to be found anywhere in civilian life to the same degree. He must be trained to set little value upon himself, since he must be prepared to sacrifice himself upon being ordered to do so. Even aside from such exceptional circumstances, in peace time and in the regular exercise of his profession, discipline requires him to obey without question and sometimes even without understanding. (Durkheim [1897] 1951, p. 234)

Indeed, the crux of the legal issues at the Abu Ghraib trials was whether the officers were responsible for the unlawful orders that were issued or whether the soldiers were responsible for their failure to disobey the unlawful orders. Yet society expects soldiers to obey commands without question or understanding (for a detailed discussion of the complex issue of the soldier's duty to disobey an unlawful order versus the officer's responsibility via the doctrine of command responsibility, see Mestrovic (2008). There is no easy solution to this dilemma, but our approach is to distinguish sharply between a soldier's normal altruism in a normal military setting versus unnecessary suffering in anomic forms of social functioning.

The term anomie was coined by Emile Durkheim in *The division of labor in society* ([1893] 1984) and in *Suicide* ([1897] 1951). Durkheim refers specifically to *dérèglement* as the synonym for anomie: "*l'état de dérèglement ou d'anomie*" ([1897] 1983, p.287). Anomie is depicted by Durkheim as a general societal

condition of *dérèglement* or derangement – literally, "a rule that is a lack of rule" ([1897] 1951, p.257), or in the original French: "*consciences déréglées et qui erigent en règle le dérèglement dont elles souffrent*" ([1897] 1983, p.287). Andre Lalande [1926] 1980 uses Durkheim's original understanding of anomie. Jean-Marie Guyau preceded Durkheim in using this concept in the year 1885: "*C'est l'absence de loi fixe, qu'on peut désigner sous le terme d'anomie*" (Guyau [1885] 1907, p.165). French dictionaries such as the *Littré* refer to *dérèglement* as a state of corruption, evil, agitation, torment, impiety and intemperance which leads to general suffering and torment.[3] It is significant that these terms can be applied to the social conditions and experiences of both soldiers and prisoners at Abu Ghraib as revealed in testimony and reports and are in line with Durkheim's general assumptions about anomie that it is a disorganised social condition that leads to unnecessary suffering and distress (see Mestrovic and Brown 1985). Extreme suffering and distress, in turn, can lead to scapegoating and the vendetta (Durkheim [1912] 1995, p.404).

Emile Littré was an important disciple of Auguste Comte, who in turn influenced Durkheim. Given that Comte posited a progression of societies from theological through metaphysical to positivistic stages and that the effects of the previous stages are not entirely eliminated, one may suppose that Littré and Durkheim both took very seriously the ancient meanings of words. Like the *Oxford English dictionary*, *Littré's* dictionary ([1863] 1963) seeks out the meanings of words based upon their empirical usage in ancient texts. For example, even if it is true that in contemporary French the statement that one's refrigerator is *dérèglé* means that it is miscalibrated, the more important point is that the ancient meanings that the refrigerator is possessed by evil spirits (theological) or is not functioning in accordance with its essence (metaphysical) are not entirely lost. It is common for modern people to refer to their computers, watches and other machines as "possessed", even if this is said in jest and even though they seek to repair the machines by scientific standards. We wish to make two points in this respect. Firstly, we take seriously Durkheim's precise choice of *dérèglement* as the word to convey the meanings he intended based upon usage extant in his time as well as historical usages, which is a theme consistent with his overall approach to all social facts. Secondly, to state that the military unit at Abu Ghraib was "miscalibrated", according to contemporary French linguistic usage, is still preferable to the claim that it exhibited "normlessness", which is a purely invented word with no long history of usage.

Durkheim treats anomie as acute and temporary as well as chronic and long-lasting. In *Suicide*, as well as other works such as *Moral education* and *Professional ethics*, he also addresses several varieties of anomie, among them conjugal, economic, marital, religious, political, military and intellectual, among others pertaining to various social institutions. Durkheim's scaffolding for understanding anomie includes Arthur Schopenhauer's philosophy in which the imperious will is unrestrained by rational categories or representations (Baillot 1927), theological understandings of *anomia* as sin (Lyonnet and Sabourin 1970) and various other European philosophers (Mestrovic 1985). Again, we stress that the notion of anomie as a kind of sin automatically carries with it the ideas of expiation, scapegoating, suffering and justice; concepts that are important to Durkheim's overall project of sociology conceived as the science of morality.

Thus, Durkheim's overall meaning of *dérèglement* seems to be that it is a severe form of collective derangement. Literally, anomie seems to imply a condition of collective insanity, or more precisely, a societal analogue to a state of individual personality disorder. This connection between individual and collective psychic pathology is not surprising, given that several of Durkheim's contemporaries, especially Sigmund Freud, frequently made the analogy between individual and collective consciousness vis-à-vis deranged psychic structures. Henri Ellenberger (1970) offers what seems to be one of the most comprehensive analyses of the many thinkers from Durkheim's era who subscribed to this point of view. It is worth noting that Durkheim and his contemporaries were writing at a time in which the disciplines of sociology, psychology, psychiatry and other social sciences were not sharply distinguished from each other in the manner in which they are today. For example, Freud held that psychoanalysis was a

tool to be used for apprehending culture, not just the individual. Furthermore and in line with Durkheim's overall assumptions, this perspective on collective derangement should not be reduced to the contemporary version found in Christopher Lasch (1971), for example, wherein a culture of narcissism is reduced to a society of numerous individuals who are deranged narcissists. To be true to Durkheim's assumptions, one should argue instead that to conceive of Abu Ghraib as a deranged (anomic) society is to grasp that it was a place full of violence of many sorts (including psychological and cultural abuse, post-traumatic stress disorder, learned helplessness and physical hardship) that led to many varieties of suffering for all concerned.

While the *dérangement* or madness of Abu Ghraib was patently obvious to all who witnessed the testimony at the trials at Fort Hood, Texas, along with the suffering that it entailed, this connection between anomie and suffering in the case of Abu Ghraib is obscured and sometimes invisible in general as well as scholarly discourse. Regarding the derangement, we note that the Fay Report as well as testimony showed that 90 per cent of the prisoners were not terrorists and were not hostile to the USA; that they had no information to give; that naked prisoners were routinely forced to wear panties in their heads; that the abuse occurred as part of a de facto policy that was not related to interrogation techniques; that the prison was in the middle of a war zone and did not have adequate supplies of food, water, generators and bullets. Soldiers testified that Abu Ghraib was not a normal prison, that they called it "Bizarroworld" and said that it was "hell on earth". Our point is that Durkheim's very precise definition of anomie as derangement fits the facts as they were presented in open trial.

As for suffering, one of the so-called rotten apples (corrupt soldiers) testified that the nights at Abu Ghraib were filled with moans and screams from prisoners who were shackled in painfully contorted positions. The physical suffering of the prisoners may perhaps seem obvious, but other forms of psychic suffering are not as obvious: isolation, humiliation, hopelessness, panic, confusion. But the least obvious suffering was that of the soldiers themselves. Far from the happy, fraternity party atmosphere described by the information media, testimony revealed that the accused soldiers suffered from post-traumatic stress disorder, insomnia, depression and anxiety, in addition to the physical hardships of unlawfully long work shifts, lack of adequate cooling and heating in the work environment, unlawful ratios of guards to prisoners, lack of water and food, inadequate toilet facilities and a host of other factors including but not limited to the fact that most soldiers slept in jail cells. All these facts, verified in open court, are in line with Durkheim's neglected observation that anomie produces suffering of many sorts in various degrees for all participants in an anomic society.

Contrast with conventional perspectives on Abu Ghraib

The facts that were disclosed during testimony and in US Government reports are in line with Durkheim's very precise understanding of anomie as the derangement that produces widespread and unnecessary suffering. In other words, anomie is itself a form of irrational violence (in its many forms, from psychic to physical) that does not and cannot promote social solidarity. Moreover, the anomic job of the soldiers at Abu Ghraib was primarily to inflict suffering on prisoners and the soldiers suffered as they performed these anomic role obligations. Over and over again, we heard soldiers testify on the witness stand that they perceived themselves as punishing prisoners, even as the prosecutor was arguing passionately that the abused prisoners were innocent of any crimes. According to Durkheim ([1893] 1984, p.46), "punishment has remained an act of vengeance, at least in part". But Durkheim distinguishes sharply between the vendetta as a pure form of the vengeance exhibited by the soldiers and the sort of attenuated vengeance exhibited by the prosecutor in a military court martial. Nevertheless, as we have stated from the outset, Durkheim's ([1893] 1984, p.48) overall position is ambiguous: "All that can be said is that the necessity for vengeance is better directed nowadays than in the past".

The truth about Abu Ghraib has been obscured in the general and scholarly discourse into a plethora of inaccurate myths: that the abuse was performed by seven corrupt soldiers, when testimony and reports show that the abuse was part of a widespread pattern of abuse that had migrated from Guantanamo Bay and US-run prisons in Afghanistan as well as elsewhere in Iraq;[4] that the abuse was the result of applying interrogation techniques when in fact prisoners were abused ad hoc in stairways, hallways and places and times that had no relationship to interrogation; that the abuse was the result of obedience to authority when in fact the testimony drove home the point that there was a vacuum of authority and leadership at Abu Ghraib.

There is something deceptively rational about these and other explanations for the abuse because they attempt to mask the derangement uncovered by Durkheim as the most important feature of anomie. If the seven rotten apples can be scapegoated as the root cause of the abuse, then the widespread, systemic and irrational nature of the abuse does not have to be confronted. If the abuse is somehow linked to following rational techniques, then one does not have to face the madness of a de facto policy of torturing prisoners who were not hostile to the USA and who had no information to give. If the abuse was merely the result of following orders then it somehow makes sense, even if such a defence does not sway judges who hold that the soldier is obligated to disobey an unlawful order. In fact, the concept of anomie is not typically used to comprehend the abuse at Abu Ghraib or other sites of war crimes since Durkheim's era – and if it is implied, it is a distant echo of the Parsonian version of anomie as normlessness that emerges, not Durkheim's version as derangement.

Durkheim's perspective was changed considerably by the most influential American sociologist of the twentieth century, Talcott Parsons (1937). Parsons elaborated anomie into the meaning of "the war of all against all" (Parsons 1937, p.407). His most famous disciple was Robert K. Merton, whose "Social structure and anomie" (1957) became the most cited article in sociology. According to Merton (1957, p.161): "as initially developed by Durkheim, the concept of anomie referred to a condition of relative normlessness in a society or group". It is a curious fact that despite the popularity and esteem afforded to Merton's

notion of normlessness, sociologists and criminologists have been relatively silent on the many
instances of anomic war crimes that have
occurred since Durkheim died in the year 1917,
including but not limited to the Holocaust and
genocide in Russia, Yugoslavia and Rwanda, as
well as ethnic cleansing or war crimes in
Vietnam, Cambodia, Afghanistan and elsewhere
(see Gutman and Rieff 1999). In summary, the
concept of normlessness has become a sort of
cottage industry in explaining domestic crime in
the USA, but is seemingly irrelevant in explaining war crimes throughout the world over the
course of a century of discourse on abuse in war
time.

The prosecutor at the court martials
revealed in open court that all of the abused
prisoners were not a threat to US citizens and
had no information to give them (Mestrovic
2007, p.11). In fact, it is highly irrational, chaotic
and deranged to use torture for the sake of
obtaining information on prisoners who had no
information to give. Even if the soldiers who
abused the prisoners did not always know that
their victims did not have information to give
them, the more important Durkheimian point is
that there were no established social mechanisms
in place for ascertaining this important fact (for
example, there was no screening, no judicial
review boards, no assumption that prisoners
were innocent until proven guilty, no implementation of the Geneva Conventions on processing
and treating prisoners and so on). All this
uncertainty, unpredictability, social chaos and
capriciousness seem to support Durkheim's
characterisation of anomie as derangement
more than normlessness.

What does "normlessness" really mean?
Parsons, Merton and other functionalists never
define the term. From the perspective used here,
that Durkheim's understanding of anomie as
derangement must lead to widespread yet
unnecessary suffering, it is interesting that the
functionalist understanding of "normlessness"
is emotionally neutral and does not imply
suffering. Sociologists who have followed Merton's lead seem to believe that normlessness will
lead to crime and deviance, but not suffering.
The more important point, from Durkheim's
perspective, is that the violence produced by
anomie goes far beyond crime and includes
many forms of torment, agitation, sorrow and

suffering, including psychic pain. Moreover,
regarding Abu Ghraib, it is not true that the
Geneva Conventions and other norms ceased to
exist – it is more accurate to observe that these
and other norms were not followed. Finally, the
functionalist perspective assumes that social
systems are self-correcting – but the military
society at Abu Ghraib did not self-correct. In the
words of Captain Jonathan Crisp, defence
counsel for Lynndie England, the dysfunctional
social system at Abu Ghraib not only failed to
self-correct but was self-perpetuating (Mestrovic
2007, p.175). Durkheim ([1897] 1951) assumes
that anomie becomes chronic until self-conscious and deliberate remedies are sought from
outside the dysfunctional system.

In general, functionalists who follow
Parsons and Merton assume that society is a
stable, self-maintaining and self-correcting system made up of norms, values, beliefs and
sanctions.[5] All these assumptions can be questioned with regard to the reality of abuse at Abu
Ghraib. At Abu Ghraib the international norms
(exemplified by the Geneva Conventions) were
sometimes out of sync with national norms
(based upon the US Constitution as well as US
Army field manuals) as well as local norms
(memorandums and competing interpretations
of permissible interrogation methods). US values concerning the importance of democracy
were out of sync with the dehumanising atmosphere established at Abu Ghraib. The collective
belief that the USA was a liberator was out of
sync with the belief that US soldiers acted like
tormentors at Abu Ghraib. The sanctions
exemplified by court martials of low-ranking
soldiers are out of sync with sanctions for grave
breaches of the Geneva Conventions, which call
for the prosecution of high-ranking leaders, or
what is referred to as the doctrine of command
responsibility (see Human Rights Watch 2006).
This doctrine exists as a sort of dead letter:
officers are supposed to be held accountable for
abuses committed by their subordinates on the
grounds that officers knew or *should* have known
of the abuse. In practice, officers are exempt
from responsibility. In the courtroom at Fort
Hood, the military judge hardly bothered to
respond to arguments concerning the doctrine of
command responsibility.

But the most serious flaw in the functionalist misreading of anomie is its excessive

The mall, a place for shoppers and zombies alike (2005). flickr/Mister Wind-Up Bird

rationalism. Merton's depiction of innovation as a discrepancy between socially prescribed goals and the illicit aims used to attain them fails to capture the reality or motivations of the soldiers who abused prisoners at Abu Ghraib. Merton's conceptualisation rests on the Parsonian model of rational social action. But why were the soldiers abusing the prisoners in the deranged ways described above? In private conversations, convicted soldiers told us bluntly that they were told that the prisoners were terrorists who were planning to or already had harmed Americans and to treat them "like dogs" in order to save American lives in the future. The vigilante punishment of potential terrorists who had not been tried is not a socially prescribed goal in American society. If Merton's concept of innovation must be used, we hold that the soldiers were implementing a deranged, anomic form of innovation: both the goals and means used were out of sync with the values of US society.

Anomie in a post-emotional society

Thus far, we have highlighted the discrepancies among perceptions of the abuse at Abu Ghraib from Durkheimian, functionalist and conventional points of view. How can these discrepancies be reconciled? From our perspective, the postmodern reply that social life consists of a sea of circulating fictions (Baudrillard 1986) that can be redefined any way that one chooses is not satisfactory. In his book *Pragmatism and sociology* Durkheim ([1950] 1983) took up the Nietzschean perspective, which has become the intellectual bedrock for much of postmodern discourse, and rejected it. While he agreed with Nietzsche that truth was seemingly malleable and reality was open to many interpretations, Durkheim regarded as sacrilege the Nietzschean rejection of what Durkheim called the cult of truth. We propose that many of these, as well as other discrepancies in conceptualising the Abu Ghraib saga, can be captured in the concept of post-emotionalism – with regard to both the sociology of knowledge involved in grasping the meaning of anomie and the layperson's grasp of the abuse at Abu Ghraib as the result of a few rotten apples as distinct from systemic derangement. The drama of the evils committed at Abu Ghraib using sex, violence and humiliation occurred in the context of what may be called a post-emotional society (Mestrovic 1997).

The post-emotional society harks back to the past in order to create synthetic emotional responses in the present and post-emotionalism is defined as "the tendency for emotionally charged collective representations to be abstracted from their cultural contexts and then manipulated artificially by self and others in new and artificially contrived contexts" (Mestrovic 1997, p.2). Examples range from the Serbs invoking a grievance from the year 1389 in order to justify their violence in Yugoslavia in the 1990s, Greece using the memory of Alexander the Great in order to block the existence of Macedonia in the 1990s and again in the year 2008 to block Macedonia's entrance into NATO, to France and the UK still nursing their wounds at losing their stature as founders of civilisation and the Enlightenment. Similarly, the USA used the moral code of America as the beacon of democracy set upon a hill found in de Tocqueville's ([1848] 2004) *Democracy in America* to justify war against Iraq when the real enemy was Osama bin Laden. President Barack Obama frequently claimed during his campaign that the war against Iraq was a diversion from capturing or killing bin Laden. In Obama's words: "Because of a war in Iraq that should never have been authorised and should never have been waged, we are now less safe than we were before 9/11" (Obama'08 2007). But it took nearly 8 years for a highly visible politician to make this obvious point. Moreover, it seems that few people read or recall the other portions of de Tocqueville's classic, which deal with slavery and the extermination of Native Americans. It is

as if the sinister side of US history emerged at Abu Ghraib in the form of post-emotional racism, humiliation and violence. A moral code that used to evoke genuine emotions among the Puritans was used at the beginning of the present millennium in an attempt to depict US motives in the war against Iraq as noble even if the means involved disregard for the Geneva Conventions.

We note that all the illustrations used above are variations of what Durkheim and Fauconnet call the vendetta. According to Durkheim ([1893] 1984, p.49), "the vendetta was originally the first form of punishment" The vendetta involves vengeance by families and clans against other families and clans. The difference between the vendetta and justice lies in the fact that just expiation is "vengeance for something sacred", namely, a cause that promotes social integration (p.56).

While Mestrovic uses several theoretical perspectives for the intellectual scaffolding of post-emotional theory, including Freud, Riesman and Durkheim, the Durkheimian element will be emphasised in the present analysis. Durkheim ([1893] 1984, p.44) put forth a sociology of passion: "In the first place, punishment constitutes an emotional reaction". All his writings are loaded with concepts pertaining to his general claim that "nearly every collective representation is in a sense delirious" (Durkheim [1912] 1995, p.220). This passionate element in his sociology perhaps derived from but was certainly reinforced by the popularity of Arthur Schopenhauer's ([1818] 1965) philosophy at the time he was writing, stands in sharp contrast to the emphasis placed by Parsons and other functionalists on cognitive, rational aspects of so-called rational social action. In a real sense, Parsons gutted Durkheim's emotionally laden concept of anomie of its emotional import. Moreover, post-emotionalism in general is made possible in a modern society dominated by the information media which intellectualises, rationalises and denatures the emotional import of events. In a word, developments since Durkheim's death in the year 1917 point to a progressive de-sacralisation of the social world, which is the essence of post-emotionalism. In addition, post-emotionalism itself is a form of anomie or societal derangement that leads to widespread, unnecessary suffering (anxiety, depression, feelings of helplessness and so on).

This seems to be the culmination of the dramatic and relatively new development in social relations that David Riesman called other-directedness in his 1950 book, *The lonely crowd*. Riesman's ([1950] 2001, pp.240–243) explicit use of Durkheimian theory and the concept of anomie as elements of his theoretical scaffolding in this best-selling sociology book of all time has been neglected. For our purposes here, the interesting connection between Durkheim and Riesman is that both are extremely sensitive to the emotional nuances of social life and various types of suffering in different types of society.

The modern, other-directed type has mutated from Riesman's description of a shallow conformist and manipulator of self and others into the sophisticated, post-emotional voyeur of emotional drama considered as text, not reality. The Geneva Conventions are simply too inner-directed and old-fashioned to have a genuine impact on other-directed society: they were authored by individuals who possessed internal moral gyroscopes or a moral compass and who believed that moral standards should last for at least their lifetimes. The other-directed, post-emotional type is resigned to the conclusion that moral standards can and do change much more rapidly so that one is expected merely to do the best that one can under given circumstances. In David Riesman's terminology, the other-directed or what we call the post-emotional type has become the ultimate inside dopester:

The inside dopester may be one who has concluded (with good reason) that since he can do nothing to change politics, he can only understand it. Or he may see all political issues in terms of being able to get some insider on the telephone. That is, some inside-dopesters actually crave to *be* on the inside, to join an inner circle or invent one; others aim no higher than to *know* the inside, for whatever peer-group satisfactions this can bring them. (Riesman [1950] 2001, p.181)

Riesman's depiction of the helplessness of the observer to change politics applies also to the American soldier's sense of helplessness in changing policies at Abu Ghraib. Testimony revealed that numerous attempts at whistle blowing were invalidated by superiors who, when informed of abuse by idealistic, young soldiers, told them "just go back to work".

In line with Durkheim's understanding of anomie as derangement, Riesman likens an extremely other-directed or what we are calling post-emotional society to a mental health ward, as when he writes:

The ambulatory patients in the ward of modern culture show many analogous symptoms of too much compliance and too little insight, though of course their symptoms are not so sudden and severe. Their lack of emotion and emptiness of expression are as characteristic of many contemporary anomics as hysteria or outlawry was characteristic of anomics in the societies depending on earlier forms of direction. (Riesman [1950] 2001, p.244)

Note that, like Durkheim, Riesman contextualises anomie depending upon society's stage of development: anomie will differ in traditional, inner-directed and other-directed societies; even if all types of anomie are forms of derangement. And he concludes: "Taken all together, the anomics – ranging from overt outlaws to catatonic types who lack even the spark for living, let alone for rebellion – constitute a sizable number in America" (p. 245). Perhaps the numbers of anomics and of the helpless, post-emotional type of anomics have increased still further since Riesman wrote these words in 1950.

Consider, as an illustration, one of the most iconic photographs from Abu Ghraib, that of a prisoner who was named Gilligan by the American soldiers and who is shown standing on a box, hooded, waiting to be electrocuted. One of the most eerie moments of the court martials at Fort Hood, Texas, was the testimony by several soldiers that Gilligan was friendly and liked the soldiers, and that they liked him too. (Riesman emphasises that other-directed society favours the veneer of events being "nice" and falsely agreeable to the peer group). This photograph of what appears to be old-fashioned torture was redescribed in the courtroom as a friendly incident in which soldiers were doing their job trying to keep Gilligan awake and that he understood this so that he laughed and joked with them during the torture. The defence attorney insisted that Gilligan and the soldiers who tortured him were friends. It did not appear to us that the witnesses who testified to this effect were self-consciously lying. This iconic incident was redescribed as a sort of "nice", post-emotional torture – again, the behaviour and the emotions were not connected. We learned through interviewing the soldiers involved that they felt anxious and depressed doing their jobs of inflicting suffering onto Gilligan and one may surmise that Gilligan was experiencing a form of Stockholm syndrome. The real suffering in this incident is not evident from the photo or the testimony, but the anomic or deranged element of the situation emerges when one applies Durkheim's understanding of anomie. There is something crazy about the idea of friendly torture.

Another important connection between Durkheim's and Riesman's approaches to what we are calling post-emotional society is captured by Riesman's line that in contemporary societies, "just because such a premium is put on sincerity, a premium is put on faking it" (Riesman [1950] 2001, p.196). While Durkheim did not foresee the fake sincerity that has become the staple of modern propaganda, political campaigns, advertising slogans, television talk shows, spin doctors, and other aspects of culture, he was a proponent of sincere and spontaneous collective effervescence. Fake sincerity is another subtle aspect of anomie as a form of derangement that leads to unnoticed forms of suffering that stem from sincere emotions not being validated by the collective consciousness. The result is the learned helplessness of the inside dopester.

In this context, one of the most remarkable things about the abuse at Abu Ghraib is that it was framed by the culture industry primarily as an interrogation technique. Some of the following were listed as being such techniques: yelling, shouting, inducing fear, loud music, the presence of military working dogs and deception – among others. If one reads this list of behaviour, without knowing that it was from an approved list of interrogation techniques, one might think that they were a description of what angry people do in abusive relationships. The post-emotional soldier is put in the position of being able to rationalise whatever emotions he or she might be feeling – even friendly feelings – while yelling, shouting and abusing prisoners as just doing one's job of inflicting suffering. Moreover, the soldier is convinced by the peer-group that the job of inflicting suffering is beneficial to the American cause because it

might save the lives of American soldiers in the future by obtaining information (which, in reality, did not exist).

For example, the Company Commander, Captain Donald Reese, testified that he was told by his superiors that the practice of prisoners wearing panties on their heads was "an MI thing" or a "supply issue". When he first saw the prisoners wearing panties on their heads, he said that he was shocked. But his genuine emotional reaction was soon invalidated by the deranged social setting at Abu Ghraib. The "MI thing" explanation is a vague attempt to claim that wearing panties on one's head was an interrogation technique, even though such a technique is not listed anywhere and no rational-legal authority exists to support it. The "supply issue" explanation is the back-up rationalisation: one is expected to believe that the US Army was unable to procure blankets and clothing for detainees, so it had them wear women's panties (which were purchased in Baghdad) to protect them from the cold. The obvious, sincere explanation for women's panties on the heads of Iraqi prisoners is that the Army was seeking to humiliate the Iraqi detainees. But this simple, obvious explanation was never made in court and is not really obvious in post-emotional society. Instead, witnesses resorted to tortured logic and preposterous claims, which were not challenged by the judge, the attorneys, the jury or even the media. To this day, nearly 3 years after the testimony, the fact that prisoners were forced to wear panties on their heads is almost never cited or discussed in the thousands of articles written by post-emotional opinion-makers. The reason for this neglect is that this act comes across as so crazy that it is easier to ignore it than to try to explain it. The company commander's explanation was accepted without emotional reaction by the judge, jury or media, as if he had said something to the effect that he drank from a glass of water. Living in the post-emotional society feels like being in the Twilight Zone. Preposterous, crazy explanations and behaviour are tolerated so long as they can be explained with reference, however tangential, to some technique that proposes even the vaguest sort of rational action and without expressing genuine emotional fire.

We note that Captain Reese and other witnesses at the Abu Ghraib were given immunity from prosecution in exchange for their testimony against the soldiers who were literally chosen for conviction. Several witnesses testified in open court that the Army threatened to charge them with crimes that were levelled at the rotten apples unless they agreed to testify against them. Durkheim and Fauconnet could not have foreseen the increasingly standard practice of forcing testimony by intimidating and threatening witnesses with prosecution. Immunity from prosecution is also immunity from punishment. More important, it creates a rehearsed, staged and what we call post-emotional atmosphere to what used to be described in more spontaneous terms as the quest for justice.

Post-emotionalism in the sociology of knowledge used to comprehend the anomic abuse at Abu Ghraib

The conceptual tools for comprehending the anomic evils at Abu Ghraib have also become post-emotional. We have already discussed the functionalist misunderstanding of anomie, which has resulted in the seeming irrelevance of "normlessness" to issues and sites pertaining to war crimes. However, even Philip Zimbardo's (2007) famous Stanford Prison Experiment conducted in 1971, has been gutted of emotional impact. It purports to apply a controversial lesson from the Second World War – that ordinary people commit terrible acts because of obedience to authority – to a situation that does not seem connected to circumstances from Germany in the Second World War. Is the connection valid? We cannot repeat often enough that the testimony revealed an absence of authority at Abu Ghraib and that the high-ranking officers who passively allowed the abuse at Abu Ghraib and elsewhere – implicitly or explicitly – escaped culpability completely, despite the existence of command responsibility. All the blame has been shifted to the low-ranking soldiers who committed some of the abuse, which is a form of scapegoating.

The major post-emotional component to Zimbardo's (2007) efforts to comprehend the abuse at Abu Ghraib in terms of his obedience to authority paradigm is that it is a reaction to a very particular understanding of Nazi atrocities in the Second World War which may or may not be true. Like Stanley Milgram, Zimbardo attempted to synthetically apply a model derived from the Second World War Nazi era out of its proper context to Abu Ghraib. In other words, Zimbardo takes a model of abuse from the fascist era and transplants it into a non-fascist, American context.

There is no good reason to suppose that fascist models of behaviour will apply to other-directed, post-emotional societies such as the USA. There are many different social-scientific analyses of Nazi atrocities, ranging from Erich Fromm (1992) to Bauman (1990) and others who cannot be reviewed here due to the limitations of space. Moreover, the obedience to authority paradigm is still hotly debated with respect to understanding Nazis. But the important point for the purposes of the present discussion is that Abu Ghraib did not have the communication and command structure of either Nazi military units or Zimbardo's Stanford experiment. On the contrary, soldiers from Abu Ghraib testified consistently that they were not sure who was the commander at Abu Ghraib and were not certain to which chain of command they belonged. In this fundamental way, the soldiers at Abu Ghraib experienced an anomic (deranged) absence of authority, unlike the mock guards at Stanford, who were in constant contact and under the supervision of the mock warden, Philip Zimbardo.

Zimbardo admits on his websites that he orchestrated prison guard techniques based upon his understanding of Nazi Germany. Thus, Zimbardo's non-contextual imposition of Nazi techniques and the peculiarities of his total control over the Stanford experiment onto Abu Ghraib constitutes post-emotionalism, on a par with the Serbs in the 1990s pretending that they were fighting the Battle of Kosovo from 1389, or the USA attacking Iraq in retaliation for 9/11, which had no connection with 9/11 (the documentation for the fact that there is no logical connection between 9/11 and the war in Iraq and also that this connection was made by the Bush Administration, is extensive. The point is that there is no parallel among these events, which is the essence of post-emotionalism. Again, we quote the then President-elect Obama, who accused the Bush Administration of "a deliberate strategy to misrepresent 9/11 to sell a war against a country that had nothing to do with 9/11" (Obama'08 2007).

Other important differences between Zimbardo's post-emotional application of his Stanford experiment to Abu Ghraib and a Durkheimian perspective include the following: Zimbardo's students knew that they were relatively safe on the campus of a major university whereas soldiers at Abu Ghraib worked in a war zone in which they were mortared regularly and experienced daily fear that they might not survive the night. Zimbardo structured his experiment as a post-emotional response to the Second World War whereas the entire war in Iraq was a post-emotional response to 9/11. In Durkheimian terms, the emotional desire for retribution should have been aimed at bin Laden but was instead displaced onto Iraq and Iraqis became scapegoats for the pain and suffering experienced by Americans. The association of Saddam Hussein with Al-Qaida was false. To repeat, Barack Obama made his case to the American people 8 years into the War on Terror that American resources and prestige were drained by the war in Iraq instead of pursuing bin Laden. In Durkheimian language, President-elect Obama finally made the emotional connection between offence and punishment that the Bush Administration had obscured post-emotionally by punishing the wrong country.

Zimbardo emphasises that his students knew that they could have walked out of the experiment at any time, whereas soldiers in the US Army could not walk out an abusive situation without risking charges of mutiny and desertion. Zimbardo created a deranged situation in which he made use of the real Palo Alto Police Department to arrest students who were picked to act like prisoners, which must have disoriented and shocked the students. Zimbardo deceived the students along the lines of Riesman's aforementioned fake sincerity. The role of psychologists and psychiatrists in torture is a topic of recent controversy in the USA and these professions have played similar, problematic roles in the former Soviet Union (for a sampling of the complexity of this controversy, see Stanley Fish's article in *The New York Times* as well as the responses by bloggers [Fish 2008]).

Yet Zimbardo projects the scientific veneer of "an experiment" onto a situation that was so psychologically harmful to students it most likely would not have passed most contemporary university research and review boards in the USA.

Perhaps the most glaring discrepancy between the two situations lies in the notion of responsibility. Zimbardo subtly shifted the responsibility for his experiment onto the presumed complicity of the Palo Alto Police Department, the President of Stanford University and the American Psychological Association such that the students who participated in his experiment had to assume that they were relatively safe because of the implicit participation of these and other normative bodies. As such, they were absolved of real responsibility for their actions in the experiment. A different situation of what we call "post-responsibility" occurred at Abu Ghraib. Soldiers were convinced that their failure to obtain information (that did not exist) would result in the future deaths of other American soldiers. Throughout the trials we witnessed, the prosecutor hammered the point that even the release of the photographs resulted in deaths to Americans because of the hatred the photos incited. In this way, the testimony of soldiers that they took photographs to document the abuse – to engage in acts of whistle blowing – became distorted as false responsibility for the presumed effects of the photographs.

In summary, we stated at the outset that Zimbardo's experiment is typically cited to explain the abuse at Abu Ghraib and Durkheim is not cited. But Durkheim's theory is preferable to Zimbardo's because Durkheim's grand theory offers concepts (punishment, anomie, expiation, scapegoating and vendetta) that are universal and applicable to all societies, past and present, traditional and modern. By contrast, Zimbardo offers a theory based upon a specific place (Germany) and time frame (the Second World War) that he uses to explain abuse at Stanford and Abu Ghraib. And we note that from a Durkheimian perspective the profession of psychology bears some collective responsibility, for the role of psychologists in the abuse at Abu Ghraib, Guantanamo and elsewhere remains controversial (see Mayer, 2005).

Post-emotional responsibility at Abu Ghraib and in American society at large

As noted from the outset, Durkheim assumed that there were normal and healthy forms of obedience to authority by soldiers, as well as for the phenomenon of punishment. To repeat, society expects soldiers to obey authority, but it also expects authority to reflect society's standards of justice. It is not obedience to authority per se that is the culprit but anomic obedience to anomic authority, by which we mean deranged normative standards that do not make sense to the collective conscience. Similarly, Durkheim ([1893] 1984, pp.44–52) insisted that as societies become modern, punishment becomes less harsh, less an expression of retribution and more an expression of restitution. Nevertheless, and as we noted at the outset, Durkheim believed that the traditional element of emotional retribution is never entirely eliminated in modern societies, even if it may be attenuated:

Thus punishment has remained for us what it was for our predecessors. It is still an act of vengeance, since it is an expiation. What we are avenging and what the criminal is expiating, is the outrage to morality (Durkheim [1893] 1984, p.47).

Obviously, the harsh "punishments" at Abu Ghraib were an anomic departure from this normal state of affairs. An understandable response to the outrage to morality that was 9/11 resulted in yet another outrage to morality that was the abuse at Abu Ghraib. This is the post-emotional tragedy that we have attempted to describe. A witness testified at the trials that Abu Ghraib "was not a normal prison" – but this assertion presupposes, in Durkheim's fashion, that normative prisons can and do exist. Similarly, Durkheim ([1912] 1995, p.404) warned that punishment must avoid singling out individuals with less social significance "to fill the function of scapegoat". He elaborates:

When the pain reaches such a pitch, it becomes suffused with a kind of anger and exasperation. One feels the need to break or destroy something. One attacks oneself or others. One strikes, wounds, or burns oneself, or one attacks someone else, in order to strike, wound, or burn him. Thus

was established the mourning custom of giving oneself over to veritable orgies of torture. It seems to me probable that the *vendetta* and head hunting have no other origin. If every death is imputed to some magical spell and if, for that reason, it is believed that the dead person must be avenged, the reason is *a felt need to find a victim at all costs on whom the collective sorrow and anger can be discharged. This victim will naturally be sought outside, for an outsider is a subject minoris resistentiae*; since he is not protected by the fellow-feeling that attaches to a relative or a neighbour, nothing about him blocks and neutralises the bad and destructive feelings aroused by the death. Probably for the same reason, a woman serves more often than a man as the passive object of the cruelest mourning rites. Because she has lower social significance, she is more readily singled out fill the *function of scapegoat* (Durkheim [1912] 1995, p.404, emphases added)

Regarding scapegoating, he writes elsewhere:

When society undergoes suffering, it feels the need to find someone whom it can hold responsible for its sickness, on whom it can avenge its misfortune and those against whom opinion already discriminates are naturally designated for this role. These are the pariahs who serve as expiatory victims. (Lukes 1985, p.345)

Scapegoating and the vendetta, for Durkheim, seem to be an anomic miscarriage of justice. With regard to the present discussion, it seems that all of Iraq became a scapegoat for the pain and sorrow of 9/11; the prisoners at Abu Ghraib became scapegoats for the US Army's frustrations; and the so-called seven rotten apples became the scapegoats for the Army's and American society's frustration, pain, shame and other suffering. Scapegoating involves post-emotional reasoning, because by its very nature it involves the synthetic and false displacements of emotions onto false targets.

Iraq had nothing to do with 9/11, the prisoners at Abu Ghraib were mostly ordinary Iraqis, and the seven soldiers convicted at Ft Hood – though they were found guilty for some of the charges levelled against them – were part of a widespread, de facto policy of abuse towards prisoners. Thus, anomie is not limited to the prison setting at Abu Ghraib but ranges far and wide to involve a weakening of the previous high regard for the Geneva Conventions and subsequent, similar abuse at Guantanamo Bay, Bagram Air Force Base in Afghanistan and scores of other US facilities in

Iraq. In addition and in line with Durkheim's assessment in *Professional ethics and civic morals*, professional organisations such as the American Medical Association (there were doctors at Abu Ghraib who turned a blind eye to the abuse), the American Psychological Association and a number of other institutions and groups whose functioning became increasingly anomic following the events of 9/11. Respectable analysts have labelled the war in Iraq as a fiasco, the result of incompetence and as caused by a state of denial (see Galbraith 2007; Ricks 2006; Woodward 2007). All this is in keeping with Durkheim's overall assessment that "it is to this state of anomie that . . . must be attributed the continually recurring conflicts and disorders of every kind" (Durkheim [1893] 1984, p.xxxv).

Let us return to the testimony concerning abuse of the prisoner nicknamed Gilligan. The testimony revealed that a superior said to Specialist Sabrina Harman: "Do whatever you want to him, just don't kill him". This is not exactly a direct order, but more of an other-directed, ad hoc expression of de facto policy. This was the vague, post-emotional version of the normative, inner-directed moral compass or gyroscope (from Riesman) that soldiers were given to gauge their behaviour towards prisoners for whom they were responsible. Interestingly, even though this was the anomic and clearly unlawful directive that was given to Harman, the judge and prosecutor both argued that Harman should have known better than to follow this unlawful order. It is alleged that common sense should have caused Harman to disobey this unlawful order, even though such ad hoc directives were commonplace at Abu Ghraib. In a sense, the court put Harman and other soldiers in the position of judge and jury for commands given in a war zone with all the post-emotional pressures we have already discussed (the most salient being that failure to follow this unlawful order might result in the death of Americans in the future).

The defence attorney responded in court to these claims by saying, "Shame on the Army!" for expecting an ill-equipped, ill-trained junior specialist to be able to challenge an unlawful order in such an environment. The important point is that instead of the Army prosecuting the officer who gave her the unlawful order, in accordance with the established doctrine of command responsibility, the court placed the responsibility for the officer's unlawful order onto the low-ranking soldier for her failure to disobey an unlawful order (on this trend to blame the low-ranking soldier for failure to disobey an unlawful order, see also Solis 1998).

Consider Major General Geoffrey Miller's well-documented mission in the summer of 2003 to "Gitmoize" Abu Ghraib. By Gitmoize he meant that the procedures at Abu Ghraib were supposed to be modelled on the procedures at Guantanamo Bay. Brigadier General Janis Karpinski, among others, documents the fact that this was General Miller's intention and writes:

The next day we greeted another visitor, who really would change our lives. Major General Geoffry Miller, Commander of the terrorist detention centre in Guantanamo Bay, Cuba, had been sent . . . to suggest improvement. . . . His prisoners, accused terrorists of many nationalities, were not regarded as prisoners of war and thus were not subject to the restrictions of the Geneva Conventions. Ours were. It was hard to see how Miller could "Gitmo-ize" a chaotic hellhole like Abu Ghraib. (Karpinski 2005, p.197).

One of these many procedures was that the role distinctions between military police and military intelligence were supposed to be merged such that MPs would be "softening up" prisoners at times other than during formal interrogation. The Geneva Conventions were ruled not to apply to Guantanamo Bay, but were supposed to apply to American-run prisons in Iraq, including Abu Ghraib. However, once soldiers and Abu Ghraib were Gitmoized, responsibility for the abusive behaviour of the soldiers at Abu Ghraib was vehemently denied by the highest levels of the chain of command in the US Army. The military judge would not allow General Miller to testify at the trials of the soldiers. General Miller was never prosecuted and was never held responsible for the abuse that ensued following his visit – even though the doctrine of command responsibility holds that he was responsible. Thus, in another curious variation of post-emotional politics, the following logic was put forth and largely accepted by the media and American society: (a) the documented abuse at Guantanamo does not constitute a war crime because the Geneva Conventions supposedly did not apply there; (b) when similar techniques were used at Abu Ghraib, where the abuse did constitute a war crime, the responsibility for the abuse was deemed to lie solely on the shoulders of the low-ranking soldiers at Abu Ghraib.

Similarly, testimony revealed that some of the unauthorised techniques at Abu Ghraib "migrated" from Afghanistan (in addition to Guantanamo) and under similar circumstances. The Geneva Conventions supposedly did not apply in Afghanistan; they did apply in Iraq; and the soldiers in Iraq were responsible for the unlawful techniques from Afghanistan. There is a deranged (from Durkheim) or Kafkaesque element to such post-emotional logic pertaining to responsibility.

Conclusions

This thumbnail sketch survey of the change in meanings of anomie from Durkheim's era to the present has uncovered many areas for future investigation and research, including issues in the sociology of knowledge. Durkheim was a grand theorist whose concept of anomie captured universal structures in society that also go by the names derangement and sin. In contrast to Durkheim and due to a series of rebellions against grand theory that go by names such as postmodernism and Merton's middle-range theories, the concept of anomie has been stripped of its original meanings as well as connotations. The misunderstanding of anomie as normlessness has been literally useless in understanding the many instances of war crimes that have occurred since Durkheim's era, yet it continues to be quoted in textbooks and treatises.

The vacuum in meaning has been filled by concepts that we call post-emotional: instead of seeking universal concepts, scholars apply concepts from a particular era and context to a situation in another era out of context. This post-emotional tendency has been illustrated with regard to Zimbardo, who misapplies the idea of obedience to authority taken from a Second World War Nazi context to the abuse at Abu Ghraib. In addition, the abuse at Abu Ghraib was itself a post-emotional misplacement and displacement of a host of emotional reactions from 9/11 and other sites of collective effervescence that resulted in out-of-context aggression. We conclude that Durkheim's un-derstanding of anomie as literally a form of derangement seems to apply to these post-emotional instances of scapegoating and misplaced responsibility that seem to plague the times in which we live.

We draw several conclusions from this analysis. One is that Durkheim's theory should be studied in relation to abuse, war crimes, justice, punishment and related topics not only by scholars, but also by jurists, diplomats and others who work in international relations and law. Although he was writing over a century ago, Durkheim's ideas still apply and offer fresh (because they have been largely ignored) perspectives on contemporary issues such as collateral damage, surgical air strikes, the detainment and treatment of prisoners, adherence to the Geneva Conventions and other, related issues. His perspective is worthy of being rediscovered and of serious discussion. In addition, the relevance of Zimbardo's paradigm should be reconsidered. His attempt to graft a model of abuse based upon fascism onto non-fascist, American sites of abuse seems to fall flat, even though it continues to be widely cited. We believe that a vigorous debate as to who is more relevant for understanding contemporary abuse, Durkheim or Zimbardo, would be highly beneficial to the social sciences as well as policy-makers.

Also, we conclude that according to Durkheimian theory, the US response should have included the following elements. Normative standards such as adherence to the Geneva Conventions should have been strengthened rather than weakened. Professional ethical standards among physicians, psychologists, lawyers, supply officers, nurses, corrections officers and others should have been followed rigorously along the lines that he suggests for preventing anomie in his *Professional ethics*. The natural desire to avenge 9/11 should have been attenuated as far as possible and restricted to Osama bin Laden and his followers along the lines of what the military calls surgical police actions. Existing, normative institutions and structures such as federal courts and the US Constitution should be used to try alleged terrorists and the prison facility at Guantanamo should be closed. The abuse at Abu Ghraib should have been expiated by punishing high-ranking civilian and military leaders in accordance with the established doctrine of command responsibility. In all these

"A new kind of fear": Jean Baudrillard's neo-Durkheimian theory of mass-mediated suicide

Alexander Riley

Unless you happen on one of the shortened versions of the event that are to be found on the Internet, the video footage of R. Budd Dwyer's suicide is an uneventful, even boring piece of video until about 2 minutes from the end.[1] It looks for most of its duration like what it was: a televised press conference held by a relatively obscure political figure, a Pennsylvania state treasurer, to make a public statement regarding serious charges on which he had recently been tried and found guilty. Most had probably expected it would consist of an announcement of his resignation, given that he was to be sentenced on the following day. Instead, the press in attendance that day heard a long, rambling monologue about justice and injustice in the American political system, in which Dwyer compared himself to Job and the political prisoners of the former Soviet gulag, followed by the handing out to colleagues and friends of what they would only later discover were his farewell wishes to them and orders regarding the disposal of his body. With startling suddenness, a large pistol emerged from a paper bag. Some onlookers immediately grasped the scripted conclusion of this drama and cried out. Others apparently moved toward Dwyer to try to intervene; he responded by warning them "No, stay back! This thing could hurt someone!" He then quickly put the pistol to his mouth and pulled the trigger. Screams erupted from the crowd as the cameras focused for long seconds, a seeming eternity, on what an instant before had been a living man, blood pouring profusely from his nose and mouth, his unseeing eyes gazing at something we can only imagine. As the camera fixed on his dead face, there were calls from someone to stop photographing and filming, calls that went unheeded for what seemed a very, very long time.

The shocking, scandalous footage of Dwyer's mass-mediated suicide in January 1987 has been frequently discussed in the context of journalistic ethics and the moral decisions that are made to run or censor controversial footage, but as far as I know it has never been taken seriously as an object of cultural analysis. What does this document *do*? What is its meaning? What place does it occupy in the cultural world that produced it? For many, it seems, these are easy questions to answer. The most common reaction to the existence of such video evidence is revulsion: this video and others like it are an offence against common decency and only someone morbidly obsessed with the gruesome and gory could bear watching such things, much less acknowledge them as fascinating. In a book-length treatment of the fascination exercised on viewers by the photographic evidence of the cruelty and horror of war, Susan Sontag considered this position at some length. Although her central argument is that at least some of this visual evidence can perhaps do what she sees as the positive work of turning viewers morally against all martial conflict, she notes several times in the text that there are arguments, in her view often difficult to counter, that such images can only ultimately be a way of numbing the conscience, or, worse, a form of depraved

Alexander Riley is the author of *Godless intellectuals?: The intellectual pursuit of the sacred reinvented* (2010). He currently teaches cultural sociology at Bucknell University.
Email: alexandertriley@gmail.com

pleasure at the spectacle of the death of others. She is tormented on the issue, even criticising her own earlier argument to the effect that repeated exposure to such extreme photographs inevitably dulls sympathy (Sontag 2003, p.105). It is a troubling aspect of the modern condition that bombardment with information, visual and otherwise, tends to provide additional possibilities for viewers to distance themselves from the real and take on a cynical stance vis-à-vis even the most serious and disturbing information. The evidence for this phenomenon can be found in the comments sections at any of the various web pages where images of serious accidents and death are viewable. Many of the commentators are deliberately flippant and seem engaged in a kind of unannounced contest to see who can respond in the most uncaring, outlandish, cynical manner possible. As Sontag puts it, "Some people will do anything to prevent themselves from being moved" (Sontag 2003, p.111). This fact alone, she notes, should be sufficient to make us wary of the work that is likely done by images of the snuffing out of human lives.

Sontag is undoubtedly correct that some of the reaction to such images will involve cynicism and numbing to suffering. But we have no reason to believe this exhausts the possibilities of what such images do. Indeed, she gives us no compelling reason even to believe that the paired and opposing readings she presents (moral reaction against violence versus immoral numbing to violence) come close to covering the spectrum of potential effects or readings. Similar binaries are frequently presented in discussions of the effects of violent video games: do they numb players to violence or do they instead perhaps impress them with the cruelty of violence without the necessity of actually inflicting it? But what if these are not the only options? Perhaps there are other things going on. Perhaps our examination of this cultural object should include an examination of just how much such a framework of possible responses and effects is itself generated by a cultural nexus of values and beliefs that also requires explanation and perhaps critique.

In this chapter I attempt to use the neo-Durkheimian thought of Jean Baudrillard[2] to shed some light on the strange subject of mass-mediated suicide. The adjective is essential here;

this is not an essay on suicide. I make no effort here to discuss the psychological or sociological factors that lead particular people to attempt suicide; though this was Durkheim's central preoccupation in his own classic work on the subject, I argue in what follows that Baudrillard's status as a neo-Durkheimian derives not from that but from other parts of the Durkheimian corpus. Nor am I interested in the specific consequences that suicides have on relatives and associates of the suicide victim, a common focus in much of the socio-psychological literature on suicide. I take mass-mediated suicide as a cultural object more broadly conceived, that is, as a phenomenon that generates meaning for people who encounter it precisely in its mass-mediated form. This means we are considering a media event, not simply a socio-psychological one. It is the possible ways in which those who encounter mass-mediated suicide from the relatively culturally distanced position of media viewers construe its meaning that are my central concern here. It goes without saying that suicide is a morally charged and controversial topic and that much scholarly commentary on the topic is addressed fundamentally to its status as a social problem and thus to ways to intervene in the lives of those prone to suicidal thoughts in order to attempt to prevent at least some suicidal acts from taking place. This essay tackles this topic from a different theoretical optic and therefore has different goals.

Symbolic exchange and suicide

Though there is much discussion about the shift in the trajectory of Baudrillard's thought over the years from Marxism to post-Marxism and from early structuralism to later postmodernist musing, there is a consistent vision of the particular role occupied by violent death in capitalist modernity evident from one of his first books to the essay he wrote about the September 11, 2001 attack on the World Trade Center. In the first chapter of *The consumer society* we find a discussion of "the consumed vertigo of catastrophe" that is essentially a meditation on the public's fascination with televised accounts of violent destruction and death. Here,

Baudrillard's analysis is still in development, yet already the point and its genealogy are clear. The "collective sacrifice of sheet-metal, machinery and *human lives*" ([1970] 1998, p.46 we see violently consumed in automobile accidents on the nightly news and elsewhere are in fact nothing more or less than capitalist society's particular way of handling what Georges Bataille called the *part maudite*. Tracking this idea to its intellectual origins in Marcel Mauss, we can speak of such mediated experiences as our reconfigured potlatch (Baudrillard [1970] 1998, p.47). Auto accidents fascinate us and the mass media that provide us with much of our common symbolic culture, because they hearken to the fundamental social need to see excess violently destroyed. A few years later, in *The mirror of production*, he again explicitly invokes this Bataillian/Maussian framework on economy and excess as his chief theoretical counterweight to the standpoint of Marx that had previously been so important for his studies of capitalist modernity:

If there was one thing Marx did not think about, it was discharge, waste, sacrifice, prodigality, play and symbolism. . . . The social wealth produced [by Marxist labour] is material; it has nothing to do with symbolic wealth which, mocking natural necessity, comes conversely from destruction, the deconstruction of value, transgression, or discharge. . . . According to Bataille, "sacrificial economy or symbolic exchange is exclusive of political economy" (Baudrillard [1973] 1975, pp.42–43).

This analysis, however, does not achieve its most detailed exposition until a few more years later, in the fifth chapter of his *Symbolic exchange and death*. Here, he embarks on an anthropology of capitalist death that is thoroughly Durkheimian, though he is perhaps required to make Durkheimian thought bend and even cry out as he shapes it to the task at hand.[3] The central point in his analysis is that death has been excluded from our cycle of exchange. Leaving the symbolic order and entering the modern productivist mode of exchange fundamentally shifted our relationship to the dead and death. Where once there was a sacrificial putting to death in order to "extinguish what threatens to fall out of the group's symbolic control and to bury it under all the weight of the dead," an act that is "neither violence nor an acting out of the unconscious" (Baudrillard [1976] 1993, pp.138–139), death in

the modern world is reformulated by our desire to obliterate it with our rationality and science. In a form that parallels the emergence of racism, we systematically exclude the dead from our social networks, eager to privilege one side of the binary life/death in the same way that racist social orders privilege one side of the white/non-white binary. From this perspective, the "natural death" has today become "the only good death" in so far as it is death "defeated and subjected to the law" (Baudrillard [1976] 1993, p.162). Only death that can be economistically calculated as the triumph of life is acceptable; this is the death that comes "at the end of a long, productive life" that we see extolled constantly in newspaper obituaries. The "early" death by accident or disease or any other cause is a failure, in productive terms. Science and the administration of social life have not done their work effectively enough when anyone is permitted to die in an accident or of disease before she has been productively exhausted and used up over a span of 70+ years of work and consumption. Baudrillard cites Weber's protestant ethic thesis as a key explanatory mechanism for the emergence of this new view of death and the dead (Baudrillard [1976] 1993, p.145). The "political economy of individual salvation" established by the reformers is generalised throughout the capitalist west, beginning in the sixteenth century. Life, in Franklin's Poor Richard aphorisms, becomes synonymous with economic value; time is money and so the more the better. Extend life, sequester death, "life as accumulation, death as due payment" (Baudrillard [1976] 1993, p.147).

Primitive death, on the other hand, had always been "social, public and collective and it is always the effect of an adversarial will that the group must absorb" (Baudrillard [1976] 1993, p.164). Here, the body is transformed into a symbolic relation in an exchange with the society of the dead. Baudrillard directly invokes the work of Durkheim and his student Robert Hertz in discussing the relationship those still immersed in the symbolic order have with their doubles and comparing it to what emerges with the modern notion of the soul. It is a movement away from a "non-alienated duel-relation with his double . . . [for h]e really can trade . . . with his shadow", while we cannot, as death has been robbed of its collective character

(Baudrillard [1976] 1993, p.141). But the movement from one relation to another is not complete. Even in capitalist modernity, we recognise the power of that primitive relationship, in some profound if unclear way and are motivated to seek forms of death that transgress the modern law of death:

All passion then takes refuge in violent death, which is the sole manifestation of something like the sacrifice, that is to say, like a real transmutation through the will of the group. And in this sense, it matters little whether death is accidental, criminal or catastrophic: from the moment it escapes "natural" reason and becomes a challenge to nature, it once again becomes the business of the group, demanding a collective and symbolic response; in a word, it arouses the passion for the artificial, which is at the same time sacrificial passion. (Baudrillard [1976] 1993, p.165)

Accidents, catastrophes, unplanned disaster are all anathema to the logic of life as capital because they elude our calculations and our control and thus our efforts to maximise the return on our investments. In this, intriguingly, we are more primitive than the primitives, Baudrillard claims, for they have ways of accounting for the violence of chance that we have long since rejected as unscientific (Baudrillard [1976] 1993, p.161). Yet this systemic logic is still countered at some unconscious level by the half-obscured cultural memory of the world that preceded the present one. Still we yearn for the death that eludes planning and sequestration. At bottom, this is because, well beneath the veneer of individualist modernity, we recognise the redemptive power of the group and the symbolic strength of a social system that brings death and the dead back into play. It is a "passion for the artificial," that is, a collective desire to invoke death at our social discretion as a term of exchange, instead of seeing it as the province of nature, and derive collective energy from the ritual process by which we bring it about (Baudrillard [1976] 1993, p.165). The sacrificial death for the primitives is a refusal of what we moderns term the nature/social divide; through it they bring the natural into their cycle of social exchange and thereby empower the collectivity. 'We are equal partners in this exchange,' they are saying.

In our modern world, of course, sacrificial death has long been morally rejected as unciv-ilised and inhuman. But the legal work required for that redefinition is never sufficient to wholly destroy the symbolic longing for total exchange-ability. The state endeavours to fully control death, but there are always deaths that elude that control. These, in Baudrillard's view, retain something of the effervescent energy of the sacrifice (Baudrillard [1976] 1993, p.175). Suicide is the primary case of a kind of death that escapes the logic and law of the natural death. Indeed, it is "the form of subversion itself" because it consists precisely in ritually destroy-ing (in a Bataillian act of violent *dépense*) the "parcel of capital [we have] at [our] disposal" (Baudrillard [1976] 1993, pp.175–176). So radi-cally transgressive is this act that the state will in fact judge and condemn successful suicides in criminal trials, despite the patently ridiculous nature of such acts (Baudrillard [1976] 1993, p.176). Even when no such condemnation occurs, the contemporary order consistently endeavours to disqualify the suicide by, for example, "beatifying" the deceased instead of embracing the fact that such "disappearance" is in fact "in certain extreme situations the only true act", as did the French Socialist Party when, in 1993, Pierre Bérégovoy, a failed minister in the last years of the Mitterrand administration, killed himself in disgrace (Baudrillard [1995] 2007, p.80). Prisoners who commit suicide perhaps most clearly defy the state's monopoly on death, but all suicides constitute an "infini-tesimal but inexpiable breach" in the system's intent on total control (Baudrillard [1976] 1993, p.175). Ultimately, the suicide's act is a response to a repression that seeks to be total, which labels itself innocuously as security but is in fact something rather more sinister:[4]

It is necessary to rob everyone of the last possibility of giving themselves their own death as the last "great escape" from a life laid down by the system. Again, in this symbolic short-circuit, the gift-exchange is the challenge to oneself and one's own life and is carried out through death. Not because it expresses the individual's asocial rebellion (the defection of one or millions of individuals does not infringe the law of the system at all), but because it carries in it a principle of sociality that is radically antagonistic to our own social repressive principle (Baudrillard [1976] 1993, p.177).

So, and this is crucial, it is not an individual act of resistance or revolution that is entailed in the

R. Budd Dwyer seconds before committing suicide on 22 January, 1987. Screen capture.

Gary Miller/Associated Press

suicide; it is an allusion to a collective vision of human reality that constitutes a challenge to the system precisely in its rejection of the logic of individualism.

The suicidal attacks of terrorists receive considerable attention in Baudrillard's later work. In *Seduction*, Baudrillard directly juxtaposed two kinds/types of seductive "event" that parallel the pure and impure sacred (about which I will say more shortly). The seductive power of the cinematic star turns the masses away from the productive, but so too does the "black light" of terrorism (Baudrillard [1979] 1991, p.96). The black magic of terrorism derives its power precisely from the fact that it has no goals and not even a clear enemy, as terrorists "strike at a mythical, or not even mythical, anonymous, undifferentiated enemy; a kind of omnipresent global social order" (Baudrillard 1983, pp.51, 55). Their acts are essentially indistinguishable from natural catastrophes (Baudrillard 1983, p.56). They are "our Theater of Cruelty" in so far as they offer "a condensed narrative, a flash ... a ritual, or

that which, of all possible events, opposes to the political and historical model or order the purest symbolic form of challenge" (Baudrillard 2001, p.130).

Baudrillard's earliest discussion of terrorism focused on New Left and Palestinian terror acts of the 1970s and 1980s. The startling events in Mogadishu and Germany in October 1977 were the subject of one of his first substantive interventions on this theme. On 13 October Palestinian Arab terrorists hired by the German terrorist group, the Red Army Faction (RAF), hijacked a Lufthansa flight, killed the German pilot and demanded the release of several RAF prisoners being held in Stammheim prison in Germany, threatening to blow up the plane otherwise. These terrorists were spectacularly killed by German anti-terrorist police after landing in Mogadishu, then shortly thereafter the RAF prisoners in Stammheim orchestrated a carefully planned suicide pact. The ritual their action produced and constituted was, in Baudrillard's perspective, effective, that is, "subversive" precisely "because insoluble" (Baudrillard 2001, p.130). It escapes the conventional games of signification (for example, crime versus law; evil versus good) by constituting a total ambivalence of meaning. There is no final truth or meaning in the *dénouement* of the actions at the airfield in Mogadishu or in the cells at Stammheim, however furiously the media and other forces of power attempted to construct it. Was the hijacking botched because it did not succeed in freeing the prisoners? Did the jailers kill Baader and his comrades in Stammheim, or were they suicides? These are questions that can be asked only from within a framework that is no longer adequate. Baudrillard suggests that the real stakes of the Mogadishu conflict were not in getting prisoners released, but rather in "oppos[-ing] to the full violence and to the full order a clearly superior model of extermination and virulence operating through emptiness ... the abolition of value, of meaning, of the real ... [in a] paradoxical death which shines intensely for a moment before falling back into the real" (Baudrillard 2001, p.132).

Baudrillard also discussed the suicidal act that culminated in the destruction of the World Trade Center towers as an act deriving its power from its contribution to symbolic exchange. Suicide terrorism of this mass and novel type challenges the system in a way well beyond even the limited suicide bombing of the Palestinians, but not because it promises an adequate military challenge to the capitalist west (Strenski [2003b] has already addressed suicide bombers from a Maussian gift-exchange perspective). On the contrary, its challenge is profound precisely because it does not attempt to take a place in that game, but instead changes the game back to a symbolic one. The goal is not to destroy capitalism, but to humiliate it and make it "lose face" (Baudrillard 2002, p.26). This is accomplished by attacking the "zero-death system" of capitalism in precisely the "collective sacrificial" terms to which it cannot respond, except by its own suicide and disappearance (Baudrillard 2002, pp.16–7, 22). The stakes are changed and raised once the terrorists place their own deaths as stakes in the game (Baudrillard 2002, p.19). In combining the "twentieth century's two elements of mass fascination ... the white magic of the cinema and the black magic of terrorism", the September 11 attacks accomplish what a conventional military response (that is, a

declaration of war by one sovereign state against another and a subsequent military engagement in the terms set forth by international agreement) could never achieve (Baudrillard 2002, pp.29–30). The victims of global capitalism would simply and quickly be annihilated in traditional military conflict with the capitalist west. But the terrorists manage to exploit both western capitalism's obsession with the control of death and the vertigo-inducing fact that very few of us are willing to acknowledge: that we in the west have ourselves wished, in the abstract and in our unguarded moments, for just this kind of spectacular, cataclysmic event (while watching and enjoying its spectacular cinematic simulation in a dozen action films) as an escape from the tentacles of the very system to which we consciously pledge our allegiance. This part of Baudrillard's argument is, for many, too scandalous to be countenanced, yet there is evidence to support his speculation. For instance, the online journal Salon.com (2009) featured an article in September 2002 that offered a small sample of "forbidden thoughts" entertained by readers concerning the attacks. Among those featured were a teen's description of the collapse of the Towers as "the best special effects I ever saw" and a film producer's awed account of the attacks in earthy Baudrillard-ese: "what a great fucking action scene".

Though such thoughts are indeed "forbidden" and cannot easily find expression, especially in the morally charged immediate aftermath of the attacks, they do indeed exist and Baudrillard endeavours to give us a framework for understanding why they do and what they tell us about the acts in question. The wager made by the terrorists, he argues, is effective precisely because any effective response to them would have to acknowledge and address our own deep desire for the symbolic violence they performed, which it can never do (Baudrillard 2002, pp.5–6).

Media ritual and the catastrophic failure of capitalist individualism in suicide

So much for Baudrillard's analysis of mass-mediated suicide. But there is yet an important unanswered question: what precisely makes Baudrillard's thought here neo-Durkheimian? It is obviously Maussian, at least in so far as it engages the framework of gift-exchange set forth in *The gift*, albeit in ways that Mauss himself might have questioned. It is perhaps even more clearly Bataillian, in borrowing the language of the *part maudite*, which Bataille himself had adapted from his own idiosyncratic reading of Mauss. But how is it Durkheimian? If we put the complicated question of the actual substance of Durkheimianism aside, we might start, as noted above, by recalling that Durkheim wrote a book-length study of the phenomenon of suicide.[5] However, that study does not touch in any real way on the perspective Baudrillard generated with respect to the subject 70 years later and it clearly has very different intellectual goals.

Durkheim's study of suicide, nonetheless, shares at least one important point with Baudrillard's reflection on the topic: both view the seemingly individual act of suicide as an indication of something that is actually going on in social or cultural structures. In each of Durkheim's four types of suicide, the causes and meanings of the act itself can only be discerned by analysing one of two structural variables, social integration and moral regulation. If there is too much or too little integration in a given society, altruistic or egoistic suicide, respectively, will increase; if too much or too little moral regulation is present, we should see, respectively, more fatalistic or anomic suicide. In similar structural terms, Baudrillard relates suicide back to a social and cultural matrix of organisation and meaning, namely, that of symbolic exchange. When particular modes of symbolic exchange are closed off by, for example, the development and expansion of a neoliberal capitalist economic system, the structural requirement for that exchange remains and we can expect it to be carried out in ways that are not (yet) preempted by the system.

But despite this similarity, the real evidence for the Durkheimian nature of Baudrillard's case on suicide lies elsewhere. I would suggest the key location of elements of Durkheim's thought regarding the meaning of self-inflicted violence is in the intriguing discussion of piacular rites in the ninth chapter of book two of the *Elementary forms*. There, Durkheim points out that rites of mourning in those most elementary religious systems that are the object of his study often include the inflicting of great damage on the self, up to and including death (Durkheim [1912] 1961, p.444). Mourners of the deceased will slash their thighs, savagely beat themselves with clubs, inflict deep knife wounds on and severely burn themselves in a collective ritual act of response to the offence felt by the group at the removal of one of its members.

The indigenous understanding of this violent ritualistic phenomenon is linked to beliefs in malevolent spiritual entities, evil shades or demons that must be warded off via effective action, but the actual cause, Durkheim argues, is the sense of vulnerability the group experiences at the death of one of its members. If individual members can perish, the entire group is also vulnerable to extermination and this threat must be addressed. The collectivity must respond through a reaffirmation of its common bond and the various death rituals constitute just such a reaffirmation. They build up common sentiments to a frenzied level at which the energy created is expended in violent self-wounding.

Just as the violence of the mourners is fundamentally framed by the collective needs and energies of the group in crisis, so too the suicide's act, in Baudrillard's analysis, is wholly informed by the collective crisis that is capitalist economy and its destruction of the symbolic exchange that is such a deep part of our cultural unconscious. Mourners who perishes as a result of their self-inflicted wounds constitute a counter-challenge to the malevolent spiritual powers that have challenged the stability of social order through their rending of a group member from the ranks of the living and the suicide should be seen similarly as a symbolic response to the challenge capitalism makes to death. Tellingly, it is at precisely this point in Durkheim's magnum opus that he turns to the binary structure of the sacred revealed in piacular ritual. Just as there is a pure sacred of beneficence that is invoked with joyful enthusiasm in many rites of the cult, there is also an impure sacred of terror, disorder and suffering that is to be engaged with in other rites, such as many of those dealing with death. However different they appear, though, the effect of both kinds of rite is functional in the final analysis; each contributes to the continued existence and well-being of the social order and the chain of exchange. Roger Caillois' elaboration of the Durkheimian theory of the festival extends Durkheim's argument regarding the impure sacred and related rituals and shows precisely how even radically transgressive violence operates in a manner that is ultimately geared to seeking equilibrium and order (Riley 2005b, 2005c). So, in Baudrillard's reading of mass-mediated suicide, there is at once a transgression and an effort to re-establish equilibrium.

More fully tracing the Durkheimian character of Baudrillard's thought on suicide requires a discussion of his engagement with a topic that has had to be grafted onto Durkheimian theory largely after the fact, due to the real historical circumstances of its emergence. The mass media were not a central topic of consideration for Durkheim and the others with whom he worked closely in the *Année* school precisely because much of what we mean by that term had simply not been invented yet. But since then, it has been broadly recognised that visual media, especially television and later the Internet, have changed the field in which we talk about the Durkheimian theory of ritual and the sacred. While some (Collins 2004) have argued that ritual requires actual physical co-presence in order to work optimally, many others have pointed to the substantial power that media ritual can have (Dayan and Katz 1988). It is certainly the case that media rituals cannot be simplistically viewed as spaces for the unproblematic construction of consensus and we need to be quite aware of the possibilities for diverse experiences of the same media event; thus, Dayan and Katz speak of the multivocality of meaning in media events (Dayan and Katz 1988, p.162).

Notwithstanding this fact, it is also true that mass media make it possible for collective experiences to be much more broadly and widely collective than they would otherwise be. If this is true of the pure sacred media ceremonies, such as coronations and presidential debates, focused on by Dayan and Katz, why should it not also be true of impure sacred media rituals concerning death, such as those discussed by Baudrillard? Indeed, some of the same media events can be experienced by different audiences, or by the same audiences at different times or in different contexts, as relating either to the pure or impure sacred.

The harrowing events of September 11, 2001 and the various ritual experiences that followed from them could be experienced not only by those physically in lower Manhattan at the time, but by millions across the globe because of the omnipresence of video cameras and the appropriate technology for instantly transmitting the images they captured all around the planet (Friend 2006). Moreover, as we have already indicated, they could be experienced by those distanced audiences in very different ways. Some of these were perfectly consonant with the moral framework most often presented by American political and other public commentators and generally therefore involving the pure sacrality of a group solidarity of benevolence and empathy that sought to extend as far outward as possible, even to the global level (Tiryakian 2005, p.315). Other interpretive frames, like that described by Baudrillard, might have allowed a collective experience of the acts as a transgressive counter-gift responding to the global challenge presented by American empire to the rest of the world.

Dwyer's "new kind of fear"

Dwyer's suicide was covered widely in Pennsylvanian and national news on the day it occurred. According to a *New York Times* story on 23 January 1987 at least two Pennsylvania television stations (WPVI-TV in Philadelphia and WPXI-TV in Pittsburgh) showed the actual moment of the final shot on air, while numerous others showed at least some of the footage, some stopping before the final event but carrying the live sound along with an image frozen just before the fatal moment. WCAU-TV in Philadelphia, for example, showed the footage up to the point at which he inserted the gun into his mouth and then cut away. Most Pennsylvania stations chose to omit the actual suicide from their footage, although this did not prevent them from teasing viewers with provocative allusions to the "awful" act that their cameras had captured (Matviko 1988, p.6).

One can ultimately only guess how many people actually viewed the footage on that day. But since then the footage has taken on an impressive life of its own. The images and sounds have been widely sampled in numerous rock songs and at least two specific musical tributes to the event and to Dwyer have been recorded. The Chicago punk group Rapeman (fronted by Steve Albini of Big Black and apparently named after a controversial Japanese comic book character) released "Budd" the year after Dwyer's suicide, in 1988. The lyrics included excerpts of Dwyer's final discourse ("this will hurt someone") and fairly clearly presented Dwyer in heroic terms, calling him a god, pristine, and pure genius. In 1995 the Cleveland industrial rock group Filter scored a hit with "Hey Man, Nice Shot," which peaked at number 76 in the Billboard Top 100 that year. The lyrical content of this song is still more explicit than that of "Budd" in its admiration for Dwyer's suicide, which is presented as the courageous act of a man surrounded by powerful enemies who yet finds a strategy to escape without losing face and to leave those enemies with "a new kind of fear". A documentary film about Dwyer, entitled "Honest Man," is apparently currently in the works from Eighty Four Films (n.d.). The trailer, which speaks of Dwyer's act as something that "shock[ed] a nation", can currently be seen online (Eighty Four Films (n.d.). As already noted, the footage of the suicide can be easily found on the Internet, where it has achieved a kind of legendary status. There exists at least one tribute site to Dwyer online, which contains links to the video and newspaper articles covering the story, several photos of Dwyer's grave in Blooming Valley, Pennsylvania and a partial transcript of Dwyer's speech. On the front page of the site, the author makes it clear that the pages are not intended to be mere exploitation of the graphic suicide, but a tribute to a victim of the persecution of the justice system (Fortune City, n.d.). Someone has even created a posthumous MySpace page for Dwyer (MySpace n.d.); he currently has five friends on the service.

The fact of the ready availability of the video and photo images of Dwyer's suicidal act separates it from some other documents that approximate its status as a media object of this kind. In July 1974 a Florida news anchorwoman named Christine Chubbuck, apparently unhappy with the increasing emphasis at her station on salacious stories and images, shot herself live on the air. Though at least some viewers would have seen the event while watching the broadcast live, it seems that the footage was not aired later by stations reporting the story and there exists no publicly accessible video record of the event, although there is considerable speculation about it online. The fact that the actual footage is not publicly available has not completely prevented Chubbuck from receiving some adulation and attention; there exists a website dedicated to her (http://www.christinechubbuck.net) at which still images of her at work and a lengthy biographical essay can be found. Yet the absence of a readily available media object that can mobilise the attention of the public has prevented the Chubbuck suicide from taking on the significant cultural tenor of Dwyer's.

More recently, a number of additional suicides have been carried out before media audiences of various kinds. I am aware of at least two recent cases of individuals who committed suicide while logged on via webcams to online chat rooms: a British man who hanged himself in March 2007 and a 19-year-old Florida man who died of an intentional drug overdose while recording himself at justin.tv just a few weeks before the writing of this chapter in November 2008. As in the Chubbuck case, there were viewers who were actually logged in to those sites at the time who saw the suicide take place, but the video of both events was quickly removed and is not now readily available online. Coincidentally, on the very day I write these words, another such story broke from Argentina, involving a former police commander facing charges related to alleged crimes committed during the Argentinian dictatorship of the late 1970s and early 1980s, who shot himself dead at his home during an on-air interview with a television station. Apparently, though the station ran the footage once to its audience, a Buenos Aires judge has barred them from showing it again and the video is not available online.

It goes without saying that we do not know precisely how many readers of the Dwyer suicide video understand the event as Baudrillard suggests they might; indeed, we even have some reason to believe that survey research might not allow us to fully inquire into this issue, as there are compelling reasons that such forbidden thoughts might not be readily admitted by at least some respondents who actually entertained them. But I would suggest the evidence online and in the popular culture I have just discussed is more than enough to lend significant empirical support to Baudrillard's speculation, however much we would like and need to more systematically explore the case. As I have elsewhere argued with respect to gangsta rap music (Riley 2005b), theories that appear controversial should not be rejected out of hand simply because of that controversy and especially if we cannot even admit that this is the reason for their dismissal and instead resort to specious claims about a failure to comply with sketchy empirical evidence. Indeed, if Dayan and Katz are right that media events are inevitably multivocal, and I certainly believe they are, we should not expect monolithic interpretations, nor should we limit ourselves to theoretical speculations confined by assumptions about meaning that are monolithic as well. Baudrillard suggested that the work of cultural theory cannot be restrained by overly narrow understandings of the means by which theoretical insights can be empirically demonstrated. One might even suggest that a certain genealogical relationship can be detected in those who would reject out of hand Baudrillard's interpretive framework as inconsistent with what actual public groups indicate and others who, a century ago, attacked Durkheim's argument about what was actually going on in religious ritual because it failed to coincide with the accounts given by those actually engaging in the rituals.

Notes

1. A shortened version of the entire event can be seen at Live Leak (2006).

2. Reading at least some parts of Baudrillard's work as consonant with certain elements in the late thought of Durkheim (especially *The elementary forms of religious life*) and in the thought of several members of the *Année sociologique* team who worked closely with Durkheim (Marcel Mauss, Robert Hertz and Henri Hubert) has over the past several decades become more and more common, in large part due to the influential work of Mike Gane (1991, 2000). The present author has also taken up this line of interpretation in much more detail elsewhere (Riley 2002b, 2005a).

3. I intentionally mimic the language of Foucault (2001a, p.1621) in describing how he used Nietzsche's thought without the slightest consideration of whether or not commentators on Nietzsche would find that usage "faithful".

4. Foucault (2001b) spoke to this same issue, albeit in a slightly different register, in an interview on the topic of social security, where he raised the idea of a right to suicide (1201).

5. Philippe Besnard (1983) long ago made the powerful argument that we must think "*Année* group" when we think Durkheimianism and I have examined some specific aspects of this in my own work (Riley 2002a, 2005a).

From political emergencies and states of exception to exceptional states and emergent politics: a neo-Durkheimian alternative to Agamben

Ronjon Paul Datta

This chapter explores the possibility of a neo-Durkheimian approach to understanding the relationship between the sacred, the political and violence. I aim to outline an alternative to the negative and state-centred conception of the sacred and the political found in Agamben's *Homo sacer* (1998), based on the optimism of Durkheim's sociology. I pose the question of violence in terms of the sacred to reread Durkheim's sociology of the sacred and politics symptomatically (see Pearce 2001) and retheorise a conception of the inherent, but not necessarily actualised violence of politics that threatens systems of rule. Central to my argument is Durkheim's theorem that the sacred is constituted by and refers to "that which is set apart and forbidden" (Durkheim 1995, p.44), especially set apart from profane everyday affairs that amount to the routine actualisation of societal rule. Durkheim's theorem however, is suggestive of the radical, sacred difference of politics itself. This alternative provides the means to shift from focusing on the phenomenon of a political emergency to which states of exception, decided by sovereign power, are a violent response (which is Agamben's focus), to exceptional states of an emergent politics grounding the sacred force of popular sovereignty in which a politics may emerge that results in violence against rule.

Dr Ronjon Paul Datta is an Assistant Professor in the Department of Sociology at the University of Alberta. His interests include contemporary and classical social theory, aleatory materialism and justice, the sociology of the sacred and political sociology. He was awarded a Governor General of Canada Academic Gold Medal in October 2008 for his doctoral work. Email: rpauldatta@gmail.com

The political, inclusion and exclusion in contemporary social theory

Since the English publication of *Homo sacer* (1998), mechanisms of inclusion and exclusion have received increased attention alongside the concern with exclusion in the post-Marxisms of Rancière, Laclau and Butler, for example. In Rancière (1999) the properly political subject is the demos. It consists of all of those persons in a society subjected to its political structure who, while formally included, are in practice excluded from decisions about a shared fate; a fate moreover, to which they are subjected to a greater extent than the fully included ruling classes. For Laclau (2007a), any act of signification (that is, the basic stuff of socio-political life) depends on a totality of signifiers that at the same time differentiates itself "from something *other* than itself" (Laclau 2007a, p.69). This other is that which is constitutively excluded from the totality of significations but nevertheless subtends the very condition of possibility of societal organisation and direction. Judith Butler, drawing on Bataille's and Kristeva's concept of abjection as radical exclusion, also stresses how "the subject is constituted through the force of exclusion and abjection, one which produces a constitutive outside to the subject" (Butler 1993, p.3). While there are differences in how exclusion is conceptualised in these theorists, they each stress that it plays an important role in mechanisms of domination. At the same time, for each of them, what is excluded remains, not least as a threat to those who benefit from the privileges of membership and as a force that can develop an alternative life of its own (see Laclau 2007b, p.14). Contemporary neo-Durkheimians have also returned to Durkheim's sociology of the sacred as a means to understand political phenomena like the non-rational volatility associated with sacrifice and moments of creative collective effervescence as found in political protest (Pearce 2001). Alexander's magnum opus, *The civil sphere* (2006) draws on Durkheim and Mary Douglas to highlight how profanations negatively charge symbols and groups and become the basis of exclusions in civic life.

Now, this attention to exclusion is somewhat surprising given Foucault's impact on contemporary social theory and his positive conception of power relations as the basic productive substratum of social relations (Foucault 1994, p.94). Foucault, in the context of his polemic against French Marxism, rejected a focus on negative exercises of domination such as exclusion, as he classifies it, as useful and pertinent to comprehending the contemporary political field. Nevertheless, as Pearce (2006) and Pearce and Woodiwiss (2001) argue, his debts to the Durkheimianism of Georges Bataille, Georges Dumézil and Lévi-Strauss make their presence felt in his own discussions of exclusion and sacralisation. These Durkheimian elements indicate that Foucault considered both positive and negative types of power (such as exclusion), even though the later are underdeveloped. For example, *The history of madness* (Foucault 2006) argues that there is a constitutive division between reason and madness that subtends the very possibility of the human sciences, the prototype of which is sacralisation (Foucault 2006, pp.ix–x, 5, 10). Foucault sustained this position in attenuated form in his genealogical concern with the productivity of power relations (Foucault 1980, pp.183–184). He also relied on Lévi-Strauss since, for Foucault, cultural analysis "was a matter of not knowing what is affirmed and valorised in a society or a system of thought but of studying what is rejected and

excluded" (Foucault 1998b, p.355). A Durkheimianism also makes its presence felt in Foucault's use of the concept of sacralisation to analyse heterotopias (spaces of difference) in terms of "a certain number of oppositions that cannot be tampered with, that institutions and practices have not ventured to change – oppositions we take for granted, for example, between private space and public space" (Foucault 1998a, p.175). That said, the challenge remains of theorising exclusion and sacralisation with more positive conceptions of power and the political. I suggest that rereading Durkheim's sociology of the sacred and politics can do so, providing reasons for inverting Agamben's analytic.

Agamben's conception of *Homo sacer*

Agamben's *Homo sacer* (1998) explicitly attempts to rethink Foucault's conception of modern biopolitics, in which life is the primary object and concern of rule, in terms of the problem of the sacral exclusion of people by sovereign power. Agamben's project, drawing on Schmitt, Foucault and Arendt and his readings of archaic legal statutes concerning banishment and exclusion, endeavours to show how politics is constituted in and through the power of political sovereignty to exclude human subjects in such a way that they are reduced to a naked living existence, stripped of social and political significance. Sacral exclusion is argued to be the foundational relation in the formation of western polities. Sacral exclusion exemplifies the farthest reach of sovereignty, the archetype of which is the Ancient Roman figure of *homo sacer*. And yet this sacred position is not one of total exclusion because it is still defined in relation to the political community, even if precisely by exclusion. Moreover, sovereignty reveals that its constitutive power lies in its capacity to reduce the subjects of a polity to a state of naked existence without significance. In particular, Agamben offers a concept of the object of bio-political sovereignty by showing how sovereign power is constitutive of this naked life and hence what counts as life does not pre-exist its constitution by the sovereign power.

Agamben thus contends that modern western politics needs to be understood in terms of three main theses:

1. The original political relation is the "ban" (the state of exception as a zone of indistinction between outside and inside, exclusion and inclusion).
2. The fundamental activity of sovereign power is the production of bare life as an originary political element and as threshold of articulation between nature and culture, *zoe* and *bios.*
3. Today it is not the city but rather the camp that is the fundamental bio-political paradigm of the west. (Agamben 1998, p.181).

For Agamben, the originary form of modern biopolitics is traced back to the Roman category of *homo sacer.* This is the sacred man who can be killed without it being called homicide and whose life, because of his exclusion from the community, cannot be offered as a sacrifice for it (Agamben 1998, p.8). The articulation of sovereign power and biopolitics lies in the power of the sovereign to decide which subjects are to be included in this state of exception, "something that is included solely by exclusion" (Agamben 1998, p.153). Drawing on Aristotle, Agamben also argues that in western politics this sacral form involves an opposition between bare life, (*zoe*) and political or social life, (*bios*). Bare life so constituted is life outside of the biopolitical community that nevertheless remains a force that subtends it (Agamben 1998, p.9).

The exclusion of the life of *homo sacer* is double since it is deemed without any value as concerns either the order of worldly affairs (the concern of juridical sovereignty), or the life of the cosmos as a whole (the concern of magico-religious sovereignty) (see Dumézil 1988). *Homo sacer* can thus be the object and target of the projects of sovereign power without any of the normal rules and rights belonging to human subjects who are included in a polity being applicable. In this manner inclusion, rights and citizenship are shown to be effects of the decisive power of sovereignty. According to Agamben the peculiar structure of modern politics lies in the circumstance that all subjects are reduced to the status of *homo sacer* because the very target of politics is our life itself. The paradigmatic

form of this structure is the camp. Today, life and law, become "truly indistinguishable from one another" (Hussain and Ptacek 2000, p.495). Consequently we now live in a zone of indistinction between *zoe* and *bios* (Agamben 1998, p.115): to be a subject is to have one's life subjected and, hence, "life is immediately political in its facticity" (Agamben 1998, p.153). In this configuration biopolitics all too easily becomes what Foucault calls thanatopolitics (Foucault 2000, p.416), since politics comes to involve deciding on the sovereign application of the state of exception, reducing people to the status of a life that is judged to be of no political or religious value and who can hence be killed with impunity. The book's most contentious element perhaps lie in its indictment of the liberal democratic value of inclusion, a sentiment I share: the issue is not to include everyone, but the mechanisms that are constitutive of what counts as the inside of the polity in which all are to be included. Furthermore, Agamben's appropriation of Foucault is also more than a little problematic; a point I shall elaborate on later.

In important respects Agamben's book inhabits Carl Schmitt's problematic of politics in which sovereignty is seen as being the decisive instance of social ordering (Schmitt 1985). In this regard, the problem of insurrection is instructive. Indeed, historically, the masses in the moment of uprising or revolt are not seen as being really human or civilised from the point of view of rule but are seen as a monstrous and cannibalistic (Foucault 2003a, pp.98–104.). This position also held sway in early mass psychology, as found in Freud and Le Bon for instance (Laclau 2007a), a view challenged by Durkheim (Richman 2002, pp.111–112). In this view such a mass is a manifestation of the threat of a political force that may undo the entire normative basis of a current system of rule (Foucault 1996, pp.90–91). In this regard it is exactly when people take exception to the normal course of affairs of state government that sovereignty returns the gesture of exception and claims that there is a political crisis or emergency. From this follows the typical governmental interpretation that it is dealing in exceptional circumstances and normal laws and rights must be suspended until an order, necessary to the activity of governing, is restored (see Borislavov 2005). It is precisely this immanent power of state sovereignty to suspend the law that is of concern to Agamben. His analysis, however, has its unpersuasive elements.

Some limitations of Agamben's approach

The first of these unpersuasive elements is that his entire analysis rests on the assertion that all forms of political power in western civilisation since the founding of Athens and Rome rest upon the same form of sovereignty, that is, the form of being able to decide on who can be banned and excluded from the *bios* of the community. Thus, Agamben's analytic is formalist (Žižek 2003, p. 108). This form appears to be a transhistorical essence that expresses itself in a variety of ways but we are not given any account of either how it is reproduced or any account as to why this form of sovereignty has remained decisive and persisted in western civilisation. The reader is only provided with a number of historical examples that illustrate the formal essence of inclusive exclusion (such as the Roman *homo sacer*, the archaic Germanic practice of banning people and the Nazi concentration camp). Moreover, as Laclau (2007b) has pointed out, the expression of this form is teleological, resembling a Hegelian conception of the historical unveiling of this form of sovereignty. Thus, in political modernity the structure of sovereignty comes to be expressed in each and every subjective instance of the polity: there is allegedly a progressive internalisation of this constitutive inclusive exclusion into the polity and citizenship that is finally expressed in the contemporary situation in which we are all *homo sacer*.

The result is an identity between *bios* and *zoe*, subjectivity and objectivity. The narrative amounts to a negative eschatology in which the end of history means the negation of citizenship, now collapsed into a totality of bare life. Consequently, history has a lacunary status in Agamben's work. As Althusser might say, it is ideological history in that it offers a history without any history: Agamben's account lacks a concern for the transformations and displacements in which what counts as sovereignty becomes possible, actualised and deployed. His analytic thus occludes the contingencies surrounding political interventions in a particular

conjuncture and neglects the extent to which people resist and struggle against being subjugated by systems of exclusion (Laclau, 2007b, p.22). Granted, Agamben is free to choose his own topics and hence Laclau's criticism, from the point of view of pure immanent critique, may well be seen as unfair. But In as much as Agamben offers an ambitious new theory of the political as a whole, we as readers must assess the extent to which it allows us to analyse and explain phenomena and events germane to what are conventionally regarded as the political, including things like the agonic characteristics of the political introduced into social theory by Marx, Nietzsche, Weber and Foucault. In this regard, Agamben falls more than a little short.

A second theoretical weakness of Agamben's analysis lies in his failure to consider the extent to which his theory of sovereign power is implicated in a juridico-discursive analytic of power, subjected to critique by Foucault for being inadequate to understanding the characteristically modern productivity of power (Foucault 1994, pp.92–102.). Indeed, for Agamben, politics is founded on what Foucault would describe as an exercise of medieval sovereign power – the power to say no and to forbid (Foucault 2003b, pp.25–31). There is also a conflation in Agamben's work between the juridical and magico-religious poles constitutive of the Indo-European model of sovereignty on which he draws, in which the functions of one are held to be necessary, but taboo, to the other. In this respect, together, they are mutually exclusive and jointly exhaustive functions of sovereignty (Dumézil 1988). The bipartite structure of sovereignty is correctly applied in Agamben's analysis of *homo sacer*, given the exception concerning homicide (he may be killed without it being called homicide) corresponding to the juridical function, and the fact that his life is not fit for sacrifice, which corresponds to the magico-religious pole. But, even though Agamben discusses how the criminal and the priest (as subjects respectively constituted by the two poles) occupy structurally antithetical positions, his analysis tends to reduce all sovereignty to juridical sovereignty. In doing so, he neglects how a life that is it is permitted to sacrifice is constituted, surely an exercise of inclusion through domination. A consideration of how the magico-religious function can serve as a potential resource for opposition and resistance to exercises of juridical sovereignty, a key point for Dumezil, is also lacking. A contemporary remnant of this bipartite structure can be found in the long-standing practice of seeking asylum in a church: inclusion in the magico-religious sphere renders the subject *sacred* (that is, set apart and forbidden) to the juridical function, even if confined and excluded in a church. This remains true today, as found, for instance, with people facing deportation after failed immigration or refugee claims who seek asylum in houses of worship, even if sadly, in the end, unsuccessful.

Agamben also only offers a concept of one real political subject, namely the sovereign. The rest are little more than objects of subjugation. The consequence is a model of the political field without a conception of active citizenship, a move accompanied by a reductionism in his ontology. In Agamben's, and subsequently Rose's (2001) work, politics in general and biopolitics in particular has as its real substance *zoe*, or life itself. Hence, it would be more correct for them to say that they are referring not to biopolitics, but to *zoe*-politics. However, this is at best a paradoxical term and at worst, contradictory. It implies the reduction of politics to *zoe*, and hence the eradication of politics itself as the concern with the *bios*. What is thereby lost in the process is exactly the biopolitical, that is, problematisations of and contestations over the shaping and directing of the life of the polity. This process involves debates and struggles over collective existence, its transformation, the nature of the good society and how it might be achieved and protected. This suggests that politics itself is excluded by Agamben's analytic, a point well grasped by Laclau (2007b, p.22), stemming from Agamben's failure to develop a properly historical problematic and resulting in an ontology of the political strikingly without anything resembling politics.

In many respects, Agamben's ontology also involves the spurious use of Foucault (Patton 2007). I will focus on two elements of Foucault's work: (a) biopolitics, for Foucault does not primarily refer to the kind of bare life discussed by Agamben and hence their respective ontological referents are distinct; and (b) it is not living being that is in question in biopolitics but rather development – Foucault's focus is not on "the meat" of human life but on how actualised

human practices can be improved and increased, and done so economically and efficiently. While Agamben argues that "the entry of *zoe* into the sphere of the *polis* – the politicisation of bare life itself – constitutes the decisive event of modernity and signals a radical transformation of the political-philosophical categories of classical thought" (Agamben 1998, p.4), this is not the case for Foucault. A significant contribution made by Foucault in his genealogy of the modern coordinates of projects and programmes of social ordering and coordination concerns the emergence of a new form of directing life, that is, what people do.

For Foucault the sixteenth-century idea of government, as the solution to the problem of rule, safety and the organisation and coordination of social life, introduces a *telos* and hence an end and finality into rationalities of rule (Foucault 2007, p.99). So, in contrast to the tautology of the rationality of sovereign rule in which the end of sovereignty is the perpetuation of sovereignty such that princes retain rule over a territory (Foucault 2007, p.98), government introduces a *telos* of improvement or, development. For Foucault, it is this difference in the conception of the historicity of rule that constitutes the discontinuity between the late medieval world and political modernity with its distinct concern with government. Importantly, this shift in how the historicity of rule was construed was accompanied by the emergence of new objects and targets of rule: the activities and programmes of government are directed at a population, not a territory and not an individualised collection of people. The *bios* of governmentality thus concerns things like birth rates, public health and productivity, that is, the multiplicity of events constitutive of the object and target of governmental intervention, intervention characterised by facilitation rather than the direct use of force. Agamben ignores these definitive components of Foucault's conception of biopolitics.

Moreover, when Foucault talks about biopolitics, what kind of life is he talking about? The life is what people are doing, not the stuff that they are (Foucault 2003c). Power and the body are not "bare life". Power refers to a localised set of contingently combined relations of force, some quantity of which comes to dominate others to produce a body with a particular quality, that is able to actually "do that" and not a range of other things (Datta 2007, p.287). Power and the body thus are not the stuff of a mode of existence but a stratum of it, providing the fuel or force of practices. That said, practices, conduct or actions cannot be reduced to the stratum of power relations because of the role played by thought and subjectivity in shaping and directing the loca-lised, contingent configurations of power where an action takes place (see Foucault 2003d). Furthermore, in the late eighteenth-century liberal critique of the excessive costs of *raison d'état*, the point is not to directly subject life, but to shape what people do to "structure the possible field of action of others" (Foucault 2003c, p.138). It is indeed a question of laissez faire – leave people, as a multiplicity, as a population, to do what they do, but with incentives and obstacles to facilitate some actions and make others more difficult.

Furthermore, the object of biopolitical power analysed by Foucault was an object discovered by the technology of police, not one of the rationality of sovereignty (Foucault 2003e, pp.195–200). Again, the concern of police was not bare life; rather it is all of the social actions and relationships, that is, "communica-tion", (Foucault 2003e, p.197) that people with-in a territory or jurisdiction were engaged in and their immanent forms of regulation (or lack thereof). In short, the life with which the police was concerned is eminently about social rela-tions and practices. In doing so, the technology of police supplied liberalism with its conception of civil society as a reality with a distinctive life of its own, serving as the ontological basis of trust and morality that allegedly must be assumed in the calculus of liberal governance. The conception of the reality of civil society thus provides the liberal diagram of government with the field it would attempt to structure so as to facilitate some actions and discourage others and hence exercise domination indirectly or govern at a distance (Rose 1999, p.49). This is not to suggest that there is not a vitalism that refers to something like "life itself" in Foucault (see Datta 2007; Patton 2007) but only to stress that Foucault's conception of the life that is at issue in biopolitics is pre-eminently social life. In this respect, when it comes to government as the predominant form taken by the modern political

field, we are dealing in the realm of *bios*, not *zoe*, as argued by Agamben.

This detour through Foucault is important because it provides a way to link the problem about Agamben's expulsion of politics from his conception of political modernity with the question of how liberal governmentality delimits (and so excludes and sanctions) what counts as politics.

Here I depart from the emphasis of Schmitt and Agamben concerning the manifestations and dangers of the sovereign when it comes to states of emergency; my point is more banal. In this regard, what interests me about the *Emergencies Act* and the *Anti-Terrorism Act* in Canada for example, is the delimitation of what it is that is to be protected. Briefly, and to follow Durkheim's method of examining law and sanction as a basis for understanding different modes of solidarity, to examine these Acts provides a clear indication of what kind of social life is sanctioned by the sovereign, and hence exempted from and forbidden to chal-lenge. What is sanctioned is economic develop-ment (hence the need to protect it), as is typical of liberal governmentality (Government of Canada 2001, Sec. 83.01). Economic develop-ment is deemed to be the basis of security and the necessary condition for improving the health and wealth of populations. This, it is held, is an activity that exists in the context of the relative insecurities of states imbricated in globally competitive and potentially anarchic relations with other states (hence the impor-tance of the Westphalian treaties and the subsequent system of state sovereignty over populations within their territory, together with other alliances with other states) (Foucault 2007, p.365). What thus comes to the fore in Foucault's analytic of government is that biopolitics is about sanctioning a particular historicity, namely a historicity of government that introduces ends and finality into the calculus of securing rule. In short, we have a perpetual concern with improvement and devel-opment, together with the apparatuses of measurement (such as audits, annuals reviews and reports) that are part and parcel of govern-mental programmes. In modified Foucauldian terms then, what is thereby constitutively ex-cluded in modern biopolitics is a concern with any other coordinates for organising and directing

Le Renard [The fox], Wilhelm von Kaulbach. Engraving for a 1794 edition of Johann Wolfgang von Goethe's *Reineke Fuchs.* akg-images

social life; the myopic valorisation of development means that other ways of thinking about the collective fate and how it might be shaped, are constitutively excluded and rendered sacred.

In this regard, Foucault's conception of governmentality helps us understand the genealogy of contemporary post-politics in which what counts as politics is reduced to debates about, and the concern with, the ways and means of social administration applied to a social field so as to enhance or improve its capacities (Laclau 2007b, p.x; Žižek 1999, pp.198–205). What

Foucault's conception of biopolitics and political modernity does, in contrast to Agamben, is highlight the genealogy of the historicity of the project of societal development, thus providing us with a means to displace the overly synchronic model of sacralisation in Agamben and introduce a diachronic one. The crucial biopolitical mechanism of exclusion is directed at a temporal level structuring modern rationalities of rule. This move provides the basis for retheorising post-political rule in light of Durkheim's emphasis on the temporal origin of the sacred, constituted in exceptional states of collective effervescence.

The state, social power, the sacred and sovereignty in Durkheim and Bataille

The basis of a neo-Durkheimian inversion of Agamben's conception of power and sovereignty is to be found in Durkheim's concepts of (social) power and (governmental/state) authority in which the latter is argued to depend on the former for its efficacy. The theoretical moves required are as follows: social power is sovereign in relation to governmental authority since it is the ontological terrain in which governmental decisions are accepted and followed, rejected, challenged or ignored; the originary ground of the force of social power is constituted in sacred/exceptional moments of collective effervescence; governmental rule is thus subjected to exceptional historical situations from which any force of law and rule must draw; and rule may be undone by an emergent force of new political coordinates constituted by totem-formation in moments of creative collective effervescence (Datta, 2008). This conception of sacred collective force that may undo the coordinates of subjugation to rules and ends (that is, profane existence) is a resource used by Bataille in the development of his concept of sovereignty, thus providing the basis for a Durkheimian conception of popular sovereignty.

Durkheim's conception of governmental authority and power

Durkheim's clearest statements on government and power are found in *professional ethics and civic morals* (1992, originally *Lecons de sociologie: physique des moeurs et du droit*). Crucial here is the way he distinguishes between political authority and social power. As concerns the formation of political society, it is the superiority of governmental authority that takes priority. As Durkheim argues, "we should define the political society as one formed by the coming together of a rather large number of secondary social groups, subject to the same one authority

which is not itself subject to any other superior authority duly constituted" (Durkheim 1992, p.45). Sovereignty is the name for this superior authority. "The particular group of officials entrusted with representing this authority", is called the state (Durkheim, 1992, pp.47–48). Civic morals constitute a stable relationship between individuals in a society and this sovereign authority. The activity of state government is distinguished from the rest of social life by its reflected concern for, and deliberation about, the social totality but this activity still depends on the array of collective representations constituting the psychic life of the conscience collective such as "myths, religious or moral legends" and the state works on them (Durkheim 1992, p.50). This psychic life of a political society is fairly spontaneous and unconscious. In contrast, we have the collective representations of political society constitutive of state activity, characterised by clarity (Durkheim, 1992, pp.79–84.). This reflected form of state representation is the basis of authority; however it depends upon and is governed by the prior collective representations. The state is thus not separate from society but aims to re-present its psychic life. Such collective representations have a thing-like quality relative to state officials that enables and constrains the capacities of the state.

Durkheim's position implies that because a societal organism has a life of its own, it ontologically governs the state. For Durkheim, anticipating Foucault in this regard, "power comes from below" (Foucault, 1994, p.94) and is communicated and circulated in social currents of collective representations (see Alexander 2006, pp.69–75). For Durkheim, power and authority are defined as relations between individuals constituted by the shared collective representations rendering communication possible, or between individuals and groups, but power and authority are not simply about dominance and subordination. Neither is power a relation in which the activity of the powerful is contrasted with the passive obedience of those who are ruled. Indeed, in all cases of power and authority, political actions are pulled by collective sentiments and social forces. Social reality is thus the real domain in which governmental decisions receive their efficacy (which is also to say that it is more than a matter of assent or consent). This sense is reflected in Durkheim's realism and anti-utopianism when it came to understanding the potentials and limitations of social change:

No one thinks that we can get together and alter the laws of physical nature. Yet there are few among us who realise that the citizens of a country, even if they are unanimously agreed in promoting an economic or political revolution, can only fail miserably in this enterprise if the revolution is not implied in the nature, in the conditions of existence of that society. (Durkheim 1961, p.258)

Political life, then, is found in the conscience collective that conveys and circulates social forces. The culmination of Durkheim's theory of power is encapsulated in *The elementary forms of religious life* where he states that, "It is society that has classified beings a superior and subordinate, as masters who command subjects who obey; it is society that has conferred on the first that singular property that makes command efficacious and that constitutes *power*" (Durkheim, 1995, p.370).

Durkheim's conception of the sacred basis of power

The elementary forms of religious life provides a theoretical account of the basis of social power and hence too of how and why collective representations have the kind of force that they do. Durkheim argues that collective representations are forceful and effective because they have a sacred, exceptional origin in relation to the routine activities of social life. Durkheim radically distinguishes between sacred forces and the profane life of individuals dutifully fulfilling their obligations in a complex division of labour in which they are rightfully concerned with their immediate, often egoistical concerns. Now, while Durkheim's theorem of sacralisation refers primarily to a static and synchronic structure of the radical difference of spatial differentiations and classifications of things, the sacred has its real origin in moments of collective effervescence where, when faced with the overwhelming currents of the collective assembly, individualistic orientations are overcome. The transcendence of egoism by collective activity liberates individuals from the normal bonds of duties, obligations and perceptions to constitute a moment

when exceptions to the rule are themselves the rule. It is this moment of liberation, fuelled by the intense concentration of collective activity, that makes organisational novelty possible. Exceptional states of creative collective effervescence are the origin of the social (not state) basis of power. Moreover, the archaic Indo-European referent for the sacred is that of a force of excess, referring to "a power which is full of ardour and swollen with fecundity" (Benveniste 1973, p.468). This conception of the sacred contrasts with Agamben's focus on the purely negative and narrowly juridical meaning of the sacred associated with the constitution of *homo sacer*.

Once nodal collective representations such as totems are constituted in moments of collective effervescence they remain charged by, and refer to, that sacred, exceptional moment (Durkheim 1995, pp.233–234). They can thus become the basis for institutionalised authority. In this manner, sacralisation is transposed from the temporal to the spatial (and more static) register, as found with churches and altars, for instance, which are believed to contain something of the originary sacred power. This sacred world, while part of society, is "withdrawn from general circulation. The common people cannot keep a kinship as it were, with sacred things of this kind" (Durkheim 1992, p.143). Permitted, regulated access to sacred places and things, typically facilitated by initiation rites mimetic of the violence done to profane life by collective effervescence, provides the basis for authority that re-presents (typically in the form of simulacra) this sacred force to the common people. The reason for this kind of prophylactic practice, Durkheim argues, lies in the contagious character of the sacred "that communicates this potency to any object that comes into contact with it" (Durkheim 1992, p.147). At the same time however, another moment of collective effervescence could provide the basis for new and discontinuous sacred symbols and hence the basis of counter-power. The points to bear in mind here are that the sacred is constituted in an exceptional moment in which routine social life is held in suspension; and the expression of sacrality in collective representations is the basis of both social power and authoritative institutions. Sacralisation then is not simply a matter of domination being exercised in the form of exclusion.

The sacred force of sovereignty in Bataille

Durkheim's social ontology and theory of the sacred provided an important resource for Bataille's concept of sovereignty. Bataille was interested in a kind of being that was not beholden to the profanity and profoundly dehumanising effects of capitalism and instrumentalism (Bataille 1995). He found in Durkheim's sociology of the sacred a reference point for an existential orientation that did not require recourse to the dialectical overcoming of subject–object relations. Indeed, for Bataille, the sacred was a type of anti-dialectical negativity, a negativity that could never be recuperated and that nevertheless remained the source of potential, creativity and a life free of concerns about usefulness (Derrida 1978). This is important because it provided a way to think of a means of escape from the subject–object couplet of profane life in which a subject is a subject because the world is viewed as an object and tool to be used to achieve instrumental ends. In short, the sacred is an excess of social power that is always there but in an unactualised form that has the power to negate or undo the profane life of human subjection to instrumentalism. Sovereignty is that which cannot be subordinated to any a priori value (and hence calculus of use) but finds its existential reference point in the originary power of the sacred. In short, sovereignty for Bataille means the power that comes from communion with the sacred. By linking the sacred with sovereignty Bataille makes it possible to reconceptualise sovereignty not as the power to make decisions about exceptions to the rule, but rather to conceive of sovereignty as the social power that makes decisions effective at all. Sovereignty is thus not a subject position but rather refers to a state of force and its non-subjection to the law of instrumental rationality.

The sacred power of popular sovereignty

While Agamben highlights the complexity of sovereignty with its capacity to constitute a relation of inclusive exclusion he also argues that "The actual exercise of such a power neither exhausts nor determines the potential, which is,

as it were, held in reserve by the sovereign, thus determining all present and potential situations" (Hussain and Ptacek, pp.501–502). In contrast, for Durkheim, it is the very potential of social reality itself that is held in reserve by people. The Durkheimian sense, in *The Division of labour in society* (1984), that transgression creates the rule, hints at this different social power. For example, when in the course of conversation at a house party, a friend says, "that's offside", it is not as though there is an explicit set of codified rules of what topics are taboo to a circle of friends and acquaintances. It is the transgression that brings to light the force of an implicit, immanent rule. The key here is the force that lies behind the sanctioning, not the content of the rule itself. It is only because there is a collective force behind the sanction that taking exception to what someone has said comes to have efficacy. In contrast to Schmitt and Agamben then, sovereignty is not about decisions but about the collective force that makes decisions efficacious. Durkheim's social ontology has affinities with the revolutionary democratic tradition as found in Negri for instance, for whom "constituent power refers to the power that by definition lies outside state juridical norms and has the potential of founding a new constitution and a new legal order" (Borislavov 2005, p.175). What Benjamin, another resource for Agamben, calls "law-making violence" (Borislavov 2005, p.180) can be expressed in Durkheimian terms as follows: the force of law-making violence lies in the always immanent constitutive regulative effect of social life on human conduct that has real laws of its own (Durkheim 1997). Law-making violence then is not about legislation (positive law and its enforcement) but rather refers to the real potential of collectives.

The violence of the sacred is ontological, founded in the actualisation of social potentials that manifest a right in new totem-creation (and have normative valence), discontinuous with mechanisms of rule. Moreover, to return to the etymological Indo-European terrain from which Agamben begins, the source of this power is classically that of the people. In western Indo-European dialects the proto-Indo-European root **teuto* designates the people. It is derived from the root **tew-* meaning to be swollen, powerful. Based on this material, Benveniste suggests that the general designation for the people literally means "the people as a full development of the social body" (Benveniste 1973, p.295). Read in terms of Durkheimian ontology, this suggests that it is no coincidence that the meaning of the people and the sacred as referring to "a power which is full of ardour and swollen with fecundity" (Benveniste 1973, p.468), substantially overlap. This power, in Durkheimian terms, is the ontological basis of all social order; it is sociogenic. As Bataille expresses it, "The sacred is that prodigious effervescence of life that, for the sake of duration, the order of things hold in check, and that this holding changes into a breaking loose, that is, into violence" (Bataille 1989, pp.52–53). Ontologically, we are dealing in the sacredness of politics itself since it is the very same emergent ground and event of the force that makes a future subjectivity possible at all, allowing humans to overcome appetites and so introduce freedom, contingency and morality as human concerns.

The sacred difference between politics and rule

Where Agamben's work is suggestive is in introducing the relations of the sacred, sovereignty, power and ontology. Where I differ is where the power of sacred difference is to be located. So, drawing on Foucault's concept of biopolitics instead of Agamben's, we can argue that there is a sacred difference constitutive of the modern political field that concerns the sacralisation of politics itself as the decisive relation constitutive of post-politics. In outlining an alternative, I suggest that politics is exceptional in relation to a current situation of rule and potentially constitutive of a new situation. In this sense, politics is radically constitutive, emerges and draws its force from the sovereign power of the social. Developing a concept of the sacredness of politics in this way facilitates rethinking what is meant by the political field as a relation between politics and rule. Rule can be defined as the condition that keeps things the way they are in a society. More precisely, I take rule to refer to the arrangement of places that people occupy in a society as found in the condescending phrase "Know your

place!", together with the dominant set of coordinates through which people think about their fate.

The Latin case provides a resource for deconstructing and reconstructing Agamben's model of how sovereign rule and the sacred works. Crucial here is the Latin distinction between *sacer* and *sanctus* (the Greek pairing is that of *hieros* and *hagios*). This distinction functioned to clarify the difference between the implicit power of the sacred and explicit sacredness. *Sacer* defines the outside of the community as seen from the inside or the inside of the community as seen from the outside. In contrast, *sanctus* designates the wall or the line that separates these two domains, functioning as both prophylaxis and potential threshold or door for the sacred (Benveniste 1973, pp.455, 453). *Sanctus* can be seen as referring to the repetition and reproduction of an already existing set of dominant normative coordinates governing the normal state of affairs and hence a primary manifestation of rule.

The postulated proto-Indo-European (hereafter, "proto-I-E") root of the English word "rule" is "**reg-*", meaning priest-king (Benveniste 1973, p.311), from which is derived the Latin *regula* (straight stick) and other Latin derivatives like *rex* (king) and *regina* (queen), and English derivatives like regular and regime. In Latin, *rex* was related to the verb *regere*. Benveniste clarifies the representations and practices associated with the proto-I-E **reg-*, providing a way of formulating rule as distinct from the sacred power of politics as follows:

In order to understand the formation of *rex* and the verb *regere* we must start with this notion [of straightness], which was wholly material to begin with but was susceptible of development in the moral sense. This dual notion is present in the important expression *regere fines*, a religious act which was preliminary to building. *Regere fines* means literally "trace out the limits by straight lines". This is the operation carried out by the high priest before a temple or town is built and it consists in the delimitation on a given terrain of a sacred plot of ground. The magical character of this operation is evident: what is involved is the delimitation of the interior and the exterior, the realm of the sacred and the realm of the profane, the national territory and foreign territory. The tracing of these limits is carried out by the person invested with the highest powers, the *rex*. . . . The Indo-European *rex* was much more a religious than a political figure. His mission was not to command, to exercise power but to draw up rules, to determine what was in the proper sense "right" ("straight"). It follows that the *rex*, as thus defined, was more akin to a priest than a sovereign (Benveniste 1973, pp.311–312).

Two of the English meanings of ruler, referring to a political figure and a measuring stick or straight edge have involved a separation of the effects of the same social structure and practices in which the priest-king enacted this ritual, in which both meanings were condensed.

This conception of rule at once designates the asymmetries of a social order (that is, the priest-king as the first stratum of the caste system in Indo-European societies); the ritual apparatus of delimiting a social sphere (the reference point for systems of inclusion and exclusion) and the sanctioning, in the positive sense, of what takes or holds and occupies the place so designated (namely, what goes on in the building correctly delimited). In this sense, rule is constitutive of the measure and coordinates of a structure of places within a social order. While this concept of rule refers to what it is that keeps things the way they are, this by no means commits one to a static model of rule. In this respect, Foucault's work is very helpful. In Foucauldian terms, the question of rule concerns the direction in which social life is actually headed because of how a field structuring possible actions is constituted; it is dynamic because it deals with actions. To put this is slightly different terms, actions actualise and so hold a place delimited by rule, even if that "place" refers to the temporal coordinates of development. That is to say that a ruled condition is one in which there is a predominant measure of things.

We are now in a position to consolidate a neo-Durkheimian alternative as follows. The contemporary political field is structured by the sacred difference between politics and rule; politics is constitutively excluded (that is, sacralised) from post-political rule and this difference traverses all points of the actualisation of rule (all actions that are in play in the political field). This formulation provides a way to think about the relationship between the mundane, quotidian actuality of action and what is not happening because it is constitutively excluded by sacralisation. In this regard, the power of the sacredness of politics itself lies in its real but underdetermined existence, which is to say that it has a power that is only in part actualised by an existing system of rule.

This alternative conception of the political field as being structured by the sacralisation of politics from rule also implies that a sacred difference structures and traverses the entire terrain of the political field as it is a constitutively excluded and structurally produced element. This resolves the problem with Agamben identified by Laclau, namely that his conception of the political neglects class struggles. In this case, the class struggle is between those on the side of rule and those on the side of politics, involving a war over the possible, understood as the work of thinking about real alternative forms of societal organisation and institutional arrangements that would counter-actualise sacred power. Indeed, for Bataille, the sacredness of politics is exactly what renders politics impossible and unthinkable within a dominant system of thought (Besnier 1990, p.178). This need not imply the pursuit of a pure politics perpetually and inherently undermined by the pragmatic demands of governmentalist administration and policy programming, as Foucault's work well points out, constrained as it is by policy objectives designed to facilitate some sorts of actions. Rather, the neo-Durkheimian point that I wish to stress here, in contrast to Agamben, is that the real ontological structure of the political field is an inherently volatile one in as much as contemporary systems of post-political governmental rule must constitutively exclude alternative ways of problematising the collective fate in order to secure and reproduce the normative and temporal coordinates of governmentality.

Politics and the threshold of history

What differentiates politics from rule in a predominantly post-political governmentalised world is a limit imposed on how collective fates are problematised (see Datta 2008).[1] This limit can perhaps best be described metaphorically as a threshold (limen), a conceptual focal point for Agamben (Hussain and Ptacek 2000). In *Professional ethics and civic morals*, Durkheim provides some indication of the ontological importance of thresholds. As he states, "In many countries, it was on the threshold that . . .

sanctity reached its greatest force" (Durkheim 1992, p.152). In this respect, a door and its limen is a centre at which the two realms of *sacer* and *sanctus* meet. In Indo-European terms, "This door, according to whether it is open or shut, becomes the symbol for separation from, or communication between, one world and another" (Benveniste 1973, p.254). Drawing on this figure, the space of the political field, actualised by the difference between politics and rule, can be understood as a limen, a pure differential relation between what is held *sanctus* from the perspective of the inside of established mechanisms for imposing dominant conceptions of right, and the realm of the *sacer*, constitutively excluded from it, while subtending it. The collective fate lies in this eternal limit (one not governed by the laws to which humans are subjected and hence subjectivised within a social order) in which the temporal coordinates of a historicity are suspended by the sovereign power of sociality itself (the sacred), in an exceptional state, from which another emergent politics may become possible.

The limen manifests a threshold between a historicity (the framework through which we represent and problematise the future we aim to make and how we conceive of what is possible and not), the actuality of what people do in going about living their social lives, and the real potential that another history and historical enframing can actually be made. This does not imply that this potential exists within a political field structured by the sacred differentiation between politics and rule. Rather, this potential is one that exists in the broader field of a societal formation: the way social institutions are arranged and articulate each other do not exhaust how else they might be articulated to constitute a new type of societal formation that would then produce a new range of potentials (Datta 2007). In short, from the Durkheimian point of view, the possibilities of politics lie in social ontology and not in interventions or modifications in the terrain of an existing political field. At issue is a temporal threshold in which a people may exist in the time of the gods, the moment of an eternal return to the originary site and force that founds the laws that will come to rule. The limen of the political field is the central, volatile and non-rationalisable site that relates the sacred violence of politics itself to any system of rule.

Summary: the neo-Durkheimian inversion of Agamben

To now modify Agamben's three main points, I suggest that

- the originary political relation is the ontological limit that relates and differentiates between the sacredness of politics itself and the profane (sanctioned) coordinates of actualised rule. This limit is epochal in the sense that it hints at the potential that a different, heterotopian historicity is possible.
- the fundamental activity of the sovereign power of the real force of a society is the founding force of the normative sphere, including that of re-presentative governmental superiority: there is an ontological superiority of popular sovereignty over state sovereignty.[2]
- today is it the myopic valorisation of development that is the sanctioned paradigm of rule. Post-political rule depends on the sacralisation (or constitutive exclusion) of politics to oppose the affirmation of the contingent formations of societal organisation that opens up the door of history and means of differently problematising collective fates.

Conclusion

I have outlined some stakes concerning the inversion of Agamben's analytic. I suggest that the real issue today is not about a condition of political emergency and state of exception where everyone is *homo sacer*, included by virtue of exclusion from either religious/cosmological or juridical significance to the apparatuses of the contemporary post-political administrative state. Rather, the issue for me is an exceptional state in which a politics may emerge that opens up the possibility of a real affirmation of the contingency of human existence, with no guarantee of salvation or improvement, only a chance to start again. Durkheim's work points to the sacred violence of politics and an optimism grounded in the sovereign power of the social in which lies the hope of a people and the dread of ruling classes. This should give us reason for optimism even in a post-political world that aims at the constitutive exclusion – the sacralisation – of politics itself.

Acknowledgements

*The author gratefully acknowledges the support supplied by a Social Sciences and Humanities Research Council of Canada Doctoral Fellowship and a Mount Allison University Research Grant. He thanks Frank Pearce and Alan Hunt for helpful discussions and Claudia Dinatale for encouragement.

Notes

1. This is not to suggest that rule does not depend upon, or more precisely, is subtended by, a politics. Rather, the constitutive emergence and conditions for the pervasive imposition of the normative coordinates of a system of rule is its originary political foundation. What is sacralised is the repetition of this kind of political event, that, were it to be actualised, would inherently threaten the security conditions of a system of rule and hence render the political field more volatile in much the same way as hierophanies destabilise the routine coordinates of profane existence.

2. Admittedly, as pointed out by an insightful reviewer, this bears a strong resemblance to Habermas' formulation, especially in *Between Facts and Norms: Contributions to a Discourse Theory of law and democracy* (1996). However, a serious theoretical issue to explore in this regard is the extent to which Habermas's position depends on a Durkheimian ontology, more so than perhaps Habermasians might like to admit, at which point his overly rationalist sense of discourse and his dependence on an actionist social ontology are contradicted by the Durkheimian sense of the sacred, collective, non-rational and volatile basis of the social.

References

Note: As multiple editions of key works by Durkheim have been used by different authors in this monograph works are listed under the original date of publication in square brackets. Subsequent editions that have been used in citations have been listed in square brackets after the original publication information.

AGAMBEN, G. 1998. *Homo sacer*. Stanford, CA: Stanford University Press.

ALEXANDER, J. C. 2006. *The civil sphere*. New York: Oxford University Press.

ALLIEZ, E. AND NEGRI, A. 2003. "Peace and war", *Theory Culture & Society*, 20 (2), 109–118.

ALUN JONES, R. 1981. "Robertson Smith, Durkheim and sacrifice: a historical context for the elementary forms of religious life", *Journal of the History of Behavioural Sciences*, 17 (2), 84–205.

ANDREW, C. M. AND KANYA-FORSTNER, A. S. 1971. "The French 'colonial party': its composition, aims and influence, 1885–1914", *The Historical Journal*, 14 (1), 99–128.

ARENDT, H. 1969. *On violence*. New York: Harvest.

ARENDT, H. 1993. *Between past and future*. New York: Penguin.

ASAD, T. 2003. *Formations of the secular: Christianity, Islam, modernity*. Stanford, CA: Stanford University Press.

AUROUX, S. 1998. *La raison, le langage et les normes*. Paris: Presses Universitaires de France.

BAILLOT, A. 1927. *Influence de la philosophie de Schopenhauer en France (1860–1900)*. Paris: J. Vrin.

BALAN, B. 1979. *L'ordre et le temps. L'anatomie comparée et l'histoire des vivants au XIXè siècle*. "L'histoire des sciences. Textes et études" series. Paris: Vrin.

BALANDIER, G. 1986. "An anthropology of violence and war", *International Social Science Journal*, 38 (4), 499–511.

BATAILLE, G. 1989. *Theory of religion*. New York: Zone Books.

BATAILLE, G. 1995. *The accursed share* vols II and III. New York: Zone Books.

BAUDRILLARD, J. [1970] 1998. *The consumer society*. London: Sage.

BAUDRILLARD, J. [1973] 1975. *The mirror of production*. St Louis: Telos Press.

BAUDRILLARD, J. [1976] 1993]. *Symbolic exchange and death*. London: Sage.

BAUDRILLARD, J. [1979] 1991]. *Seduction*. New York: St Martin's Press.

BAUDRILLARD, J. [1995] 2007. *Fragments: cool memories III, 1990–1995*. London: Verso.

BAUDRILLARD, J. 1983. *In the shadow of the silent majorities . . . or the end of the social and other essays*. (New York: Semiotext(e).

BAUDRILLARD, J. 1986. *America*. London: Verso.

BAUDRILLARD, J. 2001. *The uncollected Baudrillard*. ed. by Genosko, Gary. London: Sage.

BAUDRILLARD, J. 2002. *The spirit of terrorism and requiem for the twin towers*. London: Verso.

BAUMAN, Z. 1990. *Modernity and the holocaust*. Ithaca, NY: Cornell University Press.

BAUMAN, Z. 2005. "Durkheim's society revisited", *In:* Alexander, J. C. and Smith, P., eds *The Cambridge companion to Durkheim*. Cambridge: Cambridge University Press, 360–363.

BELLAMY, R. 1992. *Liberalism and modern society*. Oxford: Polity.

BENJAMIN, W. [1921] 1979. "Critique of violence", *In*: Banjamin, W., *One way street*. London: Verso.

BENVENISTE, E. 1973. *Indo-European language and society*. New York: London: Faber and Faber.

BESNARD, P. 1983. *The sociological domain: the Durkheimians and the founding of French sociology*. London and Paris: Cambridge University Press/Éditions de la Maison des Sciences de l'Homme.

BESNARD, P. 1987. *Anomie: les usages et ses fonctions dans la discipline sociologique depuis Durkheim*. Paris: PUF.

BESNIER, J.-M. 1990. "Georges Bataille in the 1930s: a politics of the impossible", *Yale French Studies*, 78, 169–180.

BIRTEK, F. 1991. "The Turkish adventures of the Durkheimian paradigm: does history vindicate M. Labriola?", *Il Politico*, 56 (1), 107–146.

BOLTANSKI, L. AND THÉVENOT, L. 1991. *De la justification. Les économies de la grandeur*. Paris: Gallimard.

BORISLAVOV, R. 2005. "Agamben, ontology, and constituent power", *Debatte*, 13 (2), 173–184.

BOSSUET, J. [1731] 1836. *Traité de la concupiscence*. Paris: Editeurs des Portes de France.

BOTTOMORE, T. 1984. "A Marxist consideration of Durkheim", *In*: Bottomore, T., ed. *Sociology and socialism*. London: Harvester Wheatsheaf.

BOUDON, R. 1994. "Fonction", *In*: Boudon, R. and Bourricaud, F., eds,

ISSJ 185 © UNESCO 2009. Published by Blackwell Publishing Ltd., 9600 Garsington Road, Oxford, OX4 2DK, UK and 350 Main Street, Malden, MA 02148, USA.

Dictionnaire critique de la sociologie. Paris: PUF.

BOURGIN, H. 1942. *Le socialisme universitaire*. Paris: Stock.

BUFACCHI, V. 2005. "Two concepts of violence", *Political Studies Review*, 3 (2), 193–2004.

BURUMA, I. 2004. "Review of Simon S Montefiore *Master of fear: Stalin and the court of the Red Tsar"*, *New York Review of Books*, 19 May.

BUTLER, J. 1993. *Bodies that matter*. New York: Routledge.

CAILLÉ, A. 2007. *Anthropologie du don*. Paris: La Découverte.

CAILLOIS, R. 1938. *Fêtes ou la vertu de la license. In:* Caillois, R. 1992. *Naissance de Lucifer*. Montpellier: Fata Morgana.

CAILLOIS, R. 1939. "Festival", *In:* Hollier, D. ed. 1988. *The college of sociology: 1937–1939*. [Trans. Betsy Wing]. Minneapolis, MI: University of Minnesota Press.

CAILLOIS, R. 1940. "Post script to *Théorie de la fête*", *In:* Hollier, D. ed. 1988. *The college of sociology: 1937–1939*. [Trans. Betsy Wing]. Minneapolis, MI: University of Minnesota Press.

CAILLOIS, R. 1950. "Post script to L'homme et la sacré", *In:* Hollier, D., ed. 1988. *The college of sociology: 1937–1939*. [Trans. Betsy Wing]. Minneapolis, MI: University of Minnesota Press.

CAILLOIS, R. 1958. *Les jeux et les hommes*. Paris: Gallimard.

CAILLOIS, R. 1963a. *Bellone ou le pente de la guerre*. [Reprinted 1994]. Montepellier: Fata Morgana.

CAILLOIS, R. 1963b. "Paroxysms of society", *In:* Frank, C., ed. *The edge of surrealism: a Roger Caillois reader*. Durham, NC: Duke, pp. 284–298.

CAILLOIS, R. 1988. *L'homme et le sacré*. Paris: Flammarion and Folio.

CAILLOIS, R. 1992. *Naissance de Lucifer*. Montpellier: Fata Morgana.

CALDWELL, R. A. AND MESTROVIC, S. G. 2008. "The role of gender in 'expressive' abuse at Abu Ghraib", *Cultural Sociology*, 2 (3), 275–99.

CANGUILHEM, G. 1984. *Le normal et le pathologique*. Paris: Presses Universitaires de France.

CHARLE, C. 1994. "Les normaliens et le socialisme (1867–1879)", *In:* Rébérioux, M. and Candor, G., eds *Jaurès et les intellectuels*. Paris: Les Editions de L'Atelier, 133–158.

CHASTENET, J. 1952. *l'enfance de la troisième république 1870–1879*. Paris: Hachette.

CHIDESTER, D. 1996. *Savage systems: colonialism and comparative religion in southern Africa*. Bloomington, IN: Indiana University Press.

CLARKE, T. C. 1973. *Prophets and patrons: the French university and the emergence of the social sciences*. Cambridge, MA: Harvard University Press.

CLASTRES, P. 1974. *La société contre l'état*. Paris: Minuit.

CLIFFORD, J. 1988. "On ethnographic surrealism", *In:* Clifford, J., ed. *The predicament of culture*. Cambridge, MA: Harvard University, 117–151.

COLLINS, R. 1988. "The Durkheimian tradition in conflict sociology", *In:* Alexander, J. C., ed. *Durkheimian sociology: cultural studies*. Cambridge: Cambridge University Press, 107–123.

COLLINS, R. 2004. *Interaction ritual chains*. Princeton, NJ: Princeton University Press.

COMTE, A. 1975. *Cours de philosophie positive*. 2 vols. Paris: Hermann.

COSER, L. A. 1960. "Durkheim's conservatism and its implications for his sociological theory", *In* Wolff, K., ed. *Emile Durkheim et al. Essays on sociology and philosophy*. New York City: Harper, 211–232.

COTTERRELL, R. 1999. *Emile Durkheim: law in a moral domain.*

Edinburgh: Edinburgh University Press.

DANNER, M. 2004. "Torture and truth: America, Abu Ghraib and the war on terror", New York Review of Books.

DATTA, R. P. 2007. "From Foucault's genealogy to aleatory materialism: realism, nominalism and politics", *In:* Frauley, J. and Pearce, F., eds *Critical realism and the social sciences: heterodox elaborations*. Toronto: University of Toronto Press, 273–295.

DATTA, R. P. 2008. "Politics and existence: totems, dispositifs and some striking parallels between Durkheim and Foucault", *Journal of Classical Sociology*, 8 (2), 283–305.

DAVISON, A. 1998. *Secularism and revivalism in Turkey*. New Haven, CT: Yale University Press.

DAVY, G. 1950. "Introduction", *In:* Kubali, H. N., ed. *Professional ethics and civic morals*. Westport, CT: Greenwood, xiii–xliv.

DAWKINS, R. 1976. *The selfish gene*. Oxford: Oxford University Press.

DAYAN, D. AND KATZ, E. 1988. "Articulating consensus: the ritual and rhetoric of media events", *In:* Alexander, J., ed. *Durkheimian sociology: cultural studies*. Cambridge: Cambridge University Press, 161–186.

DELEUZE, G. 2001. *Difference and repetition*. [Trans. Paul Patton]. London: Athlone.

DERRIDA, J. 1978. "From restricted to general economy: a Hegelianism without reserve", *In:* Derrida, J., *Writing and difference*. [Trans. Bass, A.]. Chicago, IL: University of Chicago Press, 251–77.

DESCOMBES, V. 1995. *La denrée mentale*. Paris: Minuit.

DITTMAR, G. 2008. *Histoire de la commune de 1871*. Paris: Editions Dittmar.

DOUGLAS, M. 1966. *Purity and danger: an analysis of the concepts of pollution and taboo.* London: Routledge.

DOUGLAS, M. 1999. *Comment pensent les institutions*, Paris, La Découverte and M.A.U.S.S.

DUBET, F. 1997. "Durkheim sociologue de l'action: l'intégration entre le positivisme et l'éthique", *In:* Cuin, C.-H., ed. *Durkheim d'un siècle à l'autre: lectures actuelles des "Règles de la méthode sociologique".* Paris: Presses Universitaires de France.

DUMÉZIL, G. 1988. *Mitra-Varuna.* New York: Zone Books.

DURKHEIM, E. [1886] 1970. "*Les etudes de science sociales*", *Revue Philosophique*, 22, 61–80. [Reprinted in Filloux, J. C. ed. as *La science sociale et l'action*. Paris: Presses Universitaires de France].

DURKHEIM, E. [1887] 1975. "La science positive de la morale en Allemagne", *Revue Philosophique*, 4 [Reprinted in Karady V. ed. *Textes I*. Paris: Les Éditions de Minuit: 267–343].

DURKHEIM, E. [1888] 1978. *Durkheim on institutional analysis.* ed. Traugott, M. Chicago, IL: University of Chicago Press.

DURKHEIM, E. [1890] 1970. "Les principes de 1789 et la sociologie", *Revue International de l'Enseignement*, XIX. [Reprinted in Filloux, J.C. ed. *La science sociale et l'action*. Paris: Presses Universitaires de France: 215–225]. [Trans. and ed. in 1973 by Bellah, R.N. *Emile Durkheim on morality and society*. Chicago, IL: University of Chicago Press: 34–42].

DURKHEIM, E. [1893] 1964. *De la division du travail social.* Paris: Alcan Quadrige [11th edn published in 1986 in Paris by Presses Universitaires de France. Transl. by Halls, W.D. in 1984 as *The division of labour in society*, published in London by Macmillan; transl. by Simpson, G. in 1933, 1947 and 1964, published by New York: Free Press].

DURKHEIM, E. [1895] 1982. *Les règles de la méthode sociologique.* Paris: Alcan. [Transl. by Halls,

W.D. as *The rules of sociological method*, published in London by Macmillan. Reprinted in 1993a in Paris by: Presses Universitaires de France.

DURKHEIM, E. [1897a] 1970. "Review of Antonio Labriola's "Essai sur la matérialiste conception de l'histoire"", *Revue Philosophique*, 43, 645–651. [Reprinted in Filloux J. C. ed. *La science sociale et l'action*. Paris: Presses Universitaires de France: 245–254; Transl. in Lukes, S. in 1982, *The Rules of sociological method*: 167–174].

DURKHEIM, E. [1897b] 1966. *Le suicide: étude de sociologie.* [Published in 1983 and 1993b, in Paris by Alcan. Quadrige. Trans by Spaulding, J. A. and Simpson, G, in 1952 in New York by Free Press, trans. by Simpson, G. in 1966 as *Suicide*, published in London byRoutledge and Kegan Paul, republished in 1970.

DURKHEIM, E. [1897c] 1970. "Review of Richard Gaston "Le socialisme et la science sociale"", *Revue Philosophique*, 54, 645–651. [Reprinted in 1970 in Filloux, J. C. ed. *La science sociale et l'action*. Paris: Presses Universitaires de France: 236–244].

DURKHEIM, E. [1898a] 1974. "Répresentations individuelles et representations collective", *Revue de Metaphysique et de Morale*, 6, 273–302. [Transl. by Pocock D. F and reprinted in 1974 in *Sociologie et philosophie*. 4th edn. Presses Universitaires de France. New York: Free Press].

DURKHEIM, E. [1898b] 1970. *L'individualisme et les intellectuels Revue Bleue.* 4th series. vol. 10: 7–13. [Reprinted in Filloux J. C. ed. *La science sociale et l'action*. Paris: Presses Universitaires de France: 261–278. Transl. in 1973 with Bellah, R. N. ed. as *Emile Durkheim on morality and society* Chicago, IL: University of Chicago Press: 43–57].

DURKHEIM, E. [1899] 1986. "Review of Merlino (Saviero) 'Formes et essences du socialisme'", *Revue Philosophique*, 48, 433–9. [Trans. by Giddens A. in 1986 in *Durkheim on*

politics and the state. Cambridge: Polity Press: 137–145].

DURKHEIM, E. [1900] 1970. *La sociologie en France au XIXe siècle Revue Bleue.* 4th series 13: 609–613, 647–652. [Reprinted in Filloux, J.C. ed. *La science sociale et l'action*. Paris: Presses Universitaires de France: 111–136, Trans. and ed. by Bellah R.N. as *Emile Durkheim on morality and society*: 3–22].

DURKHEIM, E. [1901] 1969. "Deux lois de l'évolution pénale", *Année Sociologique*, 4, 65–95. [Reprinted in 1969 in Duvignaud, J. ed. *Journal sociologique*. Paris: Presses Universitaires de France: 245–273. Transl. and edited in 1992 by Gane, M. *The radical sociology of Durkheim and Mauss*. London: Routledge: 21–49].

DURKHEIM, E. [1903] 1975. "Enfance illégitime et anomie sociale", *Année Sociologique*, 6. [Reprinted in Karady, V. ed. *Textes* vol. II: Paris: Les Éditions de Minuit: 237–241].

DURKHEIM, E. [1905] 1970. "Internationalisme et lutte des classes", from *Libres Entretiens* 2nd series. 7e entretien. Paris: Bureau des libre entretiens, 1906 [Reprinted in Filloux, J.C. ed. *La science sociale et l'action*: 282–292].

DURKHEIM, E. [1908] 1982. *Debate on political economy and social sciences.* Extract from the *Bulletin de la sociétéd'économie politique.* [Reprinted in Karady, V. ed. *Textes I:* Paris: Editions de Minuit: 218–225; Transl. in *The rules of sociological method* 1982: 229–235].

DURKHEIM, E. [1909] 1975. "Idéal moral, conscience collective et forces religieuses". *In:* Karady, V., ed. *Textes* II:. Paris: Les Éditions de Minuit, 12–22.

DURKHEIM, E. [1912] 1985. *Les formes élémentaires de la vie réligieuse.* 7th edn 1985,. Paris: Alcan, Quadrige, [Published in 1998 by Presses Universitaires de France. Transl. in 1961 and printed in New York by Collier. Transl. in 1995 by Fields, K. New York: Free Press.

DURKHEIM, E. [1913] 1983. *Pragmatism and sociology*. Cambridge: Cambridge University Press.

DURKHEIM, E. [1914] 1973. "The dualism of human nature and its social conditions", *In:* Bellah, R. N., (ed.) *Emile Durkheim on morality and society*. Chicago, IL: University of Chicago Press, 149–166.

DURKHEIM, E. [1915] 1986. *L'Allemagne au-dessus de tout (Germany above all". German mentality and war)*. Paris: Colin, 1991. [Selections in Giddens, A. *Durkheim on politics and the state*. Cambridge: Polity Press 1986: 224–233].

DURKHEIM, E. [1925] 1973. *L'education morale*. Paris: Félix Alcan. [Trans. as *Moral education* in 1961 and by Wilson, E.K. in 1973. New York: Free Press].

DURKHEIM, E. [1928] 1971. *Le socialisme*. Paris: Presses Universtaire de France. [Reprinted in 1971 as *Socialism*. New York: Collier].

DURKHEIM, E. [1950] 1992. *Leçons de sociologie*. No 111. Istanbul: University of Istanbul Publications of the Faculty of Law. [Reprinted in 1990 Presses Universitaire de France Quadrige. Transl. by Brookfield, C. with an intro. by Turner, B.S. in 1992 as *Professional ethics and civic morals*. London: Routledge.].

DURKHEIM, E. [1957] 1983. *Professional ethics and civic morals*. [Trans. Brookfield, C.]. Westport, CO: Greenwood Press, printed in 1992, New York: Routledge.

DURKHEIM, E. [1968] 1975. *Leçons sur la morale*. Paris: Presses Universitaire de France. [Reprinted in 1975 by Karady, V. (ed.) *Textes*, II: 292–312. Paris: Les Editions de Minuit].

DURKHEIM, E. 1905. "Contributions to discussion: sur l'internationalisme: définition des termes: internationalisme économique, patriotisme national et lutte des classes". *Passim* in *Libres entretiens*. Paris.

DURKHEIM, E. 1960. "The dualism of human nature and its social conditions", *In:* Wolff, K., ed. *Essays on sociology and philosophy*. New York: Harper and Row, 325–340.

DURKHEIM, E. 1962. *Socialism and Saint-Simon*. New York: Collier.

DURKHEIM, E. 1963. *Incest: the nature and origin of the taboo*. New York: Lyle Stuart.

DURKHEIM, E. 1969. "Individualism and the intellectuals", *Political Studies*, 17 (1), 19–30 [Reprinted in 1975 *In*: Pickering, W.S.F. ed. *Durkheim on religion*. London: Routledge and Kegan Paul: 59–73.

DURKHEIM, E. 1977. *The evolution of educational thought in France*. London: Routledge and Kegan Paul.

DURKHEIM, E. 1978. *Durkheim on institutional analysis*. ed. by Traugott, M. Chicago, IL: University of Chicago Press.

DURKHEIM, E. 1980. "Préface' to *L'année sociologique*", *In:* Nandan, Y., ed. *Émile Durkheim: contributions to L'année sociologique*. New York: Free Press, 47–58.

DURKHEIM, E. 1995. *Sociologie et philosophie*. Paris: Presses Universitaires de France.

DURKHEIM, E. 1997. *L'Individualisme et les intellectuels*. Paris: Arthème Fayard.

DURKHEIM, E. 1997. *Montesquieu*. Oxford: Durkheim Press.

DURKHEIM, E. 1998. *Lettres à Marcel Mauss*. [Edited by Besnard P. and Fournier M.]. Paris: PUF.

DURKHEIM, E. 2004. *Durkheim's philosophy lectures: notes from the Lycée de Sens course, 1883–1884*. Cambridge: Cambridge University Press.

DUVIGNAUD, J. 1965. *Durkheim: sa vie, son œuvre avec un exposé de sa philosophie*. Paris: PUF.

DUVIGNAUD, J. 1986. *Hérésie et subversion: essai sur l'anomie*. Paris: La Découverte.

EIGHTY FOUR FILMS (n.d.) "Dwyer story" available online at http://eightyfourfilms.com/dwyer_story.htm [Accessed 28 September 2009].

ELLENBERGER, H. 1970. *The discovery of the unconscious*. New York: Basic Books.

EMIRBAYER, M. 1996a. "Durkheim's contribution to the sociological analysis of history", *Sociological Forum*, 11 (2), 263–184.

EMIRBAYER, M. 1996b. "Useful Durkheim", *Sociological Theory*, 14 (2), 109–130.

EMIRBAYER, M. 2003. *Emile Durkheim: sociologist of modernity*. Oxford: Blackwell.

ESFELD, M. 2004. "L'anti-cartésianisme dans la théorie de la connaissance contemporaine", *In:* Esfeld, M. and Tétaz, J.-M., eds *Généalogie de la pensée moderne, volume d'hommages à Ingeborg Schüssler*. Frankfurt-am-Main: Ontos-Verlag.

FALK, R., GENDZIER, I. AND LIFTON, R. J., eds 2006. *Crimes of war: Iraq*. New York: Nation Books.

FAUCONNET, P. 1928. *La responsabilité*. Paris: Alcan.

FELGINE, O. 1994. *Roger Caillois*. Paris: Stock.

FILLOUX, J. C. 1977. *Durkheim et le socialisme*. Geneva: Droz.

FISH, S. 2008. "Think again". *New York Times* available online at fish.blogs.nytimes.com/2008/11/09/psychology-and-torture Accessed 1 October 2009.

FORTUNE CITY (n.d.) "A tribute to R. Budd Dwyer: the man behind the tragedy", available online at http://members.fortunecity.com/budd3/index.htm [Accessed 28 September 2009].

FOUCAULT, M. 1965. *Madness and civilization: a history of insanity in the age of reason*. New York City: New American Library.

FOUCAULT, M. 1979. *Discipline and punish: the birth of the prison*. New York City: Vintage.

FOUCAULT, M. 1980. "The history of sexuality", *In:* Foucault, M., *Power/ Knowledge*. New York: Pantheon, 183–93 and 1994, New York, Pantheon Books.

FOUCAULT, M. 1984. "The genealogy of ethics: an overview of work in progess", *In:* Rabinow, P. and Dreyfus, H., eds. *Michel Foucault: beyond structuralism and hermeneutics*. Chicago, IL: University of Chicago Press, 229–252.

FOUCAULT, M. 1996. "Confining societies", *In:* Foucault, M., *Foucault live: collected interviews, 1961–1984*. New York: Semiotext(e).

FOUCAULT, M. 1998a. "Different spaces", *In:* Foucault, M., *Michel Foucault: aesthetics, method and epistemology*. New York: The New Press, 175–86.

FOUCAULT, M. 1998b. "Madness and society", *In:* Foucault, M., *Michel Foucault: aesthetics, method and epistemology*. New York: The New Press, 335–42.

FOUCAULT, M. 2000. "The political technology of individuals", *In:* Foucault, M., *Michel Foucault: power*. New York: The New Press, 403–17.

FOUCAULT, M. 2001a. *Dits et écrits*. vol. I. Paris: Gallimard.

FOUCAULT, M. 2001b. *Dits et écrits*. vol. II. Paris: Gallimard.

FOUCAULT, M. 2003a. *Abnormal*. New York: Picador.

FOUCAULT, M. 2003b. *Society must be defended*. New York: Picador.

FOUCAULT, M. 2003c. "The subject and power", *In:* Rabinow, P. and Rose, N., eds, *The essential Foucault*. New York: The New Press, 126–144.

FOUCAULT, M. 2003d. "The ethics of the concern for the self as a practice of freedom", *In:* Rabinow, P. and Rose, N., eds, *The essential Foucault*. New York: The New Press, 25–42.

FOUCAULT, M. 2003e. "'Omnes et singulatim': toward a critique of political reason", *In:* Rabinow, P. and Rose, N., eds, *The essential Foucault*. New York: The New Press, 180–201.

FOUCAULT, M. 2006. *The history of madness*. New York: Routledge.

FOUCAULT, M. 2007. *Security, territory, population*. New York: Palgrave Macmillan.

FOURNIER, M. 1997. *Marcel Mauss: écrits politiques*. Paris: Fayard.

FOURNIER, M. 2005. "Durkheim's life and context", *In:* Alexander, J. C. and Smith, P., eds *The Cambridge companion to Durkheim*. Cambridge: Cambridge University Press, 41–70.

FOURNIER, M. 2006. *Marcel Mauss*. [Trans. Jane Marie Todd]. Princeton, NJ: Princeton University Press.

FOURNIER, M. 2007. *Émile Durkheim (1885–1917)*. Paris: Fayard.

FRANK, C. 1991. "Roger Caillois' logic of participation in the 30s: from le grand jeu to the Collège de Sociologie". PhD dissertation, Cambridge. MA: Harvard University.

FRIEDLAND, R. 2005. "Drag kings at the totem ball: the erotics of collective representation in Émile Durkheim and Sigmund Freud", *In:* Alexander, J. C. and Smith, P., eds *The Cambridge companion to Durkheim*. Cambridge: Cambridge University Press, 239–274.

FRIEND, D. 2006. *Watching the world change: the stories behind the images of 9/11*. New York: Farrar, Straus and Giroux.

FROBERT, L. 2000. *Le travail de François Simiand (1873–1935)*. Paris: Économica.

FROMM, E. 1992. *Anatomy of human destructiveness*. New York: Holt.

FURET, F. 1992. *Revolutionary France*. Oxford: Oxford University Press.

GALBRAITH, P. 2007. *The end of Iraq: how American Incompetence created a war without end*. New York: Simon & Schuster.

GALILÉE 1992. *Dialogue sur les deux grands systèmes du monde*. Paris: Le Seuil.

GANE, M. 1983. "Durkheim: woman as outsider", *Economy and Society*, 12 (2), 227–270.

GANE, M. 1991. *Baudrillard's bestiary: Baudrillard and culture*. London: Routledge.

GANE, M. 2000. *Jean Baudrillard: in radical uncertainty*. London: Pluto Press.

GAYON, J. 1992. *Darwin et l'après-Darwin: une histoire de l'hypothèse de sélection naturelle*. Paris: Kimé.

GIDDENS, A., ed 1986. *Durkheim on politics and the state*. Stanford, CA: Stanford University Press.

GIRARD, R. 1977. *Violence and the sacred*. Baltimore, NJ: Johns Hopkins University Press.

GIRARD, R. 1986. *The scapegoat*. Baltimore, NJ: Johns Hopkins University Press.

GIRARD, R. 1987. *Things hidden since the foundation of the world*. Stanford, CA: Stanford University Press.

GISLAIN, J.-J. AND STEINER, P. 1995. *La sociologie économique (1890–1920)*. Paris: PUF.

GODELIER, M. 1999. *The enigma of the gift*. [Trans. Nora Scott]. Chicago, IL: University of Chicago.

GOULD, G. M. 1935. *Gould's Medical Dictionary*. 4th edn. New York: McGraw Hill.

GOVERNMENT OF CANADA of 2001. *Anti-Terrorism Act*.

GRAEBER, D. 2004. "Give it away" available online at http:// www.revuedumauss.com.fr/Pages/

ABOUT.html#Anchor-47857 [accessed October 2007].

GRAHAM, E. T. 2007. "The danger of Durkheim: ambiguity in the theory of social effervescence", *Religion*, 37 (1), 26–38.

GRUZTPALK, J. 2002. "Blood feud and modernity: Max Weber's and Emile Durkheim's theories", *Journal of Classical Sociology*, 2 (2), 115–134.

GUILLO, D. 2003. *Les figures de l'organisation. Sciences de la vie et sciences sociales*. Paris: PUF.

GUILLO, D. 2006. "La place de la biologie dans les premiers textes de Durkheim: un paradigme oublié?", *Revue Française de Sociologie*, 47 (3), 507–535.

GURVITCH, G. 1931. *L'Idée du droit social*. Paris: Sirey.

GUTMAN, R. AND RIEFF, D. 1999. *Crimes of war*. New York: Norton.

GUTTING, G. 2001. *French philosophy in the twentieth century*. Cambridge: Cambridge University Press.

GUYAU, J.-M. [1885] 1907. *Ésquisse d'une morale sans obligation ni sanction*. Paris: Alcan.

HABERMAS, H. 1996. *Between facts and norms: contributions to a discourse theory of law and democracy*. Cambridge: Polity.

HALBWACHS, M. [1912] 1970. *La classe ouvrière et les niveaux de vie*. Paris, London and New York: Gordon and Breach.

HALBWACHS, M. 1928. *La population et le tracé des voies à Paris depuis un siècle*. Paris: PUF.

HALBWACHS, M. 1938a. *Morphologie sociale*. Paris: A. Colin.

HALBWACHS, M. [1938b] 1964. *Esquisse d'une psychologie des classes sociales*. Paris: M. Rivière.

HALBWACHS, M. [1938c] 1970. *Morphologie sociale*. Paris: A. Colin.

HALBWACHS, M. 1930. *Les causes du suicide*. Paris: Alcan.

HALBWACHS, M. 1939. "Les caractéristiques des classes moyennes", *In:* Aron, R and Bouglé, C. C. A., eds, *Inventaires III, "Les classes moyennes"*. Paris: Alcan, 28–52.

HAWKINS, M. J. "Durkheim on occupational corporations: an exegesis and interpretation", *Journal of the History of Ideas*, 55 (3), 461–481.

HERSH, S. M. 2004. *Chain of command: the road from 9/11 to Abu Ghraib*. New York: Harper Collins.

HERTZ, R. 1909. *La prééminence de la main droite. In:* Hubert, H. and Mauss, M., eds, *Mélanges d'histoire des religions*. Paris: Alcan.

HERZL, T. [1896] 2008. *L'état des juifs, suivi de essai sur le sionisme, de l'état des juifs à l'état d'Israël*. Paris: La Découverte.

HEYD, U. 1950. *Foundations of Turkish nationalism: the life and teachings of Ziya Gökalp*. London: Luzac and Harville.

HOLLIER, D. 1988. *The College of Sociology: 1937–1939*. [Trans. Betsy Wing]. Minneapolis, MI: University of Minnesota.

HOLLIER, D. 1995. *Le Collège de Sociologie: 1937–1939*. Paris: Gallimard.

HOLLIER, D. 1997. *Absent without leave: French literature under the threat of war*. [Trans. Catherine Porter]. Cambridge, MA: Harvard University Press.

HOVDE, B. J. 1928. "Socialistic theories of imperialism prior to the Great War", *The Journal of Political Economy*, 36 (5), 569–591.

HOY, D. C., ed 1986. *Foucault: a critical reader*. Oxford: Blackwell.

HUBERT, H. AND MAUSS, M. 1964. *Sacrifice: its nature and functions*. [Trans. W.D. Halls]. Chicago, IL: University of Chicago Press.

HUMAN RIGHTS WATCH. 2006. "By the numbers: findings of the detainee abuse and accountability project", *Human Rights Watch*, 18 (2), 1–28.

HUSSAIN, N. AND PTACEK, M. 2000. "Thresholds: sovereignty and the sacred", *Law and Society Review*, 34 (2), 495–516.

ISAMBERT, F. A. 1982. *Le sens du sacré: fête et religion populaire*. Paris: Minuit.

JACKSON, J. 2008. Conflict and culture II: revolution. BBC Radio 3, 29 January 2008.

JAURÈS, J. 1898. *Les preuves*. Paris: Les Editions de la Découverte 1998.

JELLINEK, F. 1937. *The Paris Commune of 1871*. London: Victor Gollancz.

KARPINSKI, J. 2005. *One woman's army: the commanding general of Abu Ghraib tells her story*. New York: Hyperion.

KARSENTI, B. 1994. *Marcel Mauss: le fait social total*. Paris: PUF.

KARSENTI, B. 1997. *L'homme total. Sociologie, anthropologie et philosophie chez Marcel Mauss*. Paris: Presses Universitaires de France.

KUBAL, H. N. 1936. *L'idée de l'état chez les précurseurs de l'école sociologique français*. Paris: Les Éditions Domat-Montchrestien F. Loviton.

KUMAR, K. 1993. "Civil society: an inquiry into the usefulness of an historical term", *British Journal of Sociology*, 44 (3), 375–395.

LACAN, J. 1990a. *Écrits: a selection*. [Trans Alan Sheridan]. London and New York: Routledge.

LACAN, J. 1990b. *Television*. [Trans. Denis Hollier, Rosalind Krauss and Annette Michelson]. New York: Norton Press.

LACLAU, E. 2007a. *On populist reason*. New York: Verso.

LACLAU, E. 2007b. "Bare life or social indeterminancy?", *In:* Calarco, M. and DeCaroli, S., eds *Giorgio Agamben: Sovereignty and Life*. Stanford, CA: Stanford University Press, 11–22.

LALANDE, A. [1926] 1980. *Vocabulaire technique et critique de la philosophie*. Paris: Presses Universitaires de France.

LAMANNA, M. A. 2002. *Emile Durkheim on the family*. London: Sage.

LASCH, C. 1971. *Culture of narcissism*. New York: Basic Books.

LASERRA, A. 1992. "Paroxysmes", *In:* Jenny, L., ed., *Roger Caillois: la pensée aventurée*. Paris: Belin.

LAYNE, N. 1973. "Durkheim as pacifist", *Sociological Inquiry*, 43 (2), 99–103.

LEMERT, C. 2006. *Durkheim's ghosts: cultural logics and social things*. Cambridge: Cambridge University Press.

LETVIN, A. O. 1990. *Sacrifice in the surrealist novel: the impact of early theories of primitive religion on the description of violence in modern fiction*. New York: Garland.

LEVEY, G. B. 2007. "Beyond Durkheim: a comment on Steven Lukes's 'Liberal democratic torture'", *British Journal of Political Science*, 37 (3), 567–570.

LINCOLN, B. 1999. *Theorizing myth: ideology, narrative and practice*. Chicago, IL: University of Chicago.

LISSAGARAY 1876. *Histoire de la Commune de 1871*. Paris: Imprimerie Ouvrière.

LITTRÉ, É. [1863] 1963. *Dictionnaire de la langue francaise*. Vols. 1–9. Paris: Gallimard.

LIVE LEAK 2006. "Bud Dwyer suicide video" available online at http://www.liveleak.com/ view?i=860c9b9f3b [Accessed 28 September 2009].

LOTRINGER, S. 1999. "Les Misérables", *In:* Lotringer, Sylvère, ed. *More or less*. Pasadena: Art Centre College of Design.

LUKES, S. 1972. *Emile Durkheim*. New York: Harper and Row.

LUKES, S. 1985. *Emile Durkheim: his life and work*. Stanford, CA: Stanford University Press.

LUKES, S. 2006. "Liberal democratic torture", *British Journal of Political Science*, 36 (1), 1–16.

LYONNET, S. AND SABOURIN, L. 1970. *Sin, redemption and sacrifice: a biblical and patristic study*. Rome: Biblical Institute Press.

MALON, B. 1871. *La troisième défaite du proletariat français*. Neuchatel: Guillaume.

MANNHEIM, H. 2003. *Group problems in crime and punishment*. London: Routledge.

MARCEL, J. C. 2001. *Le durkheimisme dans l'entre-deux guerres*. Paris: PUF.

MARCEL, J. C. 2004. "Mauss et Halbwachs: vers la fondation d'une psychologie collective", *Sociologie et Sociétés*, 36 (2), 73–90.

MARCEL, J. C. 2007. "Mémoire, espace et connaissance chez Maurice Halbwachs", *In:* Jaisson, M. and Baudelot, C., eds, *Maurice Halbwachs, sociologue retrouvé*. Paris: Presses de l'ENS.

MARCEL, J. C. 2008. "Organicisme et théorie des classes sociales chez Simiand et Halbwachs: un héritage caché de Durkheim?", *Revue d'Histoire des Sciences Humaines*, 19 (2), 143–160.

MARCEL, J. C. AND STEINER, P. 2006. *François Simiand, critique sociologique de l'économie politique*. Paris: PUF.

MATVIKO, J. 1988. "How far do you go and how much do you show?: Pittsburgh Television News. Media and the R. Budd Dwyer Suicide". Paper presented at the annual meeting of the Eastern Communication Association, Baltimore, MD, April.

MAUSS, M. 1950. *Sociologie et anthropologie*. Paris: PUF and Quadridge.

MAUSS, M. 1997. *Ecrits politiques*. Paris: Fayard, 1997.

MAUSS, M. 2000. *The gift: the form and reason for exchange in archaic societies*. [Trans. W.D. Halls and

with a foreword by Mary Douglas]. New York and London: Norton.

MAUSS, M. 2004. *On prayer*. Oxford: Berghahn.

MAUSS, M. AND BEAUCHAT, H. 1950. "Eskimo societies: a study in social morphology (1904–1905)", *In:* Mauss, M., *Sociologie et anthropologie*. Paris: PUF and Quadridge.

MAY, L. AND HOFFMAN, S. 1991. *Collective responsibility*. Totowa, NJ: Rowman & Littlefield.

MAYER, J. 2005. "The Experiment", *The New Yorker*, 11 July 2005.

MAYR, E. [1982] 1989. *Histoire de la biologie. Diversité, évolution et hérédité*. Paris: Fayard.

MAYR, E. 2001. *What evolution is*. London: Penguin.

MERTON, R. K. 1957. *Social theory and social structure*. New York: Free Press.

MESTROVIC, S. G. 1985. "Anomia and sin in Durkheim's thought", *Journal for the Social Scientific Study of Religion*, 24 (2), 119–136.

MESTROVIC, S. G. 1988. *Emile Durkheim and the reformation of sociology*. Totowa, NJ: Rowman & Littlefield.

MESTROVIC, S. G. 1997. *Postemotional society*. London: Sage.

MESTROVIC, S. G. 2007. *The trials of Abu Ghraib: an expert witness account of shame and honor*. Boulder, CO: Paradigm Publishers.

MESTROVIC, S. G. 2008. *Rules of engagement? A social anatomy of an American war crime: operation Iron Triangle – Iraq*. New York: Algora.

MESTROVIC, S. G. AND BROWN, H. M. 1985. "Durkheim's concept of anomie as dérèglement", *Social Problems*, 33 (2), 81–99.

MICHEL, L. [1898] 1999. *La Commune: histoire et souvenirs*. Paris: Stock. [Reprinted in 1999: Paris: La Découverte].

MILNE-EDWARDS, H. 1851. *Introduction à la zoologie générale ou considérations sur les tendances de la nature dans la constitution du règne animal*. Paris: Victor Masson.

MOSSE, G. 1964. *The crisis of German ideology*. New York City: Grosset and Dunlap.

MUCCHIELLI, L. 1998. *La Découverte du social, naissance de la sociologie en France*. Paris: La Découverte.

MySpace. (n.d.) "R. Budd Dwyer" available online at http://profile. myspace.com/index.cfm?fuseaction = user.viewprofile&friendID = 65697029 [Accessed 28 September 2009].

Obama'08 2007. "Remarks of Senator Obama: the war we need to win" available online at http:// www.barackobama.com/2007/08/ 01/the_war_we_need_to_win.php [Accessed 30 September 2009].

ORWELL, G. 1956. "Politics and the English language", *In:* Rovere, R. H., ed. *The Orwell reader*. New York City: Harcourt, Brace and World, 355–366.

PARLA, T. AND DAVISON, A. 2004. *Corporatist ideology in Kemalist Turkey*. Syracuse, NY: Syracuse University Press.

PARSONS, T. 1937. *The structure of social action*. Glencoe, IL: Free Press.

PATTON, P. 2007. "Agamben and Foucault on biopower and biopolitics", *In:* Calarco, M. and DeCaroli, S., eds *Giorgio Agamben: sovereignty and life*. Stanford, CA: Stanford University Press, 203–218.

PEARCE, F. 2001. *The radical Durkheim*. 2nd edn. Toronto: Canadian Scholars' Press International.

PEARCE, F. 2006. "Foucault and the 'hydra-headed monster': the *College de Sociologie* and the two Acephales", *In:* Beaulieu, A. and Gabbard, D., eds. *Michel Foucault and power today*. Lanham, MD: Lexington Books, 115–37.

PEARCE, F. AND WOODIWISS, A. 2001. "Reading Foucault as a realist", *In:*

Lopez, J. and Potter, G., eds *After postmodernism: an introduction to critical realism*. New York: Athlone Press, 51–62.

PÉGUY, C. 1957. "Notre Jeunesse", *In:* Burac, Robert, ed. *Oeuvres en prose 1909–1914*. Paris: Plèiade and Gallimard.

PERLEZ, J. 2008. "Pakistan's military chief criticizes US over a raid", *New York Times*, September 10.

PICKERING, W. S. F. 1984. *Durkheim's sociology of religion: themes and theories*. London and New York: Routledge.

POLIAKOV, L. 1974. *The Aryan myth*. New York: New American Library.

RANCIÈRE, J. 1999. *Disagreements*. Minneapolis, MI: University of Minnesota Press.

RANULF, S. 1939. "Scholarly forerunners of fascism", *Ethics*, 50 (1), 16–34.

RÉCLUS, M. 1945. *La troisième république*. Paris: Librairie Arthème Fayard.

RENOUVIER, C. [1872] 1994. *"La doctrine républicaine, ou ce nous sommes, ce que nous voulons"*. *La critique philosophique, politique scientifique et littéraire* (2 vols). [Reprinted in Douailler, S. *et al.* eds in 1994 in *Philosophie France XIXe siècle*. Paris: Livres de Poche]

RENOUVIER, C. 1864. *Introduction à la philosophie analytique de l'histoire*. Essais de Critique Générale: Quatrième Essai. Paris: Librairie Philosophique de Ladrange.

RENOUVIER, C. 1869. *Science de la morale* (2 vols). Paris: Librairie Philosophique de Ladrange.

RENOUVIER, C. 1875. *Traité de psychologie rationelle*. (3 vols). Paris: Bureau de la Critique Philosophique.

RENOUVIER, C. 1879. "Les dangers de la troisième république", *La Critique Philosophique*, 8, 177–186.

RICHARDSON, J. 2004. *Nietzsche's new Darwinism*. Oxford: Oxford University Press.

RICHMAN, M. 2002. *Sacred revolutions: Durkheim and the College de Sociologie*. Minnesota, MI: University of Minnesota Press.

RICKS, T. 2006. *Fiasco: the American military adventure in Iraq*. New York: Penguin.

RIESMAN, D. [1950] 2001. *The lonely crowd*. New Haven, CT: Yale University Press.

RILEY, A. 2002a. "The sacred calling of intellectual labour in mystic and ascetic Durkheimianism", *Archives européennes de sociologie/European Journal of Sociology*, 42 (2), 354–385.

RILEY, A. 2002b. "Durkheim contra Bergson? The hidden roots of postmodern theory and the postmodern 'return' of the sacred", *Sociological Perspectives*, 45 (3), 243–265.

RILEY, A. 2005a. "'Renegade Durkheimianism' and the transgressive/left sacred", *In:* Alexander, J. and Smith, P., eds *The Cambridge companion to Durkheim*. Cambridge: Cambridge University Press, 274–301.

RILEY, A. 2005b. "The rebirth of tragedy out of the spirit of hip hop: some suggestions for a cultural sociology of gangsta rap music", *Journal of Youth Studies*, 8 (3), 297–311.

RILEY, A. 2005c. "The theory of play/games and sacrality in popular culture: the relevance of Roger Caillois for contemporary neo-Durkheimian cultural theory", *Durkheimian Studies*, 11, 103–114.

ROBERTSON SMITH, W. 2002. *Religion of the semites*. Edison, NJ: Transaction Books.

RORTY, R. 1989. *Contingency, irony and solidarity*. Cambridge: Cambridge University Press.

ROSE, N. 1999. *Powers of freedom*. Cambridge: Cambridge University Press.

ROSE, N. 2001. "The politics of life itself", *Theory, Culture and Society*, 18 (6), 1–30.

SAHLINS, M. 2004. *Stone age economics*. London/New York: Routledge.

SALON.COM (2009) "Forbidden thoughts about 9/1" available online at http://dir.salon.com/story/mwt/feature/2002/09/07/forbidden/index1.html 1[Accessed 28 September 2009]

SAUMADE, F. 2003. *Drieu la Rochelle: l'homme en désordre*. Paris: Berg.

SCHLANGER, N. 2006. "Technological commitments: Marcel Mauss and the study of techniques in the French social sciences", *In:* Mauss, M., *Techniques, technology and civilization*. Oxford: Berghahn, 1–29.

SCHMITT, C. 1985. *Political theology: four chapters on the concept of sovereignty*. Cambridge, MA: MIT Press.

SCHOPENHAUER, A. [1818] 1965. *The world as will and representation*. New York: Dover.

SHAPIRO, K. 2003. *Sovereign nations, carnal states*. Ithaca, NY: Cornell.

SHILLING, C. 2005. "Embodiment, emotions and the foundations of the social order: Durkheim's enduring contribution", *In:* Alexander, J. C. and Smith, P., eds *The Cambridge companion to Durkheim*. Cambridge: Cambridge University Press, 211–239.

SIMIAND, F. 1930. *Cours d'économie politique*, vol 2. year 1928–29. Paris: Domat Montchrestien.

SIMIAND, F. 1932. *Le salaire, l'évolution sociale et la monnaie*. vols. 1 and 2. Paris: Alcan.

SOBER, E. 1984. *The nature of selection*. Chicago, IL: University of Chicago Press.

SOBER, E. AND WILSON, D. S. 1998. *Unto others: the evolution and psychology of unselfish behaviour*.

Cambridge MA: Harvard University Press.

SOLIS, G. 1998. *Son Thang: An American war crime*. New York: Bantam.

SONTAG, S. 2003. *Regarding the pain of others*. New York: Picador.

SOREL, G. [1908] 1950. *On violence*. Trans Hulme T. E. and Roth, J. Glencoe, IL: Free Press 1950.

SPENCER, H. 1878. *Principes de sociologie*. vol 2. Paris: Germer Baillière.

SPENCER, H. 1898 (1857). "La physiologie transcendante", *In:* Spencer, H., *Essais scientifiques*. Paris: Alcan.

STEDMAN JONES, S. 2001a. *Durkheim reconsidered*. Cambridge: Polity Press.

STEDMAN JONES, S. 2001b. "Durkheim and Bataille: constraint, transgression and the concept of the sacred", *Durkheimian Studies/Etudes surkheimiennes*, 7, 53–63.

STEINER, P. 2005. *L'école durkheimienne et l'économie*. Geneva and Paris: Droz.

STERN, F. 1961. *The politics of cultural despair*. Berkeley, CA: University of California Press.

STERNHELL, Z. 1995. *Neither right nor left: fascist ideology in France* [Trans. David Maisel]. Princeton, NJ: Princeton University.

STOEKL, A. 1992. *Agonies of the intellectual: commitment, subjectivity and the performative in the 20th century French tradition*. Lincoln, NE: University of Nebraska Press.

STRASSER, S. 2004. *The Abu Ghraib investigations: the official reports of the independent panel and the Pentagon on the shocking prisoner abuse in Iraq*. New York: Public Affairs.

STRENSKI, I. 1989. "Durkheim, Hamelin and the French Hegel", *Historical Reflections/Réflexions Historiques*, 16 (2–3), 146–149.

STRENSKI, I. 1995. "Review of Nancy A. Harrowitz, tainted greatness: antisemitism and cultural heroes", *Religion*, 25 (2), 285–288.

STRENSKI, I. 1998a. "Durkheim's bourgeois theory of sacrifice", *In:* Allen, N. J., Pickering, W. S. F. and Miller, W. W., eds *On Durkheim's elementary forms of the religious life*. London: Routledge, 116–126.

STRENSKI, I. 1998b. "Religion, power and the final Foucault", *Journal of the American Academy of Religion*, 66 (2), 345–368.

STRENSKI, I. 1998c. "Respecting power, worshiping power, and knowing the difference: rejoinder to David Chidester and Gary Lease", *Journal of the American Academy of Religion*, 66 (2), 381–383.

STRENSKI, I. 2002. *Contesting sacrifice: religion, nationalism and social thought in France*. Chicago, IL: University of Chicago Press.

STRENSKI, I. 2003a. *Theology and the first theory of sacrifice*. Leiden and Boston, MA: Brill.

STRENSKI, I. 2003b. "Sacrifice, gift and the social logic of Muslim 'human bombers'", *Terrorism and Political Violence*, 15 (3), 1–34.

STRENSKI, I. 2006a. *Rethinking Durkheim*. New Brunswick, NJ: Rutgers University Press.

STRENSKI, I. 2006b. "A Durkheimian text in Turkey: Ziya Gökalp, Hüseyin Nail Kubalı, and Muslim civil society", *In:* Strenski, I., ed. *The new Durkheim*. New Brunswick, NJ: Rutgers University Press, 303–336.

TAIBBI, M. 2005. "Ms. America", *Rolling Stone*, 20 October 2005, pp. 47–48.

TAROT, C. 2008. *Le symbolique et le sacré. Théories de la religion*. Paris: La Découverte.

TIRYAKIAN, E. 2005. "Durkheim, solidarity and September 11", *In:* Alexander, J. and Smith, P., eds *The Cambridge Companion to Durkheim*. Cambridge: Cambridge University Press, 305–321.

TOCQUEVILLE, A. DE [1848] 2004. *Democracy in America*. New York: Library of America.

TOMBS, R. 1999. *The Paris Commune of 1871*. London and New York: Longmans.

TURNER, S. 1996. "Durkheim among the statisticians", *Journal of the History of the Behavioural Sciences*, 32 4, 354–379.

VIRILIO, P. 1997. *Pure war*. (with Sylvère Lotringer). New York: Semiotext(e).

WALZER, M. 1986. "The politics of Michel Foucault", *In:* Hoy, D. C., ed. *Foucault: a critical reader*. Oxford: Blackwell, 51–68.

WEBER, E. [1962] 1964. *Action Française*. Stanford, CA: Stanford University Press and Paris: Stock.

WEBER, E. 1994. *The hollow years: France in the 1930s*. New York: W.W. Norton.

WEIL, S. 2003. *The Iliad or the poem of force*. [Trans. Mary McCarthy]. Wallingford, PA: Pendle Hill.

WILLIAMS, G. C. 1966. *Adaptation and natural selection*. Princeton, NJ: Princeton University Press.

WINOCK, M. AND AZÉMA, J-P. 1976. *Naissance et mort de la troisième republique* (1870–1940). Paris: Calmann-Levy.

WITTGENSTEIN, L. 2005. *Recherches philosophiques*. Paris: Gallimard.

WOODWARD, B. 2007. *State of denial*. New York: Simon & Schuster.

WORLD HEALTH ORGANIZATION (WHO) 2002. *World report on violence and health*. Geneva: WHO.

ZELDIN, T. 1980. *France 1848–1945: intellect and pride*. Oxford: Oxford University Press.

ZIMBARDO, P. G. 2007. *The Lucifer effect: understanding how good people turn evil*. New York: Random House.

ŽIŽEK, S. 1999. *The ticklish subject*. New York: Verso.

ŽIŽEK, S. 2003. *The puppet and the dwarf: the perverse core of Christianity*. Cambridge, MA: MIT Press.

INDEX